Contemporary Sociology

Contemporary Sociology

An Introduction to Concepts and Theories

Second Edition

M. FRANCIS ABRAHAM

OXFORD

UNIVERSITY PRESS

OXFORD
UNIVERSITY PRESS

Oxford University Press is a department of the University of Oxford.
It furthers the University's objective of excellence in research, scholarship,
and education by publishing worldwide. Oxford is a registered trademark of
Oxford University Press in the UK and in certain other countries

Published in India by
Oxford University Press
22 Workspace, 2nd Floor, 1/22 Asaf Ali Road, New Delhi 110002, India

First Edition published in 2006
Second Edition published in 2015
13th impression 2022

ISBN-13: 978-0-19-945278-1
ISBN-10: 0-19-945278-4

Typeset in Adobe Garamond Pro 11/13.5
by The Graphics Solution, New Delhi 110 092
Printed in India by Rakmo Press, New Delhi 110 020

To My Master Gurus

Shri Gopala Ganakan
Shri Bhaskaran Nair
Shri E.K. Zachariah

Contents

List of Tables and Figures		xv
Acknowledgements		xvii
Note for Teachers and Students		xix

I   THE FIELD OF SOCIOLOGY   1

  1   DEFINING SOCIOLOGY

  What is Sociology?   3
  Sociology and Other Social Sciences   5
  The Sociological Perspective   6
  The Founding Fathers of Sociology   9
  Auguste Comte 9   •   Karl Marx 11   •   Herbert Spencer 13
  •   Émile Durkheim 14   •   Max Weber 17
  Contemporary Sociology   19

  2   THEORETICAL PERSPECTIVES IN SOCIOLOGY

  What is Sociological Theory?   22
  Types of Sociological Theory   23
  Speculative Theories vs. Grounded Theories 23
  •   Grand Theories vs. Miniature Theories 24
  •   Macro Theories vs. Micro Theories 24
  Functions of Sociological Theory   25
  Mainline Theories in Sociology   26
  Evolutionary Theory 26   •   Structural-functionalism 28
  •   Conflict Theory 31   •   Symbolic Interactionism 36
  •   Exchange Theory 38
  Choosing and Using Sociological Theory   41
  Theoretical Perspectives in a Global Age   42

  3   METHODS OF RESEARCH IN SOCIOLOGY

  The Scientific Approach   47
  Basic Principles   48

Steps in the Research Process   49
Selection of the Topic 49   •   Review of Literature 50
•   Formulation of Hypotheses 50   •   Selection of Research
Design 50   •   Collection of Data 51   •   Analysis of Data 51
•   Writing the Report and Sharing the Results 52
Methods of Research   52
Surveys 52   •   Experiments 54
•   Observational Studies: Participant and Non-participant Observation 55
•   Analysis of Secondary Data 56
Quantitative vs. Qualitative Research   57
Issues in Sociological Research   59

II   THE FOUNDATIONS OF SOCIETY   61

4   CULTURE

The Meaning of Culture   63
Components of Culture   66
Beliefs 66   •   Values 67   •   Language 67
•   Norms 68   •   Technology 70
Cultural Orientation   70
Cultural Diversity   72
Cultural Change   73
Towards a Global Culture?   74

5   SOCIALIZATION

Heredity and Environment   79
The Results of Deprived Socialization   81
Theories of Socialization   82
Sociological Theories 82   •   Psychological Theories 84
Agents of Socialization   87
The Family 87   •   Peer Groups 88   •   The School 88
•   Mass Media 89   •   Adult Socialization 89
Resocialization   90
Total Institutions 90
Socialization by Caste, Religion, and Gender   91

6   SOCIAL INTERACTION

Verbal and Non-verbal Communication   93
Crystallization of Social Interaction   95

Theories of Social Interaction   98
Dramaturgical Approach 98 • Ethnomethodology 99
The Structure of Social Interaction   100
Status 100 • Role 101
Forms of Social Interaction   102
Cooperation 102 • Competition 103 • Conflict 103
• Accommodation 103 • Exchange 104
Virtual Networking 104

7   TYPES OF SOCIETIES AND GROUPS

Evolution of Societies   106
Hunting and Gathering Societies 106 • Horticultural Societies 107
• Pastoral Societies 107 • Agrarian Societies 107
• Industrial and Post-industrial Societies 108
Three Typologies   109
Mechanical and Organic Solidarity: Émile Durkheim 109
• Gemeinschaft and Gesellschaft: Ferdinand Tonnies 110
• Folk and Urban Societies: Robert Redfield 110
Types of Social Groups   111
Aggregate 111 • Societal Group 111 • Social Group 112
• Associational Group 112 • Primary and Secondary Groups 112
• In-groups and Out-groups 113 • Reference Groups 113
• Electronic Communities 114
Formal Organizations and Bureaucracy   114
Size and Group Dynamics   116
Social Organization   116

8   DEVIANCE AND SOCIAL CONTROL

What is Deviance?   119
The Normality of Crime: Durkheim   121
Consequences of Deviance   121
Theories of Deviant Behaviour   122
Biological Theories 122 • Psychological Theories 122
• Sociological Theories 123
Gender and Deviance   127
Crime and Criminals   128
Social Control   129
Informal Social Control 130 • Formal Social Control 130

III SOCIAL INEQUALITY 133

9 SOCIAL STRATIFICATION

Three Systems of Stratification 135
The Estate System 135 • The Caste System 136
• The Class System 140
Race, Gender, and Stratification 141
Dimensions of Social Stratification 143
Theories of Stratification 143
Functional Theory 143 • Conflict Theory 145
Global Systems of Stratification 145
Caste and Class in India 149
Lifestyles and Life Chances 153
Social Mobility 154

10 MINORITIES AND WEAKER SECTIONS

Prejudice and Discrimination 159
Patterns of Majority–Minority Relations 160
Minority Responses 161
Minority Groups in India 162
Persons with Disabilities 162 • The Aged 163
• Women as a Minority 166 • Women in India 168
• Dalits and Other Backward Classes 173 • Tribes in India 174
• Minority by Sexual Orientation 176

IV SOCIAL INSTITUTIONS 179

11 THE FAMILY

Types of Families 181
Marriage Patterns 183
Functions of the Family 184
The Future of Marriage and Family 185
Marriage and Family in India 186
Global Trends in Marriage and Family 191
Domestic Violence 192

12 THE POLITICAL ECONOMY

State and Government 196
Functions of the State 197
Social Control 197 • Defence 197 • Welfare 197

Types of States 198
Autocracy 198 • Totalitarianism 198 • Democracy 198
Types of Economy 199
Capitalism 199 • Socialism 200 • Mixed Economy 200
Democratic Socialism 200
Power and Authority 204
Theories of Power in Societies 206
The Power Elite Model 206 • The Pluralist Model 206
The Indian Political Scene 207
Globalization and Corporate Capitalism 209

13 EDUCATIONAL SYSTEM

Functions of Education 214
Socialization 214 • Cultural Transmission 214
• Social Placement 215 • Innovation 215
• Social Integration 215 • Critical Thinking 216
Inequality in Education 217
Education and the UN Millennium Development Goals 218
Education in India 220

14 RELIGION

Religions among the 'Primitive' People 228
Elements of Religion 229
Some Related Concepts 231
Magic 231 • Sect 232 • Cult 233
Contemporary Sociological Perspectives on Religion 234
Key Sociological Theories on Religion 237
The Functionalist Perspective 237 • The Conflict Perspective 240
Durkheim's Theory of Religion 241
Recent Trends in Religion 242
Secularization 242 • Resacralization 245
• Fundamentalism 246
Religion in India 247

V SOCIAL CHANGE 253

15 POPULATION AND URBANIZATION

The Basic Concepts 255
Fertility 255 • Mortality 256 • Migration 256
Theoretical Perspectives 257

Malthusian Theory of Population 257
• Demographic Transition Theory 258
Population Explosion: Causes and Consequences 258
A Note on Population in India 264
Urbanization 267
Theoretical Perspectives 271
Georg Simmel: Metropolis and Mental Life 271
• Louis Wirth: Urbanism as a Way of Life 271
Urbanization in India 272

16 COLLECTIVE BEHAVIOUR AND SOCIAL MOVEMENTS

Theories of Collective Behaviour 276
Contagion Theory 277 • Emergent Norm Theory 277
• Convergence Theory 278 • Value-added Theory 278
Forms of Collective Behaviour 279
Crowds 279
Dispersed Collective Behaviour 280
Rumour 280 • Fads and Fashions 281
Social Movements 282
Theories of Social Movements 282
Relative Deprivation Theory 282 • Resource Mobilization
Theory 283 • Political Opportunity/Political Process Theory 283
New Social Movements 284
The Life Cycle of Social Movements 285
Social Movements in India 287
Environmental Movements 287 • Women's Movements 288
• Caste-oriented Movements 289

17 SOCIAL CHANGE, ENVIRONMENT, AND
SUSTAINABLE DEVELOPMENT

Theories of Social Change 292
Evolutionary Theory 293 • Functional Theory 294
• Conflict Theory 295
Sources of Social Change 295
Physical Environment 295 • Technology 296
• Cultural Contacts and Diffusion 296
• Values and Ideology 297
The Process of Social Change 297
Social Change in India 301

Environment   303
Sustainable Development   309

Further Readings   313
Index   317
About the Author   328

Tables and Figures

TABLES

7.1	Characteristics of Rural and Urban Societies	111
8.1	A Typology of Modes of Individual Adaptation	124
9.1	Per cent of Population Living on Less than $2 Per day (2002)	146
9.2	Per cent of Population Living on Less than $2 Per day (2011)	146
12.1	Various Estimates of the Number Living Below Poverty Line in India (2009)	204
15.1	The World's Ten Largest Countries in Population	257
15.2	Rate of Natural Increase for Select Regions	262
15.3	World Population Growth	266
15.4	Top 10 Largest Urban Agglomerations (1975, 2000, and 2025)	268
15.5	Ranking of Select Indian Cities in Two Census Periods	273

FIGURES

15.1	Population Clock (2014)	260
15.2	Much of the World Still Remains Rural	269

Acknowledgements

For various chapters in this book I have adapted or otherwise taken passages as such, especially related to sociological thought, theoretical perspectives, religion and processes of social change, from several of my previous publications listed below:

Modern Sociological Theory: An Introduction, New Delhi: Oxford University Press, 1982.

Sociological Thought: From Comte to Sorokin (co-author with John Henry Morgan), New Delhi: Macmillan India Limited, 1985.

Perspectives on Modernization: Toward a General Theory of Third World Development, Washington DC: University Press of America, 1980.

'Religious Social Systems' and 'Small Informal Social Systems' in *Social Systems: The Study of Sociology*, Charles P. Loomis and Everett D. Dyer (eds), Cambridge: Schenkman Publishing Company, 1976.

Note for Teachers and Students

This book is a comprehensive general sociology text for beginners. There are, of course, several good standard textbooks in sociology but this one is different in some important respects. First, this text has separate, detailed chapters on theoretical perspectives and research methods. Issues pertaining to education, economy, deviance, urbanization, and environment are also addressed in separate chapters. Most key concepts and theories in the discipline are presented in detail. Second, major social institutions and organizations are extensively discussed in terms of contemporary theoretical orientations not only in sociology but also related sciences thus maintaining the interdisciplinary character of the discipline. Third, keeping in mind that current sociology is global in outlook, examples and illustrations are drawn from numerous cultural contexts. Finally, the book deals with a number of contemporary social issues which are relevant to both Indian society and the international community. These issues include emerging electronic communities, environmental movement, sustainable development, gay rights, women and minorities, and globalization and social justice. These factors make this text comprehensive, interdisciplinary, comparative, and very current.

However the task of including all major concepts, theories, methods, global perspectives, and recent trends into one manageable textbook necessarily has some limitations. In an introductory text like this one, one can only provide an overview of mainline theories; therefore, a number of theories such as quantitativism, behaviourism, phenomenology, and sociology of knowledge have not been included. Yet, in this revised edition, a number of recent developments in the field of sociology, especially new perspectives in theory have been included.

As a graduate of Gandhigram Rural University, where I studied and worked for several years, I have done extensive research in village India and published several works on the subject. I taught sociology at an American university for almost thirty years. During this time I also served as Director of International/Intercultural Studies and had the opportunity to visit over forty countries. I spent nearly three months in China and six weeks each in Thailand, Indonesia, Brazil, Mexico, Egypt, the former Soviet Union, and the Caribbean. Therefore, many illustrations have been drawn from my personal experiences in different cultures. To students, some of these examples may sound 'strange and unreal'. That is precisely the point. We share the global village with over seven billion people who live in numerous cultures with different value systems, traditions, and practices. To understand diversity is to appreciate cultural differences. Students will keep in mind that no attempt has been made to evaluate different cultural practices. For example, to say that we eat our food with our fingers whereas people in other countries use chopsticks or forks does not mean that one practice is better than the other. To say that people in East Asia eat dogs and snakes is not to say that our food habits are somehow superior to theirs. I have carefully drawn cross-cultural examples to illustrate cultural differences so that students can appreciate diversity in the global arena. There is also another compelling reason. In spite of all the talk about 'convergence', globalization, and universal outlook, there is also a resurgent interest among many communities and cultures in rediscovering their ancient roots and celebrating ethnic traditions. In other words, people take pride in their ethnic heritage and identity. This is also a significant social phenomenon around the world. Therefore, we need to understand unique and distinct cultural practices in order to appreciate the diversity of world cultures. A general sociology text can no longer be confined to conventional themes and geographic boundaries. In this contemporary text I have attempted this and I hope both teachers and students of sociology will find this useful.

M. Francis Abraham
August 2014

PART I

THE FIELD OF SOCIOLOGY

Defining Sociology

WHAT IS SOCIOLOGY?

Humans have always sought to examine themselves and their social life. In the course of time, several intellectual disciplines such as theology, history, political science, economics, psychology, and ethics were developed to explain different aspects of human enterprises. Auguste Comte (1798–1857), who is known as the father of sociology, recognized the absence of a general science that deals with society as a whole. He argued that if a class of phenomena can be divided into *n* subclasses, then there must be n+1 sciences to deal with them: n (or say, nine) disciplines to deal with each of the subclasses and an extra discipline (a tenth one) to deal with what is common to all of them and also to examine the relationship between them. In other words, it was Comte's idea that if history, economics, political science, psychology, and other subjects study different areas of social phenomena, there must be a general social science to deal with society as a whole and to examine the interrelationship among them. Comte also felt that there was no science yet to deal with such social institutions as marriage, family, and community as well as the numerous social structures and processes. Thus, there was a definite need to create a new discipline. Comte combined two terms 'socius', Latin for society, and 'logos', Greek for studying, and coined 'sociology' which literally means 'study of society'.

Comte defined sociology as the abstract and theoretical science of social phenomena. While Durkheim defined sociology as the study of social facts which are the collective ways of feeling, thinking, and acting, Weber thought of sociology as the study of social action and social relationships. *International Encyclopedia of the Social Sciences* defines sociology as 'the study of social aggregates and groups in their institutional organization, of institutions and their organization, and of the causes and consequences of changes in institutions and social organization' (Sills 1972: 1). Today sociologists are more apt to define sociology as the scientific study of society, its institutions, structures, and processes. Typically, sociology is concerned with social interaction, social groups, and social behaviour. It examines why people behave the way they do, how culture shapes human behaviour and what sorts of group dynamics influence social behaviour. The focus of sociology, therefore, is on social systems and processes, rather than individual beliefs and behaviours.

There are three major characteristics of sociology as a discipline. First, sociology is a social science that deals with social systems and processes. The older natural sciences such as physics, chemistry, biology, and astronomy deal with the physical world, material objects and their properties. They are also considered to be more mature and exact sciences because they establish more or less accurate principles and laws. But the social sciences which focus on various aspects of human behaviour in the social world cannot be an exact science. This is especially true of sociology which deals with social behaviour in different cultural contexts. It is extremely difficult to generalize human behaviour which is influenced by different values, customs, traditions, social groupings, and even geography. Every society is different and people feel, think, and act differently according to their own subcultures based on caste, class, ethnicity, language, religion, and ideology. Therefore, sociological laws can only be approximations, and not exact formulations in the tradition of hard sciences. Moreover, we cannot predict human behaviour with absolute certainty or formulate principles and laws which are universally valid. Therefore, as a social science, sociology will always remain as an inexact science.

Second, sociology is a general social science that deals with society as a whole. Other social sciences such as history, anthropology, political science, economics, and psychology deal with particular aspects of society or certain types of society altogether. Although they study several aspects of society such as economics, politics, and the evolution of culture within the context of the larger society, they are narrowly focused on their particular field. Even anthropology, though a general social science, traditionally focused on certain types of societies. Sociology deals with the big picture, the larger society, as well as the relationship among different aspects of society and the inter-connection between each of the parts and the society as a whole. Sociology is a comprehensive social science that deals with the dynamics of social structures and forces that criss-cross and mix up.

Third, sociology is a pure science, not an applied science. There is a popular misconception that sociology is somehow concerned with social welfare and that it is designed to solve social problems and build a better society. However, that is not the intent of the discipline of sociology as a scientific endeavour. Sociology is concerned with the acquisition of knowledge about society, knowledge that can be used for the betterment of society or for its destruction. For instance, if we know what holds a community together we can certainly use that knowledge for community development or for the dissolution of that community. The sociological knowledge we acquire about society will be a valuable tool for social workers who want to build a better society, or for leaders of government who want to formulate public policies. Business is the applied science that utilizes the objective knowledge gained in economics, a pure science. Similarly, pharmacy is based on the knowledge of properties and relationships of matters acquired in the pure science of chemistry. Sociology is a science of society that investigates social relationships, institutions and behaviours, and attempts to formulate some general principles. How we utilize that knowledge is left to the individuals as concerned citizens, political leaders, or social workers. But social reconstruction is not the acknowledged purpose of sociology, Comte notwithstanding, although sociological knowledge is a useful tool for that purpose.

SOCIOLOGY AND OTHER SOCIAL SCIENCES

Let us now examine the relationship between sociology and other social sciences. We have already described sociology as a general social science that deals with society as a whole, and other social sciences as specific disciplines which concentrate on different aspects of the social world. For example, political science deals with the political aspects of society, especially voting behaviour, state, and government. Sociology also deals with several aspects of political behaviour but only in relation to the larger society. Whereas political scientists look at the rise and fall of particular governments and their leaders, sociologists simply view governments as social institutions and leadership as a social phenomenon. Sociologists are not particularly concerned with the architects of India's Independence per se but in their qualities of leadership and the social forces that catapulted them to positions of charismatic authority.

Economics is another social science that is related to sociology. But economics focuses on economic behaviour, money, forces of demand and supply, industry, economic growth, and development. Economy is only one of the classes of social phenomena such as religion, politics, and education. Therefore, economics is, like political science, a specializing discipline which is primarily concerned with the economic aspects of society. Economics and Sociology are closely related and have overlapping areas. However, their focus and emphasis vary. As a generalizing science, sociology examines all other aspects of society, including economy, in relation to overriding social forces, but economists tend to concentrate on specific aspects of economy such as monetary behaviour, market, business cycle, capital, labour, and industry.

History is primarily concerned with events of the past but seeks to relate them to one another in order to provide a perspective from the past to the present and vice versa. The historian is interested in unique events, specific revolutions or particular wars. But sociologists are concerned with them as general social phenomena. Whereas historians study the French Revolution, Chinese Revolution or the First War of Indian Independence as unique events, sociologists look at revolution and war as social phenomena. In other words, history is concerned with the unique and the particular, whereas sociology is concerned with the regular and the recurrent. Historians are interested in the accurate description of past records and events but sociologists are concerned with the underlying social processes common to all those records and events or patterns and principles which help explain them. Therefore, we might say that history is a particularizing discipline whereas sociology is a generalizing science.

Anthropology and psychology are two other social sciences closely related to sociology. Anthropology may be considered a general social science because it is a comprehensive study of man. However, anthropology has traditionally focused on 'uncivilized', archaic and 'primitive' societies. Although the focus has shifted in recent years and anthropologists now study even urban social systems in modern complex societies, anthropology was originally thought of as a comprehensive study of the total way of life of rather isolated and relatively homogeneous communities. Anthropologists study every aspect of the community, its social system, culture, religion, economy, politics, family, and clan system as well as social norms and life cycle rituals.

They may study the Eskimos, the Zulus, the Rajputs, the Nairs of Kerala, or the Bodos of Assam but they cover the entire spectrum of their social world, all social institutions, structures, and processes. Although sociology is also a general social science it is far more focused; it looks for patterns and variations in social structures and processes. Sociology looks at specific social systems, one step at a time, and tries to arrive at principles and patterns and common denominators in social structures and processes. To put it bluntly in layman's terms, anthropology is often a 'package deal' whereas sociology focuses on the various components in the package but in relation to the full deal.

Psychology, as the study of human behaviour, is concerned with the individual, his personality, nervous system, intelligence, motivation, and learning. Modern psychology deals with many subject areas including cognitive functions, unconscious forces, overt behaviour or even physiological and biochemical processes. Whatever their emphasis or focus, psychologists share a common interest in human nature and behaviour. Most generalizations in psychology tend to revolve around types of personality. Social psychology, often thought of as a branch of sociology, serves as a bridge between sociology and psychology. Although social psychology continues to maintain a primary interest in the individual, it is mainly concerned with the way the individual behaves in groups. The focus is not on the individual per se or his personality system but on how he and his personality are influenced by the cultural milieu in which he lives. Sociology has no special interest in the unique individual or his personality, rather it concerns itself with the nature of social groups in which the individual lives. Whereas psychology and social psychology are interested in the nature and behaviour of individuals, sociology is concerned with the social world in which the behaviour takes place. At the risk of some oversimplification we may say that psychology is the study of individual behaviour, social psychology is the study of the behaviour of individuals in social groups, and sociology is the study of social groups and their structures and processes which exert considerable influence on the individual.

In summary, we may say that sociology is a general social science that deals with society as a whole as well as the interrelationship between different aspects of society and the relationship of each part to the total whole. Other social sciences deal with particular aspects of society, often within the context of the larger social world. Sociology also embraces other social sciences in terms of definite subject areas or fields which specialize in different aspects of society. Thus we have political sociology, historical sociology, sociology of the economy, sociology of the family, environmental sociology, sociology of religion, industrial sociology, sociology of education, sociology of the community, rural sociology, social stratification, race and ethnic relations, gender studies, criminology, and many other fields.

THE SOCIOLOGICAL PERSPECTIVE

As a general social science of society, sociology provides a unique sociological perspective on the world around us. It is a way of looking at events, forms, and processes through the trained eyes of a scientist. Sometimes it is a way of verifying common sense observations. At other times the challenge is to realize that an obvious reality may have several layers of meaning. In other words, the sociological perspective enables us to look critically at commonly held assumptions about ourselves and our society. It also tells us that we are all products of our culture. We tend to think that we are all free men and women who can independently think and act but the reality is that who we are and how we live in groups is considerably influenced by our beliefs, values, standards, institutions, and processes which are part of our culture.

How does a crowd turn into a mob? How do free-thinking individuals become sycophants of religious and political charlatans and unconditionally surrender themselves? How do we explain that caste loyalty is as strong as ever inspite of all protestations against untouchability and caste superiority? Why do Christians and Muslims in India follow several age-old Indian customs along with the practices of their adopted faiths? Why do the Todas of the Nilgiris still practise polyandry? Why do boys and girls in several communities in India grow up with the idea that they are destined to marry some preferred mates such as a sister's daughter or a maternal uncle's daughter? Answers to these questions are many and varied but they will clearly illustrate the importance of culture.

The sociological perspective has at least four dimensions:

First, human beings live in groups, and therefore, their thoughts and actions, even their nature to some extent, are influenced by the groups in which they live. An Indian child of any caste or religious group, plucked away at birth and placed among the Yanomamo Indian tribe in the jungles of South America is bound to become a hunter or warrior who is totally oblivious of the cultural heritage of India. Children in many Asian societies are socialized to be submissive to their parents and respectful of all elders. Our social groups determine the language we speak, what kinds of food we eat, ceremonies we follow, festivals we organize, whom and how we marry, and how we greet or treat one another. Some cultures encourage children to be individualistic, aggressive, and competitive while others encourage them to be passive and cooperative. Culture is often the prism through which we see ourselves and others.

The sociological perspective of a trained scientist stresses the social contexts in which people live; it enables us to see the world in a larger social context. When Karl Marx spoke of social location of ideas he was referring to the way social class influences people's ideas. We know that the rich and the poor do not think alike and when it comes to public policies their perspectives are most divergent. Similarly, the type of occupation, level of education, gender, age, and caste influence the way we perceive the world around us. The sociological perspective enables us to see the connection between the particular and the universal. It teaches us to look beyond narrow social boundaries and see social phenomena from a broader social context. C. Wright Mills (1959: 5) in his thought-provoking essay on 'Sociological Imagination' spoke of 'the quality of mind essential to grasp the interplay of men and society, of biography and history, of self and world'. The sociological perspective encourages us to be objective, to look at the world critically and not to take things for granted based on traditional beliefs and practices.

Second, the sociological perspective teaches us about the social construction of reality. What is reality? A school of Indian philosophy tells us what we see is only 'maya' or illusion. We are also told that 'seeing is believing'. We may, of course, believe what we see but it is equally true that we may also see what we believe we see. The fact is that reality has nothing to do with what is empirically true or false. If a social group believes something to be real, for all practical purposes it is the 'reality' which influences the group's thinking and behaviour. Before the global shape of the earth was scientifically confirmed people believed it to be flat, and sailors used to be advised not to go too far lest they would fall off into the abyss. If people believe in good omen, auspicious hour or horoscope, then it is a reality that guides their behaviour. If people believe in miracles, then they see miracles happening. Just look at all the 'For Favours Received' advertisements in our daily newspapers. If a group believes that gods can be polluted by the so-called 'outcastes' there is no point in arguing that the reality might be that the almighty gods, rather than being polluted by the hapless devotees, might purify whomsoever approaches them. When for years people in village India believed that smallpox is caused by a particular goddess and can be controlled only by propitiating the deity, it was a well-entrenched social reality.

The sociological perspective teaches us to differentiate between reality and socially construed reality and to interpret them from a scientific point of view.

Third, the sociological perspective informs us that reality has many layers of meaning. The obvious reality may be only a mask for a construed or contrived reality. The concept of caste superiority may not be based on foundations of purity and pollution but invented to serve the vested interests of higher castes. According to Marvin Harris, the Hindu attitude towards the cow as a sacred animal and the ban on beef-eating may be a very rational social invention. Economists have for years attempted to explain the emergence of modern capitalism but it was Max Weber who saw the relationship between Protestant ethic and the spirit of capitalism and attributed the rise of modern Western capitalism to the values embedded in Protestant ethic. Education was once the prerogative of the social elites who thought educating the lower classes would turn them into troublemakers. Whereas proponents of functionalism in sociology see religion as an integrating force which brings order and stability to society, conflict theorists such as Marxist sociologists think of religion as an 'opiate' of the people that helps hoodwink and subjugate the masses. What was characterized as 'sepoy mutiny' by the British, the Indian nationalists called the First War of Independence. An incident of communal or political violence will be variously reported by members of different political or communal groups. People tend to see reality from their own personal experiences. But sociologists as social scientists must probe layers of meaning underlying every incident and every reality. The sociological perspective helps us achieve a balanced view of the many meanings and interpretations of the social phenomena.

The fourth dimension of the sociological perspective is what C. Wright Mills (1959: 196) called 'Sociological Imagination'. Sociology is concerned with ordinary, everyday life. The sociologist investigates why people do the things they do and feel and think the way they do. He cannot simply depend on common-sense explanations. Events can transcend boundaries of space and time. Many current events make sense only in the context of historical constellations. For instance, traditional rivalries, prejudices, and conflicts from ages past may still influence many contemporary events. Similarly, sociological imagination encourages us 'to capture "fringe-thoughts": various ideas which may be by-products of everyday life, snatches of conversation overheard on the street, or, for that matter, dreams. Once noted, these may lead to more systematic thinking, as well as lend intellectual relevance to more directed experience'.

According to C. Wright Mills, sociological imagination is 'becoming the major common denominator of our cultural life and its signal feature.' The sociological perspective, rooted in such imagination enables us to see the present in terms of the historical scene, ordinary experience in terms of universal experience, and isolated events in terms of social patterns. For example, it is often said that every Indian is a prisoner of his own subcaste. Whether it is true or not, there is no denying the fact that an individual's social 'location' colours his vision. Social happenings, political issues, mass movements, and even individual opinions are to be understood in terms of relevant social patterns. A good sociologist, like a trained scientist, looks at all social phenomena in an unbiased manner. In short, the sociological perspective is the critical eye on the world which observes every social phenomenon in a larger social context.

THE FOUNDING FATHERS OF SOCIOLOGY

Auguste Comte (1798–1857)

Sociology is a science of human behaviour which emerged in the minds of men living through an age of unprecedented social and political revolutions. And of those early social scientists, Auguste Comte leads the list. Comte was startled by the destructive effects of the French Revolution which, he believed, undermined the moral fabric of the community. He wanted to establish a new social order based on what he perceived to be the moral community. The task of recreating a new social order required a new scientific discipline with objective laws. Thus was born sociology as a science of society.

At an early age, Comte stumbled upon an elder social idealist, namely, Comte Henri de Saint-Simon, who was destined to make a profound and lasting impression upon the former and his work. Comte, who became quickly enamoured of the old man's belief that science was the new spiritual power of the age and that soon both morals and politics would become positive sciences—sciences established upon objective data and empirical facts—became Saint-Simon's secretary, assisting in the production of the progressive periodical, *Industrie*. Having come under the spell of Saint-Simon, Comte coupled his own ideas about human society with the elitism and liberalism of the former. In fact, it was often difficult, when reading their papers, to distinguish the pair's individual contributions. However, soon afterwards, the two men parted company, never to collaborate or even say anything good about the other again. Saint-Simon, possibly thinking of his old age, began to press for immediate action in social reforms, while young Comte wished rather to dwell long and carefully upon the theoretical development of his grand system of 'positive physic'. This drift also led to the shift from 'social philosophy' to 'social physic' first, and later to 'sociology'.

Comte believed that the evolution of human society parallels that of the development of the individual's intellect. In other words, the individual mind, human activity, and society pass through successive stages of historical evolution leading to some final stage of perfection. Comte proposed the law of the three stages governing social evolution as follows:

1. *The Theological or Fictional (fictitious) Stage*. During this stage the human mind invokes gods and goddesses and seeks to explain phenomena by ascribing them to beings comparable to man himself. Every natural phenomenon, be it thunder, lightning, fire, or rain, is attributed to a particular god.

2. *The Metaphysical or Abstract Stage*. This is a stage in which the mind presupposes abstract forces and personified abstractions capable of producing all phenomena which are now attributed to impersonal forces rather than supernatural beings.

3. *The Positive or Scientific Stage*. During this stage 'observation predominates over imagination' and all theoretical concepts have become positive. All phenomena are now interpreted in terms of scientific principles and laws. By way of illustration we may say that if thunder and lightning were attributed to god Indra in the theological stage, the laws of physics explain the phenomena in the scientific stage.

Corresponding to the three stages of evolution, there are two major types of societies: the Theological–Military society and the Scientific–Industrial society. The former is characterized by the predominance of theological thinking and military activity. Priests were endowed with intellectual and spiritual power while the military exercised temporal authority. In the scientific–industrial society, priests and theologians are replaced by scientists who represent the new moral and intellectual power. Priests and shamans no longer determine the cause of an illness or prescribe solutions; scientists do. Comte believed that the new scientific–industrial society will become the society of all mankind. Thus, Comte's theory of progress, often referred to as the unilinear theory of evolution, involved the development of the human race to a single design: the passage of human mind and society through definite steps of evolution leading to a final stage of perfection.

Just as the human mind passes through the various stages, all intellectual disciplines evolve and develop as well. Comte ranks all sciences in a hierarchy based on the order in which each discipline becomes positive. The base of the hierarchy is mathematics, followed by astronomy, because these are the sciences in which the positive method comes to be adopted first. In time, the method will be adopted by physical sciences, natural sciences, and then social sciences. Finally, the positive method which has triumphed in all abstract sciences will essentially prevail in history and politics and culminate in the founding of a positive science of society, namely sociology, which is, in a word, the roof of all sciences. Sociology thus becomes the crowning glory of all intellectual disciplines because of man's ability to explain social phenomena in terms of scientific principles and laws which were thus far applied only in the natural sciences.

Although a confirmed positivist, Comte was sceptical about the rationality of the human animal. Man is not by nature a positivist; he is not naturally scientific. He becomes so gradually, through the evolution and progress of society and the human mind. Thus, for Comte, there was a direct correlation between the progress of the human mind and the evolution of human society. As one develops, so does the other. Comte explained: 'I mean the relational coordination of the fundamental sequence of the various events of human history according to a single design' (Abraham 1985: 11) constitutes the key to conceptual sociology. This true science—'positive physic' or 'sociology'—consists of observation, analysis, and comprehension of the capabilities of the human mind as they are revealed to us through their progressions in the course of history.

To Comte, positive method meant the subordination of concepts to facts and the acceptance of the idea that social phenomena are subject to general laws—social laws. Yet, as he consistently pointed out, owing to the complexity of human relationships, attitudes, and behaviours, these social laws are necessarily less rigid than biological laws. Positive knowledge is to be gained by sociology by employing a three-step methodology buttressed by historical analysis: *observation*, which must be guided by a theory of social phenomena; *experimentation*, which in sociology means controlled observation; and *comparison*, which includes human to animal, society to society, like to unlike, etc. Sociological method, for Comte, assured the scientific quality of 'social physics', and though the precision was quantitatively short of pure mathematics, the quality of its analysis into the complexities of social life catapulted the science of humanity to the top rung in the scientific ladder.

The scientific study of social phenomena involved two aspects of society: social statics and social dynamics. Social statics refers to the basic fact of social order, the structure and pattern, which gives every social system its stability. This social order is brought about by consensus universalis, a universal agreement among all societies of the dialectically creative role of order and progress. The concept of social dynamics, on the other hand, involves the theory of progress, the law of three stages and the inevitable evolutionary development of order. Order and evolution are thus two sides of the same coin. In contemporary sociology, though, the terms social statics and social dynamics are replaced by the concepts of social structure and social change. Indeed, in the tradition of Comte, we see that every social system has a basic structure or order but it also undergoes change and development over time.

Karl Marx (1818–1883)

Although Marx never used the term sociology, much of twentieth century sociology is eminently influenced by his writings.

Marx's genius lay not so much in his absolute originality but rather in the constellation and configuration of his ideas and insights gained from cross-fertilization. Unlike the Hegelian idealism which perceived truths in ideas, Marx claimed the contrary, namely, that ideas were not the realm of truth but rather matter is. Whereas Hegel's system could be called 'dialectical idealism', Marx gave himself over to the development of what came to be called 'dialectical materialism'. The popular image of 'turning Hegel upside down' or 'standing Hegel on his head' is illustrative of the Marxian corrective to Hegelian idealism. According to Marx (Fromm 1961: 198)

In direct contrast to German philosophy which descends from heaven to earth, here we ascend from earth to heaven. That is to say, we do not set out from what men say, imagine, conceive, nor from men as narrated, thought of, imagined, conceived, in order to arrive at men in the flesh. We set out from real, active men, and on the basis of their real life-process we demonstrate the development of the ideological reflexes and echoes of this life-process—Morality, religion, metaphysics, all the rest of ideology and their corresponding forms of consciousness, thus no longer retain the semblance of independence ... Life is not determined by consciousness, but consciousness by life.

Thus, Marx would not ascribe an independent, determinate role to ideas or philosophical conception. This is because he believed that they reflected, rather than caused, changes in social and material life. Yet, Marx did not deny the reality of subjective consciousness or its significance in social change.

The changing of society was the fundamental focus of Marx's intellectual work, for men must be liberated from the shackles which they unwittingly have produced for themselves. And in changing society, men must come to realize that they themselves can not only bring about legitimate and positive change but are personally responsible for the way things are, for 'men make their own history'. Thus, when men come to realize and accept the fact that 'human history is the process through which men change themselves even as they pit themselves against nature to dominate it', they are on their way to self-liberation.

Just as Comte distinguished three phases of human evolution on the basis of ways of thinking, Marx identified four stages of human history on the basis of modes of production: primitive communism, ancient slave production, feudalism, and capitalism. The relationship which men have with one another varies with the mode of production. Primitive communism signified communal ownership whereas ancient mode of production was characterized by slavery; the feudal mode of production by serfdom, and the capitalist system by the bourgeois exploitation of wage earners. Each of these stages, except primitive communism, constituted a distinct mode of man's exploitation of man and his struggle for freedom. Marx was committed not only to the analysis of this scenario but more particularly to its final culmination in the classless society of socialism. Marx believed that the process of dialectical materialism in which men struggle for survival in competition would end when the working people of the world (the proletariat) became sufficiently strong and politically conscious so that capitalism would be finally overthrown and socialism would be installed. This fifth and final state would constitute a classless society with no private property, and no distinctions between controllers and the controlled.

Defining Sociology ❖ 13

Although Marx did not consistently argue for a crude economic determinism, he left no doubt that he considered the economy to be the foundation of the whole socio-cultural system. Throughout their study, Marx and Engels emphasized the primacy of economics in human relationship and the centrality of the economic dimension in political structures. The economic system of production and distribution, or the means and relations of production in the Marxian sense, constitute the basic structure of society on which are built all other social institutions, particularly the state and legal system. According to Engels (Larson 1973: 43), '… the production of immediate material means of subsistence, and consequently, the degree of economic development attained by a given people or during a given epoch, form the foundation upon which the state institutions, the legal conceptions, the ideas on art, and even on religion, of the people concerned have been evolved.'

Consistent with his economic interpretation of history, Marx developed a variant of the sociology of knowledge which stressed the primacy of the economic principle in the evolution of ideologies, philosophical systems, politics, ethics, and religion. The central thesis of Marx (Johnson 1981: 133) is this: 'It is not the unfolding of ideas that explains the historical development of society (as Hegel and Comte would have argued), but the development of the social structure in response to changing material conditions that explains the emergence of new ideas.' According to Marx, ideas belong to the realm of the superstructure and are determined by the economic infrastructure. He believed that the ideologies prevailing at any particular point in time reflect the world view of the dominant class. In other words, ideas depend on the social positions—particularly on the class position of their proponents. These views, moreover, tend either to enhance or undermine the power and control of whatever class happens to be dominant at the time. If generated from the dominant class, they tend to be supportive and reinforce the predominance of the social structures. 'The ideas of the ruling class are, in every age, ruling ideas: i.e., the class which is the dominant *material* force in society is at the same time its dominant *intellectual* force. The class which has the means of material production at its disposal has control at the same time over the means of mental production' (Marx 1964: 60). Marx believed that we will fail to understand the historical process if we detach the ideas of the ruling class from the ruling class and attribute to them an independent existence. Therefore, he sought to trace the evolution of ideas to the life conditions in general, and the forces and relations of production in particular.

Marx's theory of class struggle is the most influential conflict perspective not only in sociology but in all social sciences, and we will discuss it in detail in the next chapter.

Herbert Spencer (1820–1903)

Although Comte coined the term sociology he never paid much attention to the subject matter of sociology; it was Herbert Spencer who defined the field of sociology and outlined the areas of interest which are still relevant today. Spencer's major contributions to sociology may be enumerated under three headings: organic analogy, evolutionary theory, and social Darwinism.

Organic analogy refers to the identification of society with a biological organism. Both society and organism undergo growth, development, and decay. Their parts are interrelated and their functions reciprocal. As they grow in size, they increase in complexity of structure and their parts become more differentiated. As a living organism is a nation of units, so is society. The significance of this analogy is the suggestion that society, as an organism, must be studied as a whole with interdependent parts. The analogy reminds us that any change in one part of the system is likely to affect other parts. This point of view has considerably influenced contemporary system theory and structural functionalism.

Spencer's evolutionary theory, often referred to as universal evolutionary theory, argues that every society does not necessarily go through the same fixed stages of development as Comte proposed, but the culture of mankind, taken as a whole, has followed a definite line of evolution. The theory involves essentially two processes. First, there is the necessary movement from simple societies to various levels of compound societies. Second, there is change from military to industrial society. An increase in the size of social units invariably accompanies an increase in the complexity of structure. Thus, as simple societies grow in size, they become heterogeneous and complex.

Social Darwinism, based on the principle of the survival of the fittest, was another idea that Spencer wholeheartedly endorsed. According to him, nature is endowed with a providential tendency to get rid of the unfit and make room for the better; it is the law of nature that the weak should be eliminated for the sake of the strong. Spencer was an untiring advocate of individualism and laissez-faire politics. He insisted that the state has absolutely no business in education, health, social welfare, or any programmes that seek to eliminate poverty, create jobs, or improve living conditions. Nature is more intelligent than man and it will be a fatal folly for him to interfere with the order of nature.

The ideology of social Darwinism, once very influential in American social thought, remains largely discredited today.

Émile Durkheim (1858–1917)

Whereas Comte never gained legitimate entry into academia and Spencer spurned academic opportunities, Émile Durkheim created the first course and first chair in sociology and pursued a brilliant academic career. Durkheim is considered to be the first empirical sociologist who examined massive data to formulate his original theories of religion and suicide. Durkheim's sociological realism was a frontal attack upon Spencerian individualism and much of what it stood for. A crucial concept in Durkheim's theory of solidarity is the collective conscience which is the sum total of beliefs and sentiments common to the average members of society and forming a system in its own right. This collective conscience, a distinct reality which persists through time and unites generations, is a product of human similarities.

Sociology is the study of social facts which are collective 'ways of acting, thinking, and feeling that present the noteworthy property of existing outside the individual consciousness' (Durkheim 1964). Social customs, mores, laws, institutions, religious observances, rules of professional behaviour, and even the so-called superstitions are social facts handed down by society from generation to generation. They have distinctive social characteristics; they are external to the individual; they endure through time, outlasting individuals and groups and are endowed with coercive power by virtue of which they impose themselves on the individual. Social facts are first and foremost 'things' which are social in nature and cannot be explained in terms of psychological or physiological analysis.

Durkheim rejected the assumption that the ultimate explanation of collective will emanates from human nature in general and that, therefore, sociological laws are only a corollary of the more general laws of psychology. Social processes are distinct in that they are external to the individual and independent of his will. Emphasizing the *sui generis* quality of social facts, Durkheim insisted that social phenomena cannot be reduced to individual phenomena. A whole is not identical to the sum of its parts; society is not a mere sum of individuals. The social system made up of individuals represents a distinct social reality with its own life and characteristics, and must be investigated at a higher level. From the outset, Durkheim's orientation towards the study of society required that economic and psychological reductionism be eschewed in deference to the *sui generis* quality of social facts. According to him, social facts are not merely manifestations of economic realities analysable using marketing graphs and tables, nor are they merely characteristic manifestations of psychological realities which must be analysed by studying individual personalities. Since social facts are social in nature, a science of social facts is needed to correctly analyse them. Facts, Durkheim argued, can be gathered by observing external and immediately visible phenomena, for example, religious affiliation, marital status, suicide rate and economic occupation. They must be treated as 'things', as empirical phenomena, not as concepts. Durkheim argued in *The Rules of Sociological Method*: 'Things include all objects of knowledge that cannot be conceived by purely mental activity, those that require for their conception data from outside the mind, from observations and experiments, those which are built up from the more external and immediately accessible characteristics to the less visible and more profound' (1964: xliii).

The theme of social solidarity was of foremost concern to Durkheim. His theory of social solidarity is fully discussed in Chapter 7 ('Types of Societies and Groups'). However, a few brief remarks are in order here. Durkheim did not subscribe to the notion prevalent at that time that modern industrialism and urbanism would destroy social solidarity and weaken the fabric of society. In fact, Durkheim argued that the specialization of tasks and the increasing social differentiation in advanced societies would create new and stronger bonds of mutual interdependence. Durkheim termed this type of social solidarity based on mutual interdependence 'organic solidarity' and differentiated it from mechanical solidarity based on similarities and consensus in traditional societies.

Durkheim's views on social solidarity and *sui generis* nature of society have made significant contributions to functionalism and methodology in sociology.

Durkheim's book, *Suicide*, is a monumental landmark in which conceptual theory and empirical research are brought together. He began with a refutation of several prevailing theories of suicide based on psychology, biology, genetics, climate, and geographical factors. Durkheim argued that suicide which appears to be a phenomenon relating to the individual is actually explicable aetiologically with reference to social structure and its ramifying functions. His central thesis was that suicide rate is a factual order, unified and definite. This is because, each society has a collective inclination towards suicide, a rate of self-homicide which is fairly constant so long as the basic conditions of its existence remain the same. He identified three major types of suicides:

1. *Egoistic Suicide*. Egoistic suicide results from the lack of integration of the individual into his social group. Durkheim studied varying degrees of integration of individuals into their religion, family, political, and national communities, and found that the stronger the forces throwing the individuals on to their own resources, the greater the suicide rate in society. For example, regardless of race and nationality, Catholics show far less suicides than Protestants because Catholicism is able to integrate its members more fully into its fold. Family, like a religious group, is a powerful counter agent against suicide. Non-marriage increases the tendency to suicide while marriage reduces the danger by half or more. Larger families are even more integrated and have greater immunity. Similarly, great political upheavals and popular wars rouse collective sentiments and national faith, leading to more powerful political integration, thus reducing the rate of suicide.

2. *Altruistic Suicide*. This type of suicide results from over-integration of the individual into his social group. An individual's life is so rigorously governed by custom and habit that he takes his own life because of higher commandments. Examples are legion: women throwing themselves at the funeral pyre of their husbands (sati), Danish warriors killing themselves in old age, Japanese Harakiri, self-immolation by Buddhist monks, and self-homicide by army suicide squads. In all these cases, the individual seeks 'to strip himself of his personal being in order to be engulfed in something which he regards as his true essence' (Durkheim 1951: 225).

3. *Anomic Suicide*. This results from normlessness or deregulation in society. Although this kind of suicide occurs during industrial or financial crises, it is not because they cause poverty; sudden prosperity or instant fortune can have the same effect. Durkheim attributed anomic suicide to unlimited aspirations and the breakdown of regulatory norms. There is nothing in man's organic structure or his psychological constitution which can regulate his overweening ambitions. Social desires can be regulated only by a moral force. But during abrupt transitions, such as economic disaster, industrial crisis

or sudden prosperity, society is temporarily incapable of exercising this influence and normlessness ensues. That is why, Durkheim reasons, anomie is a chronic state of affairs in the modern socio-economic system.

Additionally, Durkheim also identified a fourth type of suicide, termed *fatalistic suicide*, which results from over-regulation by society. When the individual is overly controlled by society, he or she feels powerless before it or considers himself/herself overwhelmed by fate. Durkehim thought this type of suicide will be less and less relevant in modern society.

Durkheim's work on religion is considered one of the major treatises in the field of sociology of religion as well as sociology of knowledge. See Chapter 14 on religion for a discussion of this theory.

Max Weber (1864–1920)

Generally regarded as the greatest sociologist, Max Weber made substantive contributions to almost every branch of sociology with original theories and perspectives. His scholarship has vastly enriched not only sociology but most other social sciences and humanities such as history, political science, economics, religion, art, and philosophy. Weber (1964: 88) defined sociology as 'a science which attempts the interpretive understanding of social action in order thereby to arrive at a causal explanation of its course and effects.' Social action is reciprocally oriented action which is intentional, meaningful, and symbolic. In contemporary sociology the term refers to interaction. Weber was primarily interested in the subjective meaning of action or the meaning actors give to their own actions. What intrigued Weber was the actually assigned 'reasons' for identifiable behaviour given by actors themselves. These behaviour complexes, oriented by individuals within specifiable socio-historical settings, were the subject of sociological analysis. In the absence of assigned 'meanings' by the individuals, the actions are meaningless and thus outside the purview of sociology. In this context, Weber introduced a key methodological concept called *verstehen* which means comprehending or understanding on the level of meaning. The notion of *verstehen* is based on what Weber perceived as an advantage of the social sciences over the natural sciences. In the natural sciences we can only observe uniformities and deduce generalizations about the functional relationships of elements; comprehension is, therefore, mediate. In the social sciences, on the other hand, we can understand the actions and comprehend the subjective intentions of the actors; comprehension is immediate. Our understanding of why lightning strikes or liquids freeze is mediate; they have no inside story to tell. But when students go on strike or political parties call for a hartal we must investigate the inside meaning. *Verstehen* makes possible the scientific study of social behaviour in two ways: it facilitates direct observational understanding of the subjective meaning of actions and it facilitates understanding of the underlying motive.

Max Weber is also well known for what is usually labelled the value-free approach in sociology. For Weber, values are precisely the subject matter and make possible a truly scientific study of human actions. However, values are a matter of faith, not scientific testimony; science cannot validate them. Therefore, sociologists must investigate values but cannot provide binding norms. Sociologists, Weber felt, must study what is and not what ought to be or ought not to be. They should investigate things as they are but cannot prescribe how they should be. Weber does not deny an individual scientist's right to uphold values and be guided by them. But in his scientific pursuit he must only be guided by objectivity and scientific integrity.

Weber's development of the concept of *ideal type* is a major contribution to sociological theory. An ideal type is an analytical construct that helps the researcher ascertain similarities as well as deviations in concrete cases. It is neither a statistical average nor a hypothesis; rather, it is a mental construct, an organization of intelligible relations within a historical entity, formed by exaggerating certain essential features of a given phenomenon so that no one case of that phenomenon corresponds exactly to the constructed type but every case of that phenomenon falls within the definitional framework. In the words of Shills and Finch (1949: 90), 'An ideal type is formed by the one-sided accentuation of one or more points of view and by the synthesis of a great many diffuse, discrete, more or less present and occasionally absent *concrete individual* phenomena, which are arranged according to those one-sidedly emphasized viewpoints into a unified *analytical* construct' (emphasis in original).

Weber developed three kinds of ideal types based on their levels of abstraction: 1. ideal types of historical particulars which refer to specific historical realities such as 'Western city', 'protestant ethic', or 'modern capitalism'; 2. ideal types which refer to abstract elements of the historical reality that are observable in a variety of historical and cultural contexts, such as 'bureaucracy' or 'feudalism'; 3. ideal types 'that constitute rationalizing reconstructions of a particular kind of behavior'. All propositions in economic theory may be said to fall in this category since they 'are merely ideal-typical reconstructions of the ways men would behave if they were pure economic subjects.'

The ideal type as Weber understood it had nothing to do with moral ideal, for the type of perfection implied in the ideal is purely a logical one and not to be found in pure form in any socio-historical situation. Weber cautioned against the tendency to treat the ideal typology as a *carte blanch* solution to all social analysis. It is strictly a 'methodological device' and is not intended to suggest that social phenomena are essentially rational complexes, though the ideal type is a rational grid for logical observation and analysis. Applied primarily to various types of rational behaviour, it is fundamentally a 'model of what an agent would do if he were to act completely rationally according to the criteria of rationality involved in his behaviour's sense'. In such instances, the ideal type provides a milieu of precise language and procedure for analysing specific behaviour while aiding in the formulation of theoretical explanations for behavioural instances which vary from what is called the 'ideal-typical norm'. Weber also applied this ideal-typical norm to define and classify so many other concepts such as authority/domination which are discussed in Chapter 12 ('The Political Economy').

Weber's theory of protestant ethic and the spirit of capitalism is one of the most influential pieces which have inspired numerous studies. In this Weber argued that a certain cluster of values embedded in Protestantism promoted hard work, thrift, and several similar values which fostered capitalism in the West. Weber's perspectives on bureaucracy, social stratification, and sociological methodology continue to guide contemporary sociology.

There are also other masters of sociological thought who substantially influenced the subject matter of sociology. Georg Simmel is one of the founders of mirco-sociology and formal sociology with emphasis on the study of small groups and social interaction. Ferdinand Tonnies' typology of Gemeinschaft and Gesellschaft which corresponds to 'traditional' or 'folk' communities and 'modern' or 'urban' societies has provided a powerful conceptual scheme for the analysis of social and behavioural systems. Vilfredo Pareto's conceptualization of society as a system in equilibrium remains a central theme in current structural-functionalism.

To put the history of sociology in perspective, it must, however, be pointed out that sociology as an academic discipline emerged only in the nineteenth century. Comte, Marx, Spencer and other founding fathers made substantial contribution to the development of sociology. But they were primarily social philosophers rather than social scientists. While Comte was preoccupied with the moral reconstruction of society, Marx envisioned a utopian society based on equality and justice. Whereas Spencer endorsed the process of natural evolution, Durkheim emphasized social solidarity based on consensus. There were also significant differences between European and American sociology. Marxian sociology had considerable influence in the early development of sociology in Europe, but its influence was very limited in America. Moreover, the subfields of sociology were not given equal attention in every country. For example, while American sociology was almost alone in its attempt to develop research methodology as a special field, European sociology made substantial progress in the sociology of knowledge and the study of values.

Although it is generally accepted that Durkheim is the first empirical sociologist, it was only in 1913 that he was offered an academic position with a sociology title (Professor of Education and Sociology). In the United States, the first course in sociology was taught in 1876 at Yale University by William Graham Sumner. In 1893, the University of Chicago became the first to establish an academic department offering doctorate in sociology. Gradually, sociology began to add several fields and schools, and after World War II, sociology came to be accepted as a distinct social science almost all over the world.

Contemporary Sociology

Although France and Germany produced most of the founding fathers of sociology, the United States played a major role in the advancement of contemporary sociology. Talcott Parsons, Pitirim Sorokin, and Robert Merton emerged as the three leading figures in modern American sociology. While Sorokin focused primarily on socio-cultural dynamics, Parsons developed the general system theory and Merton proposed theories of the middle range. George Homans,

Alex Inkeles, Alvin Gouldner, Lewis Coser and many others have contributed significantly to the development of modern sociology.

In India, sociology was introduced as a course in the economics department at the University of Calcutta in 1917. Two years later, Bombay University established the first Department of Sociology. Universities of Bombay, Delhi, Agra, Baroda, and Lucknow led the way for the initial development of sociology. For example, the Lucknow School led by Radhakamal Mukherji made significant contributions to ecological and institutional theories. However, to a large extent in India, traditionally anthropologists have focused on subjects which are central to sociology. They have made significant contributions to studies in caste, joint family system, rural communities, and social change. Similarly, a number of sociologists and anthropologists especially M.N. Srinivas, G.S. Ghurye, A.R. Desai, and others have made significant contributions to our understanding of the caste system, political processes, Indian culture, economic development, urban society, socio-cultural change, and family.

Sociology has come a long way from the days of the founding fathers. Earlier emphasis on social evolution has given way to social change first and development later. Sociology is no longer confined to the study of culture and various social institutions and processes. The field of sociology has now grown to incorporate numerous subfields such as complex organizations, demography, ecology, environmental sociology, feminist sociology, military sociology, peace studies, medical sociology, criminology, social stratification, sociology of religion, sociology of sport, sociology of the Third World, industrial sociology, sociology of occupations, and many more, in addition to such traditional fields as community, rural and urban sociology, sociology of knowledge, theory, methodology, comparative sociology, and sociology of education. In recent years sociology has also become more interdisciplinary and global in outlook.

With globalization came new challenges and opportunities, and sociology responded with expansion into new fields and schools. Human sexuality, sociology of gender, sociology of mass communication, global culture, modernization, sociology of developing societies, environmental sociology, and a host of other fields found new impetus. The old concept of community based on spatial setting was transformed to embrace the concept of electronic communities based on social networking. Cultural systems based on geography and the ideology of nationalism have been overshadowed, to a large extent, by the new superstructures of globalism which, according to Jan Aart Scholte (2000), are any social phenomena which are 'supraterritorial'. Revolution in transport and communication technology, explosion of internet, waves of international migration, global consumerism, the rise of multinational corporations (MNCs), and the emergence of numerous international organizations have transformed the boundaries of social systems and social sciences. Yet, it will be an exaggeration to say that these developments have hastened the advent of a true global culture. In fact, studies suggest that several traditional cultures make use of electronic technology to strengthen their subcultures. International business corporations adapt their products and strategies to the cultural ethos of local communities. Even the Taliban uses the most advanced technology to promote fundamental Islamic traditions. Therefore, sociology, the scientific study of society, will remain as local as it is global, probably with more emphasis on comparative and interdisciplinary perspectives.

STUDY QUESTIONS

- Define the following concepts in a few sentences: social statics and social dynamics; economic determinism; and social facts.
- Write a paragraph on the following: unilinear evolutionary theory; social Darwinism; organic analogy; *sui generis* nature of society; *Verstehen*; ideal type; and value-free sociology.
- Define sociology and enumerate the distict characteristics of the discipline.
- How is sociology related to other social sciences? Explain.
- Sociology provides a unique sociological perspective on the world around us. Elucidate with illustration.
- Discuss Comte's positivism.
- Briefly summarize Comte's law of the three stages.
- Summarize Durkheim's theory of suicide.

REFERENCES

Abraham, M. Francis, *Sociological Thought*, New Delhi: Macmillan India Limited, 1985.

Abraham, M. Francis and John Morgan, *Sociological Thought*, New Delhi: Macmillan India Limited, 1985.

Berger, Peter, *Invitation to Sociology: A Humanistic Perspective*, New York: Doubleday, 1963.

Coser, A. Lewis, *Masters of Sociological Thought*, New York: Harcourt Brace Jovanovich, 1971.

Durkheim, Émile, *Suicide,* New York: Free Press, 1951.

———, Preface to the Second Edition, *The Rules of Sociological Method*, New York: Free Press, p. xliii, 1964.

Fromm, Eric, *Marx's Concept of Man,* New York: Frederick Ungar, 1961.

Harris, Marvin, *Culture, People and Nature*, New York: Crowell, 1975.

———, 'The Cultural Ecology of India's Sacred Cattle', *Current Anthropology*, 7, pp. 51–63, 1966.

Sills, David L. (ed.), *International Encyclopedia of the Social Sciences*, New York: The Macmillan Company, p. 1, 1972.

Johnson, Doyle P., *Sociological Theory*, New York: John Wiley and Sons, 1981.

Larson, Calvin, *Major Themes in Sociological Theory*, New York: David McKay, 1973.

Marx, Karl, *Selected Writings in Sociology and Social Philosophy*, London: McGraw-Hill, 1964.

Mills, C. Wright, *The Sociological Imagination*, New York: Oxford University Press, 1959.

Scholte, Jan Aart, *Globalization: A Critical Introduction*, London: Macmillan, 2000.

Shills, E.A. and H.A. Finch, *Max Weber on the Methodology of the Social Sciences*, New York: Free Press, 1949.

Weber, Max, *Theory of Social and Economic Organization*, New York: Free Press, 1964.

Theoretical Perspectives in Sociology

What is Sociological Theory?

Scholarship in the social and philosophical sciences through the ages has shown a persistent interest in theories about human behaviour and has produced an abundant crop of literature. However, there is no general agreement on the definition of theory, and the proponent of every theory seems to have his own view of what constitutes a theory. According to some sociologists, a 'theory is an explanation of the relationships between phenomena which is not solidly established as a law, but is more than a mere hypothesis' (Mihanovich 1957). To others, a theory should be stated formally in a deductive–inductive system and should be verifiable. Sociological theories differ considerably in terms of such characteristics as verifiability, precision, scope, predictive power, or the radius of the explanatory shell.

In the mainstream sociology, there are two general definitions of theory which reflect the broad spectrum of sociological thought. In the words of Abraham Kaplan (1964: 295):

A theory is a way of making sense of a disturbing situation so as to allow us most effectively to bring to bear our repertoire of habits, and even more important, to modify habits or discard them altogether, replacing them by new ones as the situation demands. In the reconstructed logic, accordingly, theory will appear as the device for interpreting, criticizing, and unifying established laws, modifying them to fit data unanticipated in their formulation, and guiding the enterprise of discovering new and more powerful generalizations. To engage in theorizing means not just to learn by experience but to take thought about what is there to be learned. To speak loosely, lower animals grasp scientific laws but never rise to the level of scientific theory. They learn *by* experience but not *from* it, for *from* learning requires symbolic constructions which can provide vicarious experience never actually undergone.

Robert Merton (1957: 39) provides a simpler and more popular definition: 'the term sociological theory refers to logically interconnected sets of propositions from which empirical uniformities can be derived.' The dominant mainstream in sociological thought as well as the greater proportion of current literature in contemporary sociological theory views theory as composed of three major realms:

1. Main currents in sociological thought, especially as manifested in the works of great masters like Comte, Spencer, Durkheim, Weber, Pareto, Simmel, Tonnies, and others.

2. General modes of sociological analysis like evolutionary theories, structural-functionalism, conflict theory, exchange theory, symbolic interactionism, and the system theory which generate a host of propositions concerning society as a whole.
3. A large number of theoretical perspectives, paradigms, empirical generalizations, deductive–inductive systems, and typologies which deal with the relationships between units within society.

A theory is a plausible explanation about social phenomena or a class of social phenomena, logically construed and systematically organized, that underscores the relationship between two well-defined variables. It is more than a hypothesis or speculative reasoning but far from a scientific law, that is supported by evidence. A theory is thus contrasted with a fact, law, and practice. A fact is an empirically verifiable observation whereas a theory is a systematized statement of relationship between facts. And a theory cannot be derived from empirical observations and generalizations merely by means of rigorous induction. A theory is a symbolic construction and theory-building is a matter of creative achievement. A theory is thus an abstract conceptual scheme that reaches out beyond itself, transcending the observable realm of empirical reality into a higher level of abstraction by means of a symbolic construction.

Types of Sociological Theory

There are three broad categories of sociological theory.

Speculative Theories vs. Grounded Theories

Speculative theory refers to an abstract impressionistic approach rooted in the philosophical system. The great encyclopedic minds of Comte and Spencer have synthesized the findings of a variety of disciplines to formulate a formidable array of impressive theoretical systems to explain social processes and organizations. But grounded theory is based on the findings of empirical research, and in the words of Glaser and Strauss, 'generating grounded theory is a way of arriving at theory, suited to its supposed uses. We shall contrast this position with theory generated by logical deduction from *a priori* assumptions' (Larson 1973: 2). A speculative theory corresponds to a conceptual ordering whereas grounded theory corresponds to an empirical generalization. The former generates a host of assumptions, philosophical and methodological, as well as theoretical entities and conceptual schema; the latter produces specific sociological laws, principles, and empirical generalizations. Speculative theories usually give rise to theoretical laws, and grounded theories to empirical laws. Speculative theories usually rely on historical method whereas grounded theories make use of positive methods and mathematical procedures. The philosophical treatises of Comte, Spencer, and Marx are counted among speculative theories, whereas beginning with Durkheim's study of suicide, all data-based theories are considered grounded theories.

Grand Theories vs. Miniature Theories

A grand theory is a broad conceptual scheme with systems of interrelated propositions that provide a general frame of reference for the study of social processes and institutions. It differs from speculative theory only in that its propositions are somewhat anchored—although not solidly—in the empirical world, whereas the propositions emanating from the speculative theories are essentially assumptions rooted in the philosophical system. The difference is only a matter of degree, not of kind. A grand theory is a comprehensive formulation generating a host of propositions and it provides a master scheme of general sociological orientations. Grand theories abound in jargon, tendency-statements, and intuitive generalizations. Parsons' general system theory and Sorokin's theory of socio-cultural dynamics are examples of grand theories.

Miniature theories are partial theories, rather than inclusive theories. They are often centred on a single proposition or a simple hypothesis. Then there are what Merton (1957: 5–6) calls 'theories of the middle range: theories immediate to the minor working hypotheses evolved in abundance during the day-to-day routines of research, and the all-inclusive speculations comprising a master conceptual scheme from which it is hoped to derive a very large number of empirically observed uniformities of social behaviour.' They are more specific and their frame of reference is considerably limited; they generate a manageable number of propositions concerning specific units within society. They are less pretentious than the high-sounding all-inclusive grand theories. Merton's theories of anomie, relative deprivation, and reference group, Homans' theory of elementary social behaviour, and Festinger's theory of cognitive dissonance are examples of theories of the middle range.

Macro Theories vs. Micro Theories

On the basis of the radius of their explanatory shell, theories may be classified as macro and micro or molar and molecular theories. Macro theories are broader in scope, and encompass an extended range of laws. Micro theories have a narrow frame of reference and focus on a limited range of phenomena. Early masters of social thought were almost exclusively concerned with grand, cosmic issues or total societal patterns and thus they expounded great macro theories of society. Micro sociology is concerned with 'interactions among the atoms of society'. Psychological reductionism, role theory, and small group theories represent micro tradition in contemporary sociology. The distinction between the two types of theories is based on the size of the unit of analysis rather than the level of analysis. Macro theorists, for example, study the factory as a social system; micro theories, on the other hand, seek to analyse workers' behaviour within the industrial establishment. While macro theory deals with the caste system within the Hindu social organization, micro theory might focus on the lifestyle of a particular subcaste. The former delineates the social structure; the latter explains social roles and individual behaviour that mediate the structure. Macro theories deal with society as a whole; mirco theories deal with the subsystems that make up the whole.

Macro theories are a species of grand theories and can be verified only in a preliminary fashion. Micro theories belong to the tribe of miniature theories and can be 'tested' in a 'scientific' sense. This is why many scientists claim that micro theories are intrinsically more satisfactory and fruitful in the pursuit of scientific inquiry. However, this position is untenable in the social sciences. Money cannot be reduced to coin; nor can social phenomena be reduced to individual phenomena. Society is more than an aggregate of individuals because of the qualitative jump involved in the transformation of the units into the social system. There are many sociological phenomena for which molecular theories cannot provide any satisfactory explanation because of the multiplicity of the variables included and the complexity of their relationships. Hence we choose between types of theories depending on the social phenomena and the range of variables involved.

FUNCTIONS OF SOCIOLOGICAL THEORY

We may summarize the major functions of sociological theory as follows:

1. *Theory suggests potential problems and produces new investigative studies.* A fruitful theory is a storehouse of meaningful hypotheses and a continuous source of inspiration to the process of sociological inquiry. And many empirical investigations lead to theory-building just as they proceed from well-formulated theories.
2. *Theory predicts facts.* Based on intuitive knowledge, historical analysis, and observation of social uniformities, a theoretical system often provides a secure ground for prediction. Usually expressed as tendency-statements, such theoretical postulates increase the fruitfulness of research by providing leads for further inquiry.
3. *Theory systematizes matters and their relationships into convenient conceptual schema.* Not only does it explain observed regularities and social uniformities, it also simplifies laws and establishes order in congeries of facts. A 'mental shorthand' so to speak, theory summarizes relationships between variables in a conceptual framework.
4. *Theory establishes a linkage between specific empirical findings and general sociological orientations, thus enhancing the meaningfulness of research.* Unrelated findings of isolated studies suddenly assume new meanings when they are put in the proper sociological perspective. Theory mediates between specific empirical generalizations and broad sociological orientations rooted in the intellectual tradition.
5. *Theory guides research and narrows down the range of facts to be studied.* Theory supplies hypotheses, provides direction to the investigation, and helps the researcher look for certain variables and overlook others. Just as theory points to clues which give us insight into what we are to find, it also helps the researcher ignore an array of factors which may or may not yield results.
6. *Theories serve as tools of inquiry.* They aid in the formulation of a research design, in conducting experiments, in the selection of measurements, in the quantification of data,

and in the final interpretation of data. This function corresponds to the instrumentalist view of theories.

7. *Theory points to gaps in our knowledge and seeks to fill them with intuitive, impressionistic or 'existential generalizations'.* To use the words of Kaplan (1964: 303): 'What is important is that laws propagate when they are united in a theory: theory serves as a matchmaker, midwife and godfather all in one. This service is what is delicately known as the "heuristic function of theory".'

MAINLINE THEORIES IN SOCIOLOGY

There are five mainline theories which provide general perspectives in sociology. They are:

1. Evolutionary Theory
2. Structural-functionalism
3. Conflict Theory
4. Symbolic Interactionism
5. Exchange Theory

In addition to these five, sometimes system theory is mentioned as a separate general theory in sociology. However, system theory may be regarded as a variant of the more general theory of structural-functionalism which involves a prior conceptualization of 'system'.

Evolutionary Theory

Early sociologists and anthropologists were so preoccupied with the process of evolution that they laboured to show the lawful nature of societal growth through systematically defined stages, such as hunting-and-gathering, horticultural, agrarian, and industrial, that human culture treaded. The theoretical structure erected by the early evolutionists inhered the notion of cumulative development in human culture and considered progress, defined as an intrinsic goal, inevitable and universal. Although nineteenth century evolutionism has fallen into disuse, models of man and society derived from it continue to exercise some influence on contemporary sociology.

There are at least four variants of evolutionary theory:

1. *Unilinear Evolutionary Theory.* Based on the assumption that human culture has undergone progressive and cumulative growth, unilinear evolutionary theory posits that man and society are progressing up definite steps of evolution leading to some final stage of perfection. As we saw in the first chapter, Comte believed that every society will pass through three stages and culminate in the inauguration of a scientific–industrial society

characterized by progress in all aspects of life. Lewis Henry Morgan traced the unilinear development of societal progress 'from savagery through barbarism to civilization'.

2. *Universal Evolutionary Theory.* This perspective traces, as Spencer has done, the development of human communities from simple to more complex forms with all its attendant consequences, particularly those of increasing differentiation of parts and the integration of structure. It is not concerned with fixed stages or a unilinear sequence of development; nor does it assume that every society goes through the same stages. The universal evolutionary theory posits that human society as a whole has followed a discernible path of evolution with varying consequences and patterns in different cultures.

3. *Cyclical Evolutionary Theory.* According to this perspective there is no straight line evolution but there are discernible stages or cycles which a society or a long-enduring culture may go through more than once or even repeatedly. The famous rise and fall theory of civilization expounded by Oswald Spengler best illustrates the cyclical evolutionary perspective. Rejecting all previous conceptions of historical time, Spengler argued that there was not one linear time but as many times as there were historical civilizations. Thus, each society, like an organism, has birth, adolescence, youth, maturity, decline, and decay. The rising phase of society is referred to as culture and its declining phase as civilization. In a similar vein, Arnold Toynbee proposed the 'circular staircase theory of history'. The main thrust of his work is that while the course of its history as a whole is cyclical, every long-enduring culture climbs to great heights, each succeeding step a little bit better than the one preceding it. Pitirim Sorokin's theory of social and cultural dynamics also fits the cyclical evolutionary perspective in that it describes the course of history as a continuous but irregular fluctuation between sensate and ideational cultures. Sensate systems are based on the testimony of our senses which dictate that nothing is true or genuine beyond what we can see or feel. Ideational systems are based on faith in supernatural forces and the perception of transcendental reality. There is also the idealistic culture which represents a synthesis of both sensate and ideational cultures. The Golden Age in the history of every society reflects idealistic culture whereas the declining phase of civilization devoid of moral values but dominated by the urge to satisfy greed, sensual needs, and desires represents sensate cultures.

4. *Multilinear Evolutionary Theory.* Contemporary evolutionists have abandoned the grand theories of evolution that make sweeping generalizations about the cumulative development of human civilization; they focus, instead, on the processes and consequences of types of change in a given society. With the whole-scale repudiation of unilinear evolutionism at the turn of the century the entire evolutionary perspective fell into disuse. But in recent years the works of several leading anthropologists have largely revived an interest in evolutionary perspective. Similarly in sociology, Parsons, Bellah, Eisenstadt, Wilbert Moore and others have formulated explicit conceptions of evolution to explain the processes of structural differentiation and functional specialization. Then

there are numerous sociologists, especially the proponents of various modernization theories, who use an essentially evolutionary frame of reference without acknowledging it. As Wilbert Moore (1963: 39) puts it, 'What is involved in modernization is a "total transformation" of a traditional or pre-modern society into the types of technology and associated social organization that characterize the "advanced", economically prosperous, and relatively politically stable nations of the Western world.' Similarly, Lerner (1968: 386) defined modernization as 'the process of social change whereby less developed societies acquire characteristics common to more developed societies.'

Although many sociologists would deny it, the advocates of structural-functionalism and the proponents of diachronic theories of modernization often utilize an evolutionary frame of reference. The unilinear theory of evolution, of course, stands discredited. The concepts of evolution and progress, regarded as value-laden, were replaced by those of change and differentiation, apparently value-free. But the evolutionary perspective provides a powerful conceptual tool for the analysis of the processes and patterns of change. However, it must be emphasized that the evolutionary perspective is more a descriptive typological tradition than an explanatory theoretical system; it is primarily an approach to the study of social change in different societies, not a generalized theory of any particular social system.

Structural-functionalism

The theory of social structure and the theory of functionalism are closely linked; every structuralist deals with function of the social structure and every functionalist studies the structure of the social system. Therefore, for all practical purposes, we may treat structural-functionalism as one theory.

Levi-Strauss conceived of social structure as a logic behind reality. He insisted that the 'term social structure has nothing to do with empirical reality but with models which are built up after it'. He took Radcliffe-Brown to task for not distinguishing between social structure and social relations. While social relations constitute the raw materials out of which the models making up the social structure are built, the structure itself cannot be reduced to an ensemble of social relations; rather such relations themselves result from some pre-existing structures. The structure exhibits the characteristics of a system and is made up of several elements, none of which can undergo change without effecting changes in all other elements.

Whereas Levi-Strauss regards social structure as a model behind reality, Nadel views it as reality itself. He regards the role system of any society, with its given coherence, as the matrix of the social structure. Nadel's conception of structure is based on three criteria: repetitiveness of the social phenomena (that is, when some definable state of affairs can be said to reproduce itself); durability of the social phenomena (that is, when particular social phenomena last for a long time or run their full course); and moving equilibrium (when a regular state of affairs, on being upset by some identifiable disturbance, reasserts itself or returns to status quo). Thus, Nadel views structural analysis in quasi-static terms, as an attempt to capture the uniformities in the underlying processes.

The history of functional analysis may be traced to Comte's consensus universalis, Spencer's organic analogy, Pareto's conception of society as a system in equilibrium, and Durkheim's causal-functional analysis. Comte viewed society as a functionally organized system, its components in harmony. To him, consensus universalis, the necessary correlation between the elements of society, was the very foundation of social structure. Spencer (1971: 615–16) presented an organic biological model and contended: 'If organization consists in such construction of the whole that its parts can carry on mutually-dependent actions, then in proportion as organization is high there must go a dependence of each part upon the rest so great that separation is fatal; and conversely. This truth is equally well shown in the individual organism and in the social organism.' However, he attributed social structures and processes to individual needs such as desire for happiness, a contention rejected outright by Durkheim. In the anthropological tradition, Radcliffe-Brown and Malinowski elaborated and codified functionalism as the basis of anthropological—and sociological—thinking.

Malinowski's functionalism is often termed as individualistic functionalism because of its treatment of social and cultural dynamics as collective responses to fundamental biological needs of individuals modified by cultural values. Social structures and processes, institutions and values, are all regarded as functional responses to individual physiological needs such as hunger and sex, which prompt cultural usages and social institutions, which, in turn, shape the way these basic drives express themselves. However, Radcliffe-Brown rejected Malinowski's individualistic functionalism and, following Durkheimian tradition, emphasized structured social relationships. But he substituted Durkheim's term 'needs' by 'necessary condition of existence' to avoid teleological interpretations. Having rejected Malinowski's emphasis on stated motives of individual participants, Radcliffe-Brown chose social structure as the unit of analysis and sought to explain numerous interpersonal relationships and socially patterned ways of minimizing built-in strains inherent in such relationships. Radcliffe-Brown focused primarily on the function of each element—in the maintenance and development of a *total* structure—and largely overlooked functional consequences of specific elements for differentiated parts of the whole and for the individual components.

Modern sociological theory has been profoundly influenced by structural-functional, or simply functional, analysis which became enormously popular at the turn of the century. Today functional analysis has become the principal, if not the only reigning, paradigm of contemporary sociology with more adherents than any other mode of sociological analysis or school of thought. Functionalism is simply a view of society as a self-regulating system of interrelated elements with structured social relationships and observed regularities. It is a sociological perspective which seeks to explain a social element or cultural pattern in terms of its consequences for different elements as well as for the system as a whole. Although functionalism manifests itself in a variety of approaches, there is one common element: 'an interest in relating one part of a society or social system to another part or to some aspect of the whole' (Cancian 1968: 29). When functional analysis looks at any social institution such as the joint family, the caste system, religion, a political party, or an industrial complex, it looks at it as a social system with interrelated parts, and seeks to explain how the parts are related to one another and to the whole and what functions they all serve. Similarly, every social usage, behavioural pattern, even the so-called superstitions are analysed in terms of their functions. In short, functional analysis seeks to describe the consequences of a given cultural usage or social element; explain the persistence of an observed pattern of behaviour; and analyse the specific contribution of a part of some whole to other parts and to the whole.

Functional analysis involves the prior conceptualization of a system and a definite emphasis on the primacy of the system over elements. In other words, functionalists view all social institutions and arrangements as social systems, and a system is considered to be more than a sum of its parts. The focus is on the relationships among its parts and the contribution of the elements to the maintenance of the system. Society, like an organism, is perceived as a system of functionally interrelated components each of which, like an organ, performs a function essential to the survival of the system. The normal operation of one element, then, requires the normal operation of other elements. For example, conventional wisdom in early anthropological analysis has portrayed traditional societies as coherent, harmoniously interwoven cultural systems with greater internal consistency, uniformity, and homogeneity. Although modern societies are complex, rather than homogeneous, and characterized by greater structural differentiation, they are still regarded as systems with interdependent parts.

Every element of a social system has a function which contributes positively to the continued operation of that system or, negatively, towards its disintegration and change. In this context, Merton distinguished between manifest and latent functions and between function and dysfunction. Manifest functions are those consequences that are intended and recognized by the participants in the system of action concerned, and latent functions are those consequences neither intended nor recognized by participants. Positive function is any activity or usage that contributes to the adaptation or adjustment of the unit to its setting. However, the same social arrangement can have, or may be perceived to have, both positive and negative consequences. Religion is perceived as means of salvation by the faithful but it is characterized as the opiate of the people by Marxists. What is functional for some may be dysfunctional for others. The rain that saves a crop spoils a picnic. What is in the best interest of the individual may be detrimental to the solidarity of the collectivity. The caste system may have been functional for the upper castes but it was certainly disastrous for the lower castes who were oppressed and suppressed through the ages. The typology of manifest and latent functions is equally illuminating. Most customs and activities have certain intended functions but they may also have some unintended consequences. The Muslim who undertakes the traditional pilgrimage to Mecca and the Hindu who organizes an elaborate ritualistic ceremony to write the name of his favourite deity a million times are both trying to acquire spiritual merits, the intended function of the activity, but the latent function may be a substantial enhancement of the status and prestige of the individual actor. Furthermore, latent functions of certain activities are recognized by interested groups although not intended by the sponsors of those activities. For example, the intended function of establishing a new college in a small town is to serve the needs of higher education. But the latent function may be a significant boost to the local economy. Thus, functionalism looks at all the consequences of social actions, institutions, customs, and practices.

Functionalists also see society as a relatively persistent structure of elements with built-in mechanisms for self-regulation. Using the principle of homeostasis, Parsons and his associates view society as a self-regulating system, attempting by more or less automatic adjustments to redress the balance of its equilibrium when it is upset by internal or external forces. Initially, the functionalists regarded society as a stable system of patterned interaction or structured social relationships. In this view, basic relationships among system components change little over time, and the emphasis was on such concepts as order, stability, structure, integration, and persistence. Later, faced with the criticism that equilibrium meant maintenance of status quo with no scope for fundamental changes, the functionalists introduced the concept of dynamic equilibrium. According to this view, change is not only possible but the original position may not be restored, and the new balance may create a new order and a new equilibrium.

The thrust of the functionalist position is that the dominant condition of society is order, reinforced by stability and consensus. Parsons views the entire social system as resting heavily upon shared values. Thus, the functionalists tend to exaggerate homogeneity, stability, and integration of the social systems. This view is derived from anthropological studies of simple pre-literate societies which were more or less homogeneous social systems. Although its application to modern complex societies with considerable structural differentiation and functional specialization is extremely limited, many functionalists continue to stress the integrative function of values. Functionalism also has largely underplayed conflict and structural strain. Having overstressed integration and consensus, functionalists overlook conflicts, especially contradictions inherent in social structure.

Conflict Theory

Whereas structural-functionalism has established itself as a dominant mode of sociological analysis, conflict theory is still in its infantile stage. As a matter of fact, there is no such thing as *the* conflict theory of sociology; rather, there are several conflict theories which seek to explain specific aspects of social phenomena. Generally speaking, conflict theories tend to be specific, restricted to the interrelationship between two or more units within society. Caste and communal conflicts, political violence, class war, strikes, protests, student movements, revolutions, peasant uprisings, and the like often become subjects of analysis. Karl Marx and

Ralf Dahrendorf represent macro-level conflict theories; C. Wright Mills' theory of the power elite is also a general theory but its frame of reference is limited to American society.

Karl Marx: The Theory of Class Struggle

Marx believed that human society passed through different stages of development and that each stage contained the seeds of its own destruction. However, Marx did not see history as a monotonous succession of struggles between the rich and the poor. Although the class war has always been between the oppressor and the oppressed, the leading contenders in the social drama of conflict differed markedly in different historical periods. The capitalist society, however, is based on the concentration of the means of production and distribution in the hands of a few. The bourgeoisie use the state as an instrument of economic exploitation and consolidation of self-interests. Inherent in capitalist society is a tendency towards the radical polarization of classes into two hostile camps, bourgeoisie and proletariat, the capitalists who own the means of production and distribution and the working classes who own nothing but their own labour. The poverty of the proletariat grows with increasing exploitation of labour. As the wealth of the bourgeoisie is swelled by profits, the workers become poorer and poorer. The economic exploitation and inhuman working conditions lead to increasing alienation of man. Work is no longer an expression of man himself, only a degraded instrument of livelihood. And the product of work becomes an instrument of alien purpose. With the development of industry, the proletariat not only increases in number, it becomes concentrated in greater masses and becomes conscious of its existence and its strength. Workers unite and begin to fight for their rights. At the height of the class war a violent revolution breaks out which destroys the structure of capitalist society. The bloody revolution terminates capitalist society and leads to the social dictatorship of the proletariat. The revolution is violent but does not necessarily involve mass killings of the bourgeoisie; since property is wrested from them, the bourgeoisie will cease to have power and be transformed into the ranks of the proletariat. Socialization of effective private property will terminate class and thereby the causes of social conflict. The state will eventually wither away as it becomes obsolete in a classless society in which nobody owns anything but everybody owns everything, and each individual contributes according to his ability and receives according to his need.

This, in a nutshell, is Karl Marx's theory of social conflict. Marx had only limited influence on the development of early sociology in the nineteenth century which was dominated by evolutionists, but the mid-twentieth century witnessed a rebirth of Marxist sociology which remains today at the centre of dialectic and conflict analysis. However, the original premises and postulates of Marx are considered too simplistic. Marx misjudged or grossly exaggerated the polarization of society into two hostile classes, the extent of alienation and total powerlessness of workers, and the ushering in of a utopian classless society without the state. However, Marx's overall theme of the struggle between the 'haves' and the 'have-nots' continues to be influential in the analysis of social conflicts. Conflict sociologists make effective use of Marxian theoretical schema to explain the processes of class conflict and revolutionary social movements around the world: conflicts between landless peasantry and landed aristocracy, between political and military elites, between workers and management in industrial societies, populist movements and conservative counter-revolutions, and various ideological warfare. Contemporary Marxist sociology has accumulated a considerable amount of evidence to substantiate the Marxian postulates that economic position is the major determinant of one's lifestyle, attitudes, and behaviour, and that a strategic position in the economic structure along with access to effective means of production and distribution hold the key to political power. The modern theory of power elite is only a variation of the Marxian theme of economic determinism which argues that economic dominants in a community are also potential power wielders.

Like Marx, Weber also recognized the emergence of capitalist mechanism in modern economic development. However, he saw capitalism as only one of the major factors shaping social development, and stressed the importance of non-economic factors such as values in the development of capitalism itself. Again like Marx, Weber also believed that modern societies are fraught with class inequalities which are basic to their very nature, and as such he attributed positions of power—dominance and submission—to such economic inequalities. However, Weber did not subscribe to the Marxian notion that class struggle will eventually overthrow capitalism. Rather, he stressed the process of rationalization which involved the development of science, modern technology, and bureaucracy.

The Frankfurt School and Critical Theory

The Frankfurt school is so called because of its association with the Institute for Social Research in Frankfurt, Germany, which was established by a group of young neo-Marxists to undertake an independent study of Marxism. The most outstanding members of the Institute were Theodore Adorno, Max Horkheimer, Herbert Marcuse, Eric Fromm, Leo Lowenthal, and Franz Neumann. The theoretical system of the Frankfurt school is essentially conflict-oriented and owes a great deal to Marx. However, its proponents are by no means orthodox Marxists. They draw heavily on the early writings of Marx and also employ 'conventional' sociological analysis of Max Weber and Karl Mannheim. Additionally, they attempt to tie together psychoanalysis and Marxism by synthesizing the Marxist theory of social structure and change and the Freudian theory of individual motivation and personality.

Convinced that the orthodox Marxist theory of capitalism can no longer account for the basic contradictions of the advanced industrial society, Jürgen Habermas, one of the most articulate spokesmen for the school, developed his own model of critical theory with particular attention to the recent developments in the capitalist system. Unlike Marx, Habermas saw three different types of capitalist societies: 1. Liberal capitalism—the nineteenth century capitalism that Marx theorized about; 2. Organized capitalism that characterizes western industrialized societies; and 3. Post-capitalism of the 'state-socialist societies' with 'political-elitist disposition of the means of production'. Like Marx, Habermas saw contradictions inherent in each of the systems which will ultimately lead to its disintegration and change, and emphasizes the role of ideas and consciousness in bringing about such changes.

Critical theory has become an influential school of thought within conflict sociology. Schroyer (1978: 251–4) defines critical theory 'as that kind of inquiry which is capable of analyzing the supposed and actual necessity of historical modes of authority and which presupposes the interest of the emancipation of men from law-like patterns of nature and history.' He continues:

'Construction of a critical theory follows the principle of an immanent critique. By first expressing what a social totality holds itself to be, and then confronting it with what it is, a critical theory is able to break down the rigidity of the object. Hence, Marx's identification of the ideology of "equivalence exchange" as the self-image of capitalist society is contradicted by the formulation of the "developmental laws of capitalism". The phenomenal appearance of capitalism is negated by its own internal dynamics. Marx's critical theory is, in his mentor's terms, a "determinate negation" of capitalism, and has remained till our time the foundation for critical research.'

In the continental tradition of critical theory, Pierre Bourdieu, a French sociologist, proposed the theory of power and practice. He emphasized the role of practice and embodiment in social dynamics. According to him, individuals occupy a position in their social space and are not defined by social class (as Marx would have argued) but by the relative amount of symbolic, social, economic, and cultural capital. A staunch opponent of modern forms of globalization, Bourdieu saw sociology as a weapon against social oppression and injustice. Indeed, he referred to sociology as a combat sport to defend against the 'domination of symbolic systems and the imposition of distorting categories of thought'. Bourdieu theorized that dispositions have two parts: the habitus which is the ensemble of dispositions towards action and perception that operates from within social agents, and the practice which the habitus generates. According to him human behaviour is recursive, relational, and reflexive. Therefore, any analysis of human behaviour must take time into consideration, for, time gives behaviour 'its form, as the order of succession, and therefore its direction and meaning'. Practices are reflexive in the sense that they carry with them their own interpretation, which means that they organize the relationship between individuals and society in a way that is circular. The actor's course is guided by a dialectic, and as a social being he is always subject to the orientations and limits of the habitus. Taking a cue from Marx, Bourdieu argued that it is the objective character of social conditions that produces a class habitus. Bourdieu studied how relations of domination shake an actor's subjective aspirations in a wide variety of social and cultural contexts. His even-handed concern for both the actor's point of view and social structure has won him a number of admirers. 'Exploring practice theory as a way to tie together consciousness and structure, action and its temporal horizon, as well as Weber and Marx, theorists have applied Bourdieu's thinking to case studies that range from gift-giving, saving, and consuming to gender, sexual difference, class relations and colonial encounters' (*International Encyclopedia of the Social and Behavioural Sciences*: 1968).

We may summarize the most outstanding features of contemporary critical theory as follows. First, its proponents believe that intellectuals should assume an active role and develop a critical attitude to society. Second, critical theory holds that people's ideas are a product of the social system in which they live and, therefore, it is impossible to be entirely objective and to eliminate completely the biases that are culture-bound and time-bound. Third, critical analysts emphasize the importance of society's economic organization, especially 'the class-related form of work', property and profit, and its impact on culture, personality, and polity. Fourth, unlike orthodox Marxists, critical theorists reject pure economic determinism, and assign culture and ideology an independent role in society. Fifth, critical theory emphasizes the 'rational constitution of society' and seeks to judge the present social order in terms of Hegelian humanism and reason. Finally, it has concentrated to a great extent on a critique of mass culture, the causes and consequences of alienation, and the interaction between personality and social structure.

Ralf Dahrendorf: The Rulers and the Ruled

The conflict theory of Dahrendorf is based exclusively on the relations of authority. To him, social organizations are imperatively coordinated associations rather than social systems. Authority structure, which is an integral part of every social organization, results in the creation of a dichotomy of positions of domination and subjection. Some are entrusted with the legitimate right to exercise control over others who are subordinate to the former. This distribution of authority leads to the formation of two conflict groups corresponding to the two positions of control and subjection—those who give orders and those who take orders. Since the interests of the two groups are divergent, conflicts between the rulers and the ruled are inevitable. Dahrendorf (1973: 102) argued that authority structure is an essential part of every social organization and cannot be done away with; therefore, it is impossible to eliminate conflict altogether. Although conflict is inherent in the social structure, it is not always violent or manifest. Social conflict can be latent, regulated or temporarily suppressed or channelled but 'neither a philosopher-king nor a modern dictator can abolish it once and for all.'

Dahrendorf has summarized the essential elements of conflict theory as follows:

1. Every society is subjected at every moment to change; social change is ubiquitous.
2. Every society experiences at every moment social conflict; social conflict is ubiquitous.
3. Every element in a society contributes to its change.
4. Every society rests on constraint of some of its members by others.

Lewis Coser: Conflict Functionalism

In the tradition of Simmel, Lewis Coser has written extensively on the positive functions of social conflict. Conflict allows expression of hostility and the mending of strained relationships. It leads to the elimination of specific sources of conflict between parties and enables redress of grievances through the establishment of new norms or the affirmation of old ones. Hostility towards the outgroup, a community or caste, unifies the ingroup. When the need for greater solidarity is felt, members of the ingroup tend to exaggerate conflicts with other groups, and where such conflicts exist, any deviation from the group norm is severely condemned. Social conflicts not only generate new norms and institutions but also new coalitions and alliances; they bring about technological improvements, revitalize the economy, and lubricate the social system; and they facilitate the release of tension and frustration and enable the social system to adjust itself. Social conflicts and movements have often resulted in significant reforms and positive social changes. Therefore, conflict is not always or necessarily dysfunctional.

Symbolic Interactionism

Symbolic interactionism is essentially a social–psychological perspective that is particularly relevant to sociological enterprise. Instead of dealing with abstract social structures, concrete forms of individual behaviour, or inferred psychic characteristics, symbolic interactionism focuses on the nature of interaction, the dynamic patterns of social action and social relationship. Interaction itself is taken as the unit of analysis; attitudes are relegated to the background. Both the human being and the social structure are conceptualized as more complex, unpredictable, and active than in the conventional sociological perspectives. Societies are composed of interacting individuals who not only react but perceive, interpret, act, and create. The individual is not a bundle of attitudes but a dynamic and changing actor, always in the process of becoming and never fully formed. He has not only a mind but also a self which is not a psychological entity but an aspect of social process that arises in the course of social experience and activity. Above all, the entire process of interaction is symbolic, with meanings constructed by human ingenuity. The meanings we share with others, our definition of the social world, and our perception of, and response to, reality emerge in the process of interaction.

Charles Horton Cooley and George Herbert Mead are the major architects of symbolic interactionism. Cooley's concept of 'looking glass self' is one of the major contributions to sociology. Cooley (1968: 121–2) was fond of saying that self and society are twin-born. For him, to be aware of oneself was to be aware of society, thus social consciousness and self-consciousness are inseparable. These consciousnesses of society and self are located in the mind, that is, human imagination. 'The imaginations which people have of one another are the solid facts of society, and that to observe and interpret these must be a chief aim of sociology' (ibid.). The self is not either individual or social primarily or firstly, but rather is a creation of dialectics between the individual and his social environment. An individual's awareness of himself is a reflection of his perception of other's ideas of who he is, a process of one mind responding to other minds. Thus, looking glass self is one's image of oneself based on one's perception of the images of others. As the individual perceives others' estimations of his appearance, his self develops accordingly. Not only is he aware or able to imagine how he appears to others, he becomes also conscious of others' judgements and evaluations of his appearance. Family and peer groups play a major role in the development of the individual's self-image.

It is Mead who has given us the most elaborate exposition of what has come to be called the symbolic interaction theory. Mead insisted that the self is neither a psychological organism nor a biological entity but essentially a social structure which arises in the process of social experience and activity. Social interaction, communication, and group processes introduce the self into which the individual organizes all his experiences. Thus, an individual comes to acquire the concept of self from the social group with which he has meaningful interaction. How does a girl, for instance, come to formulate her self-concept of being very beautiful? Now, according to the symbolic interaction theory, she is not beautiful because she thinks she is beautiful, and she is not beautiful because others think she is beautiful, but she is beautiful because she thinks others think she is beautiful. It is the response of the 'boys' and her experience with her peers that give her the self-concept of being very beautiful.

According to Mead, the self is composed of two parts: the 'I' and the 'me'. The 'I' is the initial response of the organism to the attitudes of others; the 'me' is the organized set of attitudes of others which one assumes. The attitudes of the others constitutes the organized 'me' and then one reacts towards that as an 'I'. In other words, the 'I' represents the spontaneous behaviour of the human infant—that behaviour which is unconditioned and undisciplined. Over time, the process of continuous interaction with parents and others, gives rise to the concept of 'me' which seeks to restrain and regulate the behaviour of 'I' in accordance with the established norms of the group or society. Mead delineates three stages in which the concept of self arises and develops: the stage of imitative acts, the play stage, and the game stage. The imitative stage occurs about the second year of life during which time the young child mimics the mannerisms and behavioural patterns of his parents, siblings, and others in his immediate social environment. The play stage begins about the third year which is characterized by the child's growing interest in assuming various roles of his 'significant others'; for example, playing mother, father, elder sister, etc. During the third and final stage of self-consciousness development called game stage, a unified self emerges. At this time, the child has developed the capacity to 'take the role of the others', not just of one other and not just one role, but he is able to assume the attitudes of several people comprising his social group all at one time. This stage is, of course, very complex and indicates real maturity in the consciousness of the self and others. Through the growth and development of the self emerges the generalized other which represents that stage at which the individual is finally able to relate to himself—as object and subject, as 'I' and 'me'—the attitudes and values of his social environment. The generalized other is identified with an organized community or social group which fosters a sense of, and commitment to, an individual's self-unity. The generalized other nurtures a sense of enduring selfhood, of continuous self-integrity and personal identity through a continuously expanding number of social circles. In short, the individual does not experience himself directly but only indirectly from the attitude of the generalized other. The individual's self-consciousness is, then, a product of social interaction or more specifically, of his perception of the responses of others towards him. In short, a primary group with which an individual identifies himself may make him a 'coward', an 'intelligent' person, a 'handsome' fellow, a good 'mixer', or a 'bashful introvert' depending on the self-concept the group has helped foster. This is precisely why symbolic interactionism is an important theory of socialization which reminds us that families need to strive to give children positive images in their formative years.

After Mead's death, a group of his students at the University of Chicago proposed new variations and elaborations upon Mead's thought. Prominent among them was Herbert Blumer. Agreeing with Mead that society is continuously modified through the interactions of individuals, Blumer continued to emphasize the 'processual' nature of society over the somewhat rigid structural analysis of the functionalists. Society is essentially not a structure with a function but a dynamically unfolding process. For Blumer, meaning does not inhere in objects; rather, objects have meaning attributed to them by individuals in a definition of the situation. Significant meaning exists only to the extent that individuals have mutually agreed upon a particular definition of a specific object—whether it be a rock, a chair, or an idea. Research methods, therefore, says Blumer, must attempt to get at the definitions of those individuals interacting in the social environment under analysis, by means of such materials as personal documents, case studies, participant observation, and life histories.

Blumer considers the following to be the central features of symbolic interactionism:

1. Human society is made up of individuals who have selves. The self constitutes the central mechanism which enables the human being to make indications to himself of things in his surroundings, to interpret the actions of others, and to guide his own action by what he notes.

2. Individual action is constructed or built up instead of being a mere release; it is built up step by step by the individual through a process of self-indication, through noting and interpreting features of the situation in which he acts.

3. Group or collective action consists of the aligning of individual actions, brought about by the individuals' interpreting or taking into account each other's actions. In taking a role, the individual ascertains the intention or direction of the acts of others and forms and aligns his own action on the basis of such interpretation of the acts of others.

Exchange Theory

The theory of social exchange is a mixture of utilitarian economics, functional anthropology, and behavioural psychology. The intellectual roots of exchange theory may be traced to the utilitarian thought which views men as rationally seeking to maximize their material benefits from transactions with others in a free and competitive marketplace. Contemporary exchange theorists, however, recognize that men are not always rational and that they do not always try to maximize profit in every exchange but their interactions are often governed by cultural values and symbolic meanings. When individuals enter into social exchange transactions, they are performing certain social roles in accordance with well-defined norms and traditions. One of the most significant norms is, of course, the norm of reciprocity which is a kind of generalized obligation which compels one person to make a return for the benefit received from other persons. Benefits exchanged by two parties may not be identical or equal; usually the parties return something more or less in value than the benefit received. This institutionalized norm is reflected in several social customs and practices such as weddings, religious ceremonies, Christmas gifts, and similar social obligations.

The first explicit formulation of exchange theory was the work of Sir James Frazer. In studying various kinship and marriage practices among primitive societies, Frazer was particularly struck by the strong preference of the Australian aboriginals for cross-cousin marriages and their prohibition of parallel cousin marriages. He sought to explain the custom in terms of the familiar utilitarian economic thought: the Australian aboriginal who had no equivalent in property to give for a wife was obliged to get her in exchange for a female relative, usually a sister or daughter; in other words, men enter into institutionalized patterns of exchange to satisfy their basic economic needs. Malinowski was the first to draw a clear distinction between economic exchange and social exchange. In sharp contrast to the utilitarian perspective of Frazer, Malinowski recognized the symbolic meaning of exchange which was intended to strengthen a network of interpersonal relationships. Malinowski recognized the importance of basic psychological needs in explaining social behaviour but rejected the assumption of persuasive economic motives in social explanation.

Levi-Strauss, one of the most influential structuralists, rejected both Frazer's utilitarian interpretation and Malinowski's psychological conceptualization, and formulated the most explicit and elaborate structural exchange perspective. He argued most emphatically that 'it is the exchange which counts and not the things exchanged' and that 'goods are not offered primarily or essentially, in order to gain a profit or advantage of an economic nature' (Coser 1956: 78). Obviously, for Levi-Strauss, the items of exchange are culturally defined and their values are not intrinsic but extrinsic and symbolic. And the primary function of exchange is structural integration of the larger society. He also emphasized that the patterns of exchange varied with types of social organization and that they are regulated by the norms and values of a society.

George Homans: The Behavioural Perspective

Labelled as an individual self-interest theory, Homans' formulation represents a unique combination of elementary economics and behavioural psychology. Eminently influenced by Skinner's behavioural psychology, Homans argued that the principles of psychology derived from the study of animal behaviour will form the core of a deductive system of propositions explaining social behaviour. Turner (1974: 222) has neatly summarized those theoretical generalizations in behaviourism that found their way into sociological exchange theory:

1. In any given situation, an organism will emit those behaviours that will yield the most reward and least punishment.
2. Organisms will repeat those behaviours which have proved rewarding in the past.
3. Organisms will repeat behaviours in situations that are similar to those in the past in which behaviours were rewarded.
4. Present stimuli that on past occasions have been associated with rewards will evoke behaviours similar to those emitted in the past.
5. Repetition of behaviours will occur only as long as they continue to yield rewards.
6. An organism will display emotion if a behaviour that has previously been rewarded in the same, or similar, situation suddenly goes unrewarded.
7. The more an organism receives rewards from a particular behaviour, the less rewarding that behaviour becomes (due to satiation) and the more likely is the organism to emit alternative behaviours in search of other rewards.

In short, Homans' exchange theory postulates that human beings enter into exchange situations expecting a reward and will continue to sustain the relationship so long as the reward is satisfying. This perspective has been severely criticized by Peter Ekeh and others who argue that social exchange is a symbolic act with meanings assigned by cultural values. Symbolic behaviour is not only behaviourally creative, it is also normative behaviour shared by persons within a value system. That is why it is not always the value of the things exchanged that counts but the meaning and thought behind the interaction itself.

Peter Blau: The Structural Perspective

Blau begins his analysis of social exchange using basically the same psychological perspective on behaviour at the elementary level as Homans but rejects the latter's behavioural perspective and psychological reductionism. Having analysed the characteristics of interaction, Blau shifts the micro-level analysis to incorporate macro structures such as social systems which have their own 'dynamics with emergent properties.' He also deals with the consequences of the patterns of exchange for power, social integration and so on in terms of all three major theoretical frameworks in modern sociology–symbolic interactionism, functionalism, and conflict theory.

Blau regarded social life as a marketplace in which actors negotiate with each other to make a gain—a material benefit or a psychological reward. And the individual who has received some benefits is obligated to reciprocate in order to continue receiving them in the future. Thus, the norm of reciprocity serves as a 'starting mechanism' of social interaction and group structure. The exchange relations also may lead to power relations. A person on whom others are dependent for vital services has the power to extract compliance in an exchange relationship. Those who have monopoly over limited supply of materials and resources as well as those who control the means of production and distribution have the power to dominate exchange relationships.

As Blau shifts his emphasis from elementary exchange to macro-level structures, shared values and standards and the processes of competition, differentiation, integration, and opposition assume greater significance. Exchange relations among complex structures are typically institutionalized, and largely patterned by common standards and values. Such values are viewed by Blau as 'media of social transaction'. They are internalized in the individual members in a society through the process of socialization. Institutionalized as common standards and judged as appropriate by the collectivity, they mediate complex exchange systems and define principles of reciprocity and fair exchange. But there are also values in a society that are not institutionalized into the exchange system. These 'opposing values' provide a counter-institutional component in the macro-structure generating forces of dissension and imbalance. For example, the exploitative or oppressive exercise of power by those who command valued resources provokes social disapproval and, even hostility and rebellion.

Evolutionary theory, structural-functionalism, conflict theory, symbolic interactionism, and exchange theory are regarded as mainline theories in sociology because they deal with larger systems in general. There are numerous special theories which deal with issues in different subfields and schools of sociology. We will consider some of them in relevant chapters. In this chapter, our focus has been on general theories in the sociological mainstream.

CHOOSING AND USING SOCIOLOGICAL THEORY

In the behavioural sciences, the quest for a true theory could be a futile exercise; every theory holds some pieces to the picture puzzle of the social world. A complete picture of social phenomena emerges only through the integration of a variety of social theories. Quine has put it succinctly: 'Knowledge normally develops in a multiplicity of theories, each with its limited utility.... These theories overlap very considerably, in their so-called logical laws and in much else, but that they add up to an integrated and consistent whole is only a worthy ideal and happily not a pre-requisite of scientific progress' (Kaplan 1964: 309).

No theory is absolutely true, and no theory is a final formulation because new knowledge is pouring in all the time which modifies or even repudiates existing theories. Even the theories that remain downright repudiated today have had their days of glory. For instance, ever since Comte expounded the unilinear theory of evolution, generations of early sociologists—and, to some extent, contemporary experts in modernization—have used it to describe the dynamics of evolution and progress in total societies. A theory is not judged productive or otherwise solely in terms of the answers it gives; equally, indeed, the value of a theory lies in the number of questions raised. A productive theory must suggest potential problems, generate fruitful hypotheses, provide new perspectives, and guide sociological inquiry. In this sense, theories may very well be ends in themselves, just as they may be means to other ends.

Theoretical bias is one of the ailments afflicting social scientists. It borders on scientific ideology of some sort, either a fixed point of view, or a rigid frame of reference. Theoretical bias creeps in when sociologists grow too fond of a particular theory and become identified with it so deeply as to preclude considerations of other factors or perspectives. It is true that all theories are not applicable to all situations at all times; therefore, selective perception is inevitable and useful. Sociologists must choose between—sometimes conflicting—theories depending on the themes and contexts of their inquiry. They must also learn to live with diversity. It is not the existence of diverse theories but their abuses that must concern us. A product of creative achievement and intellectual sophistication, sociological theories must reflect the thought processes of the imaginative mind. Knowledge about the social universe grows in myriad ways; therefore, the search for a true theory is like the pursuit of a mirage.

Theoretical Perspectives in a Global Age

During the past three decades, societies have undergone major transformation, moving from modern to postmodern to global systems, with attendant shift in structuralism, nationalism, and integration. Let us consider some of the postmodern theoretical perspectives.

Advocates of postmodernism claim that founding fathers saw history in progress as premodern societies moved towards modernism in a rather predictable fashion. They argue that not only there is no defendable notion of 'progress' but the concept of history itself is irrelevant. Postmodern world is not defined by any particular ideology or process, be it Marxian socialism or Weberian rationalization. Rather, it is dominated by the new media which instantaneously exposes multitudes of people simultaneously to new ideas, values, images, and events which have no basis in history. The postmodern world is constantly changing; it is characterized by flexibility, mobility, diversity, differentiation, and information systems. The new mass media is the most powerful agent, not necessarily of change but of image making. According to Jean Baudrillard, the electronic media has cut us off from the past and created a new world based on hyperreality. People are not directly moved or affected by the events seen on television but by the images created by the media. In other words, people are not touched by the reality on the ground, but by the reality manipulated by the media.

It is true that revolution in electronic media and the vast popularity of internet, new information techniques, mass mobility, new international organizations and world systems, more fluid movement of people across national borders, development of cosmopolitan cities and multicultural societies, and systemic linkage of world financial markets have ushered in a postmodern era. Yet, these same processes and technologies have been evolving over time, creating new products and processes. If history is dead as postmodernists claim, then the term postmodernism itself is a misnomer because 'postmodernism' makes sense only in its historical relation to 'modernism'. That is why postmodern sociologist Zygmunt Bauman has now moved away from the term 'postmodern' to 'liquid modernity' which implies our world is in a constant flux evolving and changing all the time.

So, modernism is not dead; postmodernism is only a more advanced state of modernism which serves as a period of transition to globalization. Jan Aart Scholte (2005) defines globalism as 'a reconfiguration of geography, so that social space is no longer wholly mapped in terms of territorial places, territorial distances, and territorial borders'. According to him, globalizing processes are at work whenever and wherever phenomena are 'supraterritorial'. Manuel Castells calls the new global economy 'automation' driven by information technologies. He is concerned that we no longer control the world we have created because of the enormous power of commercialized means of mass communication.

Ulrich Beck also rejects the the notion of postmodernism and posits that the world is moving into a phase of what he calls 'the second modernity' in which all institutions are becoming global. According to Beck, the second modernity is characterized by 'the world risk society'. Beck (1992: 21) defines risk as 'a systematic way of dealing with hazards and insecurities induced and introduced by modernization itself. Risks, as opposed to older dangers, are consequences which relate to the threatening force of modernization and to its globalization of doubt.' For most of human history, societies faced *natural risks* such as floods and epidemics. But contemporary society is characterized by *manufactured risks* that are human-made. Pollution, injury to the environment, destruction of forest reserve, accumulation of toxic/nuclear waste, overuse of limited resources, and the creation of new superbugs or drug-resistant bacteria are only some of the examples. Such contemporary risks threaten the very existence of human species. In the first place, modern societies consume unsustainable amount of natural resources. Yet, the production of wealth still takes precedence and the gobal ideology encourages high mass consumption. Second, contemporary risks are invisible and hard to measure. Global warming, climate changes, and even the presence of toxins and antibiotics in our food are not easily detected or measured. Third, contemporary risks involve social inequalities. 'Wealth accumulates at the top, risks at the bottom', says Beck. The global poor are exposed to more risks than the global rich. Fourth, contemporary risks are not just limited to national boundaries. Think of nuclear accidents like Chernobyl, air pollution, and pollution of major waterways. Fifth, contemporary risks create winners. Managing risks and offering protection from risks is a big business such as those of health and pharmaceuticals. Finally, risks generate new social conflicts leading to new debates and social movements.

According to Anthony Giddens, another globalist, we live in a 'runaway world' marked by new risks and uncertainties. Giddens' theoretical perspective is centred around two notions of trust and reflexivity. In a world of rapid transformation, traditional forms of trust based in the local community give way to confidence in 'abstract systems' such as telebanking, stock markets, fund managers, and other global marketing systems. Living in an information age also means, according to Giddens, an increase in social reflexivity. 'Social reflexivity refers to the fact that we have constantly to think about, or reflect upon, the circumstances in which we live our lives' (Giddens 2010: 100). In traditional societies, people followed socially patterned way of life in a more or less 'mechanical' fashion but in contemporary global society, people are exposed to more ideas, choices, and opportunities which require more social reflexivity.

Now, let us put these postmodern and global theoretical orientations in perspective. Postmodernists are pessimists who pronounced modernism and history dead. Their assumption that the mass media, new technologies, and ideas have no connection to the past is false. The assumption that instant communication, exposure to new cultures, values, and ideas, and globalization will break up traditional systems and usher in a world culture is equally false. An assessment of themes in contemporary television serials shows that they depict traditional paternalistic and male-dominated families. Some of the most popular shows deal with gods, witches, spirits, saints, miracles, and almost daily personal appearance of gods to the devotees. Even the powerful media empire of Murdoch had to bow to the court of public opinion. The democratic uprisings across the Middle East, with slogans of liberty, fraternity, and equality, are reminiscent of French Revolution. The anti-corruption movement launched by a frail old man called Anna Hazarre evoked the images and messages from Indian struggle for independence, and the government of the largest democracy in the world is trembling. Internet and mobile technology are widely used by these and other social movements. At the same time, the Taliban uses the same advanced technology to hasten a return to Islamic fundamentalism. Even in the United States, political influence of conservatives and religious fundamentalists is on the rise. What is the point? The point is that history is not dead; humans are not completely controlled by the big media, ruthless despots, or mighty business. We have not lost control of our lives or our sense of history.

Classical thinkers like Comte, Spencer, Marx, Durkheim, and Weber could not, of course, foresee the development of modern mass media, mobile technology, global market, and international monetary systems. But the theories they proposed dealt with the inevitable evolution of societies from simple to various levels of complex societies. Spencer spoke of doubly compound and trebly compound societies. Durkheim spoke of complex societies based on organic solidarity. Weber spoke of the development of science, technology, and bureaucracy, a process he called rationalization. Today's postmodernists and globalists talk of contemporary societies as complex, pluralistic, and multicultural.

Now, let us take a fresh look at the first two mainline theories: evolutionary theory and structural-functionalism. The central theme of these theories may be summarized in two phrases: structural differentiation and functional specialization. That is, the study of the structure of social systems and their functions over time. Today's powerful mass media, global markets, international monetary systems, and intergovernmental organizations are systems with highly differentiated structures and highly specialized functions. Therefore, structural-functionalism, as a general theoretical perspective in sociology, is just as appropriate for the analysis of premodern societies as it is applicable to postmodern and global societies. With the development of science and technology, new systems (information systems, for example) develop with new structures and new functions. Why can't we use the framework of structural-functionalism to study the global society and its subsystems as well as their differentiated structures and specialized functions? In this perspective, the manufactured risks of global society that Beck spoke of are the latent dysfunctions, to use functional terminology. Structural-functionalists were, perhaps, overly concerned with order and stability. Can anyone argue that it is no longer of any consequence? With the economic meltdown in America and the debt crisis in the Eurozone, the watchword today is stability of the world economic order. Developed nations and international monetary systems are striving hard to establish some kind of equilibrium in the world economic system. Indeed, Radcliffe-Brown (1952: 193) saw this interconnectedness of the world in 1950 when he wrote: 'It is rarely that we find a community that is absolutely isolated, having no outside contact. At the present moment of history, the network of social relations spreads over the whole world, without any absolute solution of continuity anywhere.' So let us look at theories as perspectives, a logical way of looking at things; let us not throw out the old just because they are old.

STUDY QUESTIONS

- Define socioloigical theory, keeping in mind different interpretations.
- Define and differentiate between the following: speculative vs. grounded theories; grand theories vs. miniature theories; macro vs. micro theories; manifest and latent function; and function and dysfunction.
- Enumerate the functions of sociological theory.
- Discuss the different variants of evolutionary theory.
- Evaluate structural-functionalism as a dominant theory in sociology.
- Critically examine Marx' theory of class struggle.
- Write a paragraph on the following: Frankfurt School and critical theory; Dahrendorf's theory of conflict; conflict functionalism; and anthropological perspectives on functionalism.
- Discuss symbolic interaction theory with special reference to Cooley, Mead, and Blumer.
- Briefly review the anthropological perspectives on exchange theory.
- Compare and contrast Homans' and Blau's theories of exchange.
- Evaluate classical theories in the context of postmodernism and globalization.
- What are your considerations in choosing a sociological theory?

REFERENCES

Abraham, M. Francis, *Modern Sociological Theory: An Introduction*, New Delhi: Oxford University Press, 1982.

Aron, Raymond, *Main Currents in Sociological Thought*, Garden City: Doubleday, 1970.

Beck, Ulrich, *Risk Society: Toward a New Modernity,* London: Sage, 1992.

———, *World Risk Society*, Cambridge: Polity Press, 1999.

———, *Cosmopolitan Vision*, Cambridge: Polity Press, 2006.

———, *World at Risk*, Cambridge: Polity Press, 2008.

Blumer, Herbert, 'What is Wrong with Social Theory?', *American Sociological Review*, 19, 1954.

Bourdieu, Pierre, *Outline of a Theory of Practice*, Cambridge: Cambridge University Press, 1997.

Cancian, Francesca M., 'Varieties of Functional Analysis', in David Sills (ed.), *International Encyclopedia of the Social Sciences*, Vol. 6, New York: Macmillan Company, 1968.

Cooley, C. H., *Human Nature and Social Order*, New York: Schocken Press, 1968.

Coser, Lewis, *The Functions of Social Conflict*, New York: Free Press, 1956.

Dahrendorf, Ralf, *Class and Class Conflict in Industrial Society*, Stanford: Stanford University Press, 1959.

———, 'Toward a Theory of Social Conflict', in Amitai Etzioni and Eva Etzioni-Halevy (eds), *Social Change*, New York: Basic Books, 1973.

Durkheim, Émile, *The Rules of Sociological Method*, New York: Free Press, p. 72, 1964.

Giddens, Antony, *The Third Way: The Renewal of Social Democracy*, Cambridge: Polity, 1998.

——— (ed.), *The Global Third Way Debate*, Cambridge: Polity, 2001.

———, *Runaway World: How Globalization is Reshaping Our Lives*. London: Profile, 2002.

———, *Sociology*, New Delhi: Wiley India, 2010.

Kaplan, Abraham, *The Conduct of Inquiry*, San Francisco: Chandler Publishing Company, 1964.

Larson, Calvin, *Major Themes in Sociological Theory*, New York: David McKay Company, 1973.

Lerner, Daniel, 'Modernization: Social Aspects', in *International Encyclopedia of Social and Behavioural Sciences*, New York: Macmillan Company, 1968.

Levi-Strauss, Claude, *Structual Anthropology*, New York: Basic Books, 1963.

———, 'The Principle of Reciprocity', in Lewis Coser and Bernard Rosenberg (eds), p. 78, 1971.

Mead, George Herbert, *Mind, Self and Society*, Chicago: University of Chicago Press, 1934.

Merton, Robert K., *Social Theory and Social Structure*, Glencoe: Free Press, 1957.

Mihanovich, Clement S., *Glossary of Sociological Terms*, Milwaukee: Bruce Publishing Co., p. 24, 1957.

Moore, Wilbert, *Social Change*, Englewood Cliffs: Prentice-Hall, 1963.

Radcliffe-Brown, A. R., *Structure and Function in Primitiue Society: Essays and Addresses*, London: Cohen and West, 1952.

Scholte, Jan Aart, *Globalization: A Critical Introduction*, New York: St. Martin's Press, 2000.

———, *Globalization: A Critical Introduction*, Basingstoke: Palgrave Macmillan, 2005.

Schroyer, Trent, 'A Reconceptualization of Critical Theory', in Alan Wells (ed.), *Contemporary Sociological Theories*, Santa Monica: Goodyear Publishing Company, 1978.

Spencer, Herbert, 'Social Structure and Social Function', in Lewis Coser and Bernard Rosenberg (eds), *Sociological Theory*, New York: Macmillan Company, 1971.

Turner, Jonathan, *The Structure of Sociological Theory*, Homewood: Dorsey Press, 1974.

Methods of Research in Sociology

The Scientific Approach

Before Copernicus, people believed the earth to be flat and sailors used to be advised not to go too far lest they would fall off into the abyss. In the past, people with mental illness were thought to be possessed by evil spirits. In many rural communities people believed that smallpox was caused by an angry deity who must be appeased. Years ago, Christian farmers in Kerala used to invite priests to come and sprinkle holy water on ginger crops in order to save them from pests and diseases. Smoking is known to cause cancer. A sedentary lifestyle with regular intake of fatty foods is supposed to contribute to obesity and heart disease. The earth's ozone layer is being continuously depleted by emissions of chlorofluorocarbons.

These examples fall in one of two categories: common sense and scientific truth. Common sense is based on 'what everybody knows' or what people think they know; it is not supported by scientific evidence. However, scientific principles are based on irrefutable evidence, and can be proved time and again.

Science refers to a systematized body of knowledge on any given subject as well as the process of acquiring that knowledge. Here, social sciences and natural sciences differ considerably. In chemistry and physics we can count, measure, break, mix, burn, or otherwise experiment with objects in myriad ways. For instance, we can combine hydrogen and oxygen and make water in the laboratory. We can also clearly document other principles of physics. Even in biological sciences we can experiment with animals and test the efficacy of different drugs. These are all exact sciences whose laws can be verified under given circumstances. However, human beings cannot be treated as guinea pigs and experimented with; we have to depend on the conscious responses of the behaving individual. The problem is that we may not ask the right questions, and even if we do ask the right question, we may not get the right answer. People may not perceive the meaning of the questions correctly or they may even lie about them. And, because of people's beliefs and the way they feel about certain things, they might assume their answers are correct. Above all, the investigator and his subject may carry their own prejudices which colour the way they perceive the situation. It is always difficult to measure the intensity of people's feelings, comprehend their thought processes or understand the meaning they give to particular situations. Therefore, sociology can only formulate some general principles about social behaviour and social relationships. Such sociological principles or laws cannot claim the measure of exactitude that principles of natural sciences—or even principles of economics—have.

Yet, sociology as a science is a logical system which bases its knowledge on systematic procedures and objective principles.

Basic Principles

Sociologists study social relationships in a systematic way. Such a study requires the understanding of several concepts and their interconnectedness. The first is the concept of *variable*, a factor whose values change over time and from case to case. Caste, class, level of income, gender, type of occupation, or religious and political affiliation are significant sociological variables which influence people's thinking and their social relationships. In studying patterns of social behaviour and social interaction, sociologists examine the relationship between variables. An *independent variable* is considered a potential cause or a factor that influences other factors. A *dependent variable* is the effect. When we say smoking causes cancer, smoking becomes the independent variable and cancer the dependent variable. Discrimination on the basis of caste, dowry, and the decline of joint family are generally treated as independent variables which cause considerable trauma in contemporary Indian society.

The relationship between independent variable and dependent variable is one of *causation*, a situation in which one or more variables lead to certain consequences. One has to exercise extreme caution in determining the cause-and-effect relationship. First and foremost, the researcher has to rule out the possibility of any other independent variable influencing the outcome. He must also be able to demonstrate that changes in the independent variable result in corresponding changes in the dependent variable. This requires keeping all other independent variables constant while assessing the impact of a said independent variable on a particular social phenomenon. Establishing causation in the social sciences requires not only extreme caution but also an objective outlook.

Correlation is another concept which explains the relationship between variables. Researchers speak of correlation when two or more variables are found together, but when they are found together more often, they settle on a statistical description of the relationship called *correlation coefficient*. If two variables are always present together, their relationship is called positive correlation. The number +1.0 indicates the strongest possible relationship, which means not only that the two variables are always found together but also that an increase or decrease in the independent variable causes a corresponding increase or decrease in the dependent variable. Two variables can also have a perfect negative correlation represented by the number −1.0 which means that when one variable is present the other is always absent or that the changes in the value of an independent variable produce the opposite effect on the dependent variable. However, in real life we seldom find a perfect positive or negative correlation. This means the association between two variables ranges from very weak to very strong.

Even if there is a strong correlation, one should not jump to the conclusion that causation exists. Several studies have found strong correlation between alcohol abuse and spouse abuse: men who frequently get drunk often batter their wives. We cannot always conclude that alcohol abuse prompted spouse abuse. It is possible that men used to beat their wives before they turned to alcohol. Even if the two conditions always coexisted we still cannot say that alcoholism caused spouse abuse. This may be the case of a *spurious correlation*, a condition in which two variables are always present but the effect is actually the work of a third undetected variable. The men may be suffering from other psychological conditions that incite the abuse. That is why researchers have to use proper scientific *control* to neutralize the effect of other intervening variables. The fact that the suicide rate is high in Kerala cannot be attributed to a single factor such as dowry, economic deprivation, or mental illness. How to arrive at causation from correlation is one of the great challenges facing sociologists.

Reliability and *validity* are two other important concepts. *Reliability* refers to consistency in measurement. A reliable instrument will produce the same results with repeated measurements. A scale that gives out a different weight each time you step on it is unreliable. *Validity* is a condition in which an instrument measures exactly what it is supposed to measure. An instrument may be reliable without being valid. A ruler or a measuring tape with an inch missing will always give out consistent measurement but it does not reflect precise measurement. In sociology the challenge is to ask the right questions to elicit the right answers. When we say someone is 'very happy' or 'very religious' how do we really measure happiness or religiosity? For instance, is a person who goes to temple or church every day truly 'very religious'? Going to the church or temple does not necessarily measure the 'religiosity' of a person. Therefore, a researcher has to make sure that the questions and instruments he uses give out precisely what they intend to measure. This is a tough challenge for sociologists.

Steps in the Research Process

Scientific research involves at least seven steps. Given below is an overview of the steps in general terms, and it does not reflect the actual sequence of events in every study.

Selection of the Topic

The first step in the research process is the selection of a researchable topic. Sociologists may choose a topic because of their personal interest in it; the current popularity of the topic, the availability of data or financial support for the study, or because of the potential contribution such a study would make to current literature in sociology. Causes of suicide in Kerala, consequences of the dowry system in India, female infanticide, and incidents of communal violence are hot topics. It is also important to examine the justification for the study in terms of its relevance to society, science, and the individual researcher.

Review of Literature

Once you have decided on the research question, you will have to find out what other researchers have done in the area. It is possible that your question has already been answered or that some related questions are far more important than your original idea. You must also find out what models and techniques other scientists have used, and with what results. A review of literature helps the researcher narrow down the problem, focus on the most relevant issues, identify appropriate theories, and choose the right tools. Above all, it helps the researcher define his problem more precisely, sharpen his focus, and stay the course. A literature review also helps identify the appropriate variables and their definition. At the same time, one must also keep in mind that the review of literature is not necessarily only the second or third step in the research process, but it is an ongoing process to be engaged in throughout the study.

Formulation of Hypotheses

Based on his experience the researcher may assume possible relationships between certain sets of variables. He may also infer such relationships from the literature review. Now he formally states his expectations in the form of a series of hypotheses. A *hypothesis* is statement of the relationship between two or more variables. For example, you might state that there is a positive relationship between alcoholism and spouse abuse or between the practice of untouchability and inter-caste conflict. Now, a formal statement of a hypothesis also requires an *operational definition* of concepts, that is, a precise and measurable definition of variables. Terms like 'old people' or 'senior citizens' are meaningless for scientific inquiry but if we say persons sixty years of age and older, we have an operational definition of the variable. Similarly, hypotheses must be testable; 'God exists' may be a wonderful idea but it is not a researchable question.

Selection of Research Design

The research design depends largely on whether the researcher is interested in qualitative research or quantitative research. Qualitative research features researchers themselves as observers and participants. The researcher is a participant in or a witness to the lives of others. This is quite different from other kinds of research in which the investigator is not a sustained presence in a naturally occurring situation or setting. According to Lofland and Lofland (1995: 3):

The central reason for undertaking this ongoing witnessing of the lives of others is the fact that a great many aspects of social life can be seen, felt, and analytically articulated only in this manner. In subjecting him- or herself to the round of lives of others and living and feeling those lives along with them, the researcher becomes an *instrumentality* or *medium* of the research. The researcher seeks to witness how the studied others perceive, feel, and act in order to grasp these seeings, feelings, and actings fully and intimately. The epistemological foundation of field studies is indeed the proposition that only through direct experience can one accurately know much about social life.

Quantitative research, on the other hand, is interested in the collection of data in numerical form. Quantitative data are obtained through enumeration and measurement. Investigators rely on documents, fixed interviews, experimental simulations, and other sources which are at least one level removed from *direct* observation. In quantitative research, data may be collected directly in quantitative form, or data originally in qualitative form may be quantified.

In order to collect data, the researcher must choose a scientific method, and the research design stipulates possible methods, tools, and techniques appropriate for the proposed study. The researcher may have his preference for a particular method but the research question often dictates certain methods. One of the basic questions the researcher must decide is whether the study calls for *qualitative* or *quantitative* methods. Qualitative research is open-ended; it is about feelings, meanings, social relationships, and sociocultural dynamics. Quantitative research involves measurements and statistical analysis. For example, market research that involves the study of consumer preferences often requires formal questionnaires and surveys. But the inner workings of a cult or prison system can only be studied by 'infiltrating' it, a form of participant observation.

Questionnaires and interviews are important tools for sociological research. A questionnaire is a form containing a set of questions. The answers to them should be filled in personally by the respondents. If an interviewer writes or records the responses on the form, it is called an interview schedule. An interview is a conversation between an investigator and an informant for the purpose of gathering information. The researcher lists a number of questions to structure and guide his questioning of a respondent. The use of an interview schedule allows the respondent to ask for clarification and explanation of unclear questions. It also allows the interviewer to record responses not directly anticipated in the design of the study. However, interview schedules may be highly structured with the interviewer simply reading the questions and recording the answers based on predetermined alternatives.

Collection of Data

Gathering the data is obviously a tedious task but something that must be done conscientiously. If it is a qualitative study the researcher may have to do it himself. But in the case of large quantitative studies such as public opinion polls, market research, and other surveys, the researcher may use trained interviewers. The key to the success of the study is the researcher's ability to keep an accurate record of all pieces of information in the process that might fit the picture puzzle in the long run.

Analysis of Data

First, organize your data in terms of the research design, in qualitative or quantitative terms. Data analysis requires the use of appropriate statistical procedures. Then, you examine the data to see if your hypotheses are confirmed or rejected. Do the data point to unexpected relationships, new leads, or gaps in current knowledge? Do your findings conform to any existing theories? In social research there are always alternative ways to interpret the findings. Sociologists also try to relate their specific findings to theories and literature in the field in order to enhance the value of their research.

Writing the Report and Sharing the Results

Having analysed the data, a researcher begins to prepare a detailed report of the findings. The report must, however, deal not only with a summary of findings but also the various steps involved in the research process including a statement of methods and tools utilized so that other researchers can replicate the study. The researcher also reports how his findings are related to existing theories and literature and how they support or refute popular assumptions. Sharing the results is an important professional obligation. The results may be published in scientific journals or popular magazines depending on the scope of the inquiry.

METHODS OF RESEARCH

Sociologists use a variety of methods and techniques to collect their data. Methods of research usually fall under four categories: surveys, experiments, observational studies, and analysis of secondary data.

Surveys

In social sciences a survey is probably the most used method of gathering data. A survey is a research method that uses carefully constructed questions to elicit information about attitudes, behaviour patterns, social relationships, or other aspects of a social system. Manufacturers use the survey method to identify the lifestyles of persons who use their product. Pollsters use surveys to gauge public opinion. Sociologists may use a survey to determine how a particular community has been affected by a natural disaster or the closure of a large local industry. A survey usually relies on one of two techniques: *questionnaire* or *interview*. A questionnaire is a set of questions usually mailed out to select respondents who write their answers on the form itself. An *interview* occurs in a face-to-face setting or over the telephone in which the researcher records the answers. The questions may be close-ended or open-ended. The former involves checking one of the predetermined responses. The respondent simply checks 'yes' or 'no' boxes or one of the multiple choices. The open-ended question allows the respondents to write in their own responses.

Before proceeding with the survey, the researcher has to determine the category of persons whom he wants to question. The entire target group is called *population*. In a public opinion poll, the population consists of the entire public. If you want to study the effect of the dowry system, the population will consist of the entire group of people who paid or received dowry.

Now it is quite obvious that in terms of time, money, and other resources, 'questioning' the entire population is almost an impossibility. Therefore, we must select a *sample*, a limited number of respondents carefully chosen from the population. Since the researcher has to get his responses from a select group of people, rather than the entire population, he has to make sure that the sample is representative of the population. If the sociologists want to know whether people are satisfied with ration shops, they must first identify the people who frequently use the ration cards. People's experience with ration shops may vary with gender and social class. Therefore, a representative sample must include men and women as well members of different social classes.

There are different types of samples based on the procedures we use. First, there is the *random sample*, a procedure which assures that every individual in the population has an equal chance of being included in the study. The best example is to drop all names in a bowl and draw the required number at random. Let us say that we want to survey the attitude of college students towards a hartal or a bandh. We select a college with 1,000 students and we can interview only 100 students. Now, how do we select 100 students out of the total population of 1,000? The random sampling technique suggests we write all 1,000 names on separate pieces of paper, roll them up and mix them in a bowl or bucket and choose 100 names at random. We may then proceed to interview them. But it might so happen that the sample consists of a disproportionately large number of men. It is also possible that male students' opinions differ substantially from those of female students. In the random sample we might even have a disproportionately large number of students who are sympathetic to a political party that has just called for a bandh. The sample may include too many final-year students and not enough first-year students, and we have reason to believe that their opinions are markedly different. Now the challenge is to make sure we have a representative sample, that is, our sample consists of all categories of students in accordance with their proportional size in the student population. This is accomplished by the *stratified random sample*, a technique which breaks down the population according to various categories and their proportion to the size of the population. Now we make separate lists of male and female students, first-year and final-year students and so on and throw them into different bowls and choose at random as many from each category as their size in the total population warrants. This procedure is definitely superior to the random sample because it represents all shades of opinion in the population. Imagine a survey of the attitude of students to abortion using a sample that consists of a disproportionately large number of Christian students! Or, in a caste-driven election, pollsters interviewing too many members of a particular caste and making a prediction on the outcome! Such samples are biased.

Some researchers also use the *systematic sample*, which involves selecting every *n*th case from an arbitrary list. In the aforementioned example we selected 100 students from a population of 1,000 by random sample. If we were to choose the systematic sample we would prepare an alphabetical list of all 1,000 students and choose every tenth student on the list. The first student is however chosen from among the first ten students by random sampling and then every tenth student from that number is selected for an interview. When pollsters want to conduct large surveys, they choose every twenty-fifth or fiftieth person from a telephone directory. As you can see, the systematic sample suffers from the same disadvantages as the random sample; we cannot simply ensure that it is representative.

Surveys are cost-effective and provide a quick means of gathering data from a large population. Without a huge investment in time and money, thousands of people can be asked hundreds of questions. Since questions are usually standardized and everyone is asked the same questions with the same choice of responses, the findings can be easily translated into numbers and quantified. But there are also problems associated with the technique. First and foremost, we have to ensure that our samples are representative. Second, if we depend on questionnaires, many in the sample may not complete or return them. Above all, in surveys we have to take people at their word; we have no way of knowing whether they mean what they say. Finally, since survey questions are to be standardized, complex issues have to be phrased into simple questions which may not elicit valid responses.

Experiments

An *experiment* is a research technique in which the researcher manipulates conditions and controls variables in such a way that the effects of independent variables may be isolated and observed. The experiment usually involves two identical groups operating under similar conditions. One is the *experimental group*, the one in which the independent variable is introduced. The other is the *control* group from which the independent variable is absent. When scientists want to study the effect of a particular drug they select two groups which are similar; then the drug is administered to the experimental group to study its effects. Testing the causation is the most important function of an experiment, that is, researchers want to know if, other conditions remaining the same, the introduction of the independent variable causes the expected effects. In the social sciences, unlike in the natural sciences, ideal controlled conditions seldom exist but researchers have undertaken some remarkable experiments.

Two of the most celebrated experimental studies in sociology are those of Muzafer Sherif and Solomon Asch. The researchers wanted to know how individuals' perceptions are influenced by the thinking of the group. Sherif conducted an experiment where he used a stationary pinpoint of light in a totally dark room. Initial subjects all reported the light to be stationary. Then the researcher gradually introduced several of his collaborators who were instructed to lie and say that the light was moving. At the end of the experiment, the original subjects who thought the light was stationary changed their minds, and their perception was overwhelmingly influenced by the group norm which held that the light was moving. Similarly, Asch developed an experiment in which subjects were asked to make perceptual judgements about relative lengths of lines on cards. The subjects could easily see that the lengths were different and accordingly gave correct answers. But then Asch's secret accomplices began to give incorrect answers, causing confusion and bewilderment among the other subjects. By the end of the experiment, Asch found that more than a third of all subjects chose to conform to the others by answering incorrectly. In both experiments the finding was that naïve subjects would yield to the pressure of a group opinion. Are the opinions and perceptions of the individuals shaped by those of the majority?

The sociology class may conduct an experiment to test the effectiveness of different teaching techniques. You may take two identical classes where the same subject is being taught. In one class, instruction is delivered solely by lectures. In the experimental group you might introduce different methods in addition to lectures such as group discussions, power point presentations, and other multimedia techniques. It will be interesting to see if the combination methods are more effective than the traditional lecture method.

Observational Studies: Participant and Non-participant Observation

Sociologists can learn by observing people. Meaningful studies require systematic observation over a long period of time, sometimes years. Researchers systematically record their observations, analyse their findings, and arrive at conclusions supported by theories or other findings. There are two types of observational studies: *participant observation* and *non-participant observation*. Participant observation is a research method in which the researcher becomes a member of the target group while observing its group processes and recording his findings. In the case of non-participant observation, the researcher observes the group from the outside without becoming involved in it. Participant observation may be of two different types. First, the researcher may be a complete participant as a member of the group. He may infiltrate the group incognito and continue to act as a member of the group which has no clue about the credentials of the researcher. Sociologists have studied prisons, religious cults, and hippie communities in this fashion. Second, the researcher may seek the acceptance of the group he wants to study and be a participant–observer. He may move into a tribal group, establish rapport with its members, and observe the group dynamics and lifestyles. Participants may study religious communities and campus politics as participant observers. Non-participant observation involves observation of children at play in natural settings or watching how the faithful perform religious or ritualistic ceremonies.

Participant observation, also known as field study, is one of the most effective tools at the disposal of the sociologist. If a sociologist really wants to study the inner workings of a religious cult he must somehow gain an entry into it and act as a full-fledged member of the group. When sociologist Yablonsky wanted to study the hippie communes in the 1960s he adorned their attire, grew long hair, and joined them. If you really want to study the homeless or slum dwellers from the inside, you have to join them as one of their own. A classic example of participant observation is William Foote Whyte's *Street Corner Society*. In the late 1930s Whyte joined a group of poor immigrant 'boys' in a rundown section of Boston. He undertook a four-year study which exposed many stereotypical assumptions the affluent people had about the inhabitants of street corners.

From the point of view of meaningful qualitative research, participant observation is the most effective tool. It allows the researcher to get close to the subjects and study the inner dynamics of the group from the inside. You can experience how people feel, instead of relying simply on what they say. Fieldwork is also flexible since it is not formatted by standardized instruments and measurements. But there are also disadvantages. In the first place, participant observation is not applicable to all situations. It is extremely difficult to infiltrate closed societies such as convents and prisons; it is impossible to identify yourself with a children's group. Since you only deal with a small group it is difficult to generalize; it is also impossible to replicate a study that is based on the subjective impressions of a researcher. Above all, there is always the danger that the researcher may become too involved in the group and consider himself part of it, feeling and experiencing the way other members do. In such cases, the researcher may lose sight of his original mission.

Analysis of Secondary Data

It is not always necessary for sociologists to gather their own primary data. In today's technological society a wealth of information is already out there. Census data gathered by the government constitute possibly the biggest source of information on a wide variety of topics. Sociologists may also depend on data collected by any number of previous studies. Court records, police reports, local government statistics, and media reports are other sources of valuable data. Personal records such as letters and diaries, literary works such as biographies and novels and historical documents provide important insights. *Content analysis*, a technique in which researchers systematically review the content of secondary sources such as journals, newspapers, novels, movies, television shows, etc., is a very useful research tool. The content analysis of movies and television shows over a period of time can yield significant information on how societies and people's attitudes have changed. Early movies almost always focused on domestic violence perpetrated by villainous mothers-in-law and sisters-in-law. Today's movies shy away from such themes and focus on economic crimes and political violence. Similarly, it will be interesting to study how often women appear in television news. In a month-long study of *News at 10* on Indian television by Media Advocacy Groups found that only thirty-two women as opposed to 290 men appeared in the news and even this number included women in the audience. Even when women's issues and development were discussed most of the discussants were men.

Historical study is an important form of secondary analysis. It takes a theme and traces its evolution over time through the study of books, media reports, films, and historical accounts. Sociologists have studied the processes of industrialization, urbanization, and modernization using extensive library research. In India, anthropologists have sought to describe the evolution of caste and untouchability over centuries. The catch words of today are globalization and privatization. It will be interesting to study the shift in the policies of successive governments, away from socialism to capitalism. Such studies require extensive use of secondary data gathered over long periods of time.

Historical cases such as revolutions, social movements, and the demise of civilizations can only be studied through the analysis of accumulated data. Thus, historical studies allow the sociologists to study rare phenomena as well as historical events. They allow researchers to analyse data gathered over periods of time and look for relationships between social phenomena. Weber's theory of protestant ethic and the spirit of capitalism and Marx's theory of communism are the results of insightful analyses of historical events and processes. However, historical studies may not be as precise as experiments or surveys because researchers have to depend on accumulated data gathered at another time and for another purpose; the accuracy of such data cannot be independently confirmed. The efficacy of historical analysis depends on historical insight and the creative imagination of the skilled researcher.

QUANTITATIVE VS. QUALITATIVE RESEARCH

Surveys and experiments rely largely on quantification and measurement. Field studies based on participant and non-participant observations primarily provide qualitative analyses. Historical and secondary analyses may use either or both approaches. A controversy has been raging in sociology—and social sciences in general—over the superiority or otherwise of quantitative or qualitative methods for the study of social phenomena. Let us briefly consider the argument.

Comte made philosophical positivism the cornerstone of his sociological thought. However, he recognized the importance of historical and comparative methods as well. But social physics or the school of neopositivism that dominates contemporary sociology owes its origin primarily to the statistical tradition that may be traced to Quetelet rather than Comte's philosophical positivism. Neopositivism takes phenomena from the physical as explicit models for social events and employs the laws of the former to explain the latter. It involves the direct application of explanatory models drawn from physical sciences to describe social phenomena. Neopositivists consider sound scientific methodology to be the first principle of sociological analysis, and what they consider to be sound scientific methodology is necessarily mathematical and other formal models that feature formalization of variables, measurement and quantification, computer techniques and language, experimental logics, laboratory experiments, and computer simulation of human behaviour. The great preponderance of articles in the mathematical verification style in modern sociological journals attests to the current popularity of formalistic models.

Lundberg, Dodd, Zipf, Ogburn, and Chapin emerged as the leading exponents of neopositivism. Goerge Lundberg, the most articulate and influential spokesman of the school, rejected the distinction between qualitative and quantitative methods of study. Scientific generalization is always and necessarily quantitative, and all social sciences can and must be quantified, he insisted. Lundberg considered quantitativism to be almost inseparable from behaviourism. He emphasized the sudy of observable behaviour and avoided any reference to mental facts. He went to the extent of asserting that a single principle borrowed from physics can explain a leaf flying before the wind and a man fleeing from a pursuing crowd. Thus, inspired by the philosophy of the natural sciences and armed with the most sophisticated computer hardware, neopositivists insist that only quantification can make sociology a full-fledged science. Mathematically formalized theories alone are empirically verifiable, and verifiability is the most important criterion by which to evaluate the scientific worth of a theory. Above all, neopositivists argue that a theory is valid and useful only if it is stated in law-like propositions and empirically verifiable statement of relationships between variables.

Critics of neopositivism argue that much of human behaviour is symbolic and normative. And as Weber pointed out, the subjective meaning of action, that is, the meaning the actor gives to his own actions, is often more important than the meaning attributed by rational scientists. Moreover, no amount of mathematical formulation or empirical verification can establish the validity or otherwise of values, beliefs, and feelings. C. Wright Mills questions the assumption of neopositivists that data on specific units can be added up and fitted together to arrive at a coherent theory of social phenomena. It must be remembered that what we get out of empirical research is information or pieces of information. To piece them together, if that is possible at all, we need a broader theoretical frame of reference, the kind which the neopositivists abandoned in the first place. Thus, empirical findings tend to become a jumble of facts and figures, unrelated to any meaningful theoretical system. Above all, it is helpful to remember Cameron's dictum that in sociology, unlike in the natural sciences, everything that counts cannot be counted and everything that is counted does not count.

Although the proponents of neopositivism claim it to be the flowering of a truly cumulative and scientific sociology, its critics call it 'quantaphenia' or a meaningless jumble of numbers and formulas. C. Wright Mills calls neopositivists the 'science-makers' who want to be scientific and administrative at any cost and who are not touched by the most substantive problems of the discipline since they believe that their method can convert the philosophies into science. Because of their reliance on frequency and measurement, neopositivists tend to study social situations and problems which repeat themselves. They also display a strong ahistorical bias because their techniques permit them to study only contemporary social problems, not historical social events. Moreover, they tend to choose those areas that lend themselves most readily to mathematical formulations, to the virtual neglect of more substantive areas of theoretical significance. Such a tendency, Coser (1975: 693) warns, 'will result, in the worst cases, in the piling up of useless information and, in the best cases, in a kind of tunnel vision in which some problems are explored exhaustively while others are not even perceived'.

The application of the laws of physics and all the sophisticated computer technology cannot illuminate complex social phenomena which have many layers of meaning and are mediated by the subjective experiences of creative individuals. In the first place, there is no reason to assume that the relations between the analogous elements in the social realm will be the same as in the physical world; in fact, they seldom are. Second, no amount of precise mathematical statements can give precision to imprecise data. Indeed, rigorous mathematization often obscures the weakness of the data. Third, mathematical formulations are based on extreme oversimplification of social reality because it cannot permeate the socio-cultural contexts of the larger system.

However, none of these critical statements are intended to assert that computers and measurements have no place in contemporary sociology. Rather, these remarks are intended to express the concern about the growing abuses of these tools of research, the assumption that everything must be quantified to make sense, and the neglect of substantive theoretical areas and interpretive analysis.

ISSUES IN SOCIOLOGICAL RESEARCH

Objectivity and ethical considerations are two key issues in sociological research. *Objectivity* refers to the researcher's ability to be free from biases or personal prejudices. As human beings, sociologists also share the values, beliefs, and opinions of their social groups. Caste, political and religious affiliation, and unique personal experiences may have shaped some of their views. Sociologists may choose a topic for study based on their personal interest. But once the research has begun they must keep an open mind and see and report things as they are. There is no room for personal feelings or group pressure. However, in the social sciences it is not always easy to maintain objectivity. It is difficult to avoid intense personal feelings in some research areas. While studying caste and communal conflicts sociologists who belong to the communities involved in the conflict will be under tremendous pressure to keep their personal feelings out. Biases also can result from sociologists' commitment to a particular theory or ideology. Marxist sociologists may, for example, carry their own ideological preferences to studies on privatization and globalization. A caste Hindu and a Dalit may approach the problem of untouchability from different perspectives. However, once the researchers become aware of their personal feelings and opinions and make a conscious attempt to keep them out of the scientific process, objectivity can be achieved. Without personal neutrality, findings of any study are worthless. One of the means of limiting distortion caused by personal prejudices is *replication*, repetition of the study by other scientists in order to test its accuracy. If other researchers from diverse backgrounds, using the same methods and techniques, come up with the same findings, we may safely conclude that the study has been objective.

There are many ethical issues involved in the research process. First of all, researchers have an obligation to protect human subjects. They must carefully consider the possible consequences in terms of the physical and emotional well-being of the individual subjects. Participants in the research process must be fully informed of the scope and objectives of the study. It is incumbent on every researcher to obtain a written informed consent of the human subjects. There are also cases where subjects have to be duped as in the experiments conducted by Asch and Sherif. Similarly, an investigator using participant observation may infiltrate a group and deliberately deceive members of the community he is studying. Although these are ethical issues, researchers may be compelled to undertake such studies in the interest of advancing knowledge. Another issue pertains to the confidentiality of the subjects. Here again, the researcher has an obligation to protect the confidentiality of the subjects especially when sensitive and embarrassing data are involved. Finally, researchers must also be sensitive to the way the findings of the study are used. They must resist the temptation to advance any personal agenda or advocate a particular ideology or political cause. They must allow the facts to speak for themselves.

STUDY QUESTIONS

- Define the following concepts briefly: dependent variable, independent variable, causation, correlation, reliability, validity, content analysis, neopositivism, hypothesis, research design, and objectivity.
- Enumerate and explain the steps in the research process.
- Discuss survey as a key research method in sociology.
- Evaluate the role of experiments in sociology with illustrations.
- Write a paragraph each on participant and non-participant observations.
- Discuss the role of secondary analyses in sociology.
- Examine the ethical issues involved in sociological research.
- Compare and contrast quantitative and qualitative approaches in sociological research.

REFERENCES

Asch, Solomon E., *Social Psychology,* New York: Prentice-Hall, 1952.

Babbie, Earl R., *The Practice of Social Research,* Belmont, Calif.: Wadsworth, 1983.

Coser, Lewis A., 'Presidential Address: Two Methods in Search of a Substance', *American Sociological Review,* 40: 693, 1975.

Friedman, Bruce D., *The Research Tool Kit,* Pacific Grove: Brooks/Cole Publishing Company, 1998.

Lofland, John and Lyn H. Lofland, *Analyzing Social Settings,* New York: Wadsworth Publishing Company, 1995.

Sherif, Muzafer, 'An Experimental Approach to the Study of Attitudes', *Sociometry,* 1, pp. 90–8, 1938.

Part II

The Foundations of Society

4

Culture

What distinguishes man from non-man is his possession of culture which is the result of communal living. Culture is a key concept in both sociology and anthropology. Culture shapes our values, beliefs, norms and, to a great extent, our attitudes and the way we perceive the world around us. Although we assume human beings are creative and free-spirited individuals, much of what we own, learn, and dream are part of our culture. How we dress, what language we speak, what and how we eat, how we greet one another, and what structures and institutions we build are determined by our culture. Think of the variety of costumes, languages, festivals, and ritualistic ceremonies found in different parts of India. In the traditional society caste system determined what occupations people followed and where they lived. Although some traditional barriers have collapsed, membership in a caste, community, or religious group influences many of an individual's behaviour patterns.

It is important to distinguish between society and culture, for people sometimes loosely use the term cultures to refer to other societies. A society is a group of interacting individuals who share a common culture. So culture is what members of the group have in common, the material things they own as well as the intangible non-material things such as beliefs, values, and rules of behaviour which they share. After leaving their remote caves, human beings began to live in settled communities where they cultivated crops and domesticated animals. Communal living necessitated shared rules and standards, common beliefs as well as specialized occupations, and culture began to develop rapidly. Technological developments and secular orientations have transformed the way modern society organizes itself. Today, the miraculous achievements in transport and communication have made it possible for us to appreciate the unity and diversity of human culture. Yet, we realize that every society also has a unique culture which guides its members.

THE MEANING OF CULTURE

The classic definition of culture, which inspired most other definitions in anthropology and sociology, was given by Edward B. Taylor (Theodorson and Theodorson 1969: 95) in 1871: 'That complex whole which includes knowledge, belief, art, morals, law, custom, and any other capabilities and habits acquired by man as a member of society.' This inclusive use of the term 'culture' continued to influence anthropologists for generations. However, two theories of culture dominated anthropological thinking between 1900 and 1950. They are: the process-pattern theory derived from the works of Boas and Kroeber; and the structural-functional theory of Malinowski and Radcliffe-Brown. 'While the process-pattern theory takes the concept of culture pattern as basic and the structural functional theory takes social structure as basic, both theories cover the full range of Tylor's culture concept' (Singer 1972: 539). Kroeber and Kluckhohn reviewed several hundred definitions of culture and arrived at a summary formulation which, they thought, would be acceptable to most social scientists:

Culture consists of patterns, explicit and implicit, of and for behavior acquired and transmitted by symbols, constituting the distinctive achievement of human groups, including their embodiments in artifacts; the essential core of culture consists of traditional (i.e., historically derived and selected) ideas and especially their attached values; culture systems may, on the one hand, be considered as products of action, on the other as conditioning elements of further action. (*International Encyclopedia of the Social Sciences* 1972: 528)

In summary, anthropological tradition defines culture as a total way of life of a social group, meaning everything they are, they do, and they have. It is a complex system that consists of beliefs, values, standards, practices, language, and technology shared by members of a social group.

Culture refers to learned ways of behaviour. Cultural objects are not organic or biological; they can only be acquired through social life. Like all other animals, human beings also must eat, sleep, reproduce, protect their young, and adapt themselves to the environment. Whereas other creatures largely depend on their instincts, human beings have deliberately adopted a highly variable and changeable set of cultural responses. For example, hunger and sexual urge are biological facts, but it is culture which determines how these biological urges are channelled. Culture influences not only what we eat but how we eat and how often we eat. Most Hindus do not eat beef. Pork is taboo for Jews and Muslims. The French love their snail (escargot); people of East Asia relish dogs and snakes which are sold in local markets and found on the menu in many restaurants. Indians eat with their fingers, the Chinese and Japanese use chopsticks, and the Westerners use forks and knives. Patterns of marriage and family are also products of culture. In the West, young people choose their own partners through dating and romantic love. In India, families, relatives, marriage brokers, and matrimonial ads play an important role in the selection of mate, especially in the countryside. Among the royalty in the old Polynesian society a brother could marry his sister. How people get married is also a function of the culture of the group. In India dowry is still common whereas in Africa men must offer a price to get a spouse. For thousands of years, polygamy, ritual prostitution, and untouchability were part of Indian culture. But cultures do evolve and many learned ways of behaviour now stand discredited. Attitudes to slavery, discrimination, genital mutilation, corporal punishment, nudity, sexual orientation, all have changed over long periods of time. Today, in India's cosmopolitan cities, lifestyle of the middle classes reflects many Western values.

Culture refers to a group's social heritage that has been transmitted from generation to generation. Scientific knowledge, philosophical systems, literary traditions, art forms, and customs and manners are handed down from one generation to the other. To begin with, we do not even choose our religion or language. Thus, culture is the sum total of what we receive from previous generations. Culture is also defined as social adjustment, that is, the means by which man adjusted to his environment. In other words, it is his means of survival. It is obvious that man's necessary adaptation to changing conditions had to be made culturally, not biologically. Man has the capacity to learn from experience and devise ways of adjusting to the physical environment in order to ensure his survival.

The three characteristics of culture just discussed—learned behaviour, social heritage, and social adjustment—are at the centre of nature *vs.* culture dichotomy. They stress the non-biological nature of culture. In a word, nature is organic, culture is superorganic.

Culture encompasses not only non-material things such as values and beliefs, but also material objects such as tools, technology, fashions, jewellery, and buildings. Culture includes all means of human survival which includes man's inventions and inventories as well as the means by which man adjusts to his environment. For thousands of years, people in the tropics saw no need to wear clothes. When they began to wear clothes, a wide variety of designs and rules came into existence. Also based on where they lived, people used leaves, cement blocks, or ice to construct their dwellings. Changes in technology and human values have transformed many cultural practices. Even today archaeologists examine tools, utensils, pottery, objects of art, and fabric to study the process of cultural development.

Culture is symbolic. A *symbol* is something the meaning or value of which is bestowed on it by us. It is an object often with no intrinsic meaning but infused with a profound meaning that is created and transmitted by culture. Therefore, the meanings of symbols are mostly arbitrary, a matter of cultural invention, and the meaning exists only as long as people share it. A national flag is not just any piece of cloth; a soldier is willing to die defending its honour. To the Christians, a cross is a symbol of salvation, and during the days of Roman persecution thousands died because they refused to deface the cross. In Indian culture the Sawastika stands for good luck and prosperity but the Nazis reversed it and used it as a symbol of racial purity. An engagement or wedding ring represents a serious commitment between partners in love. Prayer beads, religious rituals, fasts, the colours black and white, the sound of Om, gestures and languages, all represent different meanings to different people. Gestures provide an excellent example of symbolic meaning. Although gestures are used in all cultures, their meanings vary considerably. A common gesture which conveys a very ordinary meaning in North America is an obscene gesture in South America. Nodding the head up and down means 'yes' in India but 'no' in Turkey. In most Eastern cultures, to offer or receive a gift with your left hand is considered offensive. Language is another important component of symbolic culture. It involves not only the alphabets and grammar, but also literary works, philosophical and mathematical systems, acquired knowledge, and the process of communication itself.

We may also distinguish between ideal culture and real culture. *Ideal culture* is the culture people think they have as it is mandated by society's norms and expectations; *real culture* is the culture people actually have. It is obvious that societies cannot always live by lofty ideals and principles which simply serve as signposts; reality is often different. The United States was founded on the principle that 'All men are created equal' but the founding fathers who penned that profound principle owned slaves. Greece is touted as the home of democracy but half the population consisted of slaves. In theory India is wedded to the principle of a 'casteless and classless society' but the reality is nowhere near the ideal. We believe that God is half male and half female and we worship goddesses in the temples as most of our important deities are women; yet we debase women at home and discriminate against them in society. Our political parties condemn corruption and communalism but the alliances of convenience condone both. In every culture there is a big gap between ideal culture and real culture.

COMPONENTS OF CULTURE

Although cultures have evolved over thousands of years and vary considerably, in general terms we may identify at least five broad categories of components: beliefs, values, language, norms, and technology. The content of each of these categories varies tremendously from culture to culture; in other words, although every culture has beliefs and values—some may even be common—they may also be unique to specific cultures.

Beliefs

A *belief* is an idea or statement about reality which people accept as true. It may be based on their experiences in the past, scientific evidence, religious faith, or public opinion. Some beliefs are scientific and empirically verifiable. However, belief in God and beliefs about soul, hell, and heaven are based solely on faith. Many people in India have unshakable beliefs about horoscope, astrology, and auspicious hour. Hindu weddings are always scheduled on the most auspicious day and hour. People do different things to prevent the evil eye from befalling small babies or new buildings under construction. The bride must step into her new home with the right foot. In Thailand, people never step on the threshold of the door because they believe the good spirit that protects the home resides there. Most Asians believe that their ancestors watch out for them and have important days set apart to please them. The Christian faith is deep-rooted in creation and the Hindu belief in rebirth. People may also believe in magic, witchcraft, and several superstitions. Americans believe that the number thirteen brings bad luck. The Hong Kong Chinese will pay lakhs of rupees to get a license plate for their automobile with certain lucky numbers. Beliefs also change over time. People no longer believe that the earth is flat. Most people no longer believe that mental illness is caused by the evil spirit residing inside the head; ancient Egyptians used to drill a hole into the head to let the evil spirit escape. A sympathetic understanding of people's beliefs is essential to comprehend why people in different cultures view the world differently.

Values

Values are shared agreements among members of a society as to what is desirable or undesirable in social life. Values are generalized standards by which people define what is good or bad, beautiful or ugly. Since they are generalized standards and only provide broad behavioural preferences, people are free to disagree on specific goals, norms, or practices. Freedom, justice, equality, patriotism, and democracy are some of the almost universal values. Generally speaking, capitalism, materialism, and individualism are supposed to be integral parts of the Western value system. It is expected that people stand to attention and maintain silence when the national anthem is being played. Children are expected to be polite and respectful in front of elders. Dignity of labour is the hallmark of the American work ethic. Even graduate students from rich families undertake any type of part-time work: cleaning public toilets, digging burial pits in the cemetery, waiting at tables, or washing dishes at the cafeteria. In India people with means and education consider manual labour below their dignity. Competition is a highly desirable value in most modern societies but several tribal societies devalue competition and encourage collective cooperation. Matrimonial advertisements in India indicate a strong preference for fair, 'homely' and convent-educated girls. Since values guide our choices and our behaviour, they are the key to the understanding of how people conduct themselves in a given society.

Language

Language is the most important element of symbolic culture. Language is a form of symbolic communication through structured and sound patterns which are infused with shared meanings. In language, written words and arbitrary sounds assume significant meanings. Every word and every sound is a symbol with culturally infused meaning. Language itself is universal but the words and meanings vary from culture to culture. Language is part of a society's cultural heritage; language expresses and preserves that heritage. In the Arab world where people depend on camels for their livelihood, there are over 3,000 words for camels. In English there is only one word for 'snow', but the Inuits of Canada have many different words for snow because it has an important influence on their daily life; in several Indian languages, there is no word for snow. In English there may be four words which refer to death but in Malayalam there are a dozen words, often reflecting the status of the person who died. Have you ever thought how the English came up with words like, drumstick, snake gourd, and bitter gourd for Indian vegetables. Indian words for these vegetables have no 'adjectives' but the English words reflect the taste or appearance of these vegetables. These examples illustrate how language and culture are thoroughly intertwined.

James Henslin (1997) identifies five functions of language: 1. Language allows human experience to be cumulative. It is only through language we can transmit knowledge, ideas, beliefs, and attitudes to the next generation. Language allows us to organize our experiences and what we have learned from these experiences and pass them on to the next generation. 2. Language provides a social or shared past. Without language, our memories would be extremely limited. Language enables us to recall past events with the totality of their meanings and comprehend shared events of the past. 3. Language provides a social or shared future. Without language we cannot agree on times, dates and places; we cannot even plan an event and send out an invitation. 4. Language allows shared perspectives. How do we make sure others get the same meanings and ideas we intend to communicate? This is possible only because of the shared meanings and perspectives inherent in the language. 5. Language allows complex, shared, and goal-directed behaviour. Language allows us to establish the meaning and significance of events. Without language we cannot meaningfully talk about events in connection with festivals, birthdays, weddings, or holy days.

Language is a product of culture but culture is also shaped by language. Language develops in response to the needs of a culture. Many words and phrases in a language have no meaning outside the culture. A culture that celebrates love, bhakti, or afterlife will be replete with words, phrases, and songs that address these themes. Similarly, words and phrases, in turn, influence the nuances of our culture. Edward Sapir (1961) and Benjamin Whorf (1956) question the common assumption that words are mere labels we attach to things. They argue that language has embedded within it ways of looking at the world. It is not only that events and objects enter into the language with specific meanings but the language itself shapes the way we see those events and objects. In other words, when we learn a language we not only learn the words and the grammar but also a particular way of thinking and perceiving. Thus language not only reflects our cultural experiences but also shapes them. Language even determines our thought. Sapir and Whorf's hypothesis is based on their study of Hopi Indians in south-west United States. The Hopi Indians have no words in their language for 'time', 'day', 'hour', 'minute', 'second', 'late, 'yesterday', or 'tomorrow'. They believe that all forms life follow their own schedule and things happen when they happen. But in the English language time is a linear concept. When the Africans encountered the first white man, they had no word in Swahili to describe him. So they called the white man, *oinubu*, the one who has been peeled.

When we think of language as an element of culture, it is important to remember that we include all systems of knowledge such as science, philosophy, art, music, and mass communication. Poetry, fiction, newspapers, journals, and technical know-how are all expressions of language with specific meaning structures.

Norms

Norms are established standards of social behaviour which individuals in a group are expected to follow. They are simply rules of conduct which prescribe (pay your taxes) and proscribe (you shall not kill). Norms provide guidelines to patterns of behaviour and define them as appropriate or inappropriate according to specific social situations. Some norms are explicit while others are implicit. *Explicit norms* are those norms that are stated formally. Several schools and colleges have explicit rules about the uniforms their students are required to wear. *Implicit norms* are not written rules but those generally understood by members of the group. Boys and girls do not hug or kiss each other. Although this is a standard form of behaviour in the West, implicit norms embedded in Indian culture consider such behaviour inappropriate. There are also ideal norms and real norms. *Ideal norms* refer to high standards requiring strict conformity whereas *real norms* reflect standards of behaviour in real situations. For example, the old adage, 'Honesty is the best policy,' states an ideal norm. But we do know that people lie about small things all the time. We tell stories about why we are late, why we missed the class, or why we cannot accept an invitation. Similarly, politicians make promises before elections and forget about them completely soon after. Although such behaviours are not necessarily condoned, they are simply accepted as facts of life.

Norms are often situational in that same norms apply to certain situations but not to others. The dress that is appropriate for one occasion may not be appropriate for another. In the playground you can make all the noises you want but in the library you are supposed to observe silence. In the United States you drive on the right side of the street but in India you drive on the left side. Norms also vary from time to time. Years ago the practice of untouchability was an established standard of behaviour in India but no more. Slavery, discrimination, and corporal punishment are no longer approved forms of behaviour. Think of the many customs and practices which were, once upon a time, very common in India but are now considered unlawful or disgraceful.

Norms are classified into three types: folkways, mores, and laws.

Folkways are appropriate ways of doing things. They consist of thousands of informal rules which regulate our everyday life. They simply specify the way things are customarily done. Their violation may result in a raised eyebrow or a murmur of disapproval but no punishment. Matters of etiquette are the best examples of folkways. Cover your face when you sneeze in front of other people; vacate your seat on the bus in favour of an elderly passenger; hold the door open for the lady; reciprocate a greeting and say 'thank you' when appropriate; do not pick your nose in public; do not get up and leave in the middle of a discussion or a concert. Since folkways are not strictly enforced, they leave room for forms of eccentric behaviour.

Mores are norms considered to be vital and morally important. Most of the mores are embedded in the system of morality shared by members of a social group. Their violations are punishable in various ways. It is important to remember that many of the mores are backed by law and enforced by the government but others are not. Forgery, rape, murder, and child abuse are violations of mores as well as the established laws of the state. But cheating in a friendly card game, spreading ugly rumours about your neighbour, and premarital sex are violation of mores. Even in societies where adultery and prostitution are not punishable offences, they may be regarded as violation of mores. Even a simple act as cutting into the line of people who have queued up may be considered a violation of mores because the group feels strongly about it. Inappropriate behaviour at funerals and religious ceremonies are violations of society's 'sacred' norms. A violation of mores always invokes sanctions which vary from ridicule, avoidance, excommunication, and formal punishments.

Laws are rules which are formally established by the state or other organizations. Laws are usually formulated by governmental authorities and enforced by the police. They vary from simple laws such as fastening the seat belt in your automobile or wearing a helmet while riding a motorcycle, to payment of taxes, and prevention of corruption and homicide. Rules formally established by associations and organizations, although not usually labelled as laws, must be lumped in this category. The difference between mores and laws is that the former may or may not be written but the laws are always explicit and recorded.

Sanctions are the means by which a society enforces its norms. They involve punishments for violations or rewards for conformity. Thus, there are positive and negative sanctions. A *positive sanction* expresses approval of good behaviour. It may be as simple as a smile, a 'thank you', a pat on the back, a pay raise at the job, or an award, or a trophy. Parents reward children's good behaviour with a smile or a piece of candy. Governments give out awards or titles. A *negative sanction* refers to punishments for violation of norms. It may vary from a frown, a murmur of disapproval, avoidance, excommunication, suspension and dismissal, to fines, imprisonment, and capital punishment. Every unit of society, from a peer group or playgroup of children to formal organizations such as governments, colleges, and corporations, has its own means of enforcing sanctions. In families and peer groups, the sanctions may be subtle and informal but in large formal organizations, they are strict and well formulated.

Technology

Technology refers to all material things as well as the accumulated knowledge about them. Technology ranges from the most primitive tools of the caveman to the most refined modern computers, space shuttles, and weapons of mass destruction. Some sociologists argue that material items should not be considered as part of culture but only the technical know-how regarding them. Unless we want to make a rigorous distinction between culture and civilization, we believe that a comprehensive definition must include all material objects at the disposal of each culture. Indeed, it is technology that sets modern man apart from his ancestors. New technology creates new occupations and new attitudes. Hundreds of years ago we had no astronauts, pilots, or computer programmers, or the kind of time-consciousness these jobs involve. Anthropologists sometimes classify societies in terms of the technology at their disposal. Cultures have evolved over thousands of years from the Stone Age through the Iron Age and the Industrial Age to the modern computer age. Just think of the call centres. They involve not only knowledge about technology but also about time and language. Above all, those who man call centres must be culture-sensitive since they are dealing with people in different cultures.

CULTURAL ORIENTATION

It is obvious that values and beliefs vary from culture to culture. Certain practices which are an integral part of one culture may be downright repudiated as vulgar or even criminal in other cultures. Naturally, people have a tendency to think of their culture as superior and other cultures as inferior or even primitive.

Ethnocentrism is the tendency to evaluate one's own culture as superior. Culture preserves social heritage, instills pride, and fosters loyalty among members of a society. It has so profound an influence on individuals that they come to believe that everything that their culture stands for is the best in the world. Many people have no chance to travel outside their country, province, or even the village; thus they have no idea of how other people live. Therefore, they tend to believe that their way is the only way. Some people in India may be shocked to learn that the Chinese eat dogs, rats, snakes, and silkworms. People in poor countries think that every American is filthy rich, although poverty and hunger exist in America. People of north India and south India as well as Brahmins and Dalits have several stereotyped notions about each other, most of them unfounded. Indians think that Americans are all materialistic and greedy with loose morals. Many Americans still believe that Africa is a dark continent inhabited by primitive tribes always engaged in warfare. It is often said that one half of the human race regards the other half as lazy, dirty, cunning, and immoral. However, many of the ugly stereotypes are based on ignorance, lack of exposure to other cultures, or innocent misunderstandings.

Xenophobia, or an irrational fear of foreigners, may be one of the outcomes of ethnocentrism. Several countries in Europe are experiencing anti-immigration movements fuelled by the fear of foreigners. At one time, the United States and Australia had some of the toughest immigration laws. Many other governments have systematically tried to exclude foreigners even from visiting their countries.

Culture shock refers to the psychological and social maladjustment people suffer when they travel to a different culture. People are suddenly exposed to a number of norms, practices, and beliefs that are so different from their own that they need time to adjust and adapt. Indians who walk on to certain beaches in Brazil will be shocked to see that the entire family—mother, father, and children—enjoys swimming together in the nude. They will be horrified to see that the Masai in Kenya extract blood from a live cow, mix it with milk and drink it on a regular basis. An Indian Muslim who goes to pray in a Middle Eastern or Indonesian mosque might wonder why women in his own culture are not allowed to worship in the mosque. Westerners are horrified to see that so many Indians urinate and defecate so shamelessly in public places.

Cultural relativism refers to the principle that an aspect of culture can be evaluated or judged only in terms of the culture as a whole. Every element of a culture has a function unique to the group which shares the culture; indeed, many beliefs and standards are preserved by society precisely because they play an important role. Therefore, a custom or practice in a culture cannot be judged as right or wrong, good or bad in absolute terms; rather, it must be understood in terms of its functions. Many Americans wonder why the starving Indian farmers refuse to eat their fat cow? Marvin Harris, the anthropologist, pondered this question and undertook a detailed study. He concluded that the Hindu taboo against beef-eating is a very rational decision reinforced by religion. In the West, couples divorce when they realize that they are no longer compatible; divorce may be very tough on their young children but they rationalize that splitting up is better than raising kids in an unpleasant home where parents are always fighting. However, faced with a similar dilemma in several African cultures, a wife will start looking for another wife for her husband. The argument goes that everyone is happy when the family stays together. One of the explanations given for polyandry is that in certain extremely difficult conditions of scarcity, it takes more than one husband to support a family. However, the principle of cultural relativism shall not be invoked to justify harmful customs and practices which are part of many cultures. Slavery, genital mutilation, female infanticide, honour killings, and many other forms of discrimination are examples of cultural practices which cannot be justified under any circumstances.

Cultural Diversity

Societal culture refers to the culture of a society as a whole whereas *subculture* means the culture of a specific group within that society. There are as many subcultures as there are linguistic, caste, religious, political, occupational, racial, and ethnic groups in a society. Many elements of the culture are shared by the general population. For example, Indians as a whole share Indian culture which is not synonymous with Hindu culture. They cherish the rich cultural heritage, take pride in the great civilization and share the many traditions. In addition to the saree, which is generally regarded as the national dress, Indians also share many symbols of nationalism, types of music, and folk and literary traditions.

But subcultures also abound in India. Not only Brahmins and Dalits but each subcaste has a separate culture. The Todas of the Nilgiris, Nairs and Ezhavas of Kerala, Rajputs of Rajastan, the Sikhs, Bodos of Assam, and the Parsis all have their separate subcultures. Subcultures have distinct values and norms that set them apart from the rest of the population. Religious beliefs, food habits, agricultural practices, marriage customs, festivals, dresses and ornaments, and languages may be different. Subcultures are not partial or miniature cultures; they are complete cultures unique to the particular social group. In the highly diverse Indian society, caste, religion, and language serve as the three primary determinants of subculture. But there are thousands of subcastes each with its own lifestyle. Similarly, although all Muslims share many common values, beliefs, and norms, the Muslims in Kerala have a subculture that is distinctly different from that of the Muslims of Gujarat. There are also distinct subcultures that evolve around occupations, political parties, and geographic regions. Finally, there are also deviant subcultures which are associated with the lifestyles of criminal gangs, the mafia, drug addicts, and alcoholics.

A popular concept in the current literature on culture is *multiculturalism* which is a principle of coexistence of different cultures which fosters understanding and appreciation of different cultures. A number of cultural groups exist side by side in the same culture. Multiculturalism is not just mere tolerance of diverse cultures but a deep appreciation of their richness as well as contribution to the culture as a whole. India is a land of many cultures; there is enormous diversity not only in languages but also dress styles, food habits, customs and manners, life cycle ceremonies, faiths and festivals, art and architecture, and even rural settlement patterns. Indian nationalism is based on the two themes of 'unity in diversity' and 'national integration'. The idea is that different cultures must not only coexist but they must also maintain their cultural identity while subscribing to the unity of Indian culture.

Are there *Cultural Universals* or elements of culture which are universally accepted by all cultures in the world? This question is not as simple as it sounds. George Murdock, an anthropologist, listed over sixty elements which he considered cultural universals. They included family, housing, cooking, feasting, folklore, exchange of gifts, forms of greeting, music, medicine, and others. But these are broad categories of culture components, the content of which varies considerably. It is true that all cultures consist of the broad categories or components of culture we have identified earlier. In other words, they all have values, beliefs, norms, language, and material things. But the content of each of these components varies drastically and often contradicts one another. Yet, human beings make up one species and share a common evolutionary heritage. Although they must adapt themselves to drastically different natural environments and depend on different sources of food, they must all develop some tools, means of communication, and systems of social organization with established norms. Marriage and family are often thought to be almost universal institutions. A culture regulates sexual access between male and female, determines who can marry whom and even how many, and how the marriage is to be legitimized. The institution of family is found in almost every culture because it is the most effective social arrangement for reproduction, and the upbringing and socialization of the young. Most cultures also have some life cycle ceremonies and rituals which mark rites of passage. For example, the birth of a child, attainment of puberty, marriage, and death are occasions which in some fashion or other are observed in most cultures.

Incest taboo or proscription of sexual relations among members of the immediate family is another cultural element which is almost universal. Brothers and sisters and parents and children are strictly forbidden to marry each other. There were notable exceptions in the past, among the royalty of ancient Egypt, the Polynesians, and the Incas of Peru. However, today incest taboo is probably a universal norm.

Most cultures also celebrate belief in a superior power or force. They may identify it as God, high spirit or simply as omen. But the idea that there is a supernatural force with an overwhelming influence on human destiny is generally shared by most cultures. It does not, however, mean that all members of a particular society share the same belief.

CULTURAL CHANGE

Culture is not a static system; elements of culture change from time to time. Cultures have evolved over thousands of years. Societies have abandoned many of the belief systems and cultural practices which are not consistent with scientific evidence today. Empirical evidence provided by scientific investigation has exploded many myths and undermined numerous superstitious belief systems. Think of how our cooking and eating habits have changed, and think of the numerous changes in the caste and joint family systems over the years, changes in the field of education and politics, and the transformation in transportation and communication systems.

Diffusion is the process by which elements of culture spread from one society to another. Developments in transportation and communication have brought the world closer together. Fast foods, coca cola, blue jeans, and rock music have spread to all corners of the earth. Democracy, freedom, equality, and human rights are now generally accepted values. Specialists in mass communication have written extensively on the diffusion of innovations and demonstrated how mass media play an important role in the spread of ideas and technology. Think of how western music, dance, fashions, and food habits have made an impact on the campus subculture.

Culture lag is a concept introduced by William Ogburn to explain how various elements of culture change at a different pace and with what consequences. Theodorson and Theodorson (1969: 99) define it as 'A situation in which some parts of a culture change at a faster rate than other, related parts, with a resulting disruption of the integration and equilibrium of the culture.' Usually the elements of culture related to technology change faster than non-material elements as a result of new inventions. But society is considered to be a system in equilibrium with interrelated parts. Therefore, when some parts of society change more rapidly than others, such changes cause disruption in the social system. It takes time for all related parts of society to change and adapt to the new situation. This delay, known as cultural lag, affects every society. When the bicycles first came out with leather seats many Hindus refused to ride them because of the belief that leather pollutes. Soon, the seat was covered with plastic or fabric. Birth control technologies are readily available but certain religious and cultural beliefs resist their adoption. In some parts of India people still refuse vaccinations against polio and measles. In many cities people who use to pull manual rickshaws have changed over to autorickshaws. Changes in technology bring about changes in occupations and lifestyles.

Towards a Global Culture?

Changes in the world economy since the 1970s and 1980s have led to serious intellectual debates on postmodernism and post-Fordism, based on de-monopolization of economic structures with the de-regulation and globalization of markets, trade, and labour. Some of these changes are: increase in the numbers of international agencies and institutions, the increasing global forms of communication, explosion in travel and tourism industry, the acceptance of unified global time, the preponderance of global financial networks, the phenomenon of global competitions and prices, the development of standard notions of citizenship, rights, and competition of humankind. These developments, especially the revolution in mass communication, have exposed individuals even in rural communities to other, especially Western, cultures. One of the most important consequences of this exposure may be the emergence of consumerism and consumption-based lifestyle. Such consumerism embraces not only gadgets of convenience but also taste, fashion, and entertainment. Michael Jackson and James Bond, hamburger and Coca-Cola, pop music and fast dance, blue jeans and T-shirts, and internet and flip video have come to represent global consumer culture. Consumerism typifies contemporary middle class lifestyle the world over.

Another concept being tossed around in the context of globalization is that of cultural imperialism which may be defined as an attempt to impose one's culture on other societies. During the periods of colonization, attempts were made to 'civilize' the so-called 'primitive' or 'premodern' societies. Native Americans and Australian aboriginals bore the brunt of cultural imperialism. But the concept is of limited value in the age of globalization. There is no explicit attempt to force one's culture on others. In fact, captains of modern industry as well as international governmental and non-governmental organizations strive hard to adapt to local cultures. However, some may regard proselytization and Western attempts to impose their view of democracy, human rights, and rule of law on other societies as examples of contemporary cultural imperialism.

The globalization process which points to the extension of global cultural interrelatedness can also be understood as leading to a global ecumene, defined as a 'region of persistent culture interaction and exchange': a process whereby a series of cultural flows produce both: firstly, cultural homogeneity and cultural disorder, in linking together previously isolated pockets of relatively homogeneous culture which in turn produces more complex images of the other as well as generating identity-reinforcing reactions; and also secondly, transnational cultures, which can be understood as genuine 'third cultures' which are oriented beyond national boundaries. (Featherstone 1991: 2–6)

Postmodernism questions the earlier assumptions of cultural imperialism, Americanization, and mass consumer culture which alleged a homogenizing process leading to a proto-universal culture. Instead, we see a paradigm shift which recognizes 'the diversity, variety and richness of popular and local discourses, codes and practices which resist and playback systemicity and order'.

Appadurai (Featherstone 1991) also argues that globalization of culture is not the same as its homogenization. Although globalization involves the use of a variety of instruments of homogenization such as armaments, advertising techniques, language hegemonies, clothing styles, etc., the flow of culture is increasingly in non-isomorphic paths. Appadurai conceives of five dimensions of global cultural flow. First, there are *ethnoscapes*, the landscape of persons such as tourists, immigrants, refugees, guest workers, other moving groups and persons who affect the politics of and between nations to a hitherto unprecedented degree. Second, there are *technoscapes*, the global configuration of technology, both mechanical and informational, which multinational enterprises move at high speeds across previously impervious boundaries. Third, there are *finanscapes*, produced by the rapid flows of money in the currency markets and stock exchanges. Fourth, there are *mediascapes* which refer both to the distribution of electronic capabilities to produce and disseminate information (newspapers, magazine, television, film industry, etc.) and the images they create around the world. And finally, there are *ideoscapes* which frequently have to do with ideologies of states and the counter-ideologies of movements which consist of notions and images such as 'freedom', 'justice', 'rights', 'sovereignty', and 'democracy'.

Anthony Smith (Featherstone 1991) contends that intensification of contacts between cultures does not necessarily lead to tolerance for the globalization process. He emphasizes the resilience of the ethnic communities, the ethnic cores of nations, the pre-modern traditions, memories, myths, values, and symbols woven together and sustained in popular consciousness. According to him, 'A world of competing national cultures seeking to improve the ranking of their states, offers the prospect of global "cultural wars" with little basis for global projects of cultural integration, *lingua franca*, and ecumenical or cosmopolitan "unity through diversity" notions, despite the existence of the necessary technical communications infrastructures.' In short, there is little prospect of a unified global culture, rather, there are global cultures in the plural. Yet, 'the intensity and rapidity of today's global cultural flows have contributed to the sense that the world is a singular place which entails the proliferation of new cultural forms for encounters. While this increasingly dense web of cosmopolitan–local encounters and interdependencies can give rise to third cultures and increasing tolerance, it can also result in negative reactions and intolerance.'

Indeed, the onslaught of globalization has not only failed to weaken or homogenize local cultures but in fact there has been a resurgence of localism in recent years. Many ethnic groups around the world have sought to revive their traditional cultures and reaffirm their identity. Regions and communities now embrace the idea of cultural renewal or reaffirmation. Wolfgang Sachs coined the term cosmopolitan localism to refer to the assertion of diversity as a universal right and the identification of locality as globally formed. According to Sachs (1992: 112), 'Today, more than ever, universalism is under siege. To be sure, the victorious march of science, state and market has not come to a stop, but the enthusiasm of the onlookers is flagging…. The globe is not any longer imagined as a homogeneous space where contrasts ought to be leveled out, but as a discontinuous space where differences flourish in a multiplicity of places.' Peasants in India, Peru, Mexico, and many other places are recovering and implementing traditional peasant culture and technologies rooted in indigenous ecology. For example, in1993, the Karnataka Farmers Association protested against the intentions of Cargill Seeds to patent germplasm and launched a campaign to encourage grass roots organizations to resist the development of transgenic crops and to promote regional varieties. Similarly in 1996, a small village in Kerala (Pattuvam), declared its absolute ownership over all genetic resources within its jurisdiction. A group of young villagers came up with the idea of documenting local plant species and crop cultivators growing within the village's boundaries. By registering its biodiversity in local names, the village moved to claim ownership of local genetic materials and deny the possibility of corporate patents applying to these materials.

In the words of McMichael (2000: 269):

Cosmopolitan localism takes a variety of forms. One that is spreading across the world is a dialogical method of privileging the local worldview, including an evaluation of modern Western knowledge from the local standpoint. This means learning to value local culture and developing a contextualized under-standing of foreign knowledges, so that they do not assume some universal truth and inevitability, as sometimes claimed by Western knowledge and its officialdom. In this sense modernity is understood as a peculiarly Western cosmology arising from European culture and history, which includes universalist claims legitimizing imperial expansion across the world.

In short, the forces of globalization and westernization have not homogenized indigenous cultures; in some cases they have actually revived and revitalized many of the traditional cul-tures and local ethos.

STUDY QUESTIONS

- Define the following concepts: symbol, sanctions, ethnocentrism, xenophobia, culture shock, cultural relativism, multiculturalism, cultural universals, diffusion, and culture lag.
- Define culture and examine the different interpretations of the meaning of culture.
- Discuss the various components of culture.
- Differentiate between: ideal culture and real culture; folkways, mores, and laws; explicit norms and implicit norms; positive and negative sanctions; and societal cultures and subcultures.
- Are we moving towards a global culture? Critically examine the different perspectives.

REFERENCES

Featherstone, Mike (ed.), *Global Culture: Nationalism, Globalization and Modernity,* London: Sage Publications, 1991.

Geertz, Clifford, *The Interpretation of Cultures: Selected Essays,* New York: Basic Books, 1973.

Harris, Marvin, *Culture, People, and Nature,* New York: Crowell, 1975.

———, 'The Cultural Ecology of India's Sacred Cattle', *Current Anthropology,* 7, pp. 51–63, 1966.

Henslin, James M., *Sociology: A Down to Earth Approach,* Boston: Allyn and Bacon, 1997.

Sills, David L. (ed.), *International Encyclopedia of the Social Sciences,* New York: The Macmillan Company, 1972.

Kroeber, A.L., *The Nature of Culture,* Chicago: University of Chicago Press, 1952.

McMichael, Philip, *Development and Social Change: A Global Perspective,* Thousand Oaks, California: Pine Forge Press, 2000.

Sachs, Wolfgang (ed.), *The Development Dictionary,* London: Zed Books, 1992.

Sapir, Edward, *Culture, Language and Personality,* Berkeley: University of California Press, 1961.

Singer, Milton, The Concept of Culture, *International Encyclopedia of the Social Sciences,* New York: Macmillan, 1972 (first ed. 1968).

Theodorson, George A. and Achillees G. Theodorson, *A Modern Dictionary of Sociology,* New York: Thomas Y. Crowell Company, 1969.

Whorf, B., *Language, Thought, and Reality,* Cambridge: MIT Press, 1956.

5

Socialization

Many people think that Chinese and Japanese languages are hard to learn; yet every child in China and Japan knows his or her language. These children also use chopsticks so skillfully that they can pick up not only rice but even a single peanut. Children go to temples, mosques, or churches with their parents. While women in India wear sarees, in many Islamic societies women wear the burka. The Christian wedding is a relatively simple function in a church. But the traditional south Indian Brahmin wedding may take days to complete the entire process. How do we explain such variations in social phenomena?

These phenomena can only be explained by *socialization*, the process by which individuals learn the culture of their own society. Socialization is a life-long process which enables the individual to learn the content of his culture and the many behavioural patterns of the group to which he belongs.

The processes and effects of socialization are most pronounced in early childhood when the family consciously or unconsciously teaches the child certain types of behaviour as well as beliefs. Toilet training is often a deliberate process. But religious beliefs and practices as well as several food habits are gradually learned. In the neighbourhood playgroup the child learns other rules of behaviour from the peer group. The school exposes the child for the first time to formal rules and standards of behaviour laid down by the larger society. When we accept a job the workplace introduces new norms and socialization processes. Marriage, the birth of a child, retirement, and other life cycle events require new adjustments. Indeed, the Varnashrama Dharma of Indian culture is based on the four distinct stages of socialization.

Regardless of where we live, we are all products of socialization. Human beings are social animals, and we need socialization to learn the cultural and behavioural patterns of the group to which we belong. We are also different from the herds of animals, even the ones which live in well-knit groups. First of all, animal behaviour is determined by instincts. Second, animals learn by experience, not from it. Third, animal behaviour is repetitive, not creative. Finally, there is nothing symbolic about animal behaviour. Only man, the most intelligent animal, has this fantastic ability to attribute meanings to things which have no intrinsic meaning (such as flag, cross, trishul, etc.) and is willing to die or kill for it. Socialization makes us aware of who we are, what we believe, and how we do things. Much of our personality, our beliefs, and our perception of the world are the result of socialization. Socialization is the only way an individual can become a full member of society. It is the only way we can transmit our social heritage from one generation to the next.

HEREDITY AND ENVIRONMENT

A continuing controversy in the social sciences centres on the relative importance of heredity and environment. The *nature* vs. *nurture* argument has many followers on both sides.

The nature school argues that human beings are primarily a product of their genetic make-up; in other words, biological or hereditary factors are far more important than cultural or environmental factors. This was the dominant theme in the nineteenth century and had a large following among scholars. Charles Darwin's *On the Origin of Species* argued that living organisms have changed over long periods of time and that the process of natural selection has enabled them to adapt themselves to changing environments. Variations in genetic traits allow species to try out different adaptation strategies, and finally, those genes found to be most advantageous in the evolutionary process become dominant. In other words, the process of natural selection gave the species superior genetic traits needed to cope with each stage in the evolution. Later, Herbert Spencer coined the term 'survival of the fittest' to explain the process of natural selection in society. Spencer's thesis was eagerly embraced by millionaire businessmen who thought that their superiority is the product of natural selection; the poor, the handicapped and the mentally retarded, and all those who failed to succeed in the competitive process of natural selection were inferior. The same idea was reflected in the initial attempts at colonization by the West. The white man considered himself superior and the coloured people in Africa, Asia, and the Americas, inferior. He felt that he not only had a right to conquer but also 'civilize' the 'inferior' races in the world.

Later in the early part of the twentieth century, the instinct theory became popular in social psychology. Scholars began to explain almost every behaviour in terms of an instinct. Men and women mate because of the sexual instinct. They earn money because of the acquisitive instinct. They play games because of the competitive instinct. Thus, if there were limitless behaviours, there were limitless instincts, so it appeared. Soon scholars realized that it was too easy and meaningless to explain human behaviour in terms of a large repertoire of instincts. Indeed, as we indicated earlier, much of the human behaviour cannot be explained in terms of instincts. Of course, human beings experience hunger, sexual urge, jealousy, fear, and several other feelings but even here their expression is mediated by culture. Human beings are poorly equipped with instincts. A calf as soon as it is born 'makes the move' to find the milk. The human infant has to be carried, fed, and cared for for a long time. Again as we indicated earlier, much of the human behaviour is creative, meaningful, and symbolic.

Ivan Pavlov's study of conditioned behaviour demonstrated that even apparently involuntary responses could be taught. In his experiment, dogs began to associate bell ringing with the arrival of food. The dogs were so conditioned that they began to salivate when they heard the bell even when there was no food with it. An American psychologist, John Watson came up with similar conclusions in 1924. Watson, who founded the behaviourism school, argued that nurture is the most important factor in human development and that a child can be turned into anything depending on how he or she is raised:

Give me a dozen healthy infants ... and my own specified world to bring them up in, and I will guarantee to take any one at random and train him to become any type of specialist that I might select—doctor, lawyer, artist, merchant-chief, and yes, even beggar-man and thief—regardless of his talents, penchants, tendencies, abilities, vocations, and race of his ancestors. (Watson 1930: 104)

B.F. Skinner is even more emphatic. He wrote extensively on conditioned behaviour and argued that human behaviour can be modified in any way by means of appropriate rewards and punishments. Anthropologist Margaret Mead was another outspoken proponent of the 'nurture' view. According to her: 'The differences between individuals who are members of different cultures, like the differences between individuals within a culture, are almost entirely to be laid to differences in conditioning, especially during early childhood, and this conditioning is culturally determined' (1963: 280).

In recent years *sociobiology* emerged as a separate school of thought within sociology. Sociobiology is the study of the way in which biological factors influence human behaviour and culture. Edward Wilson, the founder of sociobiology, argues that many patterns of human behaviour such as territoriality, aggression, selfishness, and the tendency to form hierarchies are innate and universal. Human beings have acquired them through the evolutionary process, and over time they have come to influence not only human behaviour but also many cultural patterns. As an example, sociobiologists refer to gender differences in the process of biological reproduction. A man releases hundreds of millions of sperm in a single ejaculation which, technically speaking, can impregnate millions of women. But a woman usually releases a single mature egg cell from her ovaries each month, and can give birth to only a limited number of children. She also has to carry the child for nine months and take care of the young for several years. These gender differences have laid the foundation for several cultural patterns such as the nature of the family, discrimination against women, and male domination over women.

It is certainly obvious that several biological forces influence human behaviour as well as cultural patterns. As we said before, sexual urge, jealousy, aggression, and many other biological forces influence human behaviour. At the same time, culture also mediates and channels them. Talents for painting, music, and dancing may be part of the biological repertoire. One who faints at the first sight of blood cannot make a surgeon. And, everyone does not have the same physical stamina or ability to excel in sports. But, such biological factors only account for minor variations. Unlike animals, human beings have to invent things to survive. Some animals go into hibernation and can stay alive for months without food or water; humans cannot. In order to protect them from extreme cold, animals may have thick hide, long body hair, or the ability to store fat in their bodies; humans have to build shelters. The Eskimo may have a little more tolerance to the cold compared to others but ultimately he has to protect himself from the cold by wearing warm clothing and living in suitable shelters. The dark-skinned people in the tropics may have a little more melanin in their skin which protects them from exposure to the sun but ultimately they too will succumb to it. There are not enough instincts, biological forces, or genetic factors that can be substitutes for culture. A Brahmin boy plucked away at birth and placed among the Yanomamo in the jungles of the Amazon will learn to hunt and fish, and he will master the art of survival in his environment. However, regardless of his vast innate talents it is highly unlikely that he will become a classical musician or a brain surgeon if he continues to live in that kind of social environment! Social roles are products of culture and individuals are trained into them by the process of socialization. Therefore, the environment or culture is far more important in the full development of the human potential. It does not, however, mean that biological forces or hereditary factors are not important; they provide the basic data or the essential raw materials which are fine-tuned by culture.

THE RESULTS OF DEPRIVED SOCIALIZATION

It is obvious that we learn our language, standards of behaviour, and beliefs through socialization. A human child who is raised by animals in the jungle has no way of learning a human language. What about physical and psychological development? Can a child who is deprived of human interaction develop a normal personality? Of course, we cannot conduct experiments which deprive the children of their development potential. But there are several documented cases of children who had very little or no contact with humans.

One of the rare cases is that of the feral children of India, two girls, who were kept alive by animals. The girls were eight years and a year and a half old when they were discovered among a pack of wolves and brought to an orphanage. 'Wolfish in appearance and behaviour, they walked on all fours, their tongues permanently hung out, and they prowled and howled at night' (Lindsey and Beach 2004: 117). Since they had had no human contact, they learnt the ways of the animals which raised them. They were physically deformed, mentally retarded, and showed no signs of human intelligence.

There are at least two well-documented cases of deprived socialization in America. They were both studied by Kingsley Davis in 1948. The first was the case of Anna, an illegitimate and unwanted child, who was forced to live alone in an upstairs room. Her mother and grandfather who lived in the house maintained no contact with her except to leave her food in the room. The child was almost six years of age when she was discovered by a social worker. She could not walk, talk, smile, or show any signs of emotion or intelligence. She was brought to an institution where she received proper care and extensive human contact. However, nearly six years of physical and mental isolation had left her permanently damaged. At age eight her mental and social development was less than that of a two-year-old child. Anna died at the age of ten from a blood disorder which was probably related to her long years of abuse.

The second case is that of Isabelle who also spent the first six years of her life in virtual isolation. Her mother was deaf and mute, and the two spent their time together in a dark room. They could communicate only by gestures. When she was discovered it seemed she was absolutely incapable of forming relationships. However, unlike Anna, Isabelle was fortunate enough to be treated by psychologists and other specialists. Within a few days she began to speak and within two years she was able to read and write. She benefited a great deal from the intensive efforts of psychologists and in about two years she had made up for the lost six years. And, she continued to progress steadily in school.

Another interesting investigation is that of Rene Spitz who compared infants raised by their own mothers with infants of the same age raised in an orphanage. The children who were raised by their mothers had extensive involvements with them and others, and developed normally. The orphans were isolated in cubicles with no human contact except feeding, changing, and medical help. After eighteen months, one third of the orphans were dead, and the rest were handicapped physically, mentally, and socially. The children who were raised at home were mentally and physically healthy.

All these cases point to an undeniable fact: human beings need human contact to learn their culture, or even to be human. Children raised in isolation cannot learn the language, and they cannot develop mentally, socially, and even physically.

Theories of Socialization

Sociology and psychology have developed several theories to explain the process of socialization. The key difference between them is that psychological theories are primarily concerned with personal identity in explaining attitudes and behaviours whereas sociological theories are primarily concerned with social identity that arises from social experience over a long period of time. Both sociological and psychological theories agree that the self is the key concept, the development of which is the primary function of socialization.

Sociological Theories

Symbolic interactionism is by far the most important sociological theory of socialization. Since this theory is fully explained in Chapter 2, here we will provide only a brief overview of the socialization process as seen by symbolic interactionists. Cooley and Mead are undoubtedly the chief proponents of the theory.

Cooley focused his attention on the complex relationship between individual and society. The two are not empirically separable but a differentiated coincidence of the same phenomenon—no society without individuals and no individual apart from society. Cooley concentrated his analytical skills upon the development of his fundamental dictum—'The imaginations people have of one another are solid facts of society.' This mental picture of oneself is what Cooley called the 'looking-glass self'. The social self is an empirical self; it is a product of social interaction, emerging from one's perception of one's self as reflected in the perceptions of others. As an individual develops a sense of 'I' he also develops simultaneously an awareness of, and sensitivity to, others as 'you', 'he', or 'she', and 'they'. Through interaction with other selves, self emerges. Not only is the individual aware of or able to imagine how he appears to others, he also becomes conscious of others' judgements and evaluations of his appearance. The result of this dual mental image, that is, how he appears to and is evaluated by others, is a responsive feeling on his part to this evaluation—of pride or mortification or self-doubt, etc.

George Herbert Mead built the three-fold foundation of his theory on Mind, Self, and Society. The mind is an emergent phenomenon of personal awareness on the part of an infant individual, of meaningful gestures selected out of a whole range of indiscriminate, experiential physical motions. The mind develops with the child's capacity to distinguish his and others' nonsense motions and significant gestures or conventional gestures. As the child's mind develops, there is simultaneous increase in social communication skills. The more developed the mind in terms of symbolic interaction skills, the more sophisticated the level of meaningful communication among individuals. The ability to use and interpret social gestures greatly facilitates the development of the mind, self, and society.

The mind emerges out of this maturing capacity of the child to distinguish and discriminate the symbols of interaction, by perceiving, conceiving, and interpreting gestures and language. By so doing, the child develops the capacity to assume the posture or perspective of the one with whom he is interacting. Mead calls this the ability to 'take the role of the other'. Thus, the mind evolves when the child is able to: 1. understand and use conventional gestures; 2. 'to employ the gestures' and to 'take the role of the other'; and 3. to imaginatively rehearse alternative lines of action. Man is not primarily an animal with instinctual behaviour of stimulus–response, but is human with a mind for rational judgement and freedom of decision. The identity of the self develops in the process of symbolic interaction or as Mead puts it, 'the symbol arouses in one's self what it arouses in the other individual'. The mature self arises when a generalized other is internalized so that the community exercises control over the conduct of its individual members. The self for Mead was not simply a bag of social attitudes picked up in the environment. He used such concepts as 'self-image', 'self-concept', 'taking the role of the other', and 'significant others' to explain the creative balance which exists between individual and society. His suggestion that through the development of a mature self-consciousness, the individual becomes both an object and a subject to himself is a profound insight.

Structural-functionalism is another theoretical perspective that explains the process of socialization. However, functionalism tends to exaggerate the homogeneity, stability, and integration of the social system in the internalization of values. This view is derived from anthropological studies of simple societies on remote islands or remote quarters of the globe. Although its application to modern complex societies with considerable structural differentiation and functional specialization is subject to review and modification, many functionalists continue to overstress the integrative function of values in the socialization process. Parsons, for example, has generally overplayed consensus on values and ideas and the almost complete internalization of norms by social actors. Parsons views society as a well-integrated system held together by value consensus and shared expectations. Actors in Parsons' scheme of system always comply with each other's expectations because of 'institutionalization' or 'complementarity'.

Denis Wrong's (1961) essay on the 'Oversocialized Conception of Man' represents the sharpest attack on internalization theories. He notes that socialization provides man with social identity but the individual is creative and has the ability to evaluate critically the social reality and take an autonomous stand towards concrete social roles. In other words, although the individual internalizes the norms and values of society in the process of socialization, he is also a creative individual who thinks and acts imaginatively.

Psychological Theories

Whereas sociologists usually focus on social interaction and group contexts, psychologists have focused on the individual and his attitudes and experiences. We will now look at a few major theories of socialization in psychology.

Psychoanalytic Theory

Sigmund Freud, the father of psychoanalysis, based his theory on two fundamental premises. The first, the genetic approach, emphasizes that early childhood experiences play a critical role in shaping one's development. In fact, Freud believed that the bare foundations of an individual's development were laid down by the tender age of five. The second premise is that a certain amount of sexual energy (libido) is present at birth and thereafter it progresses through a series of psychosexual stages that are rooted in the instinctual process of the organism. Freud also emphasizes that inherent in human nature is a tendency for different impulses and biological forces to pull in opposing directions. The spontaneous, selfish part of the nature wants something here and now; but there is another part which says there is a right way and a wrong way of having it. The raw nature wants to steal this textbook from the library but the second nature says it is wrong to do it. Tonight you would like to watch a movie and party afterwards. Then something tells you that you have to stay in the room and study for a test tomorrow. If people always followed their impulses and desires for pleasures, society would disintegrate. Socialization requires individuals to sacrifice their selfish desires in favour of the greater good of the society. Thus, socialization is a process that channels our desires and impulses in culturally accepted ways.

Freud identified three distinct parts of the personality: *id*, *superego*, and *ego*. The *id* is a bundle of biological drives; it is spontaneous, unconscious, selfish, and irrational. The id is constantly seeking to maximize pleasure and avoid pain. It propels the impulses and desires that make us want to do the things we want and when we want without any regard for other individuals or social norms. But human beings cannot do anything and everything just to maximize their pleasure. That is where the *superego* comes in. The *superego* refers to the internalized standards of society. It stands for the values, norms, and morals that are learnt through socialization. Thus, the *superego* is the conscience of the individual into which society's expectations and standards are organized. In the aforementioned examples you did not steal the book from the library and you stayed in the room and studied because of your *superego* which specifies what is right and what is wrong. The *ego* is the mediator between the *id* and the *superego*. The *ego* mediates between the impulses of the *id* and the moral standards of the society in which we live. Newborn babies are totally *id*-driven because they have not yet internalized the norms of society. But grown-ups also have the impulses, desires, and drives which make them seek pleasure at any cost. The *superego* opposes such drives, and there is this constant struggle between the *id* and the *superego*. It is the role of the *ego* to adjust our desires and impulses to the reality of the world and convince us to conform to the standards of society. The *id* and the *superego* always stand in opposition. Just as it is impossible to gratify all our needs and desires, it is extremely difficult to restrain them all. As a mediator, the *ego* adjusts the needs of the individual to the demands of society. This process of adjustment which goes on throughout life is the essence of socialization.

Psychosocial Approach

Erik Erikson's psychosocial approach outlines eight stages of personality development:

1. Trust vs. mistrust (Hope—birth to one year)
2. Autonomy vs. shame and doubt (Will—1–3 years)
3. Initiative vs. guilt (Purpose—3–6 years)
4. Industry vs. inferiority (Competence—6 years to puberty)
5. Ego identity vs. role confusion (Fidelity—puberty to adulthood)
6. Intimacy vs. isolation (Love—young adulthood)
7. Generativity vs. stagnation (Care—middle adulthood)
8. Ego integrity vs. despair (Wisdom—old age)

Each stage involves conflicts between the child's needs or feelings and external obstacles, and the development of a healthy personality depends on the successful resolution of these conflicts. Erikson believed that the eight stages are a universal feature of human development. But there are cultural variations in the way people in different societies deal with the problems of each stage and in the possible solutions to those problems. For example, in America an infant may be bottle-fed on a rigid schedule. But in Indian villages, the child may be breast-fed whenever it cries. In the West, the infant may be weaned within the first year but in India it may take twice that long, and even afterwards, the child is frequently carried by the mother or the elder sister. Thus, cultures impose different standards on the child, who must learn to cope with them. The thrust of Erikson's argument is that at each stage of development the individual confronts a specific crisis unique to that stage and that the individual must devise solutions to meet the crisis. The development of a healthy personality depends on how often the crisis has been managed successfully. A satisfactory resolution of the crisis at each stage forms the basis of the child's identity which is the acceptance of both self and one's society.

Cognitive Development Theory

Piaget's vision of human development was based on two overriding assumptions about intelligence:

1. it is a form of biological adaptation, and 2. it becomes organized as the individual interacts with the external world. Thus, for Piaget, thinking exhibits two inborn qualities. The first is adaptation, a tendency to adjust or become more attuned to the conditions imposed by the environment. The second is organization, a tendency for intellectual structures and processes to become more systematic and coherent. Just as arms, eyes, lungs, heart, and other physical structures assemble and take shape to carry out biological functions, so do mental structures array themselves in ever more powerful patterns to support more complex thought. These changes, however, depend on the opportunity to look and touch, handle and play with, and construct and order the rich assortment of experiences stemming from action on the environment. From the abundant encounters provided in common place physical and social experiences, the child confronts unexpected and puzzling outcomes that ultimately lead to reorganizations in thought. (Bukatko and Daehler 2004: 21)

Piaget identified four principal stages in which cognitive abilities develop. They are:

1. *The sensorimotor stage (first two years of life).* During this stage the human infant experiences the world through sensory contact and learns to coordinate sensory experiences with motor activities. Children imitate the actions and sounds of others but they do not comprehend the meaning of symbols.
2. *The preoperational stage (two to seven years of age).* Children begin to think about things they cannot sense directly by touching or grasping; they begin to engage the world mentally. At this point language and other symbols develop. Yet their ability to attach names and meanings is limited.
3. *The concrete operational stage (seven to eleven years of age).* During this stage children begin to master cognitive skills and comprehend abstract concepts such as weight, speed, time, and cause-and-effect. More importantly, they are able to understand the feelings and outlook of others and alter their own feelings and actions.
4. *The formal operational stage (ages eleven to fifteen).* During this period children comprehend highly abstract thought and logic. They are for the first time able to reason in terms of abstract qualities rather than concrete situations. As they develop their imagination, they can also comprehend different social roles and see themselves in those roles.

Like Cooley and Mead, Piaget also thought of the human mind as active and creative, and that through the process of socialization, children learn to shape their social world.

Learning Theory

Albert Bandura's learning theory is one of the most influential theories in developmental psychology. According to Bandura, learning does not always require direct enforcement; learning may also occur merely as a result of watching someone else perform some action, which is known as observational learning or modelling. He also calls attention to another class of reinforcement called intrinsic reinforcement or intrinsic rewards. Bandura's most important contribution is the emphasis on cognitive (mental) elements in learning. The great strength of this view of social learning is that it seems to give an accurate picture of the way in which many forms of behaviour are learned. Children's behaviour can change if the reinforcement system or their beliefs about themselves change. Learning theories represent a very different theoretical tradition, one in which the emphasis is more on the way the environment shapes the child than on how the child understands his experiences. Although learning theories disagree a good deal on the particulars, all would agree with Bandura when he says that human nature is characterized by a vast potentiality that can be fashioned by direct and vicarious experience into a variety of forms within biological limits. Learning theorists see human behaviour as enormously plastic, shaped by predictable processes of learning.

AGENTS OF SOCIALIZATION

Individuals acquire the culture of their society through participation in a variety of groups and institutions. From his family the child learns the first words of his language, religion, and several role definitions. But the family cannot teach everything. At every stage of life we learn new rules and behaviour patterns as we interact with others. The primary agents of socialization are the family, peer group, the school, and mass media.

The Family

The family is the most important institution of primary socialization. Since children spend their early and impressionable years under the care and protection of the family, they acquire a large part of their values, beliefs, and knowledge from the parents. Indeed, it is membership in a family that gives the child his first social identity. Family is the source of the first set of values, beliefs, and attitudes. This explains why children who grow up in different cultures think and behave differently. American kids usually leave their parents' home when they are eighteen; in India they may live with them for much of their adult life. In rural communities where people's livelihood depends on land and farming, parents and their grown-up sons continue to live and work together. Families confirm and perpetuate caste identity, religious traditions, and kinship obligations.

Many researchers have stressed the importance of family atmosphere and the quality of emotional relationships among members of the family in determining whether or not the child will react passively or actively, constructively or destructively, in the quest towards perfection. For instance, Adler thought that children who are pampered or neglected are particularly predisposed to a faulty style of life. The pampered child is one who is excessively spoiled and protected from life's inevitable frustration. Such a child is being deprived of the right to become independent and the chance to learn the requirements of living within a social order. The neglected child, on the other hand, is virtually denied the right to a place in the social order. Rejection arouses resistance in the child, who acquires feelings of inferiority and a tendency to withdraw from the implications of social life, leading him to become socially incompetent. Adler points out that child-rearing practices frequently consist of a continuing alternation between indulgence and rejection.

Peer Groups

Peer groups consist of people of almost the same age who share similar interests. The first peer group is, of course, the neighbourhood playgroup; children who hang out together in the neighbourhood and play different games. They sometimes spend more time among themselves than with members of the family. They swim in the river, play cricket in the local school yard, or simply hang out together. Participation in such groups gives the child an important social identity such as team player, leader, resourceful person, or shy individual. Indeed, the first neighbourhood playgroups establish their leaders and followers. Children also learn the rules of the game here, their first exposure to impersonal rules which are not their parents' creation.

Later in life peer groups become more influential in school and the workplace. Unlike the neighbourhood playgroups where peers were 'simply there', in the school the child gets to choose his own friends. Friends may be chosen on the basis of physical attraction, common interests, or shared backgrounds. They share similar interests in sports, music, movies, fashions, and even ideologies. The first taste of alcohol or the first act of smoking may be peer-induced. Young adults who grow up in crime-ridden neighbourhoods are drawn into deviant subcultures.

The influence of the peer group continues in the workplace. The office norm, or the unwritten rules of behaviour, is a product of peer socialization. For example, in an industry or in a government office, there is often this shared understanding that a honest day's work is not necessary, and the peers frown upon people who are eager to complete the task in a timely fashion. At the same time friends in the workplace can help individuals tide over many life crises such as domestic problems, divorce, accidents, and death.

The School

The school is the first formal agency which exposes the child to the rules of the larger society. Here the child learns to recognize and obey rules, practise skills, and relate to people in positions of authority. Children learn to behave in group settings, sit quietly and listen to teachers, participate in social events, and accept responsibilities. The school plays the most significant role in the development of social and intellectual skills and the acquisition of society's cultural heritage. It is not only responsible for reading, writing, and arithmetic, but for the transmission of the accumulated social heritage of the community. Education refines social skills, and frequent interaction with peers and teachers helps in the formation of a healthy social identity.

The school also teaches civic sense, patriotism, and pride in the nation's shared heritage. Above all, education is supposed to foster critical thinking so that individuals can think for themselves and become creative and productive members of the society.

Mass Media

In contemporary society, mass media play a significant, although subtle, role in the socialization process. Mass media refer to all instruments of communication such as television, radio, newspapers, magazines, movies, and records. Television has become by far the most influential medium in recent years. India has come a long way from the days of the government-controlled single-channel television. With the growth of the cable industry and numerous private television channels, people have a choice. Not only is there a wide range of programmes available, but there is also an instant transmission of images, events, styles, and fashions from around the world. Young people are now able to enjoy Western music, dance, fashion and fast food, and adopt types of behaviour patterns. There are also educational channels such as Discovery, National Geographic, and History, which inform, entertain, as well as truly instruct. However, there is considerable controversy over what some people call 'cultural pollution', which is the result of the 'pernicious' influence of the West. Much of the controversy is the result of stereotypes and the comparison of our 'ideal' culture with West's 'real' culture.

It is possible that many people watch too much television and that they devote too little time to reading. Once upon a time, good books were the only form of entertainment; now we can watch television any time of the day or night. Studies in America show that pre-schoolers and young children spend almost one-third of the day in front of the television. Studies have also shown that exposure to violence in the media can contribute to aggressive behaviour, insensitivity to violence, nightmares, and feelings of insecurity. Many of the movies and video games are also full of violence. In India, parents are more likely to regulate children's viewing of television and violent movies. However, it will be worthwhile to undertake some extensive research on the impact of certain television programmes on young children.

We also depend on other agents of mass media such as newspapers and journals to transmit enormous amounts of information. There are magazines that cater to every conceivable interest—women, young adults, fashion, film industry, sports, health and fitness, news stories, politics, occupations and professions, music, religion, etc. Then there are, of course, the books—fiction, biographies, and social commentaries—which convey a host of ideas. In a sense, every book is a powerful instrument of socialization.

Adult Socialization

Socialization is a process that continues throughout life, right from the cradle to the grave, so to speak. Although the family, peer group, school, and the mass media are the most important agents of socialization, we continue to learn standards of behaviour and beliefs from a number of other agencies. Religious institutions play a prominent role in shaping our values and belief systems. There are several religious organizations that formally or informally provide moral instruction. The workplace is another important place where significant socialization occurs. A factory, a business corporation, or a government office teaches different work ethics as well as teamwork. Then there are the numerous professional organizations and clubs that people join. They have their own rules and standards. Women's groups, senior citizens' forums, farmers organizations, and labour unions all have their own agenda and seek to influence the attitudes and behaviours of their members. Meeting new friends, life cycle events such as birth of a child, divorce, remarriage, death of a partner, travel, and exposure to new experiences, all involve new learning and continued socialization.

RESOCIALIZATION

Resocialization is a deliberate and systematic effort to alter an individual's current behaviour pattern and give him a new set of values, beliefs, and standards. Resocialization may be voluntary or involuntary. A person may check into a drug rehabilitation centre for complete remedial programme. Alcoholics check into hospitals which have rehabilitation programmes. A mental patient may be admitted to a psychiatric hospital to undergo rigorous treatment. Criminals are forced to spend time in prison. Mental hospitals, drug rehabilitation centres, and prisons are institutions charged with the responsibility of modifying people's behaviour. The military is also an institution where resocialization takes place.

There are also institutions which people seek to join and where they undergo thorough resocialization. Religious institutions such as *mutt*s, convents, and monasteries provide individuals with new cultural content and social identity. Members are deprived of their former selves including names, possessions, dresses, and even family relationships and are resocialized into an entirely new social order. Religious cults and several underground social movements rely on types of behaviour modification.

Total Institutions

A Total Institution is a place of residence where individuals are systematically stripped of their old identity and resocialized into an entirely new way of life. Such places are often surrounded by high walls, bars, fences, locked doors, and manned gates. The procedures for admittance may involve degradation and humiliation. People may be stripped of their possessions including clothing and given uniforms. Inhabitants may be assigned numbers or new names. Their contacts with the outside world including family members are highly restricted. Non-conformity may be severely punished. People voluntarily join some total institutions while membership in others is involuntary. Admission procedures and rules of acceptable behaviour vary widely from institution to institution but they all have something in common: a process for almost complete resocialization. Prisons and mental asylums are typical total institutions. However, some of the ancient monasteries and mutts with limited contacts with the outside world were total institutions; their character has undergone changes in contemporary society.

SOCIALIZATION BY CASTE, RELIGION, AND GENDER

In India caste, religion, and gender seem to have an overwhelming influence on the process of socialization. In the traditional social system every individual was a prisoner of his subcaste. People of particular castes often followed the traditional occupation and lived in segregated neighbourhoods. Although untouchability has been abolished, many of the paraphernalia of the caste system still remain. People inherit their names, choose their mates, and follow many of the life cycle ceremonies according to the caste system. Since members of each caste are socialized according to its own norms and cultural practices, there are wide variations in dress styles, food habits, religious and life cycle ceremonies, customs, spoken languages, and lifestyle.

Religion also plays a very unique role in the socialization process in India. An individual's name and membership in a clan are determined by religious affiliation. We can often identify a person's religion by his name. There are several ceremonies which confirm membership in a religious group or recognize different stages in the life cycle. Think of all the ceremonies when a woman becomes pregnant, before the delivery, at the time of naming the child, for the first feeding of rice, for the first haircut, and so on. Food habits and dress styles vary according to religion too. Consider the differences in wedding ceremonies and funeral rites. Socialization is the only means by which these differences are sustained and perpetuated.

In almost every culture gender roles are defined differently. In India gender socialization involves not only role definitions but also differences in physical appearances. In much of the countryside women are expected to look like women: grow long hair, wear women's clothes, and adorn bindi. Old traditions imposed numerous restrictions on women. At the early stages of socialization women are told that they should be modest, should not cross their legs when sitting, should never consume alcohol and tobacco, should cook and serve men first, and confine their world to the kitchen. Many castes used to forbid women from pursuing higher studies. Many occupations are still taboo for women. But many of these restrictions have eased, especially in the urban areas. Today, more and more women are employed outside the home. Yet, they still end up doing most of the domestic chores; so the double burden of women has not eased. It will be worthwhile to explore how early socialization in family, caste, and religion patterns people's behaviours and attitudes.

STUDY QUESTIONS

- Define socialization with special reference to perspectives on heredity and environment.
- Discuss the different theories of socialization.
- What are the agents of socialization, and explain the role of each.

- Define the following concepts: adult socialization, resocialization, and total institutions.
- How do caste, religion, and gender influence socialization?

References

Bandura, A., *Social Learning Theory,* Englewood Cliffs: Prentice-Hall, 1977.

Bukatko, Danuta and Marvin W. Daehler, *Child Development,* Boston: Houghton Mifflin Company, 2004.

Erikson, E., *Childhood and Society,* New York: W.W. Norton, 1963.

Freud, Sigmund, *Standard Edition of the Complete Psychological Works of Sigmund Freud,* London: Hogarth Press, 1920, 1923, 1930.

Lindsey, L. Linda and Stephen Beach, *Sociology,* Upper Saddle River, New Jersey: Pearson Education, Inc., 2004.

Mead, Margaret, *Sex and Temperament in Three Primitive Societies,* New York: William Morrow, 1963.

Piaget, J., *The Child's Conception of the World,* London: Routledge and Kegan Paul, 1929.

———, *The Construction of Reality in the Child,* New York: Basic Books, 1954.

Rose, Peter I. (ed.), *Socialization and the Life Cycle,* New York: St Martin's Press, 1979.

Watson, John B., *Behaviourism,* New York: Norton, 1930.

Wrong, Dennis H., 'The Oversocialized Conception of Man in Modern Sociology', *American Sociological Review,* 26: 183–93, 1961.

6

Social Interaction

Many sociologists would argue that interaction is the basic unit of analysis in sociology. When people meet, they greet one another or otherwise engage in some form of interaction. But the nature and quality of interaction varies according to the size and structure of the group, relationships between actors involved, and the social setting. For example, the interaction between mother and child is qualitatively different from the interaction between buyers and sellers in the marketplace. Similarly, interaction between teachers and students is different from that between boss and employees. Interaction may be purely altruistic, goal-oriented, strictly formal, or very informal. Regardless of the nature and quality of interaction, social interaction is the essential building block of group life. Interaction is a sort of starting mechanism of social life. It leads to social relationships which, over time, may be institutionalized into systems. Think of a new employee in a work situation or a new student in the classroom. It does not take long for the first interaction to develop into a durable friendship.

From a common-sense point of view, interaction may be an uneventful everyday occurrence but from a sociological perspective, interaction in everyday life is the web and warf of the fabric of social structure. Words like 'Good morning', 'How are you?', or even a simple 'helo' have deeper meaning in the social context. They reflect certain shared expectations in social relationships, conform to certain norms, and reinforce established patterns of those relationships. The regularity of those interactions gives rise to stable patterns of relationships which constitute the structure of society. In fact, the concepts of social system and social structure have no meaning if daily interactions are discounted.

Verbal and Non-verbal Communication

Interaction takes place in different social settings, under various cultural norms, and in several forms. Although language is the single most important means of communication, in everyday social interaction non-verbal communication is equally significant. *Kinesics*, or the study of body movements, examines how human beings communicate with one another through nods, gestures, facial expressions, postural shifts, and other non-verbal cues. For example, facial expressions can reveal pleasure, fear, disgust, surprise, or sadness. We use fingers, hands, and head to communicate meanings. Sometimes a whole array of questions such as 'How are you?', 'Where are you going?' and 'What do you want?' are expressed in body language and the parties to the interaction seem completely satisfied. Gestures are also frequently used to substitute or supplement language. Gestures are culture-specific and the same gestures may have different meanings in different cultures. Yet gestures are an effective way of communicating feelings in every culture. There are positive and negative gestures, decent and indecent gestures, and deferential and indifferent gestures. We shrug our shoulders to show indifference; rise and bow to show respect. We may use eye contact to initiate interaction with someone in the group or avoid the eyes to discourage contacts. Men staring at women is somehow 'understood' but women staring at men is considered sexually suggestive. It is rude to point your fingers at others. But the way different fingers are positioned and pointed has different meanings in different cultures, and they often give rise to misunderstanding. A gesture that is positive in one culture may be negative in another. But it is not only gestures but also words and sounds that may be misunderstood if the social context is not properly understood. In a British comedy, friends of a woman overheard her say: 'My girl will be a mother anyday but none of us have a clue who the father is'. You can very well imagine the confusion until you know that the woman was referring to her beloved cat. Some gestures and sounds may have specifically assigned meanings understood by a few. In Kuwait, internet cafes are segregated by sex but boys and girls send messages surreptitiously across the web using certain keyboard symbols to indicate kisses and hugs.

It is not only words in the language but also voice, body movements, and facial expressions that communicate feelings in social interaction. People may fake excitement, students may lie about their absence from class, and the mother may try to restrain her emotions. But the tone and patterns of speech, facial expressions, nervousness, dilated pupil of the eye, or demeanour may expose the true situation. Non-verbal communication may also be structured by the status of the individual. For example, the boss may exhibit types of eccentric behaviour such as removing off his shoes, yawning loudly or pointing his fingers but the subordinates are expected to behave formally and 'correctly'. Staring, touching, and public displays of affection are also forms of patterned interaction. Men are known to stare more than women. On American college campuses boys and girls embrace and kiss one another. In India even husbands and wives do not display affection in public. However, members of the same sex embrace and hold hands but such behaviour is considered part of homosexual orientation in the West.

Social interaction may be active or passive, direct or indirect. Joggers in the park just wave at fellow joggers. Many drivers as well as passengers in vehicles bow their heads or otherwise show reverence when they pass places of worship. People respond to music that they hear over the radio. In several communities in India people visit the homes where death has occurred, stay for a while, and leave without a word to anyone, but their presence and feelings are understood by all concerned. In today's videocoaches people respond differently to the movies. Some really enjoy the show and react vociferously. Others just tolerate the 'inconvenience'; yet others simply ignore it. Some of these are just responses or 'reactions' to external events and do not qualify as meaningful social interaction which is 'reciprocally oriented action'. However, some of these actions may become the basis for interaction if others respond to such 'reactions'. In this context, silence itself may become a form of interaction. Members of the family, friends and neighbours, and children on the playground sometimes go into a 'silence mode' to register a protest or as a form of subtle punishment. In India, pledge of silence is a form of self-introspection—or even a prompt for action—used by sages and gurus. Acharya Vinoba Bhave has used silence as an effective form of interaction.

The dawn of globalism has really revolutionized social interaction in two specific fields: cyberspace and love. Recent technological developments in the field of communication have totally transformed the landscape of social interaction. Satellite technology, cable television, cell phones, and the internet have revolutionized communication. The internet, for example, has become an easy shorthand messaging system. The old rules of letter writing have been debunked. Phrases and jargon substitute sentences. The technological revolution has brought in new status symbols and consumer products. It has also raised the level of human consciousness and the possibilities of global interaction. In the wake of the Tsunami disaster the old adage that 'A touch of danger makes the whole world kin' has become all too real. The outpouring of sympathy, grief, generosity, and compassion would not have been possible without the global interaction networks. Thus a study of social interaction today must include not only the well-known processes of interaction but also various forms of subtle interaction as well as global orientation.

The sphere of love and romance has also been transformed by the new age of globalization. Young people who work in computer-related and other business fields and live in metropolitan areas enjoy more personal freedom and leisure time to interact with one another. They meet at trendy stores, pizza parlours, and coffee houses to exchange ideas, in addition to continuing their chat on mobile phones and personal computers. Some of the emerging trends in romance-based interaction are as follows. Many young people tend to postpone commitment but extend romance. Love is active but personal relationship is contingent upon mutual interest rather than a forever commitment based on romance. Such type of love is called confluent love which often results in plastic sexuality, that is, sexuality freed from the needs of reproduction and continually modified by partners based on personal choice. Contemporary romantic interaction is also based on sexual and emotional equality. Such pure relationships undermine tradition-bound and male-dominated patterns of relationships.

CRYSTALLIZATION OF SOCIAL INTERACTION

Social interaction is directly observable; social relationship is not. But it is the crystallization of social interaction into patterned social relationships that is the real focus of sociology. How and when does social interaction get transformed into social relationships? You meet a stranger at a party, chat for a while, and realize that you have much in common; you become friends for life. You meet someone in cyberspace, exchange information, and share common interests; you become virtual friends. In the marketplace, you bargain with a seller and settle on a price. You may not go back to the same seller next week but the social phenomenon repeats iself. Your relationship with your doctor or employer may be on a much more formal level but it is a durable relationsip, though role-specific.

The crystallization of social interaction into social relationships involves several steps and processes. In the first place, every interaction takes place in a social situation. Whether it is a park, street corner, school playground, temple compound, or workplace, the situation has established parameters. Each situation has its own rules of conduct. In a place of worship, you dress and behave appropriately; you respect the sanctity of the place and maintain decorum. In a bar, you dress casually, relax, watch television, or talk loudly. In the local market where buyers and sellers haggle over price, even 'technically rude' behaviour is socially accepted. When a homeless drunkard calls a passing woman, 'hey pretty, stop', the rules of engagement say ignore.

Second, shared expectations pattern social interaction into social relationships. In every instance just mentioned, a set of expectations are shared by all concerned. Even the quarrelling buyer and seller know that it is all part of the business. The seller is expected to glorify his wares and the buyer is expected to be suspicious, and this is perfectly understood by both parties. Third, the process of social interaction repeats itself over time. You may not greet the same person everyday but greeting as a social form repeats itself. You may not meet the same seller for weeks but the process of bargaining goes on. As children grow up, actors change but the neighbourhood play group continues. And, every phenomenon that repeats iself establishes a pattern.

Fourth, social interaction is meaningful and symbolic. Every situation, every word, and every object has a meaning that is socially constructed. In other words, meaning is not inherent but socially ordered. And to the extent meaning of social action is socially determined, the form of interaction is socially structured. Such shared meanings establish some kind of order into social relationship. For example, it is understood that a woman who wears a bindi on the top-centre of her forehead is married; that leaves no room for misunderstanding or misadventure. Fifth, it is not the individual organism but the social person that is involved in social interaction. Therefore, social interaction involves multiple statuses and roles which are socially ordered. For instance, the interaction between teacher and student, employer and employee, and doctor and patient is socially structured. Even in apparently loose social situations which involve multiple statuses and roles, there are social definitions that govern the pattern of interaction among different actors. For instance, on the beach, there are not only swimmers but also strollers, tanners, lookers, vendors, fishermen, beggars, builders of sand castle, police, and even gangs; their statuses and roles are easily understood and social interaction is accordingly patterned.

Finally, the durability of social interaction gives rise to sustained social relationships. Not only interactions based on blood relationships and friendship but many other forms of interaction based on professional and personal interests last a lifetime. Even several forms of casual interaction—with the guy in the park, girl in a store, beggar on the street, vendor in the market, and the driver of the autorikshaw—become fairly stable over time. And, the durability of interaction leads to a patterned social relationship.

Social interaction refers to reciprocally oriented action or the way people respond to one another in social settings. It is the process through which people communicate with one another through language and gestures which influence the responses of others. Social interaction is the very basis of social life; without social interaction no group activity could take place. The development of culture, the process of socialization, and the conduct of everyday life will be impossible without meaningful interaction between members of society. All our social institutions such as family, community, religion, government, business, labour unions, and associations are built upon the foundation of social interaction. Simply put, no social interaction, no social life.

Georg Simmel thought of sociology as the study of social interaction. During Simmel's time, there were two distinct schools of thought concerning the nature of society: sociological realism, which regarded society as a real entity; and sociological nominalism, which thought of society as a fictitious abstraction. The former viewpoint conceived of society as a great being, with a mission to fulfil and with the ability to create such things as custom, religion, law, language, and the like. The second perspective assumed that society is a fiction and that individuals alone are real. Carried to its logical extreme, this perspective, Simmel feels, would reduce society to an aggregate of indivisible material atoms.

Simmel not only made a self-conscious attempt to reject the organicist theories of Comte and Spencer, but he also outright opposed both 'realist' and 'nominalist' schools of thought seeking rather a middle path. For Simmel, society is neither a great collective being nor a fictitious entity, rather it exists in the process of interaction among social units, both individuals and groups. He supported the conception that society consists of a web of patterned interactions and that the task of a genuinely scientific sociology was to study the forms of these interactions as they occur and reoccur in diverse historical periods. In his view, society consists of an intricate web of multiple relations between individuals who are in constant interaction with one another. However, it must be remembered that Simmel rejected the psychological interpretation of interaction; but presented a positive conception of interaction as social action which has a certain unity based on observable behavioural regularities, and the nature of association. Thus for Simmel, the major field of study for the student of society is *sociation*, that is, the particular patterns and forms in which men associate and interact with one another.

In other words, the argument whether society is real or individual is real is meaningless because social interaction is the basic building block and, therefore, the subject matter of sociology.

For Max Weber, the combined qualities of 'action' and 'meaning' were the 'central facts' for sociology's scientific analysis. Weber's focus was on social action, or reciprocally oriented action, which in current sociological terminology means, social interaction. According to him (Weber 1964: 88–90): 'Action is social in so far as, by virtue of the subjective meaning attached to it by the acting individual, it takes account of the behaviour of others and is thereby oriented in its course.' Weber's emphasis was on social action that is traditional and value-oriented rather than purely rational and goal-oriented. Thus, social action which is intentional, meaningful, and symbolic with subjective meaning of action is the proper domain of sociology.

In *The Structure of Social Action*, Talcott Parsons focused on unit act but in *The Social System*, emphasis shifted from unit act to social system as the primary unit of sociological analysis. However, Parsons takes action as the building block of the system. According to him (1951: 55)

A social system is a system of action which has the following characteristics: (1) It involves a process of interaction between two or more actors; the interaction process as such is a focus of the observer's attention. (2) The situation toward which the actors are oriented includes other actors. These other actors (alters) are objects of cathexis. Alter's actions are taken cognitively into account as data. Alter's various orientations may be either goals to be pursued or means for the accomplishment of goals. Alter's orientation thus may be objective for evaluative judgment. (3) There is (in a social system) interdependent and, in part, concerted action in which the concert is a function of collective goal orientation or common values, and of a consensus of normative and cognitive expectations.

Social action involves at least two individuals: the actor and the alter. Each member is both actor and object of orientation for both alter (or other actors) and himself. Social action takes place in a social situation. And, the actor's orientation to the situation is both motivational and value-orientational. Motivation is based on the principle of gratification and deprivation: the actor seeks to maximize pleasures and minimize pain. However, since social actions cannot be pursued strictly for personal gratification, value-orientation kicks in and guides human behaviour in the proper direction. In other words, social interaction is normatively regulated.

THEORIES OF SOCIAL INTERACTION

Dramaturgical Approach

Symbolic interactionism is the most important theory of social interaction. Since we have fully outlined the theory in Chapters 2 and 5, here we will briefly discuss one of the schools of symbolic interactionism known as *dramaturgy*. The dramaturgical approach is the study of social interaction as though participants are actors in a play in a theatre. According to Erving Goffman, the founder of dramaturgy, the social world is not self-ordered, and the meaning is not inherent in behaviour. Rather, the social order and the meaning of a particular behaviour are significant because people attribute significance to them. In interaction, therefore, individuals not only present themselves to each other, they also attempt to 'manage' the image they present. In fact, Goffman's primary focus is the process of impression management, that is, the ways in which actors manipulate gestures to create an impression in a particular social scene. Social behaviour, therefore, is somewhat analogous to theatrical drama. The individual's identity is performed through role and consensus between the actor and the audience. Because of this dependence on consensus to define social situations, the perspective argues that there is no concrete meaning to any interaction that cannot be redefined. Hence, dramaturgical perspective is termed 'a fully two-sided view of human interaction'. Not surprisingly, Goffman employs such terms as script, audience, identity kits, performer, performance, part, onstage, mask, props, and other theatrical references. Thus utilizing the language of drama, Goffman has analysed social interaction as parts played by different actors in a play on a particular social stage. He has provided an insightful account of the presentation of self in everyday life, demonstrated how actors validate self-conceptions, how they justify their actions through gestures, how prescriptions governing proper dress, tone of voice, and choice of vocabulary represent aspects of interaction which display the salient features of the silent dialogue, and how people manipulate different social situations and adjust to them.

Ethnomethodology

Ethnomethodology is the study of the methods by which people make sense of their social world. Its focus is on interaction that is patterned by implicit or unwritten rules and the interpretations people use to make sense of social settings. Harold Garfinkel, the founder of ethnomethodology, argued that we understand numerous social situations only by taking for granted many ideas and hidden rules which govern them. He felt that the best way to understand unacknowledged patterns of social life was to deliberately break the rules which will then expose the informal patterns of interaction. Ethnomethodologists are interested in how people construct their everyday world based on their experiences and interactions. They seek to understand social interaction from participants' own frame of reference. They understand that most human actions are patterned on the basis of taken-for-granted ideas and implicit rules. In order to expose the meaning of such situations Garfinkel devised a number of informal experiments. He asked his students to go home and act as guests or boarders in their own homes. Naturally the situation created considerable confusion, anger, and embarrassment. Another simple example illustrates the situation even better. When you ask a colleague or a friend, 'How are you?' you get a simple response. But if the other person responds with 'What do you mean by "how are you?" Are you referring to my physical well-being, mental health, financial status, my school work or my relationship with my family now?' Such a response naturally complicates things and upsets the standard pattern of interaction guided by informal rules.

Ethnomethodologists do not use a common-sense method, rather, they study common-sense methods of constructing reality. The term itself, says Mullins (1973: 184), was coined by Garfinkel 'to reflect his belief that the proper subject for social science is the way in which ordinary people establish rational behaviour patterns.' Ordinary people use various methods to determine what is happening in society; 'this methodology is "ethno" in that, like "ethnobotany", it is derived from folk knowledge rather than from professional scientific procedures.' Hence, ethnomethodology is the study of the methods used by members of a group for understanding community, making decisions, being rational, accounting for action, and so on. Instead of studying the social order per se or empirically ascertaining objective reality, ethnomethodology seeks to understand how people in interaction create and maintain a conception of social reality. According to ethnomethodologists, what is most readily observable, and hence real, are the attempts by interacting humans to persuade each other that there is an order to specific social settings and to a broader society. 'What is "really real", then', explains Turner (1974: 330), 'are the methods people employ in constructing, maintaining, and altering for each other a sense of order—regardless of the content and substance of their formulations.'

The Structure of Social Interaction

Social interaction, of course, takes place in a social setting. Therefore, interaction is often patterned by the nature of the group, status of the persons involved, role definitions, and standards of behaviour. The interaction between teachers and students is markedly different from that between workers and their employers and that between members of the family. You interact with strangers in a public bus in one way and with your friends on the college campus in an entirely different way. Gender, age, and occupational status of the participants also influence the nature of interaction.

Status

Status is a recognized social position that an individual occupies. Sociologically speaking, the term status in this sense has nothing to do with power or prestige. Male, female, father, uncle, daughter, student, teacher, wife, nurse, shopkeeper, barber, Brahmin, Dalit, judge, are all statuses. There is absolutely no connotation of high and low; status simply refers to a position in society.

Every status involves certain rights, duties, and obligations. Therefore, the status people occupy guides their behaviour in a social setting. Men and women, husbands and wives, teachers and students, clergymen and shopkeepers, are all expected to act differently in situations of social interaction. In the marketplace, the interaction may be noisy and even rude. But in the classroom, students are expected to maintain silence and decorum.

Status is also a key component of social identity. A child is recognized as the member of a family just as his parents are recognized as members of a caste or a clan. Once again, when we sociologically refer to someone as a Jat, Yadav, Nair, Reddy, or Dalit, the term simply means a position in society devoid of any honorifics or system of rating and ranking.

We all occupy a number of statuses simultaneously. A girl may be a student in a college but she is also a sister to her siblings, daughter to her parents, wife to her husband, friend to her classmates, and a typist or a babysitter during her free time. Sociologists use the term *status-set* to refer to all the statuses a person occupies at a given time. Individuals can and do occupy numerous statuses at any given time. Sometimes different statuses that make up an individual's status-set do not fit together smoothly because of cultural expectations. *Status inconsistency* occurs when there is a culturally defined dysjunction between two or more statuses an individual occupies. The case of a woman president or a prime minister in an Islamic society where the traditional status of women is low is a case in point. In the United States there are cases where thirteen-year-old and eighty-year-old students are enrolled in the PhD programme. Such 'anomalies' in India would certainly be considered status inconsistencies. In the traditional caste hierarchy 'low' caste status and high status occupations usually meant status inconsistency.

Statuses may be ascribed or achieved. An *ascribed status* is one into which we are born; we acquire it involuntarily. Gender, race, and caste denote ascribed status. An *achieved status* is a position we have acquired over time. Student, teacher, president, clergyman, dancer, soccer player, are all achieved statuses. Father and wife denote achieved statuses whereas son, daughter, sister, and uncle are ascribed statuses.

All statuses an individual occupies are not equally important. One of those statuses may have an overwhelming influence on all other statuses. Sociologists call this *master status*, a social position that is exceptionally powerful and capable of determining the overall position of the individual in society. Of course, the status of a maharaja, governor or prime minister is a master status. So are the statuses of a Buddhist monk, a Catholic bishop or district collector. In the traditional Indian society a person's caste was undoubtedly his master status. This was especially true of the so-called 'low castes' in the past when a Dalit was always considered a Dalit regardless of his accomplishments and important positions. Even today caste and religion along with occupation serve as sort of loose determinants of an individual's master status in current Indian society. In a negative sense, physical disability or a serious disease such as AIDS may also determine a person's master status.

Role

Every status has a set of expectations associated with it. A role is the dynamic aspect of status. A *role* is what people do in the status they occupy. In other words, statuses are occupied, roles are played. Role expectations are guided by cultural norms. However, different people who occupy the same status perform differently. We do know that all politicians, teachers, and policemen do not perform equally well.

Sometimes the same status may involve a number of different roles. A student, in addition to being a good student, may also have to perform such roles as class president, editor of the school journal, football player, or club organizer. Robert Merton introduced the term *role set* to refer to the cluster of roles associated with a single status. Different statuses, of course, have different roles; the term role set does not apply to them. We speak of role set to refer exclusively to a set of roles attached to a single status. For example, the status of a woman as a wife has several related roles: wife to her husband, mother to her child, nurse to the sick baby, member of the Parent Teacher Association, etc.

Since individuals occupy a number of statuses simultaneously, they are also expected to perform a number of roles. Sometimes these roles are naturally in conflict. A student may also be a wife, a mother, and a daughter. While as a student she is expected to perform well, she also has obligations to her husband, her sick child, and her ageing father. Sociologists thus recognize *role conflict*, that is, incompatibility among roles corresponding to different statuses. Role conflicts are very common in modern societies. A woman who works outside the home is a breadwinner but she is also expected to perform her roles as a wife and mother.

Even the many roles attached to the same status may be in conflict leading to *role strain*. The concept of role strain refers to an incompatibility between two or more roles associated with a single status. The student who spends too much time in extra-curricular activities does not do well in his studies. Similarly, the teacher may sometimes find it necessary to bring his work home, and when he spends too much of his time in grading papers or doing research at home, his domestic obligations are strained.

There are several ways to deal with role conflict. Compartmentalization or role segregation is one such strategy: people 'compartmentalize' their lives in such a way that they perform roles linked to one status at one time and place and play the roles associated with other statuses at other times and places. For example, teachers and businessmen leave their work at the office. Mothers with young children decide to stay home for a year or two before they return to work. In recent years, there is also a growing emphasis on *role exit*, the process by which people disengage themselves from key roles that characterized their life. Examples are: a nun who leaves the order, a politician who quits politics, a doctor who becomes a social worker, and an actor who ends his/her career to marry and settle down. Nowadays many people critically examine their lives and realize that they are not satisfied with the roles they play and choose many alternative lifestyles which they find rewarding.

FORMS OF SOCIAL INTERACTION

Social interaction takes several forms. Members of a football team must cooperate to win the match. Shopkeepers compete with one another for business. Some ruthless businessmen would like to eliminate their competition. Sometimes competition leads to compromise and accommodation. Participants in interaction may also exchange gifts to solidify their relationship. In contemporary society, people meet, chat, and establish networks in cyberspace with others they may never meet in person. Broadly speaking, we may identify six forms of interaction. This conceptualization is based on the scope and universal applicability of these forms. Their range extends from micro-level interation between individuals to macro-level interation between large groups and systems. Most patterns of social interaction correspond roughly to one or more of these basic forms.

Cooperation

Cooperation is a form of social interaction in which individuals or groups engage in joint action to promote common interests or achieve shared goals. The importance of cooperation is obvious in such major projects as construction of homes and building of bridges and roads. But it is less obvious in many day-to-day activities. In the family, parents and children share many tasks. On college campuses cooperation is key to organizing several functions. Cooperation involves the division of workload and coordination of activities. Businesses can succeed only on the basis of cooperation among employees. Sociologists have studied the working of cooperation at several organizations. If a business firm offers incentives based on personal achievement when cooperation of all members is essential to achieve common goals, it might find that employees 'hoard' information for their own advantage. Similarly, individuals who sense discrimination on the basis of caste or political affiliation may withhold full cooperation. Many organizations offer special training or sponsor social events to promote team spirit.

Competition

Competition is a form of goal-oriented interaction in which opposing individuals or groups seek to accomplish the same goals within the framework of socially approved rules. In competition, the objects pursued are limited in supply and there are several parties striving for the attention of the same audience. Colleges compete with one another for more students; newspapers and telephone companies compete for more subscribers. Manufacturers have to compete among available consumers. In competition the focus is on the achievement of the goal. In fair competition opposing parties do not try to hurt or eliminate the competitor; they simply seek to improve their products or services or devise better marketing strategies. Political elections are supposed to be an example of fair competition, but violence and malpractices mar them at times.

Conflict

Conflict is a form of interaction in which parties focus on one another rather than on the goal. Often the emphasis is on the elimination of the opponent and most rules of the competition are absent. Conflicts arise when individuals and groups do not share the same values and when the goals or resources are limited. Therefore, in conflict, one person gains at the expense of someone else. However, conflict is not always manifest or violent. Many forms of conflict such as a strike end in negotiated settlements. During the election, conflicts between political parties cause considerable violence but after the election the opposing parties may form coalition governments. Conflicts are not necessarily negative either. As we saw in Chapter 2, conflict may have several positive functions.

Accommodation

'Accommodation is a process of social adjustment in which groups in conflict with each other agree to terminate or prevent further conflict by temporarily or permanently establishing peaceful interaction' (Theodorson and Theodorson 1969: 3). It is a form of interaction which involves the elements of both cooperation and conflict. In fact, much of human interaction, is based on some form of accommodation. We may never agree or disagree with someone fully, so sometimes we 'agree to disagree'. At other times we simply 'keep a low profile' or avoid dissenting remarks. In much of everyday social interaction, we 'go with the flow' and even if we do not agree with what is going on, we refrain from making embarrassing comments. Indeed, most of the interacting behaviour involves elements of hypocrisy or expedience. Accommodation allows opposing groups to maintain their independent identities and attitudes but at the same time compromise on other areas in order to avoid serious disruptive behaviour.

Conciliation, compromise, arbitration, contracts, truce, and treaties are different mechanisms of adjustment by which accommodation is accomplished. During the Cold War unwritten rules of engagement and accommodation kept the superpowers from colliding with each other. In contemporary Indian politics opposing parties form coalitions and agree to make compromises and accommodation.

Exchange

Exchange is a process of social interaction which involves culturally sanctioned 'give' and 'take'. People enter into exchange relationships for material benefit, psychological satisfaction, or for symbolic value. The relationship between employers and employees is one of exchange for material benefits. The employees do their job and are, in turn, rewarded by the employers. Chiefs of two warring tribes exchange gifts indicating cessation of all hostilities. Exchange of gifts is considered a basic obligation on many social occasions such as birthdays, weddings, and so on. People who receive a gift or reward are obligated to return the benefits. Social exchange serves as a starting mechanism of interaction as well as cements social relationships. As we have seen in Chapter 2, social exchange is probably the most basic form of interaction in every society.

Virtual Networking

Internet and mobile technology have made it possible for people all over the world to meet, chat, and form networks of durable social relationships in cyberspace. YouTube, Facebook, Myspace, Twitter, and various other forms of communication bring together diverse people whose background is largely unknown. But the medium enables them to share ideas and interests and interact on a regular basis. Such social interaction establishes virtual networking through 'electronic communities' in cyberspace which is composed of people with shared interests and sufficient feeling to continue fairly long-lasting personal relationships. Critics of virtual networking argue that cyberspace is not real; it is devoid of human emotions and no substitute for genuine social relationship. They also point out that internet technology allows people to hide behind false identities and indulge in trickery and manipulation. 'Yet', as Giddens points out, ' the arrival of the wired-up world, thus far at any rate, has not produced any of the overwhelmingly negative scenarios predicted by some critics. "Big Brother" has not emerged as a result of the internet; on the contrary, it has promoted decentralization and new forms of global social networking' (2010: 774).

STUDY QUESTIONS

- Define social interaction. Illustrate types of verbal and non-verbal communication of social consequence.
- Discuss Simmel's theory of social interaction.

- Compare and contrast Max Weber's and Talcott Parsons' views on social interaction.
- Explain the steps and processes involved in the crystallization of social interaction into patterned social relationships.
- Discuss the six forms of social interaction.
- Write a paragraph on each of the following: dramaturgical approach and ethnomethodology.
- Define and distinguish between status and role.
- Define the following concepts: sociological realism; sociological nominalism; ascribed status and achieved status; status-set; status inconsistency; master status; role set; role conflict; and role strain.

REFERENCES

Berger, Peter L. and Thomas Luckmann, *The Social Construction of Reality,* Garden City, New York: Doubleday, 1966.

Giddens, Anthony, *Sociology,* New Delhi: Wiley India, 2010.

Mullins, Nicholas C., *Theories and Theory Groups in Contemporary American Sociology,* New York: Harper and Row, 1973.

Parsons, Talcott and Edward Shils (eds), *Toward a General Theory of Action,* Cambridge: Harvard University Press, 1951.

Theodorson, George A. and Achilles G. Theodorson, *A Modern Dictionary of Sociology,* New York: Thomas Y. Crowell Company, 1969.

Turner, Jonathan, *The Structure of Sociological Theory,* Homewood: Dorsey Press, 1974.

Weber, Max, *Theory of Social and Economic Organization,* New York: Free Press, 1964.

7

Types of Societies and Groups

Human society has evolved over a period of time; from the primitive hunting and gathering societies to the modern electronic age, human beings have lived in various types of groups under different circumstances. Today we form, as well as interact with, numerous groups which vary according to size, structure, and the quality of interaction among members. We may be members of a number of voluntary groups such as political parties, clubs, and labour unions. When you attend a rock concert or a football match you are part of one type of group and when you go on a picnic with your friends you are part of an entirely different group. In a public bus full of strangers you are simply part of an aggregate group but when your school charts a bus for your classmates to go on an excursion the nature of your group is significantly different. You are a member of an intimate and informal group such as the family but you might also belong to a very formal organization such as a governmental agency or a business corporation. Individuals spend much of their time in groups which influence their attitudes and behaviour considerably. Therefore, the study of groups is a very important part of the subject matter of sociology.

EVOLUTION OF SOCIETIES

Based on the stages of socio-cultural evolution, Gerhard and Lenski (1982) classified human societies into five types.

Hunting and Gathering Societies

The earliest band of men did not know how to raise crops or animals. They hunted wild animals and collected plants and fruits from the wild. Since they occupied small areas and had limited resources, their numbers were also small. They were essentially nomads because, as food sources became depleted in any given area, they had to move from place to place. The division of labour was very simple; men, women, and children participated in food gathering. There were no specialists but shamans or fortune-tellers who claimed knowledge of the supernatural may have existed in later periods. There were no schools or teachers; all knowledge was transmitted by the family. There was no formal authority structure although the dominant male in each group may have exerted considerable influence. Since they were nomads, individuals had no use for private property. There was no competition for wealth and power. With no accumulation of wealth, class distinctions were minimal and the social structure was somewhat egalitarian. Today, very few hunting and gathering societies survive, primarily among the Australian Aborigines and in parts of Africa.

Horticultural Societies

Almost 12,000 years ago people in the Near East began to domesticate animals and cultivate crops. This meant that hunter-gatherers could now supplement their food sources by raising crops in small areas. But the technology was limited to digging sticks and hand hoes. The knowledge of agricultural practices was so limited that the people often adopted the slash-and-burn strategy. They simply burnt the ground cover, loosened the soil, and planted the seeds. Horticulture enabled them to stay put in one place much longer until the fertility of the soil was exhausted. People often returned to the same area after the soil recovered its fertility. By raising crops and animals at their pace, horticulturalists were able to produce surplus food and support larger communities. The size of the community and the surplus quantity of food also meant that some individuals could be freed from the task of food production. There emerged full-time craftsmen who devoted their time to developing better tools and shamans who took care of the 'religious' needs of the community. As families could raise more crops and animals, some individuals began to accumulate private property. With the growth in the size of the communities, some form of leadership emerged, and wealthy individuals became chieftains. Surplus commodities also meant that horticulturalists could trade with other societies which facilitated exchange of ideas and products. Such contacts may also have triggered wars. Like hunting and gathering societies, typical horticultural societies are very rare today. The Yanomamo of Brazil is often studied as a horticultural society.

Pastoral Societies

Whereas horticultural societies developed in the fertile regions of the world, pastoral societies developed in arid regions of North Africa, the Middle East, and Central Asia where people began to domesticate large herds of animals such as cattle, sheep, goats, and camels. Pastoralists were also nomads at least part of the year but their migratory movements depended on the seasons of the year. They also generated regular surplus and traded with settled communities. Those who owned large herds were wealthy and many were workers who just tended to the animals. Pastoral societies continued to endure in regions where land was not fit for cultivation. Even today southern Iran and Uganda are home to pastoral societies.

Agrarian Societies

On the fertile river valleys of Mesopotamia, India, and China, and later in other parts of the world, people began large-scale cultivation of crops. The invention of metal and development of better tools such as the plow made it possible to till the soil and raise crops year after year. People also began to use animal power for cultivation of crops and transportation of produce. The agrarian revolution also led to the development of first cities. Growth of large cities meant political organization of society and patterns of authority structure. Large numbers of people were freed from the everyday chores of production and distribution. This meant the emergence of new roles and increasing specialization of functions. Rulers, administrators, craftsmen—particularly blacksmiths, potters, weavers, and carpenters—medicine men, religious leaders, artists, and entertainers appeared. Agrarian societies also witnessed rapid expansion of human knowledge in the field of science, mathematics, philosophy, and literature. The state grew in power and took control of all public services such as roads, irrigation systems, and community halls and began to codify rules and regulations. Traditions and conventions in the previous societies now became a codified legal system. Although the family remained an important institution, other social institutions such as schools, religious organizations, and crafts centres began to assume many functions of the families. As the importance of landed property grew, wealth became concentrated in the hands of a few elites and the class system began to take root. Today, many societies of the world remain agrarian but they also have been transformed by the onslaught of the industrial and technological revolution.

Industrial and Post-industrial Societies

The Industrial Revolution, which occurred almost 200 years ago, greatly transformed old agrarian societies. Inanimate sources of energy, which replaced animal energy, made it possible for factories to turn out manufactured goods in large quantities. The steam engine was first used in England in 1765 to run machinery. Factories looking for a large labour force began to suck in workers from rural communities. With the breakdown of feudal society masses of people were thrown off the land on which they had been tenants for generations. Individuals no longer depended solely on their families, kinfolk, or small communities to provide their livelihood; they could work in big factories in urban centres. They became not only financially independent but were freed from many communal and cultural obligations. Industrialization is the single most important factor in the growth of cities and general economic development. There was considerable expansion of knowledge in the areas of science, technology, education, medicine, art, entertainment, literature, and philosophy. As concentration of wealth grew, the class system became fully established and the gap between the rich and the poor began to widen. Centralized governments expanded their role affecting almost every realm of human activity. With increasing differentiation of social structure and functional specialization, individuals became free to choose from among numerous occupations; thus achieved status became far more important than ascribed status. In general, the Industrial Revolution led to large-scale rural–urban migration, spurred economic growth, and brought about the somewhat total transformation of agrarian societies.

Today, most of the advanced industrial societies have entered a new phase called post-industrial society or the information age. The technology of the early industrial society was relatively simple and the focus was on manufactured goods. Although the manufacturing sector is still important, the service industry records phenomenal growth. Access to various sources of energy and dramatic improvements in the field of communications technology have transformed the post-industrial society. The service sector—such as computer, insurance, banking, mass media, and hospitality industry—accounts for the lion's share of the economy. The emergence of e-mail, e-commerce, and call centres have globalized the workforce and transformed the workplace. Satellite technology makes it possible for people to stay home and yet be part of the world business enterprises. Recent trends in products and services have also given rise to a new consumer culture.

THREE TYPOLOGIES

Sociologists and anthropologists have used different typologies to classify societies. It must be stressed at the outset that the terms are not to be taken as exact descriptions of any particular society. Typologies are artificial constructs of heuristic value. The types of societies do not correspond exactly to the realities on the ground, but in each case, they are selection of some elements found in a number of similar societies. Three of the most common, and in many ways very similar, types are the following.

Mechanical and Organic Solidarity: Émile Durkheim

A society based on mechanical solidarity is a relatively small, cohesive society where most people follow the same line of occupation. People are mentally and morally homogeneous; they feel the same emotions, cherish the same values, and hold the same things sacred. Communities are, therefore, uniform and non-atomized. Solidarity which comes from likeness 'is at its maximum when the collective conscience completely envelops our whole conscience and coincides in all points with it' (Durkheim 1965). Thus, a society having mechanical solidarity is characterized by a strong collective conscience, that is, collective ways of feeling, thinking, and acting.

But, as societies grow in size they become increasingly differentiated and a number of new economic roles develop. As individuals follow different lines of occupation societies tend to become heterogeneous. Their mental and moral similarities have disappeared. A society having organic solidarity is characterized by specialization, division of labour, and individualism. It is held together by interdependence of parts, rather than by the homogeneity of elements. It is also characterized by the weakening of collective conscience. Durkheim believed that moral unity could be assured only if all members of a society were anchored to a common set of symbolic representations and to common assumptions about the world around them. With increasing specialization of functions, similarities in values and beliefs tend to disappear.

Gemeinschaft and Gesellschaft: Ferdinand Tonnies

In the absence of better terminology, Charles Loomis translated the German terms of Gemein-schaft and Gesellschaft into 'community' and 'society'. Ferdinand Tonnies, the German sociologist, closely followed Durkheim's typology but focused primarily on the differences between traditional and modern societies. A Gemeinschaft is a small, traditional rural community. People share the same values and beliefs and have a strong sense of belonging to the community. Customs and traditions are sacred, and family, kinship, and ascribed statuses are important. A Gemeinschaft is characterized by *natural will*, which meant relationships are personal and often end in themselves. People's actions were not motivated by profits or personal benefits but by a sense of the community.

A Gesellschaft, on the other hand, is based on *rational will*, or individual self-interest. Human actions are no longer motivated by social obligations or community well-being. Societies have grown into large urban conglomerations where individuals are free to follow their private interests. Social relationships are generally formal and impersonal. People are individualistic and may not share the same values, beliefs, and ideas. Like in the organically solitary society there is a general weakening of the sense of community.

Folk and Urban Societies: Robert Redfield

Redfield's folk–urban continuum has become a standard typology in rural sociology. This simply illustrates the difference between rural and urban societies. Rural communities are small and their population density is low. Most of the people are engaged in agriculture; other occupational roles are generally confined to traditional crafts such as pottery. Rural communities are homogeneous and cohesive. Members share the same values, beliefs, and mores. There is very little division of labour and, therefore, very little social mobility. In such traditional communities, family and kinship groups play a predominant role. They are not only social units but also economic units; therefore, kinship obligations are more diffuse and binding. The encompassing environs of the village, the 'old-fashioned' neighbourhood, small primary groups of peers, and the structure of kinship, are the most significant networks of social relationships. Since much of the social interaction occurs in face-to-face or otherwise familiar and close settings, social relationship is personal, frequent, and durable. Since the folk society is an agrarian society, without mechanization, science, and skilled labour, there is very little specialization. People share the same ideas and beliefs, and the folk society tends to be culturally homogeneous. Contrast it with sprawling urban metropolises with their complex societies, and the differences are obvious. The urban societies are large, densely populated, and heterogeneous. Social relationships are, generally speaking, anonymous, impersonal, and formal. Complex social organizations and highly specialized functions characterize multiple structures. Mass society allows considerable personal freedom which facilitates diverse interests and beliefs. Society is held together not by personal bonds, but by mutual interdependence.

The overall characteristics of rural and urban societies are summarized in the Table 7.1.

Table 7.1: Characteristics of Rural and Urban Societies

Rural Societies	Urban Societies
Small in size	Large
Low density of population	High density
Agrarian	Industrial
Homogeneous	Heterogeneous
Little or no specialization	High specialization
Personal interaction	Impersonal interaction
Informal social relationships	Formal relationships
Uniform and non-atomized	Fragmented and sectarian
Collectivistic	Individualistic
Shared values and common interests	Dissimilar values and interests
Strong collective consciousness	Weak collective consciousness
Informal social control	Formal social control

TYPES OF SOCIAL GROUPS

As human beings we are part of several social groups. When we attend a music concert or watch a movie in a theatre we are part of a group. When we say Punjabis, Bengalis, Malayalees, Indians, Hindus, Italians, Dalits, or Muslims we are referring to groups to which people belong. Then our family, the sociology class, and the local club to which we belong are also groups. Sociologically speaking, we know that these groups are all different. Therefore, we may classify groups into four general types.

Aggregate

An aggregate is a gathering of persons in physical proximity who have come together temporarily and lack any organization or meaningful social interaction. An audience, a crowd, passengers on the same bus, and a gathering of people watching a fireworks display or a football match are all aggregates. Most people in the crowd do not know one another and, therefore, there is no possibility of meaningful interaction among them. Members of the aggregate do not share common characteristics and hence do not share a sense of belonging to the group.

Societal Group

A societal group is a collectivity of persons who share certain common values and interests and have some feeling of solidarity. A sense of belonging or a consciousness of the kind is the primary characteristic of the societal group. Caste and religious groups as well as linguistic and nationality groups are societal groups. Chinese, Irish, Brahmins, Christians, Americans, Pakistanis, Tamilians, Rajputs, Jats, and Bengalis are all societal groups. Members identify themselves with such groups and are aware of their common characteristics. However, they may be scattered far and wide, and except for the consciousness of the kind there may not be any meaningful interaction among them.

Social Group

A social group is a plurality of persons who have a common identity, at least some feeling of unity, certain common goals and shared norms, and fairly high levels of interaction. Some examples are the family, peer group, your sociology class, a social club, or neighbourhood group. Members of the social group have regular channels of communication and social interaction. Members of a societal group may share a common identity and a sense of belonging but they may not know one another and may not be in a position to interact with one another. However, social groups have established means of contact and quality interaction. Some sociologists, though, lump societal and social groups together. Here we have used the term social group in a narrow sense to highlight the quality of social interaction among members.

Associational Group

An associational group is an organized group with a formal structure. Associational groups have stated purposes, written rules, criteria of membership, standards of procedure, and clearly defined authority structure. State and union governments, corporations, professional associations, labour unions, social clubs, political parties, and local panchayats are all associational groups. In a modern complex society, much of human interaction takes place in a wide variety of associational groups. Employees of a corporation or members of an all-India association may not know one another, but there are established means of communication and members do share common interests.

Primary and Secondary Groups

Charles Cooley coined the term *primary group* to refer to an intimate social group with shared values and common standards of behaviour and frequent direct personal contacts. According to Cooley, the primary group has the following characteristics:

1. Relatively small size
2. Face to face association
3. Unspecialized character of that association
4. Relative intimacy
5. Durable relationship

The family, children's playgroups, intimate friendship groups, and old-fashioned neighbour-hoods are considered to be primary groups. They are characterized by a sense of belonging, emotional warmth, and cooperation. The sense of we-feeling fosters a strong identification with the group. Fundamentally, these groups are harmonious and affectionate, but competition, self-assertion, and passionate contentions also emerge. 'These passions', Cooley (1962: 24) suggests, 'are socialized by sympathy, and come, or tend to come, under the discipline of a common spirit. The individual will be ambitious, but the chief object of his ambition will be some desired place in the thought of the others.' It must be noted here that small size and intimacy alone do not determine the primary group. Your club may have set up a three-member student committee to organize a function. Although the group is small and there is personal relationship among the three, the committee is not a primary group because it has been established for a specific purpose and ceases to exist after the goal has been attained. Similarly, in spite of the intimacy involved, the prostitute–client relationship does not qualify for primary group status because of the transient and specialized character of the relationship.

Secondary groups are those characterized by impersonal, contractual, formal, and rational relationships. In primary groups we interact with one another as whole beings; we do not fragment our personality. In secondary groups we only engage the specialized part of our personality. When we interact with a shopkeeper or a clerk at the post office, bank, or a government office, our interaction is formal and the relationship is confined to the specific purpose on hand. Therefore, social relationships in secondary groups are formal and matter-of-fact. According to Cooley, all groups that are not characterized by primary relationships are secondary groups.

In-groups and Out-groups

The distinction between in-groups and out-groups is sociologically significant. *In-groups* are those groups to which individuals belong and towards which they feel pride and have a strong loyalty. *Out-groups* are groups to which we do not belong and towards which we may feel contempt and even hostility. In-groups are 'we' groups, the group of insiders whereas out-groups are 'they' groups or a group of outsiders. These groups are not necessarily small; they can be as large as a nation or even bigger. One's identification with the in-group and loyalty towards it become particularly obvious in times of conflict between the two groups. Caste groups, religious groups, political parties, linguistic groups, and football teams are all in-groups, to people who belong to them. Whenever there is a communal or inter-caste conflict, members on each side become far more united and sensitive. During the Kargil crisis, people of India displayed a great sense of pride and patriotism. During elections, members of political parties or caste groups often forget individual differences and support candidates from their own in-groups.

Reference Groups

A *reference group* is a group which a person uses to shape his own values, beliefs, attitudes, and behaviour. This may be a real group to which the individual wants to belong or simply a social category whose standards he uses to guide his behaviour. Members of the new middle class often adopt the lifestyle of the old middle class hoping to join it. Persons who want to join a political party accept the ideology and programmes of the party. Students of the Master of Business Administration (MBA) class want to dress and act like business professionals.

A related concept is anticipatory socialization. *Anticipatory socialization* is a process by which individuals begin to learn the rights, obligations, expectations, and beliefs of reference groups to which they want to belong. Anticipatory socialization makes a person's adjustment of a status change easier. Robert Merton's research during World War II showed that soldiers who accepted the formal army standards valued by officers were more likely to be promoted than the soldiers who did not accept those standards. We often observe little children imitating grown-ups. Graduate students, computer scientists, and political status-seekers adopt the standards of the groups which they hope to join. M.N. Srinivas' concept of 'Sanskritization' is a form of anticipatory socialization. According to Srinivas, Sanskritization refers to the process by which 'low' castes are able to rise to a 'higher' positioning in the social hierarchy by adopting the symbols of higher status, thus taking over, as far as possible, the customs, rites, beliefs, and lifestyles of higher castes. In the past the dominant castes sought to punish those who encroached on forbidden ground, but the process could not be stopped and has been going on for hundreds of years.

Electronic Communities

In the information age of today, a new type of group has emerged. On the internet hundreds of thousands of people meet online in chat rooms and 'new communities'. There are also weblogs and chat rooms which specialize in a wide variety of topics from dog breeding and online dating, to information technology and world peace. Sociologically speaking, it is hard to place them but they are groups because people interact with one another and share common interests. Many chat groups are also fiercely loyal and have a deep sense of belonging.

FORMAL ORGANIZATIONS AND BUREAUCRACY

Associational groups are largely formal organizations. Modern governments, industries, business corporations, and huge trade unions are large complex organizations with a well-defined organizational structure called bureaucracy. In traditional rural communities most businesses were family enterprises. The head of the family managed the affairs with the help of kinsfolk. People learnt their jobs while working; there were no special training schools, and no specialized skills and expertise were needed. There were no written rules and no clear separation between private affairs and official business. The Industrial Revolution began to change all that. Later, with the emergence of modern governments, giant corporations with large labour force and the need for specialists and experts, the nature of work was transformed. Companies could no longer depend on families and kinship to supply the labour force; they needed engineers, electricians, technical experts, and administrators. People had to be hired with written contracts which specified conditions of work such as duties, pay, hours of work, benefits, and even the number of sick leave days allowed. The organizations worked on the basis of an administrative chart which clearly delineated the authority structure. There were stated goals and written rules which guided the behaviour of all members of the group. Thus emerged the most pervasive and influential administrative system known as the bureaucracy.

Max Weber was the first to give an elaborate account of the development of bureaucracy as well as its causes and consequences. His concept of bureaucracy is considered to be an ideal type because he analysed the characteristics of a typical bureaucracy. Weber attributed the following characteristics to bureaucracy:

1. The principle of fixed and official jurisdiction areas which are generally ordered by rules. The regular activities associated with each status are distributed in a fixed way as official duties. The structure of authority is clearly delineated and strictly delimited by rules.

2. The principle of office hierarchy and levels graded authority with a firmly ordered system of super-ordination and subordination in which there is a supervision of the lower offices by the higher ones.

3. A division of labour based on specialized functions and responsibilities.

4. A system of written documents ('the files') defining the procedure as well as the rights and duties of people in all positions.

5. Office management based on thorough and expert training.

6. Selection for employment and promotion based on technical competence, specialized knowledge, or skill.

7. Office-holding as a 'vocation'. Official work is no longer a secondary activity but something that demands the full working capacity of the official.

8. Provision for pecuniary compensation as a fixed salary.

9. Appointment of employees by higher officials, rather than by election.

10. The system of tenure for life. Normally the position of the bureaucrat is held for life as specified by contract.

11. A clear distinction between the sphere of office and that of the private affairs of the individual. The bureaucratic official is not an owner of the enterprise and therefore not entitled to the use of official facilities for personal needs except as defined by strict rules.

12. The practice of performing specialized administrative functions according to purely objective considerations and the official discharge of business according to calculable rules and 'without regard for persons.'

Although bureaucracy is a rationally ordered system of officials, all of us who have ever encountered bureaucrats at government offices and universities are painfully aware of the drawbacks of the system. Red tape, missing files, delayed action, and indifferent officials are the most common vices of bureaucracy. Bureaucrats quote rules and wash their hands off matters while the people whom they are intended to serve suffer the consequences. Formalism and the rule-bound and cool 'matter-of-factness' of bureaucratic organizations depersonalize human relationships. Weber counts the crypto-plutocratic distribution of power and increasing concentration of the materials of management among other vices of bureaucracy.

SIZE AND GROUP DYNAMICS

Georg Simmel was the first sociologist to analyse the effects of sheer numerical size on forms of interaction. In small groups, members typically have a chance to interact directly with one another. As the size of the group increases, its members become more unlike one another. Beyond a certain size, individualism and structural differentiation develop. Face-to-face interaction is replaced by formal arrangements consisting of offices, written rules, and well-defined tasks and responsibilities. Whereas interaction in small groups involves the total personality of individual members, participation in large groups is weak and restricted to a segment of personalities. Cooley recognized that primary groups are small intimate groups; as they grow in size cliques and factions develop within them. Similarly, when associations and companies become large complex organizations, bureaucratic structures develop to manage affairs and to exercise formal control. When city states grew into large nation-states, direct democracy had to be replaced by indirect, representational democracy. Thus, the size of the group affects its inner dynamics as well as its relationship to its own members and the outside world.

SOCIAL ORGANIZATION

So far in this chapter, we have discussed types of societies, social groups, and formal organizations. Now let us see how sociologists define and distinguish these concepts. A society is a group of people who share a distinct culture, occupy a particular territorial area, and have a sense of distinguishable identity. It is a comprehensive social system with all necessary social institutions and organizational forms necessary for its own survival. In a loose sense, a group is simply a collectivity or any plurality of individuals. But the type of group varies with its size, quality of interaction among its members, and the nature of its organizational form. Thus, a group may be an informal, face-to-face group such as a family, or a formal organization such as a business corporation. The nature of social organization determines the nature of the group.

According to *A Modern Dictionary of Sociology* (1969: 287), social organization means, 'A relatively stable pattern of social relationships of individuals and subgroups within a society or group, based upon systems of social roles, norms, and shared meanings that provide regularity and predictability in social interaction. In this sense social organization is essentially synonymous with social structure.' However, organization or structure must be viewed as a continuum with wholly unorganized groups at one end and highly organized groups or associations at the other. Groups may range themselves at any point on this continuum. A crowd is unorganized but a business corporation is organized. A primary group is somewhat organized with an informal structure and a social club is relatively more organized with a set of formal rules. But a government department or a corporation is fully organized. The most highly organized groups are associations that can sustain a total turnover in their membership and can last for long periods of time.

Finally, we must distinguish associations from institutions. Although the concept of 'institution' is one of the most important in sociology, it is also one of the most misunderstood and loosely used concepts. Sometimes we use the terms associations, organizations, and institutions interchangeably. For example, prisons, hospitals, and universities are often called institutions. We also refer to family and religion as social institutions. Strictly speaking, whereas family and religion are institutions, prisons, hospitals, and universities are associations. In the words of Bierstedt (1974: 328–9):

An association…is any organized group, whether large or small. Because of its organization, it has some structure and some continuity. It has, in addition, an identity and a name. An institution, on the other hand, is not a group at all, organized or unorganized. An institution is an organized procedure. An institution is a formal, recognized, established, and stabilized way of pursuing some activity in society. In succinct terms, then, an association is an organized group, an institution is an organized procedure.

As an organized group, every association has a location and we can ask where it is. It is also possible to belong to an association. By way of illustration we may say that education is an institution; a school or a university is an association. Business is a social institution, a corporation is an association. Medicine and entertainment are institutions but hospitals and night clubs are associations. Family and government are social institutions but Government of India and the Rao family (or any particular family) are associations. The last example probably needs additional clarification. The family as a social institution has no physical address and none can belong to it. But a family—any particular family—was formed originally by two individuals associating themselves with each other; it has an address and it has members. As these examples illustrate, conceptual clarification is essential for the establishment of sociology as a science of society.

Study Questions

- Discuss the five-fold classification of human societies by Gerhard and Jean Lenski.
- Bring out the distinct characteristics of industrial and post-industrial societies.
- Explain the three typologies used to classify societies, highlighting the differences between the polar types: mechanical and organic solidarity; Gemeinschaft and Gesellschaft; and folk–urban societies.
- Clearly bring out the differences between the following groups: aggregate, societal group, social group, and associational group.

- What is a primary group? Explain its distinct features as opposed to those of secondary groups.
- Differentiate between in-groups and out-groups.
- Write a paragraph on: reference groups, electronic communities, and formal organizations.
- Discuss Max Weber's conceptualization of bureaucracy and explain its salient features.
- What is the impact of size on the nature of social dynamics in a group?
- Differentiate the concepts of social organization, institution, and association.

REFERENCES

Bierstedt, Robert, *The Social Order,* New York: McGraw-Hill, 1974.

Cooley, C.H., *Social Organization,* New York: Schocken Press, 1962.

Durkheim, Émile, *The Division of Labour in Society*, New York: Free Press, p. 80, 1965.

Lenski, Gerhard and Jean Lenski, *Human Societies,* New York: McGraw-Hill, 1982.

Theodorson, George A. and Achilles G. Theodorson, *A Modern Dictionary of Sociology,* New York: Thomas Y. Crowell Company, 1969.

8

Deviance and Social Control

It will be difficult to visualize a society in which all people always conform to all norms. Types of deviant behaviour are to be found in every society. Crime, violence, unruly behaviour, dishonesty, immorality, betrayal, cruelty to animals, cutting corners, bending rules, and many other forms of non-conformity can be found in most, if not all, societies. But can we say that a society in which all people conform to all norms is an ideal place to live in? Mahatma Gandhi violated the salt law and started the independence movement. Martin Luther King and his colleagues violated the rules of discrimination and started the Civil Rights Movement in America. In South Africa, the oppressed people fought against the laws of apartheid. Therefore, sociologically speaking, deviant behaviour is neither good nor bad; it is a neutral act of non-conformity.

What is Deviance?

Deviance may be defined as a behaviour that is in violation of the norms of a society or a social group. Certain types of deviance such as murder and incest are a violation of the norms of society in general. But other forms of deviance may have meaning only within a particular social group. A Brahmin who eats meat may be a deviant in the eyes of most Brahmins. A member of a political party who votes for the candidate of the opposition may be a deviant from the point of view of his party. A member of a religious order who breaches her vow of silence is considered a deviant by the order.

Sociologists make use of three different concepts: deviance, crime, and non-conformity. Deviance, as mentioned earlier, is the violation of any rule generally accepted by the society or a social group. Deviance may consist not only of behaviours, but also of beliefs and physical conditions. For instance, atheists in a predominantly theistic society may be viewed as deviants. Similarly, people with mental illness, a physical handicap, or certain illnesses such as AIDS may be denied full acceptance by society because of perceived deviant condition. But not all deviants are treated or labelled the same way. For instance, people who pay bribe, ignore traffic signs or evade tax are not necessarily treated as deviants. Crime is a specific violation of a rule, often for a personal end. Cheating and stealing are obviously crimes. A criminal is generally so labelled by society and punished according to law. A non-conformist is one who does not conform to the rules of his social group because of personal belief. A member of a devout Catholic family who does not attend Church or believe in God is a deviant from the point of the social group. Although he may be ostracized by the social group, he may not be labelled a criminal by the general society. On the other hand, African Americans in the United States during the civil rights movement and the South African blacks during the apartheid regime who refused to obey inhuman laws, although non-conformists from a sociological perspective, were branded as criminals and punished according to the law. In general, we may say that all criminals and non-conformists are deviants but all deviants are not criminals.

While we recognize these distinctions, for our purpose we adopt the more popular view that deviance is essentially non-conforming behaviour because not conforming to the rules of any group is, from a sociological perspective, deviance from the point of view of that group. Having said that, we must keep the following perspectives in mind.

First of all, it is the culture that defines a particular behaviour as 'good' or 'bad', 'right' or 'wrong', or 'decent' or 'indecent'. Every culture has a moral code and its violation is usually considered deviant. Nudity in itself is not decent or indecent. For thousands of years people in tropical climates did not wear any clothes. Even today 'holy men' of different religious persuasions such as *sadhus* and Jain saints may appear nude in public. Polygamy and prostitution are legal in many societies. Therefore, an act of deviance can be defined only in terms of the culture of a group.

Second, deviance is always relative. Many types of behaviour which are very normal in many societies may be considered deviant behaviour in other cultures. Even violent behaviour such as murder is defined differently in different social contexts. Premeditated murder is one thing but murder in self-defence and manslaughter (accidental) are different. In a theatre of war killing is normal. The same act may be legal in one place in the same country but not in another. Even in countries where gambling is legal, it is permitted only in limited areas. In Malaysia it is restricted to a hill station. In Egypt foreigners can gamble in the basement casinos of luxury hotels. Unlike in most other states in India, in Kerala cows can be slaughtered and beef consumed. Rules are also relative to men and women. In many cultures, women may not smoke or wear short pants or even drive an automobile. What is termed deviance also varies from time to time. Untouchability and all forms of discrimination on the basis of caste are now illegal, although they defined normal behaviour for thousands of years. Thus, what is normal or deviant behaviour is judged in terms of culture, place, time, and gender.

Finally, in defining deviant behaviour, sociologists are supposed to be value-neutral. Yet value considerations always enter in the discussion. For instance, we may say that every one who fails to conform to rules is not a criminal who deserves punishment. Sociologically speaking, the concepts of deviance or crime simply refer to violation of rules. It is always possible that some rules are bad or utterly wrong and need to be replaced. Just consider all the caste rules that perpetuated untouchability for untold centuries! Mahatma Gandhi adopted civil disobedience as part of India's struggle for freedom. Martin Luther King, Nelson Mandela, and Aung San Suu Kyi questioned the rules of their political systems. Can we condemn the black South Africans who rose in rebellion against apartheid? But these are value judgements. Therefore, sociologists view crime and deviance as neutral concepts and consider any violations of rule as deviance regardless of the moral issues involved.

THE NORMALITY OF CRIME: DURKHEIM

Durkheim defines crime as the violation of an imperative or prohibition. In the sociological sense of the term, it is simply an act prohibited by the collective consciousness. Therefore, crime can only be defined from the outside and in terms of the collective morality prevalent in the group at any particular point in time. Durkheim refutes the popular assumption that crime is pathological, or an example of social morbidity. He insists that crime is normal, and has been present in all societies of all types. It is not just inevitable but 'it is a factor in public health, an integral part of all healthy societies' (Durkheim 1964).

According to Durkheim, crime is not only normal, it is also necessary. Crime brings about needed changes in society; it implies that the way remains open to necessary changes and in certain cases it even prepares these changes. Thus there is a vital link between deviance and progress.

To make progress, individual originality must be able to express itself. In order that the originality of the idealist whose dreams transcend his century may find expression, it is necessary that the originality of the criminal, who is below the level of his time, shall also be possible. One does not occur without the other. (Nisbet 1974: 219)

The conditions of flexibility in a society which allow geniuses to rise also allow criminals to appear. Thus, criminals play a definite role in social life. Indeed, there are types of crime the very existence of which is a sound indication of the healthy nature of the social order. This is the only way we can explain the progressive changes brought about by such great moral innovators as Socrates, the Buddha, Jesus, or Gandhi who rebelled against the system but for the construction of a new moral code.

CONSEQUENCES OF DEVIANCE

As Durkheim pointed out, deviance has several positive functions. It brings about social change and paves the way for progress. Deviance also unites the community in its response. For example, when collective consciousness or social morality is strong, any violation of norms will be taken seriously by the whole community. Groups such as religious communities, castes, and political parties sometimes develop an extraordinary sense of 'we feeling' and loyalty when deviance puts the group at a disadvantage in relation to an outside group. Deviance also helps define rules which are otherwise vague and untested. Certain types of deviant behaviour act as safety valves by preventing potentially more disruptive forms of behaviour. Punishment of deviance reaffirms society's trust in its norms and values.

Deviance also has disastrous consequences for society. In the first place, deviance undermines trust. The stability of the social system is based on the expectation that people will behave according to established norms. When there is widespread corruption and theft of public property, people lose trust in their leaders. Large-scale violation also disrupts the social order and creates fear and insecurity. Above all, deviance is expensive; it diverts valuable resources. Imagine the amount of money that is spent on prisons, the police, judicial system, and security.

Theories of Deviant Behaviour

Why do people deviate from social norms? This age-old question has been answered in so many different ways. There have been religious and moralistic explanations where deviants were thought to be manipulated by demons. They were characterized as 'bad' and 'sinful' people. Many of the old explanations of deviance have now been discredited. However, we will begin with one of the earliest explanations.

Biological Theories

The thrust of biological explanation is that criminals somehow look different from 'normal' people. Facial features such as protruded cheek bones, shape of the head, type of nose, and certain physical deformities were thought to be attributes of deviants. For instance, the Italian criminologist, Cesare Lombroso argued that criminals were born rather than made by society. According to him, criminals are evolutionary throwbacks whose behaviour is akin to 'the ferocious instincts of primitive humanity and the inferior animals.' He believed that criminal tendency could be identified by certain physical signs that betray people's savage nature. Later E.A. Hooten went to great lengths to analyse the height, weight, shape of the body, nose, ears, jaw angles, and foreheads of criminals and came to the conclusion that crime was the result of 'organic inferiority', and not a product of social conditions. In the 1940s, William Sheldon and his colleagues carried out body measurements of thousands of subjects and stressed the importance of inherited factors in explaining criminal types.

These simplistic biological explanations are no longer accepted. If we include bribery, corruption, sexual misconduct, dishonesty, and other forms of immorality among forms of deviance, then we know that the deviants can be 'perfect gentlemen' in appearance. However, current biological theorists focus on genetic factors, abnormal brainwave patterns, hormonal abnormalities, low blood sugar levels, presence of tumours, and many other physical and hereditary factors to determine whether certain biological factors are prone to create certain types of deviant behaviour. The research has not yielded any conclusive results. In any case, sociologists are not convinced that biological factors alone can explain social behavioural problems. The first use of a cigarette, alcohol, or a drug is often the result of peer pressure rather than a biological condition.

Psychological Theories

There are several psychological theories which vary in their emphasis on different factors which influence deviance. Some theories attribute deviance to emotional scars left over from early childhood experiences. As we saw in Chapter 5, the run-away *id* can play havoc with human personality. Because of inadequate socialization in the early years of a child's life, the *ego* and the *superego* have failed to control the irrational drives and instincts of the *id*, thus leading the individual to produce antisocial behaviour in later years. The criminals, thus, typically suffer from damaged *egos* or inadequate *superegos*. Similarly, personality theorists look for key personality traits that are disproportionately present among deviants. Aggression and the impulse for instant gratification are thought to be among the psychological attributes of criminals.

Behavioural theorists focus on rewards and punishments. Children learn the behaviour that bring positive rewards and avoid patterns of behaviour which generate punishments. If we live in a traditional community where good behaviours are consistently applauded, we tend to adopt them. But if the kids who live in a crime-infested neighbourhood controlled by gangs find that certain types of deviant behaviour are rewarding, they are likely to learn them.

Psychological theories cannot account for the wide variation among people with very similar personality types. Some become career criminals but others may become social workers. Do all children whose *egos* have been wounded during early socialization become deviants? Do we always choose to learn patterns of behaviour which are rewarding? Do we always have such a choice in real life? Although psychological theories cannot explain all forms of deviant behaviour they are very helpful in the realm of policy implications. Instead of treating criminals as 'bad' people to be reformed by punishments, psychological theories aid in the process of therapy and rehabilitation.

Sociological Theories

Sociologists have always been interested in the process of deviant behaviour, its causes and consequences. During the latter half of twentieth century a number of theories have been developed to explain deviance. We will discuss the following.

Anomie Theory

In his famous essay, 'Social Structure and Anomie', Robert Merton (1957: 179) sought 'to discover how some social structures exert a definite pressure upon certain persons in the society to engage in non-conforming rather than conforming conduct.' In sharp contrast to the Freudian contention that social structure restrains the free expression of man's innate impulses and that man periodically breaks into open rebellion against these restraints to achieve freedom, Merton contends that social structure is active, producing fresh motivations and patterning types of conduct. From among the several elements of social and cultural structures, he analytically separated two: cultural goals and institutionalized means. The goals are the acknowledged desirables in any society such as success, money, power, prestige, etc. which most people want. Institutionalized means are the acceptable modes of reaching out for these goals. To give a simple illustration: if you want to pass an examination (goal), you are supposed to study hard (means), and not to cheat at the examination.

Table 8.1: A Typology of Modes of Individual Adaptation

Modes of Adaptation	Culture Goals	Institutionalized Means
I. Conformity	+	+
II. Innovation	+	−
III. Ritualism	−	+
IV. Retreatism	−	−
V. Rebellion	±	±

Note: (+) signifies 'acceptance', (−) signifies 'rejection', and (±) signifies 'rejection of prevailing values and substitution of new 'values'.

Merton defines anomie as the disjunction between cultural goals and institutional means. Table 8.1 illustrates Merton's typology.

1. *Conformity.* This occurs when individuals accept the cultural goals and the appropriate institutional means for their achievement. There is no deviance involved here.
2. *Innovation.* This type of deviant adaptation occurs when the individual has assimilated the cultural emphasis on the goal without equally internalizing the institutional norms governing the means for its attainment. In other words, individuals accept the success-goals but are unwilling or unable to work for them; instead they resort to institutionally proscribed means of attaining them. Robbery, theft, embezzlement, forgery, cheating at the examination, and all similar cases where success-goals are sought to be attained by illegitimate means are examples of innovation.
3. *Ritualism.* Here the individual abandons or at least scales down the lofty cultural goals, but continues to follow institutional norms almost compulsively. The ritualist prefers to follow the easy and routine path and thus avoid any dangers or mistakes. The overly cautious bureaucrat who wants to conform to every rule in the book and the receptionist at the emergency wing of the hospital who wants to have every proforma filled in before the patient is admitted are ritualists; they cling to the safe routines and lose sight of the real goals of the organization.
4. *Retreatism.* This is a privatized mode of adaptation of the socially disinherited. The social outcasts and the maladjusted reject both the goals and means either because of personal inadequacy or because of their perception of limited opportunities. Among the deviants in this category are psychotics, outcasts, vagrants, vagabonds, skid-row bums, tramps, chronic drunkards, and drug addicts. In short, retreatists are social drop-outs with a deviant lifestyle.
5. *Rebellion.* This type of deviance occurs when individuals reject existing culture goals and approved means and substitute them with new ones. They perceive the existing structural arrangements as unfair or stumbling blocks to the attainment of more legitimate goals.

Organized political action, populist movements, and revolutionary upheavals all present degrees of rebellion. Bandhs, hartals, gheraos, violent strikes, the so-called people's war of the Naxalites, and similar rebellious actions fall in the category of rebellion.

Merton's theory is sociologically significant because of the emphasis it places on social factors and conditions. However, his theory cannot explain the process of deviance, when and how certain people reject either the goals or the means.

Differential Association Theory

Edwin Sutherland's theory of differential association addresses the fundamental question of how individuals learn deviant behaviour. He contends that deviant behaviour, like any other behaviour, is learnt primarily from the company you keep. It is well known that peer pressure accounts for many teenage habits such as smoking, drinking, drug abuse, etc. In the United States, studies have shown that people who go to prison for petty crimes learn better techniques and big crimes from their cell mates. The student who sneaks out a book from the library may have received some training from a friend.

The key elements of differential association theory are:

1. Criminal behaviour is learnt in interaction with others.
2. Criminal behaviour is learnt primarily from intimate social groups of friends and colleagues.
3. The learning process involves two components: learning the criminal techniques, and learning the criminal motives. The first aspect deals with the technique of committing the crime and the second with motives, drives, and attitudes which rationalize the criminal act.
4. A person becomes a deviant because of 'an excess of definitions favorable to violation of law over definitions unfavorable to violation of law'. A teenager in a rural community surrounded by traditional values will find the definitions overwhelmingly in favour of conformity. But a teenager in a crime-ridden urban neighbourhood controlled by gangs and crime syndicates will find an excess of definitions in favour of violation of laws.
5. Differential associations may vary in frequency, length, intensity, and priority.
6. The process of learning deviant behaviour in association with others is similar to the process of learning aspects of culture in society.

Labelling Theory

Edwin Lemert's labelling theory falls within the theoretical tradition of symbolic interactionism. The focus here is not on the individual deviant but the social process by which the individual becomes labelled as a deviant and the consequences of labelling for the individual. Most people violate some of the rules at least some of the time. People lie about things, pay or receive bribes, and avoid taxes whenever they can. Although dowry has been made illegal, people pay and receive it. But those who violate such norms, although deviants in the strict sense of the term, are not labelled as deviants. According to labelling theory, the crucial factor is not the act of deviance itself but the social response to it; that is, how society labels the individual. All of us may know politicians and government officials who take bribes but most of the time they are not branded deviants. However, when they get caught and are convicted, they are labelled as corrupt.

The labelling theory makes a distinction between primary deviance and secondary deviance. Primary deviance refers to the original deviant behaviours. Unless he is caught, the individual will not be labelled as a deviant and even he may not consider himself to be a deviant. Secondary deviance develops when individuals are labelled as deviants and they accept the label and continue to behave accordingly. Let us say that a young man breaks into a house and steals something. This is primary deviance. But if he is caught in the act and arrested, then he will be labelled a thief by the community and the police. He may carry that label for the rest of his life. Every time there is a burglary in the neighbourhood, he is a suspect. And if the individual accepts his label of thief it is likely that he will continue to engage in such deviant acts.

All norms are not equally important in society. Most people avoid sales tax. Bribery and dowry are accepted practices. But burglary and robbery are serious crimes. Therefore, the more serious the violation, the more likely the person is to be labelled deviant. Similarly, the social status of the individual is also an important factor. In every society wealthy and powerful individuals get away with many deviant acts. Big politicians and senior officials often escape corruption charges but low level government servants may get caught. A poor alcoholic who sells illicit liquor from his thatched hut may be dragged into the prison but the big kingpins of the illicit trade can ward off any trouble. Labelling theory also explains how many of the powerless and marginal individuals in a society are labelled deviants by others. The examples include petty criminals, juvenile delinquents, drug addicts, alcoholics, homosexuals, mental patients, and retarded individuals.

Conflict Theory

Beginning with Marxist theory, there are several conflict perspectives which attribute deviant behaviour to unequal distribution of resources in modern society. Wealth and power are concentrated in the hands of a few individuals. Economic dominants make laws in order to protect their own interests. They use their wealth and influence to manipulate the legal system. In every society, there are the rich and the poor, the 'haves' and the 'have-nots'. The rich and the powerful are in a position to bribe the politicians, police, and even judges and get away with infractions of the law.

The poor, on the other hand, find that they have no access to resources and opportunities and sometimes resort to deviant behaviour. The landless peasants revolt against the landed gentry. Those who are oppressed and suppressed for generations by the affluent and the powerful, rebel against their oppressor. Many revolutions and social movements are often analysed in terms of conflict perspectives. Violent upheavals by the Naxalites, anti-untouchability movements, and direct action by tribals are some of the examples. Note that sociologists do not make value judgements. They see deviance wherever rules are broken. But then critical theoretical perspectives are applied to analyse and explain the actions.

GENDER AND DEVIANCE

Women are less likely to commit crimes than men. They make up only a tiny percentage of prison population anywhere in the world. There are also differences between the crimes men and women commit. Women are more likely to be arrested for shoplifting and prostitution; and men are more often involved in violent crimes. It is also possible that law enforcement officials regard female offenders as less dangerous and that women are less likely to be imprisoned than male offenders. Such views represent what has been dubbed as the 'chivalry thesis'. Although chivalry thesis has not been fully confirmed, there is another aspect of 'femininity' that is pervasive in the criminal system. For example, Frances Heidensohn (1995) has argued that women are more harshly treated when they are perceived to deviate from 'appropriate' female behaviour. Young girls perceived to be sexually promiscuous are more often arrested than young boys. The idea is that boys are boys but girls must be girls. Mothers who neglect their children are more harshly treated than fathers. It is also suggested that aggression and violence are somehow natural for men, but women must conform to appropriate feminine behaviour. Another side of the chivalry thesis is the 'gender contract', that is, the way women are able to play up on their emotions and vulnerability and extract sympathy from the law enforcement officials. Feminists argue that the differences in such perceptions and treatment are part of the socialization process, and hence culturally determined. Girls are supposed to be 'nice', women 'gentle', mothers 'caring', and wives 'responsible'. Consider the case of rape within marriage. How hard it would be for a woman, especially an Indian woman, to press charges against her husband for rape? In a male-dominated society, most men may still assume that it is their natural right to have sex with their wives whenever they please.

Other areas of deviance dominated by gender considerations are rape, sexual assault, sexual harassment, and domestic violence. These are crimes in which women are overwhelmingly victims. Yet it is very difficult for women to negotiate the process of prosecution successfully. Victims of rape have to undergo humiliating medical examinations and courtroom cross-examinations and prove that the act was not consensual. Domestic violence and sexual assault on domestic women servants are two of the most common crimes of intimacy, and both are extremely hard to prosecute. Women's groups have argued that rape should not be seen merely as a sexual offence but as a type of violent crime. Feminists have undertaken several studies of female criminals and come to the conclusion that women do participate in every form of violent crime, including terrorism (suicide bombing, for example), but the rate is much lower.

CRIME AND CRIMINALS

Crime is simply an act that violates a law. Every crime is a deviant act but not all deviants are criminals. Lunatics, alcoholics, homosexuals, cross-dressers, adulterers, and all liars are deviants but they are not criminals.

Crime against persons and property is one of the most commonly reported types of crime. This includes vandalism, theft, robbery, assault, rape, fraud, embezzlement, murder, and a host of others. Generally speaking, property crimes are much more common than violent crimes. However, in India, child labour, bonded labour, and feudal serfdom account for millions of people in servitude. There are literally millions of cases where destitute women, tribals, and children as young as six years old have worked for years under the most wretched conditions and are yet unable to pay off the measly Rs 100 which was advanced to them or their parents. Women and children are kidnapped, bought and sold into prostitution. Child marriage, female infanticide, and dowry deaths are other typically Indian criminal phenomena. In all these cases, crime statistics are often not reliable. Many crimes go unreported. Victims of rape and spousal abuse often do not report such crimes and there are no reliable records of people in child and bonded labour.

Victimless crimes are another type of criminal behaviour. Gambling, prostitution, illicit drug use, and public drunkenness are included in this category. Smuggling and black marketing may also be listed among victimless crimes. When the supply of desirable goods is limited, black markets thrive. If these illegal operations become highly profitable, then organized crime syndicates are likely to step in.

White-collar crimes are one of the most common crimes in India. They are committed by people of higher socio-economic status in the course of their business activities. Bribery, embezzlement, and adulteration are three common types. Adulteration of food is so rampant and extensive that it is almost a wondrous industry by itself. Pollution of air and water by factories, illegal dumping of toxic waste, sale of defective products, and consumer fraud are also white-collar crimes. Only those who are strategically located in their organizations (banks, government offices, or businesses) and have the opportunities and access to resources can engage in white-collar crimes. Politicians, government bureaucrats, bank officials, and business executives have opportunities for corruption and embezzlement.

Contrary to public opinion, violent crimes are common in India. For years, homicide was considered an American phenomenon; the United States consistently recorded the highest murder rate in the world. However, since the fall of communism, Russia has surpassed the United States as the murder-nation of the world. Because of the unprecedented social upheaval following the break up of the Soviet Union, homicide rates have dramatically increased in eastern European countries. Yet, even today, the United States has more cities known as the murder capitals of the world than any other country. In India we often read the horror stories about guns and violence in America. While it is true that America tops the list in terms of violence against individuals, India has the highest incidence of collective violence which includes political and communal violence, inter-caste conflicts, and massacres by death squads. Political violence includes assault on opposition parties, scare tactics, and use of thugs and criminals to intimidate voters. Communal violence that occasionally flares up in different parts of the country sometimes claims thousands of victims. The massacre of Sikhs after the assassination of Indira Gandhi and the recent Hindu–Muslim carnage in Gujarat are cases in point. Even more poignant are the regular occurrences of cold-blooded murder and mayhem in villages in Bihar by the private armies of big landlords. Thugs and criminal gangs who make up the feudal militia with links to political elites roam the countryside and terrorize Dalits and landless labourers. Custodial rape as well as torture and murder by the police are also fairly common in India. Whereas underworld gang warfare and crime exist almost everywhere in the world, in India they seek to replace democratic institutions. In some states, a large percentage of legislators are convicted criminals and well-known thugs; yet people of India have no right to know about the antecedents of their representatives.

SOCIAL CONTROL

Socialization serves to produce individuals who fit into the society. That process imparts skills and values that enable them to participate effectively in the ongoing social processes. Tradition, rules, and laws serve to compel individuals to conform to appropriate ways of behaviour. But compulsion is neither the only nor the most effective means of assuring conformity. Motivation and self-control are equally important. In modern societies, there are ways of linking the individual to various kinds of social action by offering rewards for undertaking certain activities. In India, historically, people have looked up to government jobs. Although with the emergence of global business enterprises, government service has lost some of its sheen, a good proportion of people still prefer the security and permanence of government jobs. In Kerala, the competition is so fierce and the coaching centres so active that it looks like every youngster wants to be an engineer or a doctor. A host of social inducements propels individual motivation which, in turn, leads to internalized attitudes towards self-achievement. Such processes also help internalization of other attitudes such as deferred gratification, postponement of marriage, and self-restraint in social activities. However, motivation and self-control are not enough.

Through socialization, individuals have internalized the norms and standards of society. This means that individuals generally accept the values and cultural standards of the social group or society to which they belong. That is the reason we feel guilty about lying and cheating. Thus we obey most of the norms most of the time because we accept them. However, internalized standards may not always work and violations do occur. How does a social group or society make sure its members obey the social norms?

Social control is the process of enforcing conformity. It is the mechanism by which a social group makes sure that its members conform to its norms and standards. Social control is enforced through *sanctions* which are rewards or punishments handed out to encourage conformity. Sanctions may be positive or negative. Positive sanctions are rewards and include awards, prizes, titles, public recognitions, and a host of others. They vary from a pat on the back, to the Nobel Prize. Negative sanctions refer to punishments which vary from gossip, ostracism, a cold shoulder or silent treatment, to a fine, prison term, and execution. There are two types of social control: informal and formal.

Informal Social Control

Families and peer groups do not depend on the police and judiciary to enforce conformity. There are several informal means of control such as peer pressure and disapproval. An individual who ignores the queue and rushes to the head of the line faces a stare or murmur of disapproval. A man who occupies a seat on the bus marked for 'ladies' will be asked to move. In the past, a man who violated a caste norm could be ostracized by the entire village. In traditional rural communities, gossip and social disapproval are enough to encourage people to conform to group norms. Informal means of control are particularly effective in small, intimate groups.

Formal Social Control

Formal social control refers to officially established means of enforcing conformity. Informal means of control are not always sufficient to deal with serious crimes. A family quarrel even if it involves assault may not be reported. But serious crimes against property and persons are usually handled by the state. State and local governments enforce norms pertaining to pollution, building codes, and environmental protection. However, formal social control is not all about governments, the police, and judicial system. Companies use promotion, demotion, and salary adjustments to enforce conformity. The fine on your telephone bill for late payment is a form of formal social control. Your college has a number of disciplinary procedures in place which involve fines, suspension, and dismissal. In short, any officially established procedures designed to encourage conformity and discourage deviance are part of formal social control.

Study Questions

- Define deviance with special reference to crime and non-conformity.
- Write a paragraph on Durkheim's theory of normality of crime.
- Discuss the various theories of deviance: biological theories; psychological theories; Merton's anomie theory; differential association theory; labelling theory; and conflict theory.
- Critically examine different types of crime and their social consequences.
- Discuss the gender perspective on deviance.
- Define social control. Explain different types of social control with illustration.

- Define the following concepts: deviance; crime; non-conformity; social control; sanctions—positive and negative sanctions; and informal and formal social control.

REFERENCES

Durkheim, Émile, *The Rules of Sociological Method*, New York: Free Press, p. 67, 1964.

Ferrell, Ronald A. and Victoria L. Swigert, *Deviance and Social Control,* Glenview, Illinois: Scott, Foresman, 1982.

Heidensohn, Frances, *Women and Crime,* London: Macmillan, 1995.

Lemert, Edwin, *Human Deviance, Social Problems and Social Control,* Englewood Cliff: Prentice-Hall, 1972.

Merton, Robert, *Social Theory and Social Structure*, Glencoe: Free Press, pp. 132–62, 1957.

Nisbet, Robert, *The Sociology of Emile Durkheim,* New York: Oxford University Press, 1974.

Sutherland, E.H. and D.R. Cressey, *Criminology,* Philadelphia: Lippincott, 1978.

———, *Principles of Criminology*, Philadelphia: Lippincott, 1939.

Part III

Social Inequality

Social Stratification

It will be an ideal society where all members are equal. But in reality there is no society based on perfect equality. Every society has a system of rating and ranking its members based on a number of criteria. Income, occupation, education, and hereditary status are some of the most common criteria used to rank people in a social hierarchy. Children of wealthy families inherit not only money but also prestige. Celebrities and members of the aristocracy have considerable social prestige. Based on their economic status, individuals are placed in different social classes. In India the caste system is used to rank individuals and groups as high and low. Throughout history most societies have used some system of classification such as pleibians and patricians, lords and serfs, rich and poor, landlords and landless labourers, upper castes and lower castes, the rulers and the ruled, and the elites and masses.

Social stratification is a system of structured inequality which rates and ranks members of a society based on select criteria and limits access to wealth, power, privileges, and opportunities. Social stratification is not a haphazard arrangement; it is a system of structured inequality based on definite criteria. Moreover, it is not a classification of individuals based on their attributes but an established system of classifying groups. The caste system is a typical example; it is a highly complex hierarchical arrangement based on heredity and perpetuated by an even more complex system of rules and regulations. Similarly, the ruling elites close ranks in order to protect their own vested interests. Economic dominants use their power and influence to perpetuate their privileges. The poor are exploited by the rich and forced to live on the margins of society. The system of social stratification not only apportions prestige and privileges among the elites but it also restricts opportunities available to the masses.

THREE SYSTEMS OF STRATIFICATION

There are three commonly recognized systems of stratification. They are estate, caste, and class.

The Estate System

The estate system of stratification formed part of the feudal system and was prevalent in Europe during the Middle Ages. It is a closed system in which a person's social position is defined by law-based land ownership, occupation, and hereditary status. Each of the strata in the estate system has its own established rights and duties. The estate system consisted of the following strata:

1. Landed aristocracy known as feudal or manorial lords.
2. The clergy.
3. Merchants and craftsmen.
4. Serfs or landless peasants who were legally tied to the land.

Wealth was concentrated in the hands of a small group of royalty and feudal lords who enjoyed hereditary status and prestige. The aristocracy owned the land as well as the peasants who lived and worked on the land. They were supposed to be brave warriors who had the responsibility to protect their vassals. The clergy also enjoyed considerable prestige and often owned vast tracts of land. The serfs were legally tied to the land and were very similar to slaves but with significant differences. Unlike slaves, the serfs were not bought and sold as individuals; they came with the land. Also, unlike slaves, serfs had certain clearly defined rights. Nevertheless, their condition was not much better than that of the slaves. Merchants and craftsmen operated independently and were, strictly speaking, outside the estate system. They could achieve considerable wealth and influence. On the whole, the estate system involved a hierarchical order based on heredity and permitted very little movement from one stratum to the other. However, estates usually were part of the manorial system and hence, they were local rather than national systems.

The Caste System

The caste system represents a rigid form of stratification based on hereditary status, traditional occupation, and restrictions on social relationships. The typical caste system is part of Hindu social organization although many of its characteristics can be found in other social contexts. M.N. Srinivas (1962: 3) defines caste: 'as a hereditary endogamous, usually localized group, having traditional association with an occupation, and a particular position in the local hierarchy of castes. Relations between castes are governed, among other things, by the concept of pollution and purity, and generally maximum commensality occurs within the caste.' In the words of E.A.H. Blunt (1946: 50), caste is 'an endogamous group, or collection of endogamous groups, bearing a common name, membership of which is hereditary, imposing on its members certain restrictions in the matter of social intercourse, either following a common traditional occupation or claiming a common origin, and generally regarded as forming a single, homogeneous community.'

There is no single valid theory that could effectively explain the origin of caste, the oldest system of stratification. Some scholars claim that caste is a pre-Aryan institution, part of the prehistoric clan life in India and that the Aryans found it a convenient basis for race relations based on inferiority and superiority in their dealings with the natives. The 'religious' explanation, of course, is that the Brahmins proceeded from the mouth of Brahma, the Creator, the Kshatriyas from his shoulders, the Vaishyas from his thighs, and the Shudras from his feet. However, a more valid explanation could be that the caste system is a perversion of the old varna system, the functional division of labour in society. Some authors, especially in the West, equate caste system with the original varna system which classified individuals into four groups:

Brahmins: priests, scholars, teachers, astrologers, and custodians of learned tradition.

Kshatriyas: rulers, administrators, and warriors.

Vaishyas: Merchants, artisans, traders, farmers, moneylenders, and cattle-keepers.

Shudras: workers and labourers.

The trouble is that varna system does not begin to tell the story of the caste system. There are several religious and secular interpretations of both systems, and no one is sure exactly when and how either system came into existence. However, it seems safe to conclude that the varna system was a functional division of labour based on *guna* or aptitude. Any individual with an aptitude for learning could be a considered a Brahmin and any individual with an aptitude for governance or warfare a Kshatriya and so on. In other words, the varna system was a classification of individuals based on their quality or ability; it was not a classification of groups into hereditary status categories. The four-fold divisions were not mutually exclusive; an individual could become a member of any varna provided he had the required talents to qualify him as a member of that particular varna. An elightened individual with a thirst for knowledge and ability to learn sacred texts could become a Brahmin. On the other hand, the son of a Brahmin with the predominance of *tamoguna* in him was only a shudra. The varna model did not imply any gradation on the basis of ritual purity although the four groups were unequal in the status hierarchy. Since the groups were not based on hereditary status, individuals were supposed to perform the functions for which they had the necessary talent. Gradually, each stratum developed its own subculture; the Vaishyas amassed wealth and as their status improved, they joined the 'trivarnic civilization'. The Shudras were reduced to permanent backwardness as a service class. Those who resisted oppression and preferred to live independent lives retired to forests and are today counted among the tribes of India. The privileged castes, particularly the Brahmins, rewrote scriptures, introduced the theory of pollution and provided new philosophical interpretations of sacred texts in an attempt to justify their superiority and to perpetuate the serfdom of the masses of untouchables and outcastes. Thus, according to many, the caste system, based on birth, is a perversion of varna which was based on guna or aptitude.

However, according to Dumont (1970: 73–4):

Far from being completely heterogeneous, the concepts of varna and *jati* have interacted, and certain features of the osmosis between the two may be noticed. The notion of the varnas which prevails nowadays, even among anthropologists, is influenced by caste. Thus it is often said that the true Kshatriyas have been long extinct, and that the Rajputs, though having the function of the Kshatriyas in modern times, are not real Kshatriyas. It is thought that in ancient India the accession to the throne, and to the dignity of Kshatriya, by dynasties of a different origin, was an irregularity. This assumes that heredity is more important than function, which is true of caste but not of the varnas. So far as the varnas are concerned, he who rules in a stable way, and places himself under the Brahman, is a Kshatriya. Moreover, these categories were not strictly endogamous either. Probably the Kshatriyas have always been lax in this matter. The particular place given to power in the system has had notable and lasting results: in the first place, the pattern of polygyny and meat diet, which does not correspond to the Brahmanic ideal, has been quietly preserved at this and lower levels until quite recently; in the second place, since the function is related to force, it was easier to become king than Brahman; Kshatriyas and Untouchable are the two levels on which it is easy to enter the caste system from outside.

Yet, the caste system cannot be explained in terms of the four varnas. In the first place, there are thousands of castes and subcastes in India. Second, their place in the social hierarchy varies from place to place. Generally speaking, castes are mutually exclusive, often localized, groups into which individuals are born and represent minutely graded levels of social distance and a way of life influenced by a tradition of customs and taboos. Third, castes have evolved over the years; legal changes, education, new employment opportunities, urbanization, and the secular standards of human values and dignity have transformed many features of the caste system. The characteristics outlined below represent the traditional system.

1. *Hierarchy*. The caste system represents a hierarchic pyramid with Brahmins at the top, numerous low castes or Dalits at the bottom, and thousands of other castes and subcastes in the middle. In the words of A.R. Desai (1978: 38): 'It has fixed the psychology of the various social groups and has evolved such minutely graded levels of social distance and superior–inferior relationships that the social structure looks like a gigantic hierarchic pyramid with a mass of untouchables as its base and a small stratum of elite, the Brahmins, almost unapproachable, at its apex.' However, contrary to popular impression, the hierarchy is not a clear-cut one. The top and bottom layers are relatively fixed but there is considerable debate regarding the status of the numerous groups in the middle.

2. *Hereditary status*. Caste is determined by birth and there is very little room for change.

3. *Traditional occupation*. In the old system almost every caste followed a certain occupation which was handed down from one generation to the next. Temple priests, leather-workers, potters, carpenters, barbers, washermen, sweepers, village musicians, and even landless agricultural labourers came from traditional castes. Louis Dumont believes that the above three characteristics (hierarchy, heredity, and traditional occupation) are linked by religious orientation. These are not ordered strictly in terms of power relations or economic domination. According to Dumont (1970: 107–8):

> It is no accident that the specializations which are most marked in the accepted religious language are those in which the link between caste and profession is strongest, and, even nowadays, most stable. It is correct to say that these are most strictly jajmani, but at the same time one must not lose sight of the fact that they serve as a model for the others. Just as we have seen how the ideology of the pure and impure serves to express all sorts of things, so here the universal form of the relation is given by the properly religious relation, as the etymological connotation of jajmani incidentally reminded us. One employs a Brahman, a genealogist, a barber, one employs similarly a carpenter, one employs an untouchable unfree labourer: each case is always, so to speak,

on the same model. In other words, the 'religious' is here the universal mode of expression, and this is perfectly coherent if one knows that the overall orientation is religious, that the language of religion is the language of hierarchy, and that the hierarchy is necessarily, as we have seen, a matter of pure and impure.

4. *Endogamy*. Individuals usually marry within the caste, and in the past inter-caste marriages were strictly forbidden.

5. *Theory of pollution*. Relations between castes were traditionally determined by the concepts of pollution and purity which asserted that lower castes are polluting to the higher castes. The theory of pollution formed the basis of untouchability and established the most elaborate boundary maintenance system known to man.

6. *Restrictions on social interaction and access to opportunities*. Lower castes were denied many opportunities; they were not allowed to wear jewellery or finery, enter temples, or attend schools. Most were forced to live in separate neighbourhoods. In many areas, caste laws prescribed the distance that should separate them in both public and private places. For example, in parts of India, the lower castes could not appear in front of the higher castes and were considered polluting to the Brahmins even from a distance of 60 feet or more. Since different castes claim equal or superior status, the acceptance of cooked food and water was considered the most important criterion for judging social status. A caste that serves cooked food and water to another caste but will not accept the same from that caste considers itself superior and the latter caste accepts its position as inferior.

7. *Castes are localized groups*. There is no uniform standard that evaluates castes all over the country. A particular caste may be considered 'untouchable' in one region and not so in another region.

While the characteristics described above can be attributed to the caste system in general, the situation on the ground is largely determined by the nature of subcastes. The castes divide themselves into numerous subcastes and some of the restrictions such as endogamy may not strictly apply to them. Ghurye (1932), for instance, believed that although it is the caste which is recognized by the society at large, it is the subcaste which is considered more relevant by the particular caste and the individual. Therefore, Ghurye argues that in order to get a sociologically correct idea of the institution, we should recognize subcastes as real castes. But Karve insists that castes result from the aggregation of subcastes, rather than subcastes from the subdivision of castes. Once again, the situation of subcastes in relation to the castes varies with region and language.

Although much has been written about discrimination and untouchability, very little attention has been paid to the functions of the caste system. The caste system served as a great unifying force; it held together numerous culturally diverse groups in the wake of external threat and frequent aggression during the long history of Indian civilization. It also promoted efficiency and economy in the execution of traditional occupations in the absence of modern vocational training schools by encouraging artisans and craftsmen to excel in their professions. Caste also served as a mutual aid and insurance cooperative and through the institution of the *jajmani* system, it integrated the various caste groups in the locality into a well-knit community with an elaborate network of well-defined roles and social relationships.

Castes are no longer confined to traditional occupations. Untouchability has been abolished and its practice in any form or manner is made punishable under the law. India also has instituted an elaborate system of reservations for Dalits and backward castes in local elections, colleges and universities, and public services. There are also many affirmative action programmes designed to advance the welfare of the weaker sections.

In a final note on the caste system, it must be said that although the caste system is an integral part of the traditional Hindu social organization, many of its features are found among Christians, Muslims, and Sikhs in India. There are social divisions and commensal restrictions among various religious groups. Sociologically speaking, racial discrimination in the old American south and apartheid in South Africa are very similar to the caste system in India. Any rigid system of stratification based on hereditary characteristics such as birth, race, and skin colour is akin to the caste system in that the primary determinant of social status is invariably fixed. An individual may climb economically and even socially, but the ascribed status based on hereditary factors does not change.

The Class System

The class system refers to the classification of people based on their economic positions in society. As we saw in the section on the evolution of societies, classes began to emerge as individuals started to accumulate wealth. Social classes are not rigidly defined like estates or castes. Individuals move up or down the ladder as they gain or lose in the market system. Even those born in poverty have, in principle, a chance to get an education and a good job and raise their economic standing in society. Of course, individuals born into wealthy and influential families have much better access to resources and opportunities. Yet, the hallmark of the class system is individual 'achievement' rather than 'birth'.

Although sociologists have classified classes into several types, the age-old classification of upper, middle, and lower classes still holds good. The lower classes are sometimes divided into 'working class' and the poor. Among the upper classes a distinction is often made between the aristocracy of birth and wealth such as royalty (members of the old ruling families) and the new rich. The former consists of old aristocratic families which enjoyed considerable wealth and prestige in the past. The latter group is sometimes referred to as 'money bags', people who gained a lot of wealth in business, industry, or through illegal means.

Sociologists rely on a number of criteria to determine classes. Income and wealth are the most commonly used. Whereas income refers to an individual's earnings, wealth is the sum total of all assets including inheritance, real estate, jewellery, gold and precious stones, and stocks and bonds. Level of education, type of occupation, material possessions (Mercedes Benz), house-type (palatial mansion), and lifestyle are used to classify people into classes. Sometimes the place of residence—low income or poor neighbourhood, slum area, or wealthy subdivision—is important. Prestige or status which is purely a subjective criterion is also significant in social stratification. Based on certain attributes which elicit recognition and respect, people tend to evaluate individuals into different classes. In India, government jobs are generally valued much higher (at least until recently) than private jobs. The three letters IAS (Indian Administrative Service) define a prestige category unto itself.

The shape and character of class system has changed considerably. What Warner (1936: 234–37) called the upper-upper class based on aristocracy of birth and wealth is under decline. In India too the old upper class based on zamindari system of inherited wealth has shrunk. The new upper class consists of self-made men and women, captains of industry and business whose wealth and power is derived from profit-making in global markets. For example, Warren Buffett and Bill Gates continue to occupy the top of the billionaires' list. The character of the middle class has also undergone great transformation. The ranks of the contemporary middle class are swelled by professionals with specialized training in information technology, finance, and service industries. Because of the technical qualifications and credentials, they occupy strategic managerial positions in companies which provide them with great material and cultural advantages. While they are supervised by the executive class, they themselves monitor and evaluate the work of those below them in status hierarchy. In India, the expansion of government bureaucracy has also created a large middle class. In spite of the growing trend towards consumerism and the emerging 'lifestyle of comfort' among them, the middle class is neither homogeneous nor cohesive, because their interests and expectations vary widely according to their position in the occupational structure as well as their credentials and qualifications. The size and composition of the lower class has also changed. In the first place, the working class has become smaller and the proportion of those below the poverty line has shrunk. Although worldwide the income level of blue-collar workers has improved, in India the situation of manual labourers and migrant workers has only improved marginally.

RACE, GENDER, AND STRATIFICATION

Traditionally, race and gender have been determinants of inequality and differential access to rewards, privileges, and opportunities. Let us first consider race. What is race? Social scientists now agree that there are no clear-cut biological traits that establish different races but only a range of physical variations in human groups. Race is a social construct and is sociologically significant as long as it has meaning for people within a society and social relationships are patterned accordingly. Although no one accepts the so-called race science any more, biologically grounded features such as facial features and colour of skin are used to locate individuals and groups within a particular position in society and assign certain characteristics and competencies. This process of classifying people according to race is called racialization. In the United Kingdom, Indians, Pakistanis, and African blacks are racialized. For centuries Jews were forced to live in ghettos in European cities. Similarly, Gypsies were racialized and discriminated against in Europe. In America, race has always been a factor in social stratification, and even today it defines access to opportunities, resources, and rewards. Apartheid in South Africa was the most rigid system of stratification based on race. Whites who constituted 10 per cent of the population were at the top of the hierarchy, followed by 'coloureds' (mixed race), Indians, and blacks in that order. In the Middle East, migrant workers are racialized and often treated according to their country of origin.

Like race, gender, another social construct, has been the basis of stratification through the ages and in almost all societies. Gender is a determining factor in structuring roles, rewards, and opportunities. Traditionally, men have served as 'breadwinners' and women have assumed primary responsibility for child care and domestic work. In some subcultures, women were not encouraged to pursue higher education or work outside the home. They were expected to marry early, produce children, and take care of the family. Traditional agrarian societies fostered a typical patriarchy in which men exercized control over women. In India, Manu's code stipulated that women depend on their fathers in their childhood, on their husbands in marriage, and on sons in their old age. In China, the dictum of 'thrice obeying' meant exactly the same thing. Through centuries such 'admonitions' and cultural practices have fortified men's 'superiority' and dominance over women and condemned women to free domestic labour and/or as sexual objects.

R.W. Connell (1987) has put forward a general theory of gender relations. She points out that everyday interactions and practices in society gave rise to an 'organized field of human practices and social relations' which subordinates women to men. Gender relations are structured into patterned social arrangements over time, establishing the dominant–subordinate relationship between men and women. Yet, Connell argues that gender relations are not fixed or static; they are subject to change just like any other social construct. Connell argues that significant changes—near crisis—are taking place in the three most important realms which facilitated men's hegemony over women. First, there is the crisis of institutionalization. Institutions such as family and the state which have traditionally supported men's domination over women are gradually being undermined through a series of social legislations such as divorce, women's rights, domestic violence, sexual harassment, pension, and income tax. Second process is the crisis of sexuality. The traditional type of hegemonic heterosexuality is in decline. Recent revolution in human sexuality, especially gay and lesbian sexuality, has redefined masculinity. Third, there is the crisis of interest formation. Feminist movement, gay movement, and overall changes in sexist attitude have transformed gender relations. For example, today men are more willing to share household responsibilities such as child rearing, cooking, and doing dishes. These changes have at least blunted hegemonic masculinity and transformed gender relations.

DIMENSIONS OF SOCIAL STRATIFICATION

Max Weber analytically distinguished three orders within society—economic, social, and political—and corresponding to these identified three dimensions of stratification: class, status, and power. Following Marx, Weber also defined class situation essentially as a market situation. In other words, classes were defined primarily in terms of economic criteria such as wealth, income, type of occupation, and material possessions. Status situation, on the other hand, is determined by a specific, positive or negative, social estimation of honour; it is not necessarily linked with class situation. The highest prestige in a particular social group does not always belong to the richest or the most powerful. The king or queen of England has the highest status in British society but he or she is not necessarily the richest and certainly not the most powerful. A call girl, stripper, or member of the mafia may be very rich but does not enjoy high social status. Prestige or status is the social estimation of honour which is based on how members of a society evaluate certain occupations. In several sociological surveys of selected occupations in the United States, medical doctors, lawyers, and college professors ranked the highest with 86, 75, and 74 scores respectively whereas janitor and shoe-shiner ranked lowest with 22 and 9 scores respectively. According to Weber, unlike classes, status groups are communities, and status symbols such as special attire, exclusive clubs, and unique lifestyles distinguish them from other groups.

Power, the third dimension of stratification, exists in a social club as well as in the state. Power is the ability to make a decision or influence the actions of others. In a democracy, politicians, especially of the ruling parties, exercise enormous power. Marx believed that those who have economic power also have the political power. It is well known that people with money and connections influence public decisions. In short, classes are stratified according to their relations to the production and acquisition of goods whereas status groups are stratified according to the principles of their consumption of goods as represented by special lifestyles. The genuine place of classes is within the economic order, the place of status groups is within the social order but parties live in a house of power.

THEORIES OF STRATIFICATION

Structural-functionalism and conflict theory offer different perspectives on social stratification. The former looks at the functions of stratification and explains why structured inequality is essential for the stability of the social system. Conflict theorists see inequality as the result of exploitation and talk about the inevitability of class struggle.

Functional Theory

The functional theory of stratification was first proposed by Kingsley Davis and Wilbert Moore in 1945. According to them:

... the main functional necessity of explaining the universal presence of stratification is precisely the requirement faced by any society of placing and motivating individuals in the social structure. As a functioning mechanism a society must somehow distribute its members in social positions and induce them to perform the duties of these positions. It must thus concern itself with motivation at two different levels: to instill in the proper individuals the desire to fill certain positions, and, once in these positions, the desire to perform the duties attached to them. (1945: 247)

Davis and Moore identified two determinants of positional rank:

1. *Differential functional importance.* In other words, some positions are more important than others, and so society must see to it that less essential positions do not compete with more essential positions.
2. *Differential scarcity of personnel.* Some positions are easy to fill while others are hard. Also some positions require innate talent. In many cases talent may be abundant but the training is so long, costly, and elaborate that relatively few can qualify.

The crux of the argument is that in every society there are some positions that are of the greatest importance for society and that require the greatest amount of training and talent. There must be unequal distribution of social rewards in order to ensure that these important positions are filled. The position of a janitor can be easily filled. But the position of a surgeon requires not only talent but years of training and experience. Therefore, different positions must be rewarded with different ranks, salaries, and privileges. Thus, in functional perspective, society works better if most qualified people fill the most important positions and are rewarded accordingly.

This theory generated a huge debate in sociology. Melvin Tumin and others led a frontal attack on the theory saying that there is no empirical evidence that the greatest reward goes to the most qualified to perform the most needed function. Consider the case of a cricket star who receives a reward of Rs 1 crore or more. How functionally important is that position to society and how hard is the level of training? There are several other problems with the theory. In the first place, how do we determine the relative functional importance of different positions? While it is true that a medical doctor's position is important to society, it is equally true that if street sweepers do not perform their duties, everyone's health will be affected. Similarly, if movie stars and call girls get paid well, is it because of the functional importance of their positions? Second, if the most important positions in a society always went to the most qualified people, the society would be an open society based on talent. The most talented people do not always have the opportunity to get the necessary training. Families with money, power, and connections are able to get many of the plum positions in society. Therefore, the functional theory of stratification has been criticized as a rationalization of structured social inequality in society. Yet Dennis Wrong , a critic of functional theory, noted that critics of the theory 'have succeeded in showing that there are great many things about stratification that Davis and Moore have failed to explain, but they have not succeeded in seriously denting the central argument that unequal rewards are necessary in any and all societies with a division of labour extending much beyond differences in age and sex' (1959: 773).

Conflict Theory

In Chapter 2 we discussed Marx's theory of class conflict. Here we will summarize the key points. Marx believed that the history of every society through the ages is a history of class struggle. In an industrial society the two classes who stand in opposition are the bourgeoisie and the proletariat, those who own the means of production and distribution and those who sell their labour for wages. The capitalists accumulate wealth at the expense of the workers and become richer and richer. The workers, who are systematically exploited, become poorer and poorer. Eventually, the workers become conscious of their situation and organize themselves. Thus class conflict ensues. The conflict need not always be between the rich and the poor, or the capitalists and the workers. Wherever there is exploitation, the oppressor and the oppressed constitute two antagonistic classes. So the class struggle continues between the landlords and the landless labourers, between the rulers and the ruled, and between the upper castes and the lower castes. Where Marx saw conflict between two classes based on the means of production and distribution, Ralf Dahrendorf saw conflict between two classes based on positions of authority. Similarly, Weber saw conflict based on patterns of dominance and submission determined by what he called 'structures of dominance'. Like Marx, Weber also believed that class was based on economic conditions. However, according to Weber, economic conditions were not limited to the means of production and distribution but skills, credentials, and training were an equally important part of the market situation.

GLOBAL SYSTEMS OF STRATIFICATION

Global stratification refers to the division of the world into unequal segments characterized by extreme differences in wealth and poverty. To understand the level of poverty in a country, it is not enough to know the country's per capita income. The depth of poverty in a country and the average quality of life depend on how equally or unequally income is distributed across the population. For example, in Brazil and Hungary, per capita income levels are quite comparable, but the incidence of poverty in Brazil is much higher. In Hungary, the richest 20 per cent of the population receives about four times more income than the poorest 20 per cent, whereas in Brazil the richest 20 per cent receives thirty times more than the poorest 20 per cent. The World Institute for Development Economics Research of the United Nations University (UNU-WIDER 2007) has undertaken a very comprehensive global survey of personal wealth of individuals in all countries. According to the survey, the richest 2 per cent of the world population own more than 50 per cent of the global household wealth. The survey also found that the richest 10 per cent of the people owned 85 per cent of global wealth, whereas the bottom 50 per cent owned just 1 per cent.

Unequal distribution of wealth, power, and prestige on a global basis results in vastly different lifestyles and life chances among the nations of the world as well as within each nation. The current global trading and investment regime serves primarily the interests of 20 per cent of the humanity who claim 80 per cent of the planet's resources. It tends to marginalize the poor, sharpen social and economic inequalities, and weaken the state's ability to provide much needed services and cope with challenges. More than half of the world's population lives on less than $2 per day, which is the internationally defined poverty line. Table 9.1 illustrates the extent of population living under poverty line. Keep in mind that different agencies and governments use different criteria to define poverty.

Table 9.1: Per cent of Population Living on Less than $2 Per Day (2002)

Sub-Saharan Africa	75
South/Central Asia	75
China	47
North Africa	29
Latin America/Caribbean	26
Easter Europe	14
World	53

Source: Population Reference Bureau, World Population Data Sheet (2005).

Compare this with 2011 data for the following countries given in Table 9.2.

Table 9.2: Per cent of Population Living on Less than $2 per day (2011)

Democratic Republic of Congo	80
India	76
Uganda	65
Pakistan	61
Kenya	40
Vietnam	38
Guatemala	26
Iraq	25
Egypt	19
Maldova	13
Brazil	10

Source: US Population Reference Bureau (2011).

The sad truth is that the income gap between the richest and the poorest 20 per cent of the world population continues to widen. Whereas in 1960, the wealthiest 20 per cent of the world population had more than thirty times the income of the poorest 20 per cent, by 2000, the wealthiest 20 per cent had almost eighty times the income of the poorest 20 per cent (UN Development Programme 2003). Within some nations, the income disparity is even more pronounced. For example, in Brazil and Bolivia, the poorest 20 per cent of the population receives less than 3 per cent of the total national income.

Our discussion of global stratification will touch on four basic issues: classification of economies by income, social inequality, human development, and modern slavery.

Following World War II, the world was divided into developed and underdeveloped nations. This terminology soon fell into disuse. Later, the concepts of First, Second, and Third Worlds were developed. The First World consisted primarily of rich, industrialized nations based on capitalist system. The Second World comprised of socialist economies and the Third World consisted of mixed economies. Now the Second World has largely disintegrated and the Third World is no longer clearly identifiable in regard to specific geographic region or political regime. Instead Castells (1998: 164–5) adopts the term *Fourth World* to describe the 'multiple blackholes of social exclusion' that he believes exist throughout the world in impoverished rural areas of Africa, Asia, and Latin America as well as US inner city ghettos. According to Castells, 'social exclusion is the process by which certain individuals and groups are systematically barred from access to positions that would enable them to have an autonomous livelihood in keeping with the social standards and values of a given social context.' He believes that the three worlds approach is outdated and that the future will be based on a global economy governed by a network of multilateral institutions and their financial players.

The World Bank classifies countries into three economic categories based on a Gross national Income (GNI) of 2002 level: low-income economies with GNI per capita of $735 or less; middle-income economies with a GNI per capita between $736 and $9,075, and high-income economies with more than $9,076. We know that measuring wealth and poverty across nations poses conceptual problems because of the difficulty in acquiring comparable data; yet absolute poverty is internationally defined as living on less than a dollar a day (World Bank 2003).

In the 1950s and 1960s it was generally believed that poverty, diseases, and famine in less developed countries could be reduced through the transfer of technology, finance, and experience from developed nations. The assumption was that economic growth will automatically raise the standard of living which will lead to better quality of life for all. By the 1970s, disenchantment set in: increasing a country's GNI did not reduce the poverty of the poorest but in fact global poverty and inequality increased. Wealth became concentrated in the hands of a small stratum of the very rich. This realization led to a new debate on global quality of life and human development issues. So in 1990 United Nations Development Programme introduced the Human Development Index (HDI), establishing three new criteria—in addition to GDP—for measuring the level of development in a country: life expectancy, education, and living standards. According to the United Nations, human development is the process of expanding choices that people have in life, to lead a life to its full potential and in dignity, through expanding capabilities and through people taking action themselves to improve their lives. Based on the new indices of development, it is estimated that 37 per cent of the world population in low- and middle-income countries lack the essentials of well-being. The World Bank's *World Development Report 1999/2000: Entering the 21st Century* notes that 'the average per capita income of the poorest and middle thirds of all countries has lost ground steadily over the last several decades compared with the average income of the richest third ... and the absolute number of those living on $1 per day or less continues to increase' from 1.2 billion in 1987 to 2 billion by 2015. Global resources are disproportionately controlled and consumed by a small minority of the world's population, residing mainly in the First World. For example, grains fed to US livestock equal as much food as is consumed by the combined populations of India and China (McMichael 2000: 283–4).

However, income gap is only one dimension of the global stratification. Many social scientists believe that social inequality is the real cause of poverty. Gunnar Myrdal (1970) emphatically argued in the 1970s that social equality is the essential precondition for economic equality. According to Lummis (1992: 50),

The problem of inequality lies not in poverty, but in excess. 'The problem of the world's poor', defined more accurately turns out to be 'the problem of the world's rich'. This means that the solution to the problem is not a massive change in the culture of poverty so as to place it on the path of development, but a massive change in the culture of superfluity in order to place it on the path of counter development. It does not call for a new value system forcing the world's majority to feel shame at their traditionally moderate consumption habits, but for a new value system forcing the world's rich to see the shame and vulgarity of their over-consumption habits, and the double vulgarity of standing on other people's shoulders to achieve those consumption habits.

Just consider the Indian case. India ranks near the top among Third World agricultural exporters, and in 1995 India exported $625 million worth of wheat and flour and $1.3 billion worth of rice while almost 200 million Indians went hungry. Although India boasts more billionaires than China, 81 per cent of its population lives on $2 a day or less, compared with 47 per cent of Chinese. That class divide is starkest in cities like Bombay and Calcutta, where million dollars apartments overlook million-population slums. As Frances Moore Lappe and her colleagues (1998) report in *World Hunger: Twelve Myths*, the world is awash with food as agricultural production increased dramatically in the last decades. Poverty and hunger exist in the midst of plenty and because of the opulent and wasteful lifestyle of the rich.

Finally, we come to slavery, the system of stratification in which some people are owned by others. When we think of slavery, we think of an old practice that was abolished long time ago. Think again! According to Bales (1999) there are at least 27 million slaves worldwide, primarily concentrated in Southeast Asia, northern and western Africa, especially Sudan, and parts of South America. Bonded labour refers to a particular form of slavery in which people give themselves into slavery as security against a loan or when they inherit a debt from a relative. Bales is convinced that there are slaves in almost every country in the world, where they work in simple, mechanical, traditional labour such as brickmaking, cloth and carpet weaving, domestic service and prostitution. According to Human Rights Watch (Asia) hundreds of thousands of women and children are transported by a network of traffickers and pimps from Nepal and poor rural communities all across India and are kept in conditions that are tantamount to slavery (Abraham 1998). In Thailand and the Philippines vast majority of girls are trapped into flesh trade because of rural poverty but they are seldom bought or sold. But in India vast majority of them are kidnapped, sold by their families or friends, or trapped into false marriages and then forced into prostitution. The most notable forms of slavery today include child prostitution in Thailand, enslaved brickmakers in Pakistan, domestic slaves in France and the Middle East, workers in sugarcane plantations, ranches, and mines of Brazil, and women in sex trade and children in jewellery business in India. Millions of children employed in India's match industry, carpet weaving, and lock industry are also in virtual slavery. According to some estimates, child labour, bonded labour, and feudal serfdom account for almost 300 million people in servitude in India. A sum as low as Rs 100 is advanced to parents of children, tribes, destitute women, and landless labourers who are then sold in permanent bondage. The more they work, the more they sink into the debt trap as the owners and middlemen charge them a rent for tools, a fine for alleged imperfections in their products, for provision of food supplies and kindness and favours during medical emergencies, and any family obligations such as marriage. Although bonded labour is abolished by law, employers are able to get around it by using middlemen who supply labour and stay out of sight. Bonded labour is widespread in India, Pakistan, Bangladesh, and Nepal.

CASTE AND CLASS IN INDIA

Although the caste system is regarded as the traditional form of social stratification in India, it must be noted that caste and class are not mutually exclusive. Classes based on economic criteria exist in all castes. In urban areas castes and classes coalesce in such a way that traditional caste distinctions almost disappear.

Let us examine some of the recent trends in social stratification in India.

The abolition of untouchability in 1955 was a landmark legislation that transformed the face of caste system in India. Discrimination on the basis of caste and all caste-based restrictions were abolished. But law is largely ineffective in a society where customs are entrenched and resources are monopolized. Even today many temples in north India are off limits to Dalits. There are no signs which prohibit them from entering but those who dare to violate the unwritten social norms know the consequences. The poor Dalits who depend on the rich landlords for their livelihood are not in a position to take on the system. The legislation has, of course, abolished all restrictions pertaining to admission to schools, hospitals, and other public facilities.

In most of the traditional villages in rural India, different castes live in different neighbour-hoods. Indeed, even the different castes within the Dalit community do not share the same streets. Even today, the vast majority of traditional occupations in village India are performed by the same castes just as their ancestors did for thousands of years. *Dhobis* (washermen), barbers, potters, blacksmiths, carpenters, leather workers, village musicians, and several communities of agricultural labourers are traditional castes.

There is an irony in India's official approach to caste. On the one hand, the state is com-mitted to social equality and a casteless society but every individual is required to proclaim his caste for admission into schools and government jobs. And, there is an army of officials to issue caste certificates. The reality is that caste enumeration is essential if the society wants to launch special programmes for the advancement of Dalits and backward castes.

There are at least four major trends of change that affect the caste system today.

First, education has considerably altered the framework of the traditional caste system. Although free and compulsory universal education is still an elusive goal in India, many Dalits and tribals have been able to get a good education and liberate themselves from the clutches of traditional occupations. Many of them have attained jobs in public and private sectors as teachers, clerks, and officers, but their numbers are concentrated in the lower rungs of the service ladder.

Reservation of seats in educational institutions, government services, and legislatures has brought about significant changes in the caste system. A certain percentage of seats is reserved for Scheduled Castes (SCs) and Scheduled Tribes (STs) and for other backward castes (OBCs) for admission to institutions of higher education, especially professional colleges such as medical and engineering schools. From panchayats to Parliament, the law provides for the reservation of seats for SCs and STs. There is also a system of reservation in government services and certain posts can be filled by members of the general public only if suitable candidates from SCs or STs cannot be found. Generally speaking, there are three ways in which states seek to address the problem of social inequality:

1. *Preferential treatment.* If there is a competition for a job or a seat, then other things being equal the disadvantaged person will be preferred over the other. In this case, there is no dilution of qualifications; from among the candidates who have similar qualifications, a member of the SC, ST, or OBC is deliberately chosen.
2. *Affirmative action.* This includes positive actions taken to help members of the disad-vantaged castes such as special loans, scholarships, training, hostels, and other facilities.
3. *Positive discrimination.* Even if other things are not equal, members of the disadvantaged groups are given preference. In other words, people with lesser qualifications may be selected to fill the posts. This practice is not unique to India. Several top universities in the United States have used different set of criteria in order to encourage diversity on their campuses.

There is no question that reservation has worked; though the overall percentage of both the SCs and STs in public services is still much below their proportion of the population, the number has virtually doubled in ten years.

Sociologically speaking, another significant point must be mentioned here. In India, the terms caste and class are often used synonymously. Everyone knows that caste is determined by birth but then for all practical purposes the government treats a whole caste as a class. The following excerpt from a Supreme Court ruling illustrates this point: ·

It must not be forgotten that caste is also a class of citizens and if the caste as a whole is socially and economically backward, reservation can be made in favour of such a caste on the ground that it is a socially and economically backward class of citizens. (AIR 1968 SC 1012)

The third important factor affecting inter-caste relations is rural–urban migration. Every year hundreds of thousands of people leave their ancestral villages and take up residence in urban areas. Although some of them may still carry on their traditional occupations in the cities, a vast majority of them follow occupations which have nothing to with their caste. Many of the restrictions found in the rural areas can no longer be enforced in the city. People live together in crowded urban tenements. Old paraphernalia of caste has been replaced by new symbols of class. Economic opportunities rather than traditional patterns determine an individual's social status. Levels of education and income override many conventional caste taboos including inter-caste marriage.

The fourth significant trend is the emergence of castes as important pressure groups in politics. The caste system may be cracking up in the social and ritual spheres, but it plays a dominant role in Indian party politics. All political parties consider numerically large castes to be important vote banks; they field candidates, assign seats, and allot ministerial and other posts according to caste. Caste considerations influence voting behaviour and every political party is eager to exploit caste links and accentuate caste loyalties. Since the introduction of the Panchayati Raj, caste is not merely a social phenomenon but also a political force to be reckoned with. At the state and national level caste politics continues to inflame the controversy over reservation and creamy layer. The debate continues on the percentage and duration of reservation, and there is no consensus on who all should be given reservation and where. Some critics of the reservation argue that disproportionate benefits continue to accrue to a small minority of backward classes who have benefited from the system and have now entered the level playing field. Undoubtedly, these and many other issues pertaining to reservation will continue to be debated at all levels.

The violence that followed the Mandal Report and the ensuing controversy mark a landmark in the debate on contemporary caste system in India. The critics talked about 'murder of merit' and the perpetuation of mediocrity. Most sociologists seemed to have supported the anti-Mandal position, and an impression was created that merit was somehow uniformly distributed across social strata. But the truth of the matter is that merit (as in competitive examinations) largely accrues to the privileged sections of the population that send their children to the best schools and spent vast resources on 'coaching for merit'. As Satish Deshpande (2003: 106–7) states:

it is almost a truism to say that, today, the variety of occupations and professions among all caste groups is much wider than it was fifty years ago. However, this does not change the massive social reality that the overwhelming majority of those in the 'highest' or most preferred occupations are from the upper castes, while the vast majority of those in the most menial and despised occupations belong to the lowest castes. In short, while it is indeed significant that *some* members of the lowest castes are now able to occupy very high positions, or that *many* members of high castes are being forced into menial occupations today, this does not by itself demonstrate that caste and occupational status have been delinked. We must also ask if particular *occupations* continue to be dominated by particular caste-clusters, and whether this makes for a recognizable pattern systematically linking privilege and dis-privilege to caste. In other words, the caste-composition of the privileged groups in society is a critical yardstick as long as this continues to reflect the dominance of the upper castes, it does not matter even if the *majority* of the members of these castes are themselves poor or disprivileged. This would only demonstrate that while caste remains a necessary precondition for making it into the privileged group, it is not in itself a sufficient condition to ensure entry.

In a similar vein, Panini (1996) documents that the overwhelming dominance of the upper castes in professions such as engineering, medicine, banking, journalism, and academics continues (Deshpande 2003).

In short, in every field offering a promising career in the contemporary world, the upper castes dominate and the middle and lower castes are more or less severely under-represented. Almost two generations after Independence, it is no longer possible to evade these realities as being the by-product of historical inequities. We have to face up to the uncomfortable truth that caste inequality has been and is being *reproduced* in independent India. (Deshpande 2003: 120)

The subject has been further discussed in the chapter on 'weaker sections' (Chapter 10).

Finally, a note on the class system in India. In addition to the usual categories of upper, middle, and lower classes, in India we also have a large poor underclass. India still has a small group of very rich people at the top and a large proportion of lower classes and poor at the bottom. One per cent of the population is thought to be super rich even without counting the huge reserve of black money which comprises almost 30 per cent of GDP. Over 30 per cent of the rural poor merely subsist. The Planning Commission has created a big controversy by proposing a poverty line of Rs 3,905 (Rs 26 per day) for a family of five in rural areas and Rs 4,824 (Rs 32 per day) in urban areas. States and social activists argue that the Commission is grossly underestimating poverty. The percentage of people below the poverty line is supposed to have declined, from 48 per cent in 1977 to 25 per cent in 1992. However, if we use $2 per day as the poverty level, more than 70 per cent of the people are below that level. At the current price level, per capita income during 2000–1 was only Rs 16,487. But the emergence of a fairly large middle class during the last ten years is a significant demographic factor. According to some data, the upper middle class makes up about 100 million people and the lower middle class about 350 million. The significant rise in middle class consumption through sales of colour televisions, cars, scooters, refrigerators, and other household appliances has radically altered the lifestyle of the middle classes in India.

LIFESTYLES AND LIFE CHANCES

Literature on social stratification in the West deals extensively with the lifestyles of various classes. Upper, middle, and lower classes do not live in the same neighbourhoods, drive the same cars, buy the same alcoholic beverages, shop at the same shops, or frequent the same clubs or restaurants. They do not even smoke the same brand of cigarettes or subscribe to the same magazines. Such class distinctions are very pronounced in the United States. But in India, though distinctions are everywhere, they are not as sharp as in several Western societies. For instance, in several villages and small towns in India the rich and the poor live side by side. Middle and lower classes as well as the poor use the same modes of public transportation. Yet, significant differences exist.

Ownership of private modes of transportation such as automobiles and scooters as well as expensive household appliances is indicative of class standing. Even today in the villages of Tamil Nadu, bullock carts and horse carts transport children to and from schools. Upper middle class children ride private school buses or autos. Food habits vary with social classes. The vast majority of lower classes and poor people subsist on different kinds of millets and even roots and tubers whereas rice and wheat are primarily consumed by the higher classes. Not only the types of foods but also the preparations vary with classes. Toddy is the popular alcoholic beverage of the lower classes. Middle and upper classes prefer more expensive drinks. The cooking fuel is equally different. Electricity and cooking gas are not available to a majority of the people; they have to depend on dried twigs and cowdung cakes.

Children of middle and upper classes attend expensive, often English-medium, private schools; lower class children have no choice but to attend the nearest government school. Because of home pressures and other chores, poor children often drop out of school early. Their parents are not in a position to coach them and cannot afford private tuition. Therefore, very few of them graduate from high school or go on to college. Fashionable clothes, forms of entertainment, and music systems accent the lifestyles of the middle class.

Usually upper and middle class parents tend to have fewer children than the poor. They plan their families and place great emphasis on the quality of education for their children. Child-rearing practices also vary according to social class. Upper and middle class parents emphasize self-direction; they reason with their children and depend less on punishment. Lower class and poor parents are often strict disciplinarians and even resort to physical punishment.

Life expectancy is significantly higher among members of the upper and middle classes. They have better access to sanitary housing, and balanced and nutritious food. They also visit doctors and dentists fairly regularly whereas the poor see doctors only when they are seriously ill. Many kinds of preventable diseases such as tuberculosis, dysentery, typhoid, and hepatitis are common among the poor. Babies born into poverty are significantly more likely to die before their first birthday than those born into higher-income families. Mental illness is also more common among the lower classes. Studies have shown that the poor suffer from schizophrenia, manic-depressive psychosis and other mental disorders more often than middle and upper classes. Yet they are least likely to reach out for help and get rehabilitated. Alcoholism, domestic quarrels, and spousal abuse are more common among the poor. In recent years suicide rate has also increased among the poor and lower classes.

The poor are more likely to be arrested and convicted than the other classes. They are also more likely to be physically tortured or otherwise unfairly treated by the police. They are more likely to be arrested for property crimes such as burglary. Middle and upper classes have the opportunity for embezzlement and corruption. But they are less likely to be prosecuted or convicted.

There is a positive relationship between social class and self-esteem. Members of the upper and middle classes with 'respectable' jobs have considerably higher self-esteem or positive evaluation of themselves. Indian society as a whole does not value dignity of labour. In the United States where students even from upper classes do menial jobs to make money, all work is treated with respect. In India, a majority of people look down upon manual labour and other menial jobs. Since people are treated according to their occupation, people in the lower classes tend to have a negative evaluation of themselves. Also, the poor who are dependent on others for their livelihood feel that they are denied a sense of worth in the eyes of others and themselves.

Social Mobility

We have all heard about people who rose from rags to riches; they are the heroes of many Indian movies. Individuals from low income families who get a good education, work hard, and pass competitive examinations and join the Indian Administrative Service and move up the social ladder. There are also many who have lost everything and shifted downward. *Social mobility* is the upward or downward movement of a person from one social class or status level to another. It results in gain or loss of wealth, power, and prestige for the individual.

Based on the ease or difficulty of upward movement, stratification systems are classified into *open and closed societies.* There is very little social mobility in rigid systems of stratification such as estate and caste because status is hereditary. On the other hand, the class system is supposed to be an open society because it permits movement of people from one class to another. It must be noted that no society is absolutely closed or open systems, but compared to caste and estate, the class system is a relatively open society.

Sociologists have identified different types of mobility. We will define four types.

1. *Intergenerational mobility.* This involves the comparison of a parent's and a child's social class positions. We want to know whether a child's class position is higher or lower than

that of his father. If the son of a blacksmith has attained professional education and become an engineer, this is a case of upward intergenerational mobility.

2. *Intragenerational mobility.* This is the study of an individual's occupational changes in the course of a lifetime. Let us say that an individual began his career as a manager in a company but he bought the company and became a successful businessman. In rural India we also observe cases where a barber or carpenter continues to perform the same occupation throughout his life without any change in his social status.

3. *Vertical mobility.* This means movement up or down the social ladder and necessarily involves change in social status. A man marrying into a lower social class, a lower division clerk getting promoted as an upper division clerk, and a receptionist losing her job and becoming a waitress are some examples.

4. *Horizontal mobility.* This is movement of people between groups or positions of more or less equal social status. For example, a man changes his religion; an engineer becomes an information technology specialist; and bureaucrats change departments. These changes may not involve any re-evaluation of social status.

Traditionally, caste represented a fairly closed system which permitted little or no social mobility. Lower castes were denied access to education, ownership of property, and choice of occupations. With so many restrictions on inter-caste relations, the movement of people from one caste to another was almost impossible. However, according to M.N. Srinivas, the process of Sanskritization has provided some social mobility for various castes in the ritual hierarchy. Through centuries several low castes have been able to rise to higher position by adopting the rituals, beliefs, symbols, pantheon, and practices of higher castes. Sometimes it may take a generation or two before the claimant castes are conceded the higher status. Economic betterment, acquisition of political power, education, leadership, and a desire to move up in the hierarchy have all contributed to the quickening pace of Sanskritization. Srinivas (1966: 23) observes: 'Sanskritization has been a major process of cultural change in Indian history, and it has occurred in every part of the Indian subcontinent. It may have been more active at some periods than at others, and some parts of India are more Sanskritized than others, but there is no doubt the process has been universal.'

Today the situation is different. Legal changes, affirmative action, and several ameliorative measures have increased the chances of social mobility for those at the bottom rung of the social ladder. However, the situation is not much better for OBCs, lower-income groups, and the poor. Poverty continues to be a vicious cycle. If parents are poor, they are not able to give their children a good education, and without a good education their children will not be able to find a good job. Thus, parents' minimal income and lack of opportunities keep their children locked in the same low economic status. Parents' encouragement, effective education, social and political connections, and hard work are considered to be the four most important avenues of social mobility. For the children of the poor and lower classes, at least the first three conditions are difficult to be met.

Migration to the cities has also provided some impetus to social mobility in India. Poor, lower-caste members who moved to large metropolitan centres have been able to shake off the shackles of tradition in the countryside, acquire jobs that are not caste-related and gradually move up the social ladder. Similarly, thousands of young men and women from low-income families in Kerala and Tamil Nadu have moved to Mumbai and New Delhi to find jobs as stenographers and clerical workers. Migration has also helped young female nurses from Kerala to better their prospects as well as the lot of their families. Another significant phenomenon is the mass migration, especially from Kerala and other southern states, to countries in the Middle East. Thousands and thousands of people have found skilled jobs in Gulf countries and continue to transfer millions of rupees to India every year. Many of them have been able to improve the economic status of their families within a relatively short period of time.

Another significant recent phenomenon is the rapid development of software industries and other computer-related businesses in India. Many young people see their future in the computer industry and have flocked to computer-related training programmes. The software industry pays relatively well. Then there are the call centres and numerous other computer-related businesses which have opened up new avenues of social mobility for young people.

Study Questions

- Define social stratification and summarize the three systems of stratification.
- What are the main features of caste system? Compare and contrast caste system with race-based system of stratification.
- What constitutes a social class? Examine the nature of contemporary social class.
- Examine how race and gender form the basis of stratification.
- What are the three dimensions of stratification according to Max Weber?
- Critically examine the functional theory of social stratification.
- Examine the various conflict perspectives on social stratification.
- Review the nature and extent of current global system of inequality.
- Write an essay on the current status of caste and class in India.
- Summarize the impact of stratification on lifestyles and life chances.
- Define social mobility. What are the major types of social mobility?
- Discuss the factors that facilitate or hinder social mobility.

References

Abraham, M. Francis, *The Agony of India*, Madras: East West Books, 1998.

Bales, Kevin, *Disposable People: New Slavery in the Global Economy,* Berkeley: University of California Press, 1999.

Blunt, Edward (ed), *Social Service in India*, London: His Majesty's Stationery Office, 1939; reprinted 1946, p. 50.

Castells, Manuel, *End of Millennium,* Malden, MA: Blackwell, 1998.

Connel, R.W., *Gender and Power,* Polity: Cambridge, 1987.

———, *Masculinities,* Polity: Cambridge, 2005.

Davis, Kingsley and Wilbert E. Moore, 'Some Principles of Stratification', *American Sociological Review,* 10, pp. 242–9, 1945.

Desai, A.R. (ed.), *Rural Sociology in India,* Bombay: Popular Prakashan, 1978.

Desai, Mihir, 'A Justification for Reservations and Affirmative Action for Backward Castes in India', *South Asia Bulletin,* 11(1 & 2), pp. 110–30, 1991

Deshpande, Satish, *Contemporary India: A Sociological View,* New Delhi: Viking, 2003.

Dumont, Louis, *Homo Hierarchicus: The Caste System and Its Implications,* Chicago: University of Chicago Press, 1970.

Feagin, Joe R. and B. Clairece, *Racial and Ethnic Relations,* Upper Saddle River, NJ: Prentice-Hall, 2003.

Ghurye, G.S., *Caste and Race in India,* London: Kegan Paul, 1932.

———, *Caste and Class in India,* Bombay: Popular Book Depot, 1950.

Hutton, J.H., *Caste in India: Its Nature, Functions and Origins,* New York: Oxford University Press, 1963.

Karve, Irawati, *Hindu Society: An Interpretation,* Poona: Deccan College, 1961.

Lappe, Frances Moore, Joseph Collins, and Peter Rosset, *World Hunger: Twelve Myths,* New York: Grove Press, 1998.

Lenski, Gerhard, *Power and Privilege: A Theory of Social Stratification,* New York: McGraw-Hill, 1966.

Lummis, Douglas C., 'Equality', in Wolfgang Sachs (ed.), *The Development Dictionary,* Atlantic Highlands: Zed, 1992.

McMichael, Phillip. *Development and Social Change: A Global Perspective.* Thousand Oaks: California: Pine Forge Press, 2000.

Myrdal, Gunnar, *The Challenge of World Poverty,* New York: Random House, 1970.

Population Reference Bureau, World Population Data Sheet 2005, Washington, DC, www.prb.org.

Rothman, Robert A., *Inequality and Stratification: Class, Color and Gender,* Upper Saddle River: Prentice-Hall, 2001.

Srinivas, M.N., *Caste in Modern India and Other Essays,* New York: Asia Publishing House, 1962.

———, *Social Change in Modern India,* Berkeley: University of California Press, 1966.

———, *India: Social Structure,* New Delhi: Publications Division, 1969.

Vanfossen, Beth E., *The Structure of Social Inequality,* Boston: Little, Brown and Company, 1979.

Warner, W. Lloyd, 'American Caste and Class', *American Journal of Sociology,* 42, pp. 234–37, 1936.

World Development Indicators 2003.

Wrong, Dennis H., 'The Functional Theory of Stratification: Some Neglected Considerations', *American Sociological Review,* 24, p. 773, 1959.

Minorities and Weaker Sections

Through the ages, societies have used different criteria such as biological factors, cultural traits, language, religion, and place of birth to categorize people. Sociologists are interested in three such categories.

1. *Racial Group.* It is a category of people based on physical characteristics such as skin colour, facial features, eye folds, and hair colour and texture. Accordingly, racial groups are classified into Caucasoid, Mongoloid, Negroid, and Australoid. The scientific validity of any such classifications is limited; in any case race is not a factor to be reckoned with in the Indian social context. Therefore, our focus shifts to other groups.

2. *Ethnic Group.* It is a category of people who identify themselves with a distinct cultural tradition based on religion, language, province, or other common heritage. In India when we refer to Punjabis, Muslims, Christians, Tamilians, Malayalees, or Andamanese tribals, we are referring to ethnic groups. But these are also religious communities, linguistic groups, castes, and tribes. However, the emphasis is on culture rather than biological or geographic factors. Yet, in the context of caste system in India, defining ethnic groups in terms of culture is problematic. For instance, Tamil Brahmins and Namboothiris of Kerala are both Brahmins by caste but culturally they are two distinct groups. Similarly, the Moplas of South India and the Ashrafs of North India are Muslims but they have different cultural practices. Also, the same caste groups have very different cultural traditions depending on where they live and what language they speak. Therefore, in India caste as well as linguistic and religious groups considerably overlap, making it difficult, if not impossible, to define ethnicity in terms of a single criterion such as culture.

3. *Minority Group.* A minority is a group of people subjected to prejudice and discrimination in a given society. Sociologically speaking, minority groups are not necessarily numerically small groups; they are simply victims of differential and unequal treatment. In the United States, blacks are a minority, numerically and sociologically. But in South Africa under the apartheid system, blacks were the majority group, a predominant majority that was discriminated against by a small group of whites who had the power. In India, the government makes a distinction between 'minorities' and 'weaker sections'. Muslims, Christians, Sikhs, Buddhists, Zoroastrians, and Jains, as well as the handicapped and the elderly are treated as minorities. Note that these are all numerically smaller groups.

But Dalits, tribals, and backward classes are treated as 'weaker sections'. Women are also categorized as weaker sections whether or not they are numerically small. Therefore, it appears that 'weaker sections' actually mean 'minorities' or groups who suffer discrimination and unequal treatment.

PREJUDICE AND DISCRIMINATION

Literally, prejudice means 'prejudgement', which is an opinion in favour of, or against, something or someone. Sociologically speaking, however, *prejudice* means negative judgement or bias against a group. Members of a group may have highly negative opinions about members of another group. When members of one caste regard members of another caste as inferior, unclean, stupid, lazy or uncouth, then they are expressing a prejudice. Ethnic, religious, caste, provincial, and linguistic prejudices can be found all over India.

Discrimination is a form of behaviour that entails unequal treatment by means of which one group prevents another group's access to opportunities. For untold centuries upper castes have discriminated against lower castes and denied them most of the civil rights. Prejudice is a matter of attitude whereas discrimination is a type of behaviour. A person may be prejudiced but he may not discriminate or he may be afraid to discriminate because of the law preventing discrimination.

When members of a particular group have highly negative attitudes towards another group, they usually develop *stereotypes* about members of that group. A stereotype is a set of biased generalizations about a group of people that is unfavourable, exaggerated, and oversimplified. Every caste has a stereotyped image of other castes and much of the inter-caste relationship is based on such biased and inaccurate generalizations. For example, members of the upper castes may consider the lower castes to be lazy, unclean, and stupid while lower castes may characterize some upper castes to be shrewd, selfish, greedy, and clannish.

There are several sources of prejudice and discrimination. In the case of caste system, the theory of pollution was the single most important factor in the establishment of social distance between castes. Traditional rules in the old caste system clearly specified the distance to be kept among various castes. Lower castes were forced to live in poor neighbourhoods on the outskirts of the villages where there were no sanitation facilities. They were also forced into menial and 'unclean' occupations which upper castes avoided. By denying access to property, education and other opportunities, the lower castes were forced to languish at the bottom rung of the social ladder. Such conditions made it possible for the upper castes to consider the poor to be inferior but good sources of cheap labour.

Prejudice, racial and ethnic stereotypes, and discrimination are found all over the world and have existed through the ages. The concepts of ethnocentrism and xenophobia which we discussed in the chapter on culture (Chapter 4) are relevant here. Apartheid in South Africa was an extreme case of formal discrimination. Prejudice and discrimination against African

Americans in the United States, ill-treatment of aboriginals in Australia, and the systemic prejudice and discrimination against Jews and Gypsies in Europe for centuries are only some cases in point. One time the United States immigration law clearly barred the Chinese from entering the country. The recent immigration debate in several European countries borders on xenophobia. The United Kingdom's attempt to limit immigration from non-European Union countries is based on the fear that new immigrants will take away British jobs or be a burden on the state welfare system. Many countries such as Yugoslavia and Ethiopia were broken up because of ethnic conflicts. In India, in addition to prejudice and discrimination based on caste, religion, and language, there is also a north–south divide. One time, Maharashtra for Maharashtrians movement targeted non-Maharashtrians, especially people from the south, on the assumption that they are taking away jobs from the local people. States were reorganized on the basis of language, and there is still clamour for Bodoland, Gorkhaland, and Telengana (which was ultimately formed in 2014). Caste, religion, language, race, and ethnicity have always served as the basis for prejudgements and stereotypes in India.

PATTERNS OF MAJORITY–MINORITY RELATIONS

Relations between majority and minority vary from assimilation and peaceful coexistence to subjugation and genocide. Keep in mind that sociologically speaking, a minority group is a victim of discrimination regardless of whether the group is numerically small or a majority of the population. We may identify the following patterns of behaviour to illustrate possible relations between a majority and a minority.

1. *Genocide or Extermination.* Annihilation or mass murder of minority groups is the most extreme form. The Nazis murdered millions of Jews and thousands of Gypsies, and European colonizers decimated native populations in Australia, Hawaii, and Jamaica. Extermination has occurred on a smaller scale in a number of other cases.
2. *Subjugation.* This is the subordination of minority groups by the dominant and powerful majority. Caste councils, panchayats, village headmen, and even the kings perpetuated the subjugation of Dalits and other lower castes in India.
3. *Population transfer.* Forcing a group of people to leave their home territory is a case of population transfer or expulsion. In the United States, Native Americans were forced from their homelands into reservations. Idi Amin forced the Asians to leave Uganda. In India, partition resulted in large-scale transfer of population between India and Pakistan.
4. *Segregation.* Segregation refers to formal or informal physical separation of minority groups. The situation includes restrictions on place of residence, movement, contact, and interaction. The history of caste system is a history of segregation; lower castes were forced to live on separate streets away from village centre or even in separate villages.

5. *Cultural pluralism.* Peaceful coexistence of majority and minority groups as equals while maintaining the distinct cultural traditions of each group is a case of cultural pluralism. Muslims and Hindus have always coexisted in many villages and small towns across the country. They continue their religious and cultural traditions including traditional occupations, food habits, dress styles, language, and manner of speech. The Indian motto of 'Unity in Diversity' is illustrative of cultural pluralism.

6. *Assimilation.* This is a course of action which suggests that the minority groups abandon their distinct cultural traits and adopt the lifestyle of the majority. The American society is a good example of assimilation. Early immigrants to the United States who came from so many countries and ethnic groups gradually abandoned many of their cultural traits and adopted a common language and a common lifestyle. In India, where people follow several religions, speak different languages, wear different types of clothes, and eat different kinds of food, assimilation is of limited value. However, all Indians share the symbols of nationalism and many values of Indian culture.

7. *Affirmative action.* In many cases majority groups make deliberate attempts not only to end current discrimination but also to correct the imbalances due to past discrimination. In India, the system of reservation, preferential treatment, and the many special programmes for the welfare of the minorities and weaker sections are indicative of affirmative action.

Minority Responses

Minorities, as victims of mistreatment, have responded to the majority in a number of different ways. Sociologists consider acceptance, avoidance, assimilation, conversion, activism, and aggression to be common responses.

Sometimes minorities accept their subservient status out of fear of the majority or because of lack of alternatives. In the traditional caste system, discrimination was enforced with brute force. Although many in the lower castes resigned themselves to their fate, it is hard to believe that they accepted the sanctity of the caste system or were fooled by the ideology that if they remained loyal and subservient they would be rewarded in the next birth. In the old order, avoidance was not a serious option for the lower castes who remained in their ancestral villages. However, those who migrated to the big cities were able to avoid many of the burdens of the caste system. They were also able to assimilate into the ways of the city. Similarly, people from the lower castes who acquired considerable wealth, power, and prestige have successfully adopted the lifestyle of the majority. In India, the minorities have also used conversion as a form of response to ill-treatment by the majority. Led by B.R. Ambedkar, thousands of Dalits embraced Buddhism. Even today some Dalits and tribals continue to convert to Islam or Christianity in order escape unfair treatment. However, whether conversion has helped them improve their social status in the caste-oriented system is a debatable point. Activism and aggression have always been part of the minority response to discrimination. Social movements, protests, political action, unions, and organizations have always played a major role in Indian caste history. Today, more than ever before, the minorities and weaker sections in India stand united through interest groups, formal organizations, and political action committees.

MINORITY GROUPS IN INDIA

The official classification of minorities in India is not based on sociological definition. Based on their numerical size, Muslims, Christians, Buddhists, Sikhs, and Zoroastrians are considered religious minorities at the national level. Together they constitute about 18 per cent of the population. The aged and the disabled are also officially classified as minorities. Then there are minorities based on their sexual orientation such as gays, lesbians, and transvestites. All these groups are not necessarily victims of discrimination. But there are other groups which are singled out by different groups for discrimination. In Mumbai, the Shiv Sena proclaims that Maharashtra is for Maharashtrians, meaning different linguistic and provincial minorities may be discriminated against. The Pundits in Jammu and Kashmir as well as linguistic minorities in different states have complained about unfair treatment.

The Constitution of India protects the interests of the minorities and recognizes their rights to conserve their languages, scripts, or culture and establish and administer educational institutions of their choice. There is a National Commission for Minorities to evaluate the working of the safeguards in the constitution and to make recommendations to ensure effective implementation and enforcement of all the safeguards and laws. There is a 15-Point Programme for Welfare of Minorities which includes tackling the situation arising out of communal riots and preventing communal riots, ensuring adequate representation of the minority communities in employment under the central and state governments as well as public sector undertakings, and other measures aimed at socio-economic development of minorities. There is also a pre-examination coaching scheme for improving the employability of minorities and for increasing their intake in professional courses. The government has set up a National Minorities Development and Finance Corporation to support economic and development activities for the benefit of the backward sections among the minorities, preference being given to occupational groups and women among the minorities.

We will discuss religious minorities in Chapter 14. Here we will confine our discussion to the elderly and persons with disability.

Persons with Disabilities

In the field of visual, hearing, speech, and locomotor disabilities, approximately 2 per cent of the population of the country is estimated to be disabled. Physical disability accounts for twenty per thousand persons in rural areas and sixteen per thousand in urban areas. About three per cent of the children under fourteen are mentally retarded. The number of leprosy-affected persons is estimated to be about forty lakh of whom a fifth are children. On the whole, five per cent of the population is estimated to be suffering from some kind of disability. There are numerous national schemes and assistance programmes for the welfare of persons with disabilities which include schools, vocational training centres, community-based rehabilitation programmes, distribution of aids and appliances and medical and surgical correction. Artificial Limbs Manufacturing Corporation of India, a government company, markets its products through a number of public and private outlets. The National Handicapped Finance and Development Corporation promotes economic empowerment of persons with disabilities through financing technical education and self-employment ventures. There is also a 3 per cent reservation of vacancies in services for the physically handicapped.

The Aged

As life expectancy continues to climb, the proportion of the elderly to the total population also increases, reaching almost 20 per cent in some countries. Indeed, there is an unprecedented growth of population of sixty-five and older all across the globe. Nearly two-thirds of the world's elderly now live in developing countries. In the year 2000, the percentage of people age sixty-five and over was only 6 per cent in Asia; that percentage will double by the year 2030 and quadruple by the year 2050. India is expected to have 173 million elderly in the year 2026.

The United Nations World Population Prospects (2010) projects that, for the first time in history, the 0–4 years age group will decline between 2015 and 2020, having peaked at around 650 million. The sixty-five plus population is projected to exceed the 0–4 years population during that period, rising from 601 million in 2015 to 714 million in 2020, and by 2050 the sixty-five plus will be almost two and a half times the 0–4 year age group. This also means that by 2050, the number of working-age people available to support each person sixty-five and older will decline by half wordwide, straining government social support and retirement financing. In 1950, there were twelve working-age people for every person over sixty-five worldwide. Now there are seven, and by 2050 there will be only three. Yet, laws in several countries require women to retire earlier than men, despite women's longer life expectancy. In the more developed regions, about one in four people is now over the age of 60 years. By 2050, more than one in three will be so. In the less developed countries, one in twenty people is now over the age of 60 years; by 2050, one in nine will be. Already four out of five adults of retirement age or older have no retirement income from pension or government programmes. It is high time that we realize that healthy older workers represent a growing reservoir of unrealized human capital. When they remain active in the workforce, older people can contribute much to their families, communities, and countries. But this requires a rethinking of work, family, and institutional arrangements, and especially new liberal laws.

The process of ageing and the presence of a large percentage of the aged in modern societies have important consequences for society. Moreover, like casteism and sexism, ageism has also emerged as a significant sociological phenomenon. Therefore, no textbook in sociology can ignore the problems of the aged whose numbers will soon exceed those of Dalits and religious minorities. Various societies respond differently to the aged and the ageing process. Ageing is feared in some but accepted in others. In some societies like Japan the aged are highly respected and allowed to work as long as they can. The United States has abolished compulsory retirement in most cases. In India, persons in state government services are forced to retire at the age of fifty-eight, without any regard for their ability; but politicians are allowed to steer the destiny of the nation even thirty years after that. The age of retirement was set years ago when life expectancy was much lower. Now people live twenty to thirty years after retirement. The argument in favour of retirement at an early age is that society needs to make room for younger workers who remain unemployed. But we must also consider the cost of compulsorily retiring highly skilled and experienced workers in the prime of their life and paying them pension and benefits for two to three decades.

In many Asian cultures including India, China, and Japan old age is considered to be a repository of wisdom. The aged are treated with respect. Children never address the elders by name even when they are total strangers. Most older persons live with their sons or daughters or some other member of the family. They have a role in the family's decision making process. Unlike in the West, old-age homes were somehow thought to be out of sync with traditional cultures. However, the situation is gradually changing. As children move away from their ancestral homes into cities or foreign countries, many of the elderly now find it necessary to turn to old-age homes. Another recent phenomenon is the emergence of caretakers called 'home nurses'. In the traditional agrarian society where the entire family worked on the farm, it was always assumed that parents in their old age will continue to stay in their own homes with one or more of the sons. The joint family system also facilitated the home care of the elderly. However, the processes of industrialization, modernization, and urbanization have undermined the joint family and the subsistence economy. As a result family caregiving is eroding.

Ageism is an ideology that asserts the superiority of the young over the old. Even some of the terms used to describe the elderly, such as 'old', 'aged', 'over the hill', 'senior moment', and 'old-timer' betray a sense of prejudice against them. Several stereotypes about the elderly refer to their physical infirmities, senility, passivity, and lack of alertness. When older persons wear bright fashionable clothes they are accused of 'not acting their age' but if they dress blandly they are judged as shabby. Contrary to popular belief, many of the biological changes associated with ageing are not necessarily related to illness or disability; many of the physical problems of the elderly are cumulative effects of past working conditions and health habits. Research on changes in intelligence and creativity has shown that there is no demonstrable decline until advanced old age. Yet, as Betty Friedan says the 'ageing mystique' is that we define old age as a problem, as little more than decline and deterioration.

Gerontology is the scientific study of the aged and the ageing process. As the elderly emerge as a significant minority, gerontology will continue to thrive as a growing discipline. Gerontology focuses not only on the aged and the process of ageing but also on death and dying, family and kinship relations, biological, psychological and sociological explanations of ageing, productive ageing, and services for the elderly.

Theoretical Perspectives on Ageing

Disengagement Theory. A variant of structural-functionalism, the disengagement theory views ageing as the gradual and beneficial disengagement of older persons from some social responsibilities. Elaine Cumming and William Henry (1961), authors of the theory, argue that the disengagement of the elderly from paid occupational roles is a process that is functional for both the society and the elderly. The process of ageing, with its corresponding physical decline and death, threatens the society with disruption. The society has to pave the way for the orderly transfer of statuses and roles to younger members so that societal needs will continue to be met. Moreover, the younger generations are more energetic and up to date with knowledge and skills. Society benefits from this orderly transfer as positions are filled with new blood. The young people get to perform new and productive roles. The aged are relieved of stressful jobs and have more time to engage in activities that are more satisfying to them. Thus disengagement is functional for everyone.

The problem is that the elderly may still be in a position to perform for years in their productive roles and may not want to disengage voluntarily. And when forced to retire, they may not find any fulfilment in life and fall into depression. Disengagement may also mean loss of income and prestige and more social isolation. There is also no compelling evidence to back up the argument that retiring people early and appointing young people in their place is cost-effective. *Activity Theory.* In sharp contrast to disengagement theory, the activity theory suggests that a high level of activity enhances personal satisfaction in old age. In effect, the activity theory argues that successful ageing depends not on disengagement but on more active engagement. People build their social identities based on lifelong statuses and roles. They establish their social networks and interest groups in the workplace. Therefore, disengagement not only means loss of roles and steady income but also loss of meaning and fulfilment in their lives. When retirement—or disengagement—does occur, the elderly people need new and multiple roles to substitute for the old roles.

Activity theory is based on the assumption that successful ageing is linked to substantial levels of mental, physical, and interpersonal activity. Many elderly persons find satisfaction and fulfilment in reading, writing, travelling, gardening, volunteering, and club activities. Some of them take up new jobs where their past experiences are helpful. Retired teachers or musicians may tutor children. Ex-servicemen work as private security guards. Many elders volunteer for various types of community service. Research has shown that older persons who continue an active life find more joy and fulfilment in their lives.

Activity theory is consistent with the experience of ageing in agrarian societies. It must be remembered that retirement is a relatively new social creation. In the traditional societies where most people worked as farmers and craftsmen, there was no retirement. People continued to work until they were incapacitated. Even then they were required to take care of the grandchildren and play active roles in community events. In the modern industrial economy, retirement has become part of life's expectations. There is even an emerging trend for people to choose early retirement in order to pursue other, often more productive or enjoyable activities. Grandparenting also has emerged as a significant lifestyle pattern for the elderly in most cultures, including the West. This phenomenon is also necessitated by the fact that more and more women have entered the labour force.

Social isolation is one of the major problems facing the elderly. Retirement has severed their connections to the work group. Physical problems limit their mobility. The death of a spouse or a loved one aggravates social tensions, resulting in anxiety, loneliness, and alienation. Although no reliable data have been compiled, abuse of the elderly seems to be on the increase. The abuse need not necessarily be physical, it can be verbal, emotional, and financial. Very often such abuses result from the financial and emotional stress of long-term caring. There is no doubt that the so-called 'sandwich generation' is under stress; they have to take care of their growing children and ageing parents at the same time.

The population of the elderly in India is estimated to be 7.6 crore. Projection studies indicate that the number of those aged sixty plus in India will increase to 100 million in 2013 and to 198 million in 2030. Eighty per cent of the elderly live in rural areas and 30 per cent of them are below poverty line. By the year 2016, 51 per cent of the elderly population would be women. In January 1999, the Government of India announced a National Policy for Older Persons which includes financial security, health care, and nutrition, housing, establishment of a welfare fund, provision of rebates, concessions and discounts, formation of self-help groups, strengthening of family and intergenerational relationships, and promotion of research and expertise in the field of ageing. The government has also launched 'An Integrated Program for Older Persons'. Under this scheme, financial assistance upto 90 per cent of the project cost is provided to NGOs for establishing and maintaining old-age homes, day-care centres, mobile medicare units, and to provide non-institutional services to older persons. The scheme has been made flexible so as to meet the diverse needs of older persons including reinforcement and strengthening of the family, awareness generation on issues pertaining to older persons, popularization of the concept of lifelong preparation for old age, and facilitating productive ageing.

Women as a Minority

Women may outnumber and outlive men, but in almost all societies they are victims of prejudice and discrimination. Let us begin with a sociological definition of some of the key concepts. *Sex* is simply a biological distinction between male and female. It is basically a difference in chromosome and its primary relevance is to reproduction. But the concept of *gender* is a cultural definition with its corresponding emphasis on attitudes and behaviour. In other words, gender is a cultural bag which determines that each sex must be socially and culturally different. The man is supposed to be masculine, aggressive, strong, and less emotional. Women are supposed to be feminine, smiling all the time, emotional, less assertive, and more focused on looks. Based on such distinct cultural definitions, every society expects men and women to perform different *gender roles*. Thus, traditionally, men were supposed to be breadwinners and women housekeepers. Women were excluded from several jobs and they became largely clerical workers, elementary school teachers, and nurses. But these are based on cultural definitions, not biological endowments. For example, based on her classic study of gender in three societies, Margaret Mead concluded that what one culture defines as masculine may be considered feminine in another. Based on his study of over two hundred pre-industrial societies, George Murdock also came to the conclusion that societies define only a few specific activities consistently as feminine or masculine.

Sexism is an ideology that exaggerates the differences between men and women and rationalizes the superiority of men. The sexist ideology has characterized women as inferior, less intelligent, more emotional, talkative, gentle, and obsessed with their appearance. Men are supposed to be aggressive, independent, unemotional, competitive, intelligent, and possess leadership skills. Now we know from this discussion that these traits are manufactured by culture. Although men have larger muscles and are capable of tougher physical jobs, women are known to endure longer at given tasks. Whatever the arguments about intelligence, women seem to do equally well or even better in many achievement tests. Our culture emphasizes gender differences from early socialization. Girls get to play with dolls, doll houses, and cooking utensils. Boys get cars, planes, balls, and wheels. Boys are taught to be brave and independent and encouraged to form extensive peer-group contacts. Girls are expected to spend more time in meal preparation, cleaning and care of siblings. In general, culture emphasizes the idea that a woman's place is in the home. Thus, from early childhood, women are taught to be passive, docile, and less assertive. Ironically, it is culture which turns around and attributes the same traits to them and declares them unsuitable for several male-dominated professions. Sexism is also at the root of several forms of sexual harassment against women such as 'eve teasing', rude stares, and hassling. On the whole, violence against women seems to be on the rise in many societies.

Sexism is a universal phenomenon. In the old China, women were expected to live by the traditional formula of 'santsung' or 'thrice-obeying' which expected women to comply with their father or elder brothers in their youth, their husbands in marriage, and their sons after their husband's death. Women had to be faithful to their husbands even after death while a man could have a wife and several concubines, and even visit brothels. Girls' names could not be included in the genealogical tree, and thus matrilineal relatives were considered distant kinship. Sounds familiar? These were almost exact stipulations in the Code of Manu. Betty Friedan, the author of *The Feminine Mystique,* argued that modern society defined women only in sexual relation to a man, as wife, mother or more commonly, as sex object.

Consider the case of women's 'double burden' in modern society. Most men now claim to support women's entry into the labour force, and frankly, most families need the double income. Yet, when it comes to housework, it remains largely the responsibility of women. Men are all too eager to share the double income but not the double burden associated with it.

Theoretical Perspectives

From a structural-functional perspective, Talcott Parsons explains gender differences as a complementary set of roles which men and women perform for the smooth functioning of society. Men work outside the home and earn a living; women stay at home and attend to housework and the children. This arrangement is functional for the society and the individuals. Moreover, through socialization society teaches the sexes their appropriate gender roles and prepares them for it, thus avoiding tension and conflicts. Both men and women internalize their gender roles and learn to conform to society's standards. There are also mechanisms of social control which enforce conformity to socially approved gender roles.

One can easily see why gender roles are complementary functional division of labour. But it is hard to explain why such division of labour must be sex-linked. The theory does not explain why some of the roles cannot be reversed. In other words, the 'principle of complementarity' will not be affected if women with business acumen and professional skills worked outside the home while men stayed home to attend to housework.

The conflict perspective in sociology argues that men as warriors and rulers were able to consolidate their power and subjugate women. Friedrich Engels wrote extensively on the subject. As societies moved from the hunting and gathering type to horticultural and later agrarian type, social inequality began to take root. Private property led to the accumulation of wealth. Men emerged as dominant individuals and began to control not only wealth but also power. They made sure property passed on to their sons. Upper class women were not expected to work but stay home and serve the men. Gradually women came to assume a passive and subservient role in both industrial and capitalist societies. They have become victims of exploitation. The thrust of the conflict perspective is that gender inequality is the result of economic inequality between men and women. Throughout history economic dominance by men also produced for them superior social positions. Therefore, Engels believed that women's freedom from subordination and exploitation will come only with the abolition of private property and other capitalist institutions.

It is true that women have been victims of discrimination in myriad forms. However, all forms of social injustice cannot be attributed to the conflict between men and women. Placing capitalism at the center of evil also belies the point. In fact most socialist societies were marked by greater gender inequality, especially at the healm of political affairs.

Women in India

On every index of welfare and development, Indian women are at the bottom, be it literacy, medical attention, nutrition, infant mortality, poverty, death rate, or wages. Several peculiar

Indian customs such as Sati, child marriage, dowry, ban on widow remarriage, absence of civil registration of marriages, female infanticide, and the institution of Devadasi made the position of women precarious and indefensible.

According to the 2001 census, women made up 48.2 per cent of India's population. The female population grew at a slower pace of 23.37 per cent during the decade of 1981–91. The sex ratio which was 972 females per 1,000 males in 1901 declined to 927 in 1991, and went up only slightly to 933 in 2001. Although the government was expecting it to rise, it fell even behind the 1981 level. Although the 2011 census shows a small improvement in the overall sex ratio in the country, from 933 females for every 1,000 males (in 2001) to 940.27, there is a steep fall in ratio for the 0–6 years age group, from 927.31 to 914.23. This is clearly a case of 'missing girls' at birth. In fact, the *World Development Report 2012* from the World Bank says that, after China, India has the largest number of 'missing girls' at birth, that is, the numbers that should have been born in keeping with the average world sex ratio at birth. According to the report, titled *Gender Equality and Development*, were it not for China and India, an additional 1.2 million girls would have been born in the world (one million in China alone). Because of the cultural preference for sons, more and more parents seem to be eager to discover the sex of the foetus and then resort to sex-selective abortions. India and China also account for the highest excess female mortality after birth, which means large number of girls and women die prematurely. In spite of the fact that more women get educated and employed, maternal mortality in India is almost six times the rate in Sri Lanka.

India is among the very few countries with an adverse sex ratio which is attributed to higher mortality among women in all age groups right from childhood through child-bearing ages, high maternal mortality, and female infanticide. The districts with the worst child sex ratio were all in Punjab and Haryana, two of India's wealthiest states. The worst of these ten was Fathegarh Sahib in Punjab with a child sex ratio of just 766. The best of the worst was Gurdaspur, also in Punjab, with 789. Some rural districts have juvenile sex ratio (below ten years of age) as high as 1,170 males for every 1,000 females which can only mean that one out of seven or eight female babies are killed. Even in Haryana, the second most economically advanced state in the nation, there is no relief from gender discrimination. The male–female ratio of 1,000 to 865 in 1991, which is already among the lowest in the country, is on a steady decline. While the ratio of males to females at birth is about 52:48, there is a sharp decline over the years. While the sex ratio of infants is 861 females to 1,000 males the ratio plummeted to 849 by age fourteen. The situation is not much different in several other states. Now every attempt is being made to restrict even nature's own sex selection process. There is widespread use of sex determination tests which invariably lead to female foeticide. The law regulating the sex detection process has simply sent the business underground. As Kalpana Sharma wrote in *The Hindu* magazine (29 August 2005):

Sex-detection and sex selective abortions are today spreading like an infectious disease, from the rich to the poor, from the upper castes to the Scheduled Castes and even to the Scheduled Tribes.... While in 1991, the child sex ratio for STs was 985 (against a national average of 945), in 2001 it had fallen to 973. And among SCs, the figures were 946 in 1991 and 938 in 2001.

According to Sharma,

surveys in Haryana and Punjab have revealed that some women genuinely believed that if their numbers decline, their value would increase because men will not find brides. Instead, men are buying brides from other states for as little as Rs 5,000 (in Haryana a buffalo costs Rs 40,000). These women are available to all the men in the family. Instead of being valued, women are now becoming targets of violence in districts with the lowest sex ratios.

According to the *Indian Human Development Report 2011*, half of Indian women suffer from anaemia, particularly those belonging to SCs, STs, and Muslims: 'The Scheduled Caste, Scheduled Tribe and Muslims are converging with the infant mortality rate (IMR) national average. The fall in infant mortality rate has been sharper in the case of the Scheduled Tribes as compared to the Scheduled Caste.' Despite having an impressive economic growth, Gujarat had high rates of child malnutrition, with 69.7 per cent kids up to 5 years being anaemic and 44.6 per cent suffering from malnutrition. According to United Nations Children's Fund (UNICEF) data (*The Hindu*, 6 March 2013), 56 per cent of the estimated 243 million adolescent girls (15–19 years) in India are anaemic; three out of five women in the age group 20–49 were married as adolescents. Despite the ban on child marriage, 29 per cent of adolescent girls in urban areas and 56 per cent in rural areas are married before they turn eighteen. This means millions of girls, who are underweight and anaemic, become wives and mothers before their bodies are ready to bear children. They are part of the depressing statistics of maternal deaths in India.

Despite rapid economic growth, India has one-third of the world's undernourished children and one of the highest rates of child undernutrition in the world. India is expected to reach its Millennium Development Goals nutrition indicator by 2043; China has already reached it. Brazil is expected to reach the goal by 2015. In fact, India ranks behind Sri Lanka and Bangladesh. Why? An evaluation of targeted public distribution system by the Planning Commission showed that the majority of subsidized food does not reach the intended recipients. And Indian public health system spends less than 1 per cent of GDP; China spends nearly 6 per cent.

The maternal mortality rate in India is still very high accounting for over 1 per cent of the total reported deaths every year. Life expectancy is 67.95 for females as against 65.77 for males, a mere 2.18 difference which is one of the lowest in the world. Literacy rate is 82.14 for males and 65.46 for females, a difference of about 17 per cent, one of the highest in the world. Every year about 15 million girls are born in India but about 25 per cent of them do not see their fifteenth birthday. Up to the age of thirty-five years more females than males die at every age level. Girls begin to participate in domestic work earlier than boys and have far more responsibilities such as collecting firewood, fetching drinking water, taking care of younger siblings, gathering fodder, doing farm work, food processing, and poultry keeping. By the age of ten a girl works at least ten hours a day, and there is, of course, no opportunity for schooling.

The gender bias in India is so entrenched in the country's cultural heritage that right from conception and birth to womanhood and death, the female suffers discrimination at all levels. In a patriarchal society that idolizes sons, a female child is usually considered a burden and given less of the family's affection and resources; she is socialized to accept an inferior and subservient status—less opportunity, less authority, less property, and less attention. Girls are weaned very early but the boys are breast-fed much longer. Boys are fed first and girls often last. Girls are seldom taken to doctors but boys receive better medical care. Boys are supposed to grow up into economic assets but girls and women perform more difficult and back-breaking jobs. It has been estimated that a girl works ten hours a day on an average for 315 days a year, and by the time she ceases to be a child she would have contributed to the family about Rs 40,000 worth of labour; yet she is considered a liability and drain on family resources. In north India a common prayer is: 'A son for us and daughters for others'. In the south the suffix for a boy is *chiranjeevi* (one who lives long), but for a girl it is *sowbhagyavathi* (lucky), meaning she is lucky if her husband lives long. According to Manu, the great lawgiver, a woman must always be dependent on man: on her father during the early years, on her husband during married life, and on her son in the evening of her life. Even if he is 'destitute of virtue, or seeking pleasure elsewhere or devoid of good qualities, yet a husband must be constantly worshipped by a faithful wife.' This is in a country where women represent the most important and powerful goddesses who are worshipped by all men: Saraswathy, Lakshmi, Sakthi, Annapoorna, and Kali. In spite of the fact that independent India has passed several constitutional and legal safeguards to protect the interests of women, many of these are continually transgressed by the concentric circles of powerful Indian patriarchy. Women continue to be victims of violence in the family. They continue to suffer discrimination in marriage; they have almost no say in the selection of their husbands. They have almost no freedom of reproductive choice. They are almost always discriminated against in the case of divorce proceedings and seldom granted custody of their children. They are denied equal opportunity in education and seldom receive equal pay for equal work. Afraid of ostracism, the woman usually acquiesces in her oppression.

Battering of women has always been a regular feature of Indian society. Alcohol-related crimes against women are widespread in the villages. In the urban areas, extra-marital affairs, bigamy, alcohol, gambling, and dowry play a role in domestic violence. When it comes to gender-related crimes even teenage girls are not spared. A study of girls and women who died of burns in Greater Bombay showed that 61.3 per cent were fifteen to nineteen years of age and unmarried (*The Hindu*, October 1997). In spite of the ban on dowry, marriages are seldom solemnized without a dowry which is somehow never enough. The husband and his family constantly demand more money, jewellery, and household appliances, or threaten to abandon the bride. Married women who are thrown out of their husbands' homes bring shame to their families and community. Therefore, the woman and her parents are constantly harassed, and when the extortion fails to extract more from the poor family, the woman is beaten, burnt, or even killed. Thousands of such deaths occur every year and they are always reported as accidents and seldom investigated. But the sad truth is that dowry deaths are often perpetrated by educated and 'cultured' Indians, not by the illiterate poor in the villages.

Crime against women is so widespread that today only high profile cases make news. There are many cases where women have been stripped naked, paraded through village streets, and then gangraped. Custodial rape and immoral traffic in women are two of the major sex crimes in the country. The institution of Devadasi and the custom of *chooth* (untouchability) or opting out of a childhood engagement are responsible for trapping many women into prostitution. In the absence of mandatory marriage registration, girls are trapped into false marriages and forced into prostitution. Child labour and bonded labour continue to exploit and impoverish girls and women by the millions. In Rajasthan, on the auspicious day of Akhsaya Teej, mass marriages of children to old men are performed in broad daylight, and little girls are sent off to be raped by old men before they are women. Recently, a woman social worker who dared to protest the marriage of a one-year-old baby was assaulted and gangraped by hired men. According to International Planned Parenthood Federation, almost 75 per cent of the marriages in India involve minors.

There are literally hundreds of programmes launched by the government for the advancement of women. They include welfare and support services, employment and training, socio-economic programmes, Swayamsidha, Swashakti Project, Balika Samridhi Yojana, Swadhar, Plan of Action to Combat Sexual Exploitation of Women, Rashtriya Mahila Kosh, Central Social Welfare Board, and National Commission for Women. The list of programmes initiated by the government are too numerous to be listed here. Yet after more than fifty years of development, female work participation is less than 25 per cent. Here again, women made up 90 per cent of the total marginal workforce, and the total employment of women in the organized sector was under 5 per cent. And it goes without saying that in the informal sector working conditions are oppressive and exploitative with long hours of hard labour, low wages, and no benefits such as holidays, maternity leave, or medical insurance. The situation is not much different when it comes to elected representatives. During 1962–7, Parliament had 6 per cent women representatives. The percentage declined to 3.5 in 1977 and increased only to 7 per cent in 1966. In other words, it took thirty years to gain a 1 per cent increase in women's participation in the national legislatures. On the other hand, in South Africa women make up 30 per cent of the National Assembly and hold several key portfolios in the cabinet, not just welfare-oriented portfolios. The situation is equally pathetic when it comes to senior administrative appointments in India. Women make up less than 10 per cent of the Indian Administrative Service and about 11 per cent of the Indian Foreign Service. And in the private sector they make up less than 2 per cent of the executive cadre.

It has been clearly documented that investing in women rather than men leads to proportionately greater development. A mother's education has a stronger impact on the health of her child than the father's. And, income controlled by women is more likely to be spent on household needs than income controlled by men. Women bear the brunt of agricultural operations and grow at least 50 per cent the world's food in developing countries and over 80 per cent in some African countries. Yet the gender gap remains substantial in many countries and women's productivity levels remain low because of their lack of access to education and other opportunities. Social scientists generally agree that education and empowerment of women alone can achieve social justice, reduce poverty, improve the lot of children, and limit population growth.

Dalits and Other Backward Classes

In the chapter on social stratification (Chapter 9) we have already discussed the caste system, untouchability, and other forms of caste-based discrimination, and various social and legislative measures designed to advance the welfare of the backward castes. In this section we will have a brief overview of the status of these minorities.

Dalits or Scheduled Castes (SCs) constitute a little over 15 per cent of the population, Scheduled Tribes (STs) make up 8 per cent, and the Other Backward Classes (OBCs) account for 52 per cent. Thus, about 75 per cent of the Indian population is officially classified as backward and regarded as victims of centuries of discrimination.

The Untouchability (offences) Act, 1955, was comprehensively amended and renamed as the Protection of Civil Rights Act which came into force in 1976. The Scheduled Castes (SCs) and Scheduled Tribes (STs) (Prevention of Atrocities) Act came into being in 1990. These measures prescribe strict punishments and provide relief and rehabilitation. But laws can do only so much. Even today thousands of temples and community wells are off limits to Dalits. In several states, the landless and impoverished SCs remain as vassals in a semi-feudal system. Education, choice of occupation, and substantial improvement in economic status are three important factors in the socio-economic development of the backward castes. Therefore, both central and state governments have a number of special schemes such as coaching, pre-examination training, book banks, scholarships, and hostels specifically for the benefit of all backward castes. Reservation in union government services is a big part of the programme intended to offset the ill-effects of centuries of discrimination. The quantum of reservation to SCs, STs, and OBCs in direct recruitment on all-India basis by open competition is 15 per cent, 7.5 per cent, and 27 per cent respectively. In direct recruitment on all-India basis other than by open competition, the reservation is 16.66 per cent for SCs, 7.5 per cent for STs, and 25.84 per cent for OBCs. In case of promotion, percentage of reservation for SCs and STs is 15 and 7.5 respectively; there is no reservation for OBCs in case of promotion. In certain limited cases, rules also provide for relaxation of upper-age limit and exemption from payment of application fees. It must, however, be pointed out that in spite of over forty years of reservation, 75 per cent of backward castes and tribes make up only less than 10 per cent of top administrative posts in the country. Part of the problem is the lack of enough qualified candidates among the backward sections of the population. That points to lack of education which, in turn, is the result of an entrenched semi-feudal system in the villages.

Satish Deshpande (2003: 114–5) did a critical analysis of National Sample Survey data based on monthly per capita consumption expenditure and his findings are summarized as follows.

In rural India, more than half of the ST population lives below the poverty line. This proportion is only slightly less for the SCs at about 43 per cent, and lesser still for the OBCs at about 34 per cent. However, the Hindu upper castes (HUCs) are markedly different, with only 17 per cent below the poverty line. In urban India, these inequalities are even more stark. Only about 5 per cent of the HUCs are below the poverty line, while the figures are 43 per cent for both STs and SCs and 36 per cent for the OBCs. The data further show that the HUCs constitute almost 60 per cent of the non-poor urban class, whereas the urban OBCs do not resemble their rural counterparts and are much closer to the STs and SCs in profile. In fact, urban OBCs account for more than one-third of the urban below the poverty line population. The figures also show another sobering fact: in the year 2000, STs, SCs, OBCs, and Muslims together accounted for 91 per cent of the urban below the poverty line population and 88 per cent of the rural below the poverty line population. Clearly, despite decades of reservation and talks of social justice and empowerment, the dimensions of systemic inequality have not changed much.

Tribes in India

The tribal population in India has a rich and colourful history. There are approximately 500 different tribes who constitute about 8 per cent of the population of India. The most numerous tribes are Bodo, Gond, Hmar, Munda, Oran, Gaddi, Khasis, Dimasa, Chenchu, and Bhil. The Bhils mainly inhabit central and western India and are found primarily in Gujarat, Maharashtra, Madhya Pradesh, and Rajasthan. The Bhils, noted for their bravery, were often part of the royal armies during the medieval and British periods. The Gonds are concentrated in Madhya Pradesh, eastern Maharashtra, Chhattisgarh, and northen Andhra Pradesh. They are primarily agriculturalists and often practice shifting cultivation. Because of the thick forest cover, north-eastern part of India has a large tribal population. Nagaland, Manipur, Assam, and Arunachal Pradesh have tribes like Nagas, Bodos, Mizos, and Santhals. While Orans are one of the most progressive tribes in India, the Chenchus still depend largely on hunting. It is difficult to classify Indian tribes in terms of race, religion, ethnicity, or language alone. The traditional occupation or the primary means by which a particular tribe makes a living is one way of classifying them. Accordingly, we have the following categories:

1. *Hunters, fishermen and gatherers.* The original inhabitants of the Andaman Islands depended almost entirely on hunting, fishing, and gathering.
2. *Shifting cultivators.* In the hilly regions of the North-east, Madhya Pradesh, and Orissa, numerous tribes followed slash-and-burn agriculture. The practice is known as *jhum* in Assam and other states in the North-east, *podu* in Orissa and *penda* in Madhya Pradesh.
3. *Cultivators and artisans.* Many tribes all over north India practise the same kind of occupations as their neighbours in the plains.
4. *Nomadic groups.* They consist of nomads who depend on hunting in the forests and artisans who settle down in a village for a few weeks and move on to other areas.

In recent years these traditional occupations have undergone considerable changes which have been rather pronounced in the case of shifting cultivators and nomads.

According to tribal custom in most cases, land belonged to the lineage but the owner can extend the use of the land to others. There were no legal documents to establish ownership; therefore, over the years, they lost much of their land to moneylenders, rich farmers, and powerful communities. The tribal population is also adversely affected by environmental degradation because they depend on biomass-based resources for food, fuel, fodder, water, and medicinal needs. Mining operations as well as tea and coffee plantations displaced thousands of tribes from their ancestral land. Nearly 50 per cent of the people displaced by government projects such as mills, mines, and dams are tribals. Since they have no title deeds or records of having paid land revenue, their lands were seized by powerful landlords. Even when compensation was given, it was in the form of cash which was spent within a short time, and there were few serious attempts to relocate or rehabilitate them. Now displaced from their traditional homes by government projects and unscrupulous landlords, the tribals have become a large pool of unemployed migrant labourers and are easily trapped into slavery as bonded labourers.

The tribals follow religious traditions and social customs some of which are markedly different from those of mainstream Indians. Although some tribes have caste groups based on arts and crafts most of the caste-based discriminations are absent. Indeed, many of the social evils associated with the caste system find no place among the tribes. Many tribes have a bride price, a certain amount that must be paid to the family of the girl to compensate for the loss of an earning member. But the payment can be in the form of free labour on the part of the groom for the bride's family. Marriage is usually forbidden within a clan but outside the clan, boys and girls may choose their own partners. Separation, divorce, and remarriage are common. Polygamy and polygyny also exist among some tribes. Young men and women sing and dance together and in some tribes, may even engage in pre-marital sexual relations. Thus, gender bias and restrictions on social intercourse are less pronounced among the tribes than among the upper castes.

Animistic beliefs are at the centre of all tribal religions. The whole world is peopled by spirits and certain objects such as some trees or oddly shaped rocks are particularly significant. In the forest, some trees may never be touched or cut because they represent the primal grove. If someone falls ill, the general belief is that some relationship to the spirit world has been violated; there are prescribed ceremonies and rituals to restore order. Even the several tribes who converted to Christianity generations ago, still follow most of their animistic traditions.

Adivasis all over India suffer from economic deprivation, social discrimination, illiteracy, exploitation, and rampant alcoholism. In a recent study by Rani Bang *et al.* (2011), there is a graphic description of the plight of Gadchiroli women in the backward tribal districts of Madhya Pradesh. The study points out that 92 per cent of women in the region had no access to treatment for gynaecological disorders. Extremely low literacy rates make it impossible for them to look for whatever social services are available. The all-India literacy rate of the tribal population is about 30 per cent, just over half of the national average. It is no wonder that inspite of 7.5 per cent reservation, tribals are not represented in the services. There are numerous special schemes for the development of the tribal population. They include Integrated Tribal Development Projects, schemes for 'primitive' tribal groups, ashram schools, hostels, vocational training, Tribal Cooperative Marketing Federation, village grain banks and educational scholarships. But without education and economic independence, the integration of the tribals into the mainstream will remain a distant dream.

Minority by Sexual Orientation

In every country there is a small minority of people who are discriminated against because of their sexual orientation. Lesbian, gay, bisexual, and transgender (LGBT) people follow a different lifestyle. Although several countries have decriminalized their sexual behaviour, these people are still discriminated against by the majority. In July 2009, the Delhi High Court decriminalized homosexual intercourse between consenting adults. Section 377 of the Indian Penal Code was adjudged to violate the fundamental right to life and liberty and the right to equality as guaranteed by the Indian Constitution. But the decision was overturned by the apex court. The exact size of the LGBT minority in India is not known.

Study Questions

- Define and distinguish between racial, ethnic, and minority groups.
- Define and distinguish between prejudice and discrimination.
- Discuss various patterns of majority–minority relations and possible minority responses.
- Review the various theoretical perspectives on ageing. Examine the status of senior citizens in India.
- Critically examine the concept of women as a minority.
- Write an essay on the status of women in India
- Review the situation of Dalits and OBCs in terms of social justice, empowerment, and legislation.
- Write an essay on tribes in India.
- Define the following concepts: race, ethnicity, minority, prejudice, discrimination, cultural pluralism, assimilation, ageism, and sexism.

References

Abraham, M. Francis, *The Agony of India,* Madras: East West Books, 1998.

Bang, Rani, Sunanda Khorgade, and Rupa Chinai, *Putting Women First: Wmen and Health in a Rural Community,* Kolkata: Stree, 2011.

Cumming, Elaine and William E. Henry, *Growing Old: The Process of Disengagement,* New York: Basic Books, 1961.

Deshpande, Satish, *Contemporary India: A sociological View,* New Delhi: Viking, 2003.

Friedan, Betty, *The Feminine Mystique,* New York: W.W. Norton, 1963.

Jain, Devaki (ed.), *Indian Women,* New Delhi: Publications Division, 1975.

PART IV

SOCIAL INSTITUTIONS

11

The Family

If there is a universal social institution it is the family. Every society needs some form of social arrangement to regulate sexual relations and to provide for child rearing and socialization. Family has survived through the ages because it provides a number of essential social functions. Yet there are wide variations in the structure and pattern of family.

Sociologically speaking, a *family* is a social group of two or more people who live together and are related by marriage, blood, or adoption. In this sense, a family is made up of not only husband and wife, but also two brothers living together or a woman and her adopted son. A *kinship* group is a network of families related by blood, marriage, or adoption. The culture determines which family relationships are considered significant. Imperial China followed the *patrilineal system* in which members trace their kinship through the father's line of descent. In this system, generations are tied together into a kinship through the male members of a family. While this is the more common pattern in India, among the Nairs of Kerala the *matrilineal system* was in vogue. Here, the kinship system consisted of families related through maternal line of descent. In the United States and much of the West, the *bilateral system* prevails. Here an individual is considered to be equally related to both his father's and mother's relatives; descent is traced through both males and females. A *clan* is a unilateral kin group, based on either matrilineal or patrilineal descent whose members believe that they are descendants of a common ancestor. It is immaterial whether they share a common biological ancestor or not; what is important is that the members believe they do. Members of a clan are expected to marry outside the clan.

A *household* is different from a family. According to the census, a household is made up of one or more people who live in the same dwelling unit which may be a house, an apartment, or a room. A household includes not only family members but also persons who are not related to one another, if they share the same dwelling unit. Thus a person living alone or a group of employees, whether related or unrelated, living under the same roof constitute a household. A family is always a household but every household is not necessarily a family.

TYPES OF FAMILIES

There are different types of families. The *nuclear family* consists of parents and their biological or adopted children. They are two-generation families. The *extended family* is a social group that consists of parents, children, and other members who are related by blood or marriage. Other members usually include parents' siblings and their families. In traditional agrarian societies extended families were the norm. Since all members were expected to work on the family farm, adult sons continued to live in their parents' household with their wives and children. Extended families sometimes also included unmarried brothers or sisters of parents. Extended families performed several significant functions in traditional society. Of course, they supplied the much needed labour. But they were also a kind of mutual aid and insurance system. Extended families took care of their less fortunate family members, provided emotional support, and pooled resources to support members who pursued higher education or new business ventures.

Families are also divided into *conjugal* and *consanguine families*. A conjugal family is based on marriage, rather than blood relationships. Nuclear families made up of parents and children are all conjugal families. In the consanguine family the emphasis is on blood relationships, rather than marital relations. In the past, the consanguine family pattern prevailed among the Nairs of Kerala. Married women did not leave their home but continued to live in their own home with their brothers. Their husbands were simply 'visitors' to the household. The children lived with their mother and were raised by her brother whose own children were raised in another household where his wife lived with her brother. This custom is no longer practised. Yet it is worth noting that the consanguine family normally formed an extended family, usually with two or three generations living together.

Sociologists use the term *family of orientation* to refer to the family in which you are a child because it is the family that raises and socializes you. There is also the *family of procreation*, the family in which you are a parent.

Families may be classified on the basis of norms pertaining to place of residence and relations of authority.

In pre-industrial societies when a son married, he brought his wife home to his father's residence. Except in a limited number of communities which had consanguine families, the bride was expected to go with her husband to his family home or community. This pattern where a married couple lives with or near the husband's family is known as the *patrilocal system*. On the other hand, a *matrilocal system* expects the couple to live with or near the wife's family.

In modern industrial societies where a couple's livelihood no longer depends on ancestral property, the newly-weds take up an independent residence. Thus *neolocal residence* occurs when the married couple lives apart from either parent's family or community. In today's society where husband, wife, or both work away from home neolocal families are the norm.

In most societies throughout history male members exercised authority and control. Even in the matrilineal system, it was the wife/mother's uncle who made crucial decisions. A *patriarchal family* is the form of family in which the father, or the eldest male member, is the formal head and source of authority. A *matriarchal family* is one in which the mother is the formal head and dominant power in the family. It is not very clear if a truly matriarchal system has existed anywhere in the world. There have been matrilocal, consanguine, and matrilineal families in which the wife mother or eldest female member had considerable power and influence. However, such families are more likely to be *matricentric* in which the mother is the central figure in the life of the children and the position of the father tends to be peripheral. In the old consanguine system among the Nairs, the husband did not live with his wife and children, and therefore, the mother exercised considerable power and influence. Yet her elder brother with whom she stayed had real authority.

Marriage Patterns

Marriage is defined as sexual access between males and females, regulated and legitimized by society. The marriage ceremony is an important cultural institution in every society that signifies the union between a man and a woman and grants them socially-approved status as husband and wife. Every society has norms about who has sexual relationships with whom. For example, the *incest taboo* that prohibits sexual relationships between persons believed to be closely related, is a universal cultural standard. In some societies, marriage between cross cousins is preferred but the union between parallel cousins is strictly prohibited. Marriage within the clan is usually considered incest among several communities in India.

Norms usually specify who are desirable or undesirable as partners in marriage. *Endogamy* is a social custom that encourages people to marry within a social group such as caste, religion, or linguistic group. *Exogamy* requires people to marry outside of the specified social group. In traditional India people married within the caste. In the past inter-caste marriage was forbidden in India just as inter-racial marriage was forbidden in America and South Africa. Many Hindu communities are required to marry outside their clan or gotra and some even outside their village. In most societies people tend to marry those from the same socio-economic background or with similar characteristics. The term *homogamy* refers to marriage of persons with similar characteristics. It need not necessarily be a matter of law. Most marriages take place within the same caste, religion, class, ethnicity, race, or some other culturally defined status group. There is also a system of *preferential marriage* which encourages or even requires people to marry someone in a specified blood line. Among South Indian Brahmins, a man is encouraged to marry his sister's daughter. In some other communities a man is supposed to marry his maternal uncle's daughter. Some of these customs are no longer very strong but each community still defines the rules.

There are two other types of marriage: *levirate* and *sororate*. The former is a custom in which a widow marries one of her husband's brothers. The levirate may take a number of forms and obligations on the part of the brother. The ancient Hebrews and Greeks and a few communities in India had a type of levirate. The sororate involves a widower marrying a sister, usually a younger sister, of his deceased wife. Here again, in some cultures, it is only an expectation while in others it may be a requirement.

Monogamy, the common form of marriage in modern industrial societies, involves one husband and one wife. *Polygamy* involves a plurality of mates, and takes two different forms: *polygyny* and *polyandry*. Polygyny consists of one husband and several wives. Islam permits upto four wives; in most of Africa, Imperial China, and India polygyny was in practice. However, most marriages were monogamous because very few could afford to support several wives and many children. Polyandry is a form of marriage in which a woman has two or more husbands. Some tribes in the Himalayas and the Todas of Nilgiri Hills practised polyandry. In some cases the eldest brother formally contracted the marriage and all brothers shared the same woman. In other cases the men were not related. When a child is born, paternity is established by means of a social ceremony. In most societies today polygamy is against the law. But through the ages, most societies permitted more than one mate, although in reality most marriages were monogamous.

Functions of the Family

From the fact that family is a universal social institution it is clear that it has very important social functions.

1. *Procreation*. Every society needs to replace its members. Although reproduction can take place outside the marital union, it is only the family that can effectively nurture and socialize the human young to meet the needs of society.
2. *Sexual regulation*. No society can allow unrestricted promiscuity. First, every society has to ensure that statuses and roles are defined so that individuals can function effectively in assigned social positions. Second, by specifying that individuals marry within or outside certain social groups, society is establishing networks of relationships and forging useful alliances.
3. *Economic support*. In the pre-industrial society, the family was the unit of production and consumption. Today as individuals pursue independent economic activities outside the home, the family may no longer be a significant unit of production. But the family is still responsible for maintenance of the human young, education, training and material support. In India, the family's support for children does not end when they turn eighteeen; in the absence of productive employment many adults continue to depend on their parents.
4. *Social placement*. Every individual is recognized as the member of a family and thus has an inherited status. Children inherit not only the family name and material assets but also a social standing. In fact, birth into a family determines a person's caste, class, religion, language, and clan.
5. *Socialization*. The family is the most important and effective agent of socialization. The human young is dependent on his or her parents for a long time. The child also spends the most formative years of his or her life in the family. The institution of family is responsible for initiating the child into the social circles, religious groups, language, and caste. Thus the child gets socialized into the group's values, beliefs, standards, and practices.

6. *Emotional security.* This is one of the most important functions of the family. Food and shelter can be provided by other institutions such as the orphanage. Studies have shown that children who grow up in loving families tend to become mentally and physically healthier than those brought up in institutions.

Many of these functions continue to be performed in large measure by the Indian family. But some of the functions such as education, apprenticeship for economic activities, training, recreation, and religion have been taken over by schools, religious organizations, and other community clubs.

THE FUTURE OF MARRIAGE AND FAMILY

In spite of all the talk about the crisis of family and loss of family values in the mass media, many social scientists believe that there is a regeneration of the family. Riley and Riley (1993) talk about an 'expanded kinship structure' which is extended in generations and in duration. These flexible types of kinship structures offer a 'latent matrix' of kin connections. Riley and Riley (1993: 163–74) mention four features of this new family which are as follows:

First, numerous social and cultural changes—especially cohort increases in longevity—are yielding a large and complex network of kin relationships. Second, these many relationships are flexible…. Increasingly matters of choice rather than obligation. A plethora of options is potentially at hand. Third, these relationships are not constrained by age or generation; people of any age, within or across generations, may opt to support, love, or confide in one another. Fourth, many of these kinship bonds remain latent until called upon. They form a safety net of significant connections to choose from in case of need.' The 'latent matrix' loses 'the sharp boundaries set by generation or age or geographical proximity…. The boundaries of the family network have been widened to encompass many diverse relationships, including several degrees of stepkin and in-laws… and other relatives.

Similarly, Rossi and Rossi (1990) argue that a nuclear family is a lifelong and multigenerational event. It is a network of two sorts of relationships of central importance in people's lives: with their parents, lasting until their parent's death, and with their own children, usually extending through their own lifetime. Therefore, sociologists should not look at the small nuclear family as a world in itself; rather, they must see it as a latent matrix or multigenerational network. The new expanded family is not characterized by living together; it may be relatively independent and self-sufficient but the new family endures throughout adulthood and maintains core relationships with extended network. Logan and Spitze (Coltrane 2004: 451–7) found that ties between the middle and older generations are strong and durable under conditions of demographic change.

Their analyses are remarkable for the apparent resilience of parent–child ties compared to other parts of people's social networks. Whether measured as contact, visiting, help given, or help received, these family ties are at the very core of people's networks outside the home. And the most traditional of them—family neighbors, that is, parents or children living within the same neighborhood—retain a special weight in social relationships.

Thus, sociologists are now more inclined than ever before to study family issues in the context of people's whole life histories, from childhood to retirement and widowhood, rather than in terms of shift from extended families to nuclear families. The latent matrix of expanded kinship has always been at the centre of family relationships in India. Even when the influence of the traditional joint family system declined, the network of expanded latent matrix continued to dominate family ties in India.

Marriage and Family in India

A discussion of marriage and family patterns in India involves two risks. First, there is the tendency to generalize, and in the case of Indian society generalization is disastrous. Patterns of marriage, family, and kinship, as well as customs and practices vary from caste to caste and region to region. The same caste and religious community may follow very different practices in two different geographic regions. Second, the whole complex of ideas that is associated with Hinduism in the popular mind is, in fact, found only among the high castes. Not only child marriage and ban on divorce and widow remarriage but also many other customs generally thought to be part of Hindu social organization were in reality found only among a few of the upper castes. In view of these two difficulties, it is hard to discuss patterns of family and mar-riage in India unless we begin to discuss the customs and practices of every caste and religious group in India, which, indeed, is an impossible task. Therefore, we will only review some of the salient features in terms of some general concepts in the sociology of the family.

Marriage is considered to be a sacrament and a duty among all Hindus. But it becomes a sacred religious obligation for the twice-born castes because they must have a son to perform many of the religious rituals. The lower castes may not attach much religious significance to marriage which, for them, is a practical necessity to have sons to assist with work in the field and to take care of the parents in their old age. For Christians, marriage is a sacrament and cannot be dissolved. For Muslims, marriage is a contract and can be annulled very easily. Legislation in India now provides for divorce among all caste and religious groups. But there is considerable social stigma attached to divorce among some Christian and Hindu communities, especially among the upper castes. A vast majority of women, except for a few educated and independent professionals, find it difficult to break away from tradition and to destroy the only emotional, social, and economic support they have.

Most forms of marriage and family existed in some castes or communities somewhere in India. Many practices have been discontinued but others survive. History and legend are replete with examples of *swayamvara* and *Gandharva* marriages. Before registration was made mandatory, a couple could go to a temple, exchange garlands, and declare themselves married. Marriage to multiple spouses, to some blood relatives, and to in-laws upon death of a spouse all existed. Some communities even had an established tradition of kidnapping and forcibly marrying a girl or a boy. Some of these customs have undergone changes.

Preferred mate selection has played a very important role in Indian society. Marriage among certain relatives is prohibited but among others it is encouraged and even required. In most cases cross-cousin marriages are permitted; parallel-cousin marriages are prohibited except among certain Muslim communities. Among certain linguistic groups in south India marriages with cross cousins and cross nieces are preferred. Several south Indian castes including the Nairs of Kerala, Telugu Komatis, and Tamil and Telugu Brahmins, marriage with the maternal uncle's daughter is encouraged, and sometimes required. However, marriage with the mother's sister's daughter is taboo. In every case, where union between relatives was encouraged it was within the context of marriage alliance between lineages and it strengthened kinship bonds.

Polygyny and polyandry existed in India through the ages. Until the Hindu Marriages Act of 1955 came into force, every Hindu was theoretically free to have a plurality of mates. But in practice very few people practised polygamy. If a wife was barren or unable to give birth to a son, a second wife would be taken. Even then, among the twice-born castes, monogamy was considered the ideal. A Muslim is permitted to take upto four wives—provided all are treated as equal—but again in practice very few Muslims took more than one wife. Among the Hindu castes which practised polygyny, the first wife had higher status. In some communities in south India, a great deal of emphasis was placed on the first marriage which must be from within the same caste; however, subsequent wives and concubines could be taken from lower castes.

Polyandry was even less common. The Todas and Kotas of the Nilgiris, the Khasa of Jaunsar Bawar, and a few other north Indian castes practised polyandry. The Todas customarily practised female infanticide and there was a shortage of women. With the abolition of female infanticide, the Todas began to practice both polyandry and polygyny. Fraternal polyandry, or the custom of blood brothers sharing the same wife, was the common practice. The disparate system which involved unrelated men sharing the same wife also existed.

Leviratic alliances have always occurred among certain castes of Haryana, Uttar Pradesh, and Karnataka. Here the custom requires a man to marry the widow of a brother. Usually the widow is supposed to marry the younger brother, not the elder brother. The custom was known as *chadar dalna*, literally speaking 'to cover with a sheet'. The Jats of Uttar Pradesh, a landed caste, found the custom functional in that they could keep the land undivided within the family. But the custom often meant that the woman had to marry a man much younger than herself. There were reports in the 1970s that the widows of *jawans* in the war with Pakistan were forced to stay with their in-laws till their husbands' brothers grew up to a marriageable age. Sororatic alliances also occur among several castes, especially in south India.

A widower can remarry in all groups but that is not true of a widow. Widow remarriage is common among Christians, Muslims, Parsis, Jains, and most lower castes. Among several twice-born castes there is a ban on widow remarriage and in some cases the widows are supposed to shave their heads, shun jewellery and wear white. Some of these practices were designed to make women unattractive as possible mates. The Hindu Widows Remarriage Act, 1856, legalized the remarriage of all Hindus regardless of caste.

Endogamy and exogamy take some unique social forms in India. There are well-established rules which prescribe as well as proscribe alliances. Endogamy requires a man to marry within his subcaste but sometimes the endogamous unit extends to a kin-cluster. Whether we call them *jatis* or not, endogamous groups also exist among Christians, Muslims, Sikhs, and Jains. Rules of exogamy often complement endogamous rules. In north India the whole village is an exogamous unit, especially for the high castes, and they must choose their mates outside the village. In south India there is no such ban; indeed, there is some preference for marrying members of the same village.

Hypergamy is a significant custom among several castes. Traditionally, a man from a higher status group takes a bride from a lower status group. But a woman is not permitted to marry a man from a lower status group which will bring 'shame' to the whole community. Hypergamy has several important social consequences. Lower-status parents are eager to marry their daughters off to a higher-caste man. Such an alliance is supposed to bring prestige as well as clout among their sections. The Kulin hypergamy was well known. The Kulin Brahmins of Bengal were in such demand as grooms for non-Kulin Brahmin girls that a Kulin Brahmin could extract exorbitant dowry and marry several girls spread over several villages. Yet they had no obligation whatsoever to their wives or children who might never see them after the wedding night. The Kulin hypergamy has disappeared but the search for higher social status continues among other castes. However, the social advantage comes with a heavy price. The parents have to come up with a huge dowry and expensive gifts to persuade the upper-status boy to marry their daughter. This is why among the lower rungs of the Rajputs and Jats, dowry played such a vital role. But even after the payment of a huge dowry, the girl will be constantly reminded of her 'lower' status and the 'small' dowry and forced to extract more gifts from her parents. Another consequence of hypergamy was that the higher group was often left with a surplus of girls. Many of their women were forced to remain unmarried. One suspects that high rates of female suicide and female infanticide might be associated with hypergamy.

The custom of hypergamy also imposed different sexual standards for men and women. Men could marry women of lower ritual status but women could not. Since it was assumed that the women marrying below their ritual status could pollute the whole group, it was necessary to protect their sexuality early on. Thus, pre-puberty marriage became an established custom among several castes. Where pre-puberty marriage was not possible, there was even the practice of a 'mock marriage' whereby women were symbolically married to a ritually correct object. The system also allowed upper-caste men to have unrestricted sexual access to women of lower castes. The institution of devadasi and the 'right of first night' which permitted upper-caste men to have sex with low-caste women on the night before their wedding are examples. The ritual of the bride being symbolically deflowered by a Brahmin was part of the marriage ceremony of several non-Brahmin castes.

A few other important features of the Indian marriage are: the institution of marriage brokers, horoscope, dowry system, elaborate ritualistic ceremonies among high castes, and wedding extravaganzas. The barber acts as a matchmaker for non-Brahmin castes in several parts of India. There are also professional matchmakers in several communities. Traditionally, kin groups of the boy and the girl jointly make the decision based on the families' ritual and economic status; the boy and the girl may not have any say in the matter, although this latter aspect is changing. Horoscopes are reviewed to make sure they match and priests are consulted to fix the auspicious day and time for the marriage. The amount of dowry is negotiated and mutually agreed to by the kin groups. Large sums of money, gifts of jewellery, furniture, vessels, appliances, and clothes are offered as part of the dowry. The amount of dowry depends not only on the socio-economic status of the groom but also his education and job. However, it must be noted here that the dowry system is not universal, and some castes do pay a bride price. Whether the parents of the groom or the bride bear the expense of the wedding also depends on the particular caste. Among the Christians of Kerala, the parents of the groom usually pay for the wedding, but for most Hindu castes it is the responsibility of the bride's family. The extent of ritualistic ceremonies also varies with each caste. A traditional Brahmin wedding may involve ceremonies for several days but among certain Kerala tribes the ceremony is nothing more than an exchange of new clothes in the presence of both families. The wedding extravaganza is another spectacle. Vast sums of money are spent, especially by the rich and powerful, to celebrate the wedding with elaborate feasts, processions, fireworks, and entertainment.

Now let us discuss some of the recent trends of change in the Indian system of marriage and family.

One of the most frequent themes in Indian sociological literature is the decline of the joint family system. The traditional joint family lived in the ancestral home surrounded by extensive landed property. Parents and their adult sons and their wives and children lived under the same roof sharing the same kitchen and performing the rituals together. The joint family had a manager, usually a patriarch, who made the decisions on behalf of all members. The oldest male member usually arranged for the marriage of all children and grandchildren, organized the funerals, and took care of all ritualistic ceremonies. Every member had a vested interest in the ancestral property which was kept within the family and in some cases the property was impartible. All common expenses, including the education of younger brothers and children, were met out of the income from the ancestral estate. Every adult who married brought his wife to the ancestral home and, therefore, virilocality was the norm, except in the case of matrilineal families. Thus the traditional joint family was like an estate-based corporation. This type of family is now on the decline. Property gets partitioned, adult brothers move away and start new businesses, or educated children take up jobs in the city.

However, this does not mean that the joint family system is vanishing in India. In fact, new types of joint families are emerging. Remember that three or more generations living together constitute an extended family. As people tend to live much longer, parents in their old age move in with one of their children. As more and more wives enter the labour force, we find that parents or some other adult member of the family move in to help the nuclear family raise the children and keep the home. From all over south India, especially Kerala, many men go to work in the Gulf countries, and their wives and children move in with the kinfolk of either the husband or wife. Even when people move to the cities and set up nuclear families, very often a relative of the husband or wife joins them to look for a job. Because of the high cost of housing some of these relatives, even after they find jobs, continue to live with the family. As M.N. Srinivas (1969: 72) observed:

Even if figures for urban areas show a dwindling in the size of the family, it does not necessarily mean that the joint family system is breaking down. Urban families are frequently not autonomous entities but only limbs of bigger families situated elsewhere. Any crisis in the parent or offspring family will be faced as a common problem. Weddings, funerals and other ceremonies are usually celebrated in the 'parent' household. There is occasionally transference of persons from one to the other family.

In a similar vein A.M. Shah (1998: 6–7) argues that:

It would be a mistake to consider the entire urban society as moving against the joint household norm. The business class, from the richest industrialists down to petty shopkeepers, is steeped in joint family culture. So also is the lower middle class composed of clerks, school teachers, and such others. The pro-letariat composed of industrial and other workers appear to be oriented towards the nuclear family due to their being migrants from villages, but are in fact not so oriented. Even the professional class, which could be considered as having come under the maximum impact of the ideology of nuclear family and individualism, is also not uniform in its culture.

The age at marriage has been going up steadily in the last two decades. Yet India has one of the lowest, if not the lowest, median age at marriage for both boys and girls anywhere in the world. The continuing practice of child marriage only compounds the situation.

Today men and women seem to have a little more control on the choice of their spouses than earlier generations. In the past, marriage was always arranged and boys and girls had almost no voice in the selection process. Although most marriages are still arranged, men and women have some say in the matter. Among educated and independent professionals inter-caste and inter-religious marriages also occur.

There is a definite trend towards smaller families. This is particularly true of the urban middle class as well as the educated poor in the rural areas.

More and more women are entering the labour force. This phenomenon has several conse-quences for the family. Parents not only tend to have fewer children but they also space child births. Children are sent to nurseries and kindergarten; in the traditional families early childhood education was entirely a prerogative of the family. At least among the professionals, families tend to be more bilateral than patriarchal. Equal education for women, enhanced status of women and increasing participation of women in the labour force have meant a decline of the segrega-tion of the sexes in work roles. This has resulted in less stereotyped division of tasks at home. In many urban middle class families where both spouses work, there is an increasing willingness on the part of men to share some responsibilities such as cooking, washing the dishes, and baby-sitting. There is also a changed definition of children. In the old agrarian families children were considered an asset but they had inferior status. Contemporary child-rearing patterns encourage children to participate in some family discussions and decision-making processes. Finally, there is an increasing professionalization of marital and parental roles. Marriage bureaus and computer dating services are now available. There are also centres for marriage counselling and specialized magazines which focus on the affairs of the family.

Divorce is legal, and there are separate family courts to deal with issues of divorce, inheritance, and domestic violence. Yet, compared to Western countries, the rate of divorce is low owing to several factors. There is some sort of social stigma attached to divorce and many families still view divorce as a blot on their honour. Some religious communities such as Catholics oppose divorce. Moreover, divorce is not easy for women who have no alternative means of support. Women who are educated and well employed with independent income might find it easier to file for divorce. On the whole, it seems safe to say that the Indian family has withstood the onslaught of many of the modern forces.

GLOBAL TRENDS IN MARRIAGE AND FAMILY

In this section we will discuss some of the patterns including alternative lifestyles in advanced industrial societies. Although most of these practices are not very common in India, they do exist, and grow in significance as more and more young men and women become professionals and start independent lives away from their sheltered home environments.

Cohabitation, the sharing of a household by an unmarried couple, has increased dramatically during the past two decades. In the United States alone there are five unmarried couples for every hundred married couples. Because of the increased social acceptance of cohabitation many men and women do not see the need for legal marriages. In many ways, the personal lives of unmarried couples have also started to resemble those of married couples. Recent legislation in India also recognizes live-in relationship.

In many industrialized countries, the case of *one-parent families* is a significant emerging phenomenon. In some cases, this is the result of the death of a spouse or divorce. But in many cases, it is the result of deliberate choice. Many women prefer to remain unmarried but opt for a child either by birth or adoption. Nearly a third of the families in the United States with children under eighteen years of age have only one parent. Higher education and good jobs have made it possible for women to be independent. But this is only part of the story. At least one-third of the women in the United States become pregnant as unmarried teenagers, with limited opportunities for education and better jobs. This means a large percentage of one-parent families, most of them headed by women, live in poverty. Recent research has also consistently shown that children growing up in single-parent families are disadvantaged in many ways.

The rising *divorce* rate is another demographic factor in most industrialized countries. The United States leads the way with almost four in ten marriages ending in divorce. Religious sanctions against divorce have little influence. Incompatibility and strained interpersonal relationships almost invariably lead to divorce. It must be noted here that the high rate of divorce does not mean that people are rejecting the institution of marriage, for most divorced couples marry within a relatively short period of time. There are several factors that contributed to the rise in the divorce rate. Women are no longer economically dependent on their husbands. The old stigma attached to divorce has all but disappeared. Legal changes have made divorce proceedings simple and easy. But several studies have emphasized the emotional scars and developmental problems faced by children of broken homes.

The rate of *singlehood*, the percentage of people living alone, is also increasing at a significant rate. The reasons for the growth of non-family or one-person households are many. Women outlive men. Many young people tend to postpone marriage. Many women who opt for an education and a good job do not find marriage a financial necessity. As a result, over 60 per cent of women between the ages of twenty and twenty-four were unmarried in the United States. The percentage of people who chose to remain unmarried is also increasing, and strictly speaking the concept of singlehood refers to this phenomenon of people opting to stay single.

Gay and lesbian couples constitute an emerging minority in many industrialized nations. In 1989, Denmark became the first country to formally recognize homosexual marriages, thereby granting union of same-sex couples social legitimacy as well as full legal benefits available to heterosexual couples. In the United States, the legal issues are still being debated but some cities grant the benefits of a civil union. Today many gay couples raise children, either adopted or their own, through surrogate parenting. Gay and lesbian couples challenge many of the traditional values but claim the same kind of satisfaction that heterosexual couples enjoy.

In vitro fertilization or commonly called 'test tube' babies is another phenomenon. Miraculous developments in birth technologies now allow doctors to surgically harvest eggs from ovaries and combine them with sperm in a laboratory dish and implant the fertilized egg in the womb of a surrogate mother. Many couples who are unable to conceive normally opt for this procedure. It is estimated that by the end of the century 2 to 3 per cent of the population in industrial societies may be the result of such birth technologies. At present the procedure is very expensive. It also raises several legal and ethical issues such as the status of parents and the temptation to use the procedure to alter the genetic make up of the human race.

DOMESTIC VIOLENCE

World Health Organization (1966: 23) defines domestic violence as 'the range of sexually, psychologically and physically coercive acts used against adult and adolescent women by current or former male intimate partners'. In India, the SNDT University Research Centre for Women's

Studies elaborated the term 'domestic violence' as 'all acts perpetrated in the private domain of the home to secure women's subordination; and which is rationalized and sanctioned by the prevailing gender ideology. It is thus seen as going beyond the legal definitions of physical assault, to include psychological and sexual violence' (Pooncha and Pandey 1999: 72). Physical violence ranges from slaps, punches, and kicks to assault with weapons, inflicting burns to homicide. Sexual violence takes the form of forced sex or forced participation in degrading sexual acts. Psychological violence takes several forms: excluding women from decision making; making fun of family or community background; curtailment of freedom to go out or attend social functions; abusive or derogatory language; or deliberate humiliation. Psychological forms of violence are hard to measure and are seldom reported.

Most common forms of violence are intimate partner violence (IPV) and violence at the hands of in-laws. Alcohol abuse and argument over dowry are the most probable causes. In one of the pioneering studies, Sriram (2003) reviewed the then scanty literature on domestic violence in India and concluded that wife-beating more than doubled in the 1980s. In response to structured interviews, almost 50 per cent of married men confessed to having abused their wives (Martin *et al.* 1999). The study also found that abuse was more common among men who had extra-marital relations. Other studies have thrown up a number of factors that are usually associated with spousal violence: younger age of couple; low education; low income background; abuse of alcohol; lack of social networks; greater marital control by husband; history of marital violence in the family of orgin of either spouse; and female-dominated financial decision-making. On the other hand, higher levels of education, higher socio-economic status, women's economic independence, number of male children in the family, and close connection to extended family are some of the protective factors. In a study of individual and community-level influences on domestic violence in Uttar Pradesh, Koenig *et al.* (2006) found that domestic violence was associated with the individual-level variables of childlessness, economic pressure, and intergenerational transmission of violence, while community-level norms concerning wife-beating were significantly related to physical violence, and higher socio-economic status protected against physical violence but not against sexual violence. Ponnudurai *et al.* (2001) investigated the reasons for attempted suicides among wives of substance abusers. Eighty per cent of the wives of alcohol and polysubstance abusers reported frequent beating by the husbands as the primary reason for attempted suicide. Kumar *et al.* (2005) investigated mental health correlates of domestic violence and found that women who experienced any kind of violence were at increased risk of poor mental health.

India has liberal laws governing dowry, honour killing, and domestic violence. However, legislation itself can do little when customs and traditions are deep-rooted in patriarchy, gender inequality, male dominance, family prestige, and social status. The traditional attitude of machismo, which is found in most societies, is aggravated in India by traditions of patriarchy, male dominance, and gender preferences.

STUDY QUESTIONS

- Discuss the different types of family.
- Examine the different patterns of marriage with special reference to India.
- What are the functions of family?
- Write an essay on marriage and family in India.
- What are the major global trends in marriage and family?
- Write a critical review on domestic violence in India.
- Considering the recent trends of change in marriage and family, what is your assessment of the future of family?
- Define the terms: household; family; kinship; clan; nuclear, extended, conjugal, consanguine families; patrilineal, matrilineal, and bilateral systems; patriarchal, matriarchal, matricentric, patrilocal, matrilocal, and neolocal families; and endogamy, exogamy, polygyny, polygamy, homogamy, levirate, and sororate types of marriage.

REFERENCES

Coltrane, Scott, *Families and Society,* Belmont, CA: Wadsworth, 2004.

Coltrane, Scott and Randall Collins, *Sociology of Marriage and the Family: Gender, Love and Property,* Belmont, CA: Wadsworth, 2001.

Eichler, Margrit, *Family Shifts: Families, Policies, and Gender Equality,* Toronto: Oxford University Press, 1997.

Garey, Anita Ilta, *Weaving Work and Motherhood,* Philadelphia: Temple University Press, 1999.

Kapadia, K.M., *Marriage and Family in India,* New Delhi: Oxford University Press, 1966.

Koenig, M.A., R. Stephenson, S. Ahmed, S.J. Jejeebhoy, and J. Campbell, 'Individual and Contextual Determinants of Domestic Violence in North India', *American Journal of Public Health*, 96, pp. 132–8, 2006.

Kumar, S., L. Jeyaseelan, S. Suresh, and R.C. Ahuja, 'Domestic Violence and its Mental Health Correlates in Indian Women', *British Journal of Psychiatry*, 187, pp. 62–7, 2005.

Martin, S.L., B. Kilgallen, A.O. Tsui, K. Maitra, K.K. Singh, and L.L. Kupper, 'Sexual Behaviors and Reproductive Health Outcomes: Associations with Wife Abuse in India', *Journal of American Medical Association*, 282(20), 1999.

Ponnudurai, R., T.S. Uma, S. Rajarathinan, and V.S. Krishnan, 'Determinants of Suicidal Attempts of Wives of Substance Abusers', *Indian Journal of Psychiatry*, 43(3), 2001.

Pooncha, V. and D. Pandey, *Responses to Domestic Violence in the States of Karnataka and Gujarat,* Mumbai: SNDT University, 1999.

Queen, Stuart A. and Robert Habenstein, *The Family in Various Cultures,* Philadelphia: J.B. Lippincott Company, 1972.

Riley, Matilda White and John W. Riley, 'Connections: Kin and Cohort', in Vern Bengston and Andrew Achenbaum (eds), *The Changing Contract Across Generations,* New York: Aldine de Gruyter, 1993.

Rossi, Alice S. and Peter H. Rossi, *Of Human Bonding: Parent–Child Relations Across the Life Course*, New York: Aldine de Gruyter, 1990.

Shah, A.M., *The Family in India: Critical Essays*, New Delhi: Orient Longman, 1998.

Srinivas, M.N., *India: Social Structure*, New Delhi: Publications Division (GoI), 1969.

Sriram, R., 'Violence in the Family: Need for Preventive and Educational Approaches', in S.M. Channbasavanna (ed.), *Chaning Marital and Family Systems: Challenges to Conventional Models in Mental Health*, Bagalore: NIMHANS, 2003.

World Health Organization. *Violence Against Women*. Switzerland: WHO, 1966.

12

The Political Economy

Through the ages societies have evolved different types of political organization. Many tribal societies such as the Mbuti pygmies of Africa managed without any organized system of government; all decisions affecting the community were made by a group of elders. Tribal chiefs, elders, and shamans exercised considerable influence in other societies. However, in large, complex societies of today political authority has to be organized and structured.

In today's world, political and economic systems are inextricably intertwined. In both industrialized and developing societies, governments play a major role in shaping the economy. Nation-states like the United States, Japan, and Germany represent the world's largest economies. Then again, some of the private business corporations are bigger financial entities than many of the nation-states. Some governments plan and structure the economy while others provide general policy guidelines. In democracies governments are often voted in and out based on the performance of the economy. Therefore, economic and political systems share a common fate.

STATE AND GOVERNMENT

The *state* is a form of political entity by which a society is organized under an agency of government which claims legitimate sovereignty over a specified geographical area and has a monopoly of physical force. This definition has a number of key elements. The state has a territory over which it has legitimate sovereignty. It is organized under a government which exercises authority over its subjects. But there are several other forms of organizations which exercise authority over their members. The patriarchal family, unions, and clubs have legitimate authority over their members. But the state is the only entity with a legitimate monopoly of physical force, with the authority to imprison and even to execute members under its jurisdiction. The state exercises its political authority through governments at the national, state, and local levels. The concept of state must be distinguished from that of a nation. A nation is an autonomous group of politically organized people associated with a particular territory.

A *government* is an agency of the state, a complex legal system, that has the power and authority to carry out the functions of the state. Key personnel in the government may change but the authority structure continues. In modern democracies, governments formed by political parties in power formulate policies, initiate laws, and launch programmes. The government has three distinct branches: legislature, executive, and judiciary. The legislature is responsible for enacting the laws that govern the behaviour of all individuals and institutions including the government. The executive formulates policies and programmes and administers the country in accordance with the laws. The judiciary interprets the laws and safeguards the rights of all citizens.

Functions of the State

Modern nation-states perform a wide variety of functions. Although the extent of functions varies according to the type of government, every state assumes major responsibilities in the following areas.

Social Control

The state alone has the authority to enact and enforce laws. First, the state establishes the laws that formally specify what is expected of the citizen as well as what is prohibited. The laws affect almost every type of behaviour from recording childbirth, getting a baby vaccinated, to driving on the highway and paying taxes. They also prohibit types of behaviour which disrupt the social order. But it is not enough to make good laws; they must be enforced. It is the responsibility of the state to maintain law and order, to punish criminals, and protect law-abiding citizens. The police and the courts are primarily responsible for social control.

Defence

One of the primary functions of the state is to protect its citizens against external aggression. Indeed, modern states have arisen out of warfare and political alliances. Modern nation-states maintain standing armies and a significant portion of the national budget is spent on the military. Occasionally, the soldiers trained and equipped for defence are also employed for maintaining order in case of emergency domestic situations. However, most democratic nations maintain a definite functional separation between social control and defence responsibilities of the state. In totalitarian states this separation is not always emphasized as the military and civilian functions are often interchangeable.

Welfare

It is the responsibility of the state to initiate policies and programmes to provide for the general welfare of the people under its territory. Such welfare measures include, among other things, health, education, transportation, employment, public services, and pension benefits. Elimination of poverty, promotion of social justice, and cultural development are also among the goals embraced by modern nation-states. In modern industrial societies individuals cannot provide for all their needs, and communities cannot initiate all public service programmes. Money must be minted and large labour forces mobilized for construction of railroads, canals, dams, ports, and highways. Regardless of the type of government, every state is expected to ensure economic stability and general social welfare.

TYPES OF STATES

The United Nations comprised of 189 states as of September 2002. They include monarchies, dictatorships, totalitarian states, republics, and other democracies. We may classify them under three broad categories.

Autocracy

A Modern Dictionary of Sociology defines autocracy as 'A form of government in which ultimate authority resides in one person (the autocrat) who occupies the top position in a hierarchy of power and from whom authority descends to the bottom of hierarchy'. The autocrat may be a monarch who inherited the position or a dictator who captured power in a coup d'etat. The autocrat is not accountable for his actions to his subordinates or his subjects. An autocracy is authoritarian but not necessarily totalitarian. In an autocracy power and authority are vested in a single individual. Military dictatorships and absolute monarchies are examples of autocracies.

Totalitarianism

In totalitarianism the state, rather than an individual, is supreme. The monopoly of power is usually vested in a party or a group of ruling elites. The state controls and regulates all phases of life, perpetuates its power, and arbitrarily decides what is best for its citizens. The centralized system of authority discourages any form of real political participation. With the development of modern technologies and surveillance systems, totalitarian governments monitor almost every aspect of the lives of citizens. Totalitarian states control access to media and other sources of information, deny people's right to assemble for political participation, and enforce strict conformity not only to state policies but also their political ideology. Nazi Germany and the Soviet Union under Stalin and modern North Korea are examples; the Taliban and other Islamic regimes where power is concentrated in the hands of a small group of religious leaders also resemble totalitarian states.

Democracy

Democracy is a form of government in which power is exercised by the people as a whole. All modern democracies are representative democracies in which people elect their representatives to form a government on their behalf. An ideal system of democracy is based on universal adult suffrage which allows all citizens of a certain age to exercise their right to vote. People elect their representatives for a period of four or five years who must face the electorate at the end of the specified period. In some countries elected representatives may be recalled by the people before their term of office expires. The effectiveness of the democracy depends on an enlightened electorate; people have to be politically conscious and active in the democratic process. Modern democracies function through an elaborate system of bureaucracy. Elected officials formulate the budget, policies, and programmes and carry out the programmes through a network of appointed officials. Modern nation states prefer democratic forms of government which recognize that the people are sovereign and the rulers are their temporary agents.

TYPES OF ECONOMY

The type of economy often depends on the political form of government. How does the state control the flow of money, goods, and services? What is the status of private property? What is the role of free market in the economic system? The answer to these questions would illustrate the relationship between the state and the economy. Generally speaking, we may classify economy into three broad types.

Capitalism

Capitalism is an economic system based on private ownership of the means of production and distribution in which individuals are free to accumulate and invest capital. In a free-market economy individuals are motivated by profit. Competition as well as the forces of demand and supply determine prices and wages. The state plays only a minor role in the marketplace, mainly controlling monopoly and exploitation. The capitalist system operates on the basis of extensive credit, free contract, and free-labour market. Since private property allows accumulation of profit, individuals invest and reinvest in business enterprises. And market forces will determine what is produced and at what price.

Adam Smith, the father of modern capitalism, attributed four features to capitalism. First, private property is the essence of capitalism. The right to own property makes people work hard for profit and at the same time respect the property of others. Second, capitalism involves freedom of choice, that is, the right to own, rent, sell, trade, or give away the property as the individuals please. Third, capitalism is based on unregulated competition which allows the market forces to determine what is produced, how much is produced, and at what price. Fourth, Adam Smith emphasized laissez-faire capitalism, that is, almost total freedom from government interference in business or commerce. Governments are expected to maintain order, facilitate free trade, and promote competition. However, an absolute laissez-faire system is extremely rare. Governments have to make sure that powerful business enterprises do not exploit people, eliminate competition, and form monopolies. All modern governments play some role in the economy of the state.

Socialism

Socialism is an economic system in which the state has collective ownership of the means of production and distribution. Profit is no longer the ultimate goal of economic activity but public good is. The state owns the land as well as all other resources and operates farms, factories, railroads, and businesses. Usually, there is a central planning agency that sets the goals and priorities. Production of goods and services as well as the entire economic activity is oriented towards meeting the public needs rather than profit-making. In addition to collective ownership and central planning, socialism advocates overall welfare of the population through extensive public assistance programmes. The former Soviet Union, former socialist countries of eastern Europe, North Korea, and Cuba are examples of socialist practitioners.

Mixed Economy

Many developing countries have adopted a system of mixed economy which combines state ownership with many aspects of capitalism. Private property is allowed and individuals are free to accumulate and invest capital for profit. But the state also owns and operates a number of enterprises. Generally speaking, it has monopoly of some industries such as metals, minerals, petroleum, railroads, and utilities. The state also has a national planning body which sets goals, policies, and priorities, as well as allocates resources. Although private enterprises and free-market systems operate, the state assumes a significant role in health, education, and welfare of the general population. India has adopted the system of mixed economy.

Today, economists and sociologists speak of a convergence theory, the idea that capitalism and socialism are growing similar. All socialist countries suffered from production of shoddy goods and acute shortages and their standard of living was far below that of the West. Now Russia and China have reinstituted the market economy. They have auctioned off most of the state-owned enterprises, legalized private property, and are offering special incentives to attract the bourgeoisie from Western countries. Profit motive is no longer considered a sin. Convergence theory describes the coexistence of capitalism and socialism in a mixed economy.

DEMOCRATIC SOCIALISM

We must keep in mind that capitalism and socialism are not absolutely pure systems. The role of the state in economic systems varies considerably from country to country. The United States is probably at one end of the continuum and the current communist regimes such as Cuba and North Korea are at the other end. Most of the other countries fall somewhere in between. In the United States, private parties control almost entire means of production and distribution. There are no government factories; even defence equipment is manufactured by private industries. The government simply contracts with private companies to manufacture military hardware. Railroads, airlines, broadcasting companies, television and radio stations, insurance companies, and banks are all owned by private corporations. Individuals not only own the land but also the minerals, gas, and oil under their property. There is no central planning system that sets economic goals for the state. Yet, the state plays a significant role in stimulating the economy. It encourages free trade but checks on business practices and discourages monopoly. Occasionally, it bails out large corporations which are in financial trouble. It provides for the welfare of the poor through various public assistance programmes. The state also plays a role in health, education, and public pension schemes. It regulates banking and inter-state commerce. State governments establish universities and local governments own and operate electric power plants. State governments also grant tax breaks and subsidies to big companies to encourage them to establish business in the state. But by and large, the state has no major role in social welfare. With the result, 15 per cent of the population lives in poverty and millions of people are without health insurance.

At the other extreme we have the Marxist socialism of the former Soviet Union, Cuba, and North Korea. Collective farming and public distribution systems failed miserably to meet the basic needs of people. Scarcity of essential goods was so widespread that the governments had to resort to rationing. Although Cuba has an excellent public health system, production of basic items is so far behind supply that the government determines how many eggs and chicken and how much oil, milk, and rice a family will receive each month. Poverty and famine are widespread in North Korea. But Vietnam and China have moved away from Marxist socialism. China has privatized a large number of state-owned corporations and now allows foreign direct investment in most industries and businesses. Ownership of the land is still vested in the state but people can lease it for a period as long as seventy years and build private homes. People can accumulate and invest capital in private enterprises and earn a profit.

Scandinavian countries are thought to be welfare states which practise democratic socialism, 'a convergence of capitalist and socialist economic theory in which the state assumes ownership of strategic industries and services, but allows other enterprises to remain in private hands' (Tischler 2002: 402). Political parties with democratic socialism as their platform have been able to enact many pieces of social legislation aimed at the welfare of society as a whole. The state ownership is limited to some key industries such as railways, airlines, television and radio stations, hospitals, educational institutions, and important manufacturing industries. The government provides free education, free medical services, social insurance, subsidized housing, generous family allowances for young children, and old-age benefits. Private individuals and companies can own and operate a number of enterprises so long as they are responsive to the needs of the population. They are taxed heavily so that there is no heavy concentration of wealth. The state also plans investment by regulating interest rates and co-investing in new enterprises. In order to provide for all public services the state depends on heavy taxation, sometimes over 50 per cent. State planning and government welfare programmes guarantee people's well-being. There is no poverty, and the gap between the rich and the poor is narrow. In addition to Scandinavian countries and Israel, several western European countries follow some form of democratic socialism. They have a better quality of life than the United States where the gap between the rich and the poor tends to grow.

According to the Constitution, India is a 'Democratic Socialist Republic'. We have adopted the principle of democratic socialism and the ideals of social justice, social welfare, and elimination of poverty. However, we are nowhere near the ideal. A large proportion of people live below poverty line. There is no social safety net or welfare programme that mandatorily covers the entire population. While employed people are covered by Provident Fund, pension schemes, etc., there is no national scheme which people can pay into for old-age benefits. Education and medical services are not accessible to the majority of people. As in the case of other democratic socialist countries, the state owns most of the key industries but there is no national health insurance or other public assistance programme that benefits all. The Indian case is unique in several ways. India is far more socialist than the democratic socialist countries of northern Europe. But the so-called Marxist socialist China has perhaps a far more vibrant private economy than India. India also has proportionately far more people on the government payroll than China. Yet we have a much higher rate of poverty. It is worth remembering that China lagged behind India in almost every sphere till the beginning of 1970, then outpaced India on virtually every score. Today, China has surpassed the United States to emerge as the globe's leading destination for foreign investment and is already the world's second largest economy and is destined to become the largest in a short time. While China's growth rate was a robust 13 per cent India's languished around 9 per cent or under. China's number of rural poor has declined from 94.22 million in 2000 to 26.88 million in 2010, or 2.8 per cent of the rural population today. India has almost thirteen times as many. Even today the Indian economy is more socialist than China's, for over 70 per cent of workers in the organized sector in India are employed by the government but in China state companies employ only less than 35 per cent of the total workforce. When critics accused Deng Xiaoping of following a capitalist policy, he answered, 'I don't care whether the cat is black or white, can it catch the mouse?' True, China did not care about the rhetoric of socialism, they fulfilled the basic needs of the people first and then launched their country into a systematic economic take-off.

With the initiation of the new economic policy in 1991, radical reforms were introduced in policies relating to trade, import and export, industry, finance and taxation, foreign investment, exchange regulation, banking, and financial services, as well as privatization. The new policy was designed to invigorate the Indian economy with private investments from within and abroad. Sectors formerly reserved for the government, such as power, telecommunications, mining, ports, roads, rivers, banking, and air traffic have been opened to the private sector. Foreign direct and portfolio investments have been allowed in almost all sectors of industry. The results have been quite amazing. The foreign exchange reserve shot up from one billion at the end of 1990–1 to more than 100 billion today. Also a substantial middle class has emerged with an insatiable appetite for modern consumer goods.

Currently, India has an impressive 9 per cent growth rate. The Government of India has just come out with *India Human Development Report 2011*. India's HDI registered impressive gains during the last decade as the index increased by 21 per cent to 0.467 in 2007–8, from 0.387 in 1999–2000. Kerala topped the list with highest literacy rate, provision of quality health services, and the consumption expenditure of people. Delhi, Himachal Pradesh and Goa secured second, third, and fourth positions respectively. But Chhattisgarh, Orissa, Madhya Pradesh, Jharkhand, Rajasthan, and Assam continued to lag behind the national average of 0.467. According to the report, two-thirds of the households in the country now live in *pucca* (cemented) houses and three-fourth of the families have access to electricity for domestic use. However, a new study by the United Nations Development Programme said that India's significant inequalities in income, health, and education dent the country's overall human development performance. The report found that 'inequality in the distribution of human development is distinctly pronounced in India' compared to other countries. According to the study, if inequality in income and access to education and health were to be figured in, India's HDI would decrease by 32 per cent. This is yet another proof that India's booming economy has not spread the benefits of growth widely.

According to the union minister for rural development, the central government alone spends Rs 1,00,000 crore on national rural development schemes. The Mahatma Gandhi National Rural Employment Guarantee Scheme is touted as one example of comprehensive rural social welfare programme. But the programme has been plagued from the very beginning with numerous problems. In the first place, the programme operates only for a short period during the year. Although the original intent of the programme was to focus on irrigation, afforestaton, land and water management, and restoration of water bodies, much of the money was spent on unproductive work. The programme also has been riddled with other problems: endemic corruption, low wages, sometimes even below minimum wages, inordinate delay in payment to beneficiaries, etc. Recently the union minister has announced that the entire expenditure on rural development schemes will be subjected to Comptroller and Auditor General (CAG) audit.

Finally, India has to grapple with three fundamental problems ailing the political economy: poverty, child labour and bonded labour, and farmers' suicide. Let us consider the issue of poverty first. Different commissions and agencies have used different criteria to define poverty. Table 12.1 shows different estimates of poverty in India.

If we use the World Bank figure of US$ 1.25 as the standard level of poverty, 42 per cent of the population of India lives below the poverty line. While the godowns of the Food Corporation of India are bursting at the seams and the agency is wondering what to do with the additional 60 million tons of wheat and rice, and while much of the grain is rotting in the poorly maintained godowns, the National Sample Survey reports that about half of all rural families in India do not have below the poverty line cards. And according to Lakshmidhar Mishra's recent book, *Human Bondage* (2011), in free India hundreds of thousands of bonded labourers work day in and day out, live in cattle sheds, toil in agricultural fields, and live below subsistence level. According to the author, more than 500,000 labourers are trapped in various forms of bonded labour in Punjab alone, one of India's richest states. Millions of children are mortgaged or

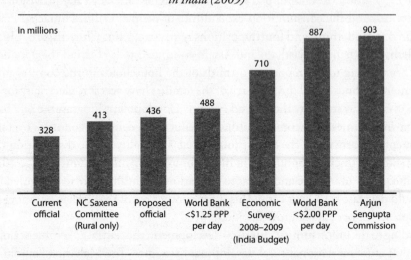

Table 12.1: Various Estimates of the Number Living Below Poverty Line in India (2009)

Source: Population Reference Bureau, based on different recent estimates of the per cent below poverty line.

sold by parents against small debts, never to be seen again. Finally, the country has seen over a quarter of a million farmers' suicides between 1995 and 2010. The National Crime Records Bureau's latest report records a sixteen-year total of 2,56,913 suicides between 1995 and 2010, the worst-ever recorded wave of suicides of this kind in human history. Maharashtra posts a dismal picture with over 50,000 farmers killing themselves in the country's richest state during the past sixteen years. Nearly two-thirds of the suicides have occurred in the five states of Maharashtra, Karnataka, Andhra Pradesh, Madhya Pradesh, and Chhattisgarh.

No wonder the United Nations Development Programme has ranked India at 134 out of 187 countries in terms of human development, whereas Scandinavian countries which practice real democratic socialism are ranked at the top.

POWER AND AUTHORITY

Force, power, and authority are three concepts which are often used interchangeably, and always incorrectly so. They are distinctly different concepts and must be clearly defined.

Power is the ability of an individual or a group to carry out its wishes regardless of resistance from others. Power often rests on the ability to use force. In other words, you have power if you have the ability to make other people act according to your wishes with or without the actual use of force.

Authority is power that is legitimized or institutionalized in a social system. This form of power is attached to a social status and is accepted as just and proper by members of the social system. The police officer who stops your car and asks for your license is exercising his authority. The thug who shows a knife and asks for your wallet has power. If a mob overpowers a police officer he is powerless but has not lost his authority.

Robert Bierstedt (1974: 357) defines these related concepts as follows.

Power is latent force; force is manifest power, and authority is institutionalized power…. Power itself is the predisposition or prior capacity that makes the use of force possible. Only groups that have power can threaten to use force and the threat itself is power. Power is the ability to employ force, not its actual employment, the ability to apply sanctions, not their actual application. Power is the ability to introduce force into a social situation; it is stance, not action; it is a presentation of the probability of force. Unlike force, incidentally, power is always successful; when it is not successful it was not, or ceases to be, power. The bankrupt corporation and the vanquished army are both powerless. Power symbolizes the force that *may* be applied in any social situation and supports the authority that *is* applied. Power is thus neither force nor authority but it makes both force and authority possible. Without power there would be no force and without power there would be no authority.

Thus power and authority are interlinked. One need not have formal authority to exercise power. Those in authority need not always resort to brute force to exercise their power; some may wield enormous power over others without any formal authority. In a democracy, unions and caste groups may have enormous power because they can force political parties to protect their interests. People have power because they can vote parties in or out of government. But the parties in 'power' (strictly speaking, authority) may be powerless to implement their agenda. Governments propose a piece of legislation or a programme; then they face stiff opposition from the people and are forced to withdraw the proposal. Thus people in authority sometimes become powerless.

Max Weber identified three types of authority based on legitimacy, that is power perceived to be proper by subordinates.

1. *Traditional authority*. This form of authority is legitimized by long-established cultural practices. It often attaches to inherited statuses. For example, tribal chiefs, village elders, and old caste councils claim authority based on traditions and customs. The authority of the oldest male member in a patriarchal family is another example. These types of authority may not be based on formal offices or legal systems.
2. *Rational–legal authority*. Authority that is attached to formal offices and established legal systems is called rational–legal authority. People exercise this type of authority so long as they hold an office. All office-holders from the Class IV officer at the local panchayat, to the president of India are part of the rational–legal authority. Also office-bearers of associations, unions, corporations, schools, and all non-governmental organizations fall under this category. Simply put, rational–legal authority is attached to any office established by formal arrangements.
3. *Charismatic authority*. This type of authority is based on extraordinary personal, almost magical, qualities of a person, actual, alleged or presumed. People with unique leadership

qualities, religious or moral influence, or enormous popular appeal are charismatic leaders. Charismatic leaders may or may not hold formal offices. The point to remember is that such authority rests on charisma or 'gift of grace' or personal magnetism of an individual. As Weber put it, the charismatic leader maintains authority 'by providing his strength in life'. Mao Zedong, Hitler, Martin Luther King, Fidel Castro, and John F. Kennedy had charisma. In India, Mahatma Gandhi, Satya Sai Baba, and Matha Amrithanda Mayi represent charismatic authority. As we can see, the charismatic leader may or may not hold a formal office and in any case charismatic leadership is not transferable.

THEORIES OF POWER IN SOCIETIES

In a democracy, people vote for a candidate or a party. The party that forms the government is supposed to be in power. But who really wields power in society? Who has the power to influence decision-making at the highest level? There are two major theoretical perspectives on power in society.

The Power Elite Model

C. Wright Mills, the chief architect of this theory, argued that economic, social, and political power in American society is manipulated by three interlocking hierarchies—the military, the industrial, and the political. The central thesis of the theory is that political leaders, chieftains of large corporations, and top military brass work together and make most decisions that affect American society. This theory is a variant of the conflict perspective and expounds the principle of a monolithic power structure. That is, all major decisions are made by a fairly autonomous few whose interests are cohesive. The elite few hail from the same kind of families, have superior education at prestigious schools, enjoy important connections, and have direct access to strategic power centres.

A close examination of the power elite model shows that it is akin to the Marxian view of the ruling class. Marx does no speak of a triumvirate but leaves not doubt that the economic dominants are the real power-wielders. The capitalists make up the ruling class and the ideas of the ruling class are the ruling ideas, Marx insisted. Thus, according to the power elite theory, the rich and the powerful in society are able to manipulate power centres and the decision-making process.

The Pluralist Model

Pluralism (Dahl, Rose, and others) contends that power is dispersed broadly among many different individuals and groups. They argue that in a modern democracy there are many contending groups, political parties, and interest groups who compete with one another for more power. In other words, pluralists reject the notion that power is concentrated in the hands of a small stratum of elites but contend that there are many veto groups who compete with one another for power and who seek to influence decisions in specific contexts with varying degrees of success. The pluralists also point out that the elitist approach invariably overlooks factional disputes and conflicts of interests within leadership groups. Instead of notions like 'monolithic political machines' and 'ruling elite', pluralism emphasizes concepts like 'multiple decision centres' and 'balance wheels'.

However, it must be emphasized that the distinction between elitist and pluralist systems is a matter of degree, rather than of mutually exclusive contrasts. As Presthus (1964: 38) contends, the two perspectives uncover two facets of social reality. In his judgement, 'To some extent, where the sociologists found monopoly and called it elitism, political scientists found oligopoly but defined it in more honorific terms as pluralism.'

THE INDIAN POLITICAL SCENE

Political sociology, an important field within sociology, investigates political processes such as grass roots participation, voting behaviour, political movements, parties, power relations, and coalition formation. Just like any other social behaviour, political behaviour is an area of concern to sociology.

First of all, let us consider which of the two models, power elite or pluralist, applies to the Indian political scene? It is difficult to identify a power elite or a ruling class in Indian society. In the first place, if there is an elite group at the very top of the social ladder it is very small. On the other hand, every political party claims to be on the side of the poor and the downtrodden. Indeed, the history of central and state legislation during the past five decades has been consistently on the side of labour and those left behind. Even the early advocates of Marxism and socialism came from the ranks of the upper social and economic strata. Therefore, it is hard to make out a case for the existence of a ruling class with ruling ideas in India. However, there are several interest groups which compete with one another for power. Many labour unions oppose privatization of public sector enterprises. Marxists are against globalization. The Bharatiya Janata Party (BJP) wants to protect the interests of the Sangh Parivar. Backward classes clamour for more reservation while the upper castes oppose any increase in reservation. Women's groups fight for reservation of seats in legislatures and Parliament. Thus pluralists might argue that the competition among various political parties, caste groups, labour unions, and other interest groups demonstrates the presence of multiple power centres in Indian politics. This argument is further emboldened by the fact that most governments are formed by a coalition of several parties with different interests. No single party can impose its will on others. Yet, Naxalites and some Marxists might argue that the failure of most Indian states to adopt effective land reforms is indicative of the strength of the power elite among the landlords.

Let us now look at some of the salient features of the Indian political system.

The role of caste in Indian politics is legendary. Numerically large castes have become important pressure groups in politics at all levels, and all political parties consider them to be important vote banks. The politics of Andhra Pradesh is dominated by the two competing castes of Reddys and Kammas and in Karnataka the rivalry between the Okkaligas and Lingay-ats dominates the political process. In Maharashtra, the Marathas, Brahmins and Mahars, in Gujarat, the Banias, Patidars and Kolis, and in Bihar, the Kayasths, Bhumihars, and Rajputs, compete in the political process. The coalition politics of Kerala sees shifting alliances among the Nairs, Ezhavas, Syrian Christians, and Muslims. Every party takes utmost care to see that its candidate in a particular constituency belongs to the caste which has a majority in the area. Elections are always fought utilizing the resources of caste loyalties. Since each caste tries to capture the reins of power at the local level, powers and functions of the castes have increased in proportion to the political power that has been transferred to the local governments.

Although several democracies in the world have multiple parties, India has the unique distinction of having multiple parties often under the same banner, professing the same goals, and subscribing to the same ideology but owing allegiance to different personalities. In India as factions grow, parties split and multiply, not to defend the interests of the constituents or the nation but to advance the personal ambitions of leaders. Often there is absolutely no difference in their ideology or programme and their manifestos do not differ from one another. There is nothing inherently wrong with a multiplicity of parties. But if parties are simply factions for domination by key personalities, then personal ambitions of individuals, rather than the larger interests of the nation, are served. Getting elected is only the first step in the spiralling staircase of personal ambition. Now deal-making begins. There is a price for everything, for loyalty, for vote, and for defection. Lakhs and crores are paid for support to the ruling party, for vote against a no-confidence motion, or for joining the rebel group. As members of Parliament and state legislatures trade their votes for plum posts or sell their loyalty in exchange for crores, the great institutions of democracy are debased and trashed.

The existence of multiple parties also makes it necessary for parties to form coalition govern-ments. In a pluralist society like India with numerous caste, religious, and linguistic groups, political alliances and multiple power centres are essential to protect diverse interests. Coalitions act as a check against dictatorial tendencies of a single party with absolute majority. India also has the unique distinction of having several regional parties, some of which have no following outside their own state, serving as equal partners in the national government.

In terms of power relations, there is another unique feature of the Indian political system that must be mentioned. That everybody is equal before the law is one of the fundamental principles of democracy. India is probably the only democracy where prosecution of public servants is deliberately designed to be a cumbersome process. In the United States all public officials including the president, members of the cabinet, and members of the Congress are routinely investigated for any violation of the law. While a state governor was addressing a meeting, the police towed away his official car which was parked in the no-parking zone and the head of state had to pay a fine and apologize to the citizens for infringement of the law. In England, the Ombudsman covers all public servants including members of Parliament. In all Western democracies, governors, prime ministers, presidents, and members of parliament are routinely investigated by law enforcement agencies, if there is a suspicion of wrong-doing. Since no one is above the law no permission is required from the boss. In India we cannot prosecute even an ex-minister without the permission of the cabinet and the governor or the president. The procedure often means that you end up getting permission from the accused or his party colleague. During the colonial rule the British had such a rule to protect British officers and their minions from the Indian legal system. But in a democracy where all citizens are equal before the law, any procedure that grants special privileges to the leaders is not consistent with the principle of the rule of law. Is this practice indicative of the presence of power elite in Indian politics?

Rampant corruption is another big problem in Indian politics. Recent movement by Anna Hazarre has called attention to multiple scams and generated some interest in the need for an effective mechanism to curb corruption. This is a theme students can investigate in the light of relevant theories of power and privilege.

GLOBALIZATION AND CORPORATE CAPITALISM

The globalization of capital is one of the important developments in the post-industrial society. According to some economists, the rise of MNCs is the greatest economic change since the Industrial Revolution. A *multinational* or *transnational corporation* (TNC) is an enterprise that owns production or service facilities in one or more countries other than the one in which it is based. As the term implies, MNCs operate across national borders. They locate their corporate headquarters in one country, manufacture their basic components in another country, assemble them in a third country, and market the finished products throughout the world. Many of the MNCs are so huge that they operate in a number countries, employ thousands of people, and earn billions of dollars in profit. Sixteen of the twenty-five most profitable corporations in the world are American.

Recent U.N. data reveal that TNCs (transnational corporations) account for two-thirds of world trade. TNCs control most of the world's financial transactions, (bio)technologies and industrial capacity—including oil and its refining, coal, gas, hydroelectric and nuclear power plants, mineral extraction and processing, home electronics, chemicals, medicines, wood harvesting and processing, and more. The top five TNCs in each major market (such as jet aircraft, automobiles, microprocessors, and grains) typically account for between 40 and 70 per cent of all world sales. Further, about 50 per cent of world trade takes place inside the TNCs, as components move within corporate networks including subsidiaries of allied firms and parent corporations in the construction of a final product.... From 1970 to 1998, the number of TNCs rose from 7,000 to 60,000, with more than 500,000 foreign affiliates accounting for roughly 25 per cent of global output. (McMichael 2000: 95–6)

There is considerable debate over the consequences of globalization. Socialists, labour unions, and conflict theorists do not take kindly to the new international systems. Especially intriguing are the popular social movements that resist transnational capitalism which is fuelled by the ideologies of neoliberalism and privatization that tend to conflict with the spirit of nationalism and the quest for social justice. They point to the global mobility of capital that is able to extract surplus from labour and gain favourable policies from nations throughout the world. As monopoly capitalism gives way to a qualitatively different capitalism, all sectors of labour decline in bargaining power, social potency, political influence, and the threat of job loss and economic stagnation force state compliance and political acquiescence. Emerging economies are faced with a new form of colonialism that forces them to surrender organizational and ideological initiative to multilateral agencies and transnational forces. Between 1985 and 1996, the portion of Chinese exports from foreign-owned plants grew from 1 to 40 per cent, but in 1995, the ratio of factory wages in China to South Korea/Taiwan to Japan was 1:30:80. Some of the giant TNCs not only exploit cheap labour in developing countries but they also interfere in the country's internal affairs. Everyone knows the story of Chile where International Telephone and Telegraph Company joined the CIA to plot a coup d'etat to assassinate Salvador Allende, the democratically elected socialist president.

The consequences of global capitalism include a variety of struggles for labour, grass roots movements against MNCs, manipulation of markets, and environmental degradation. As Philip McMichael (Smith and Borocz 1995: 37) puts it:

The objects of colonization were territories and peoples. However, in the late twentieth century nation-states, the regulators of territories and people, are being colonized. The colonization now is essentially by capital, under the banner of liberalization. While it is a universal process, it has taken its most virulent forms in the financial conditions imposed on southern states (developing countries) during the 1980s. An equally far-reaching, and arguably intentional, consequence of the debt regime (notably, global labour-cost reduction) is the challenge to the managed economies and social and political democracies of the metropolitan states. As global circuits of capital destabilize nation-states by restructuring production, markets and class relations, new ideologies of nativism, ethnocentrism, and racism have emerged, as communities and labour forces compete for economic survival. Such ideologies substitute separatist politics for the inclusive politics of social democracy.

The advocates of global capitalism argue that free trade encourages competition and greater productivity. This, in turn, lowers prices and raises the standard of living. A free market also allows unrestricted flow of goods and services. If India has to sell its rubber, tea, and textiles abroad, it has to agree to buy products from other countries. A country cannot practise socialist protectionism at home and expect to reap the benefits of free trade abroad. Today, even Russia and China, the two great champions of socialism, are chasing global capitalism.

Enter 'Occupy Wall Street Movement' that has burgeoned into a wider 'global day of rage' across Western capitals against capitalist greed. American protestors include young people, students, urban middle classes, union members, the working poor, underemployed, and unemployed. They blame bankers, speculators, and traders for the economic recession. While the vast majority of the people reel under economic crisis, the very same people who are responsible for the crisis are bailed out by the government and even paid hefty bonuses for their 'performance'. Three decades of deregulation have led to the growth of stark inequality and erosion of social mobility in America. During this period, almost all the benefits of economic growth went to the top 10 per cent, while the income of the remaining 90 per cent effectively declined. Similarly, in several European capitals, debt crises and austerity measures have prompted widespread social movements. There is an irony in all these. Unbridled capitalism and free market bred greed, intellectual dishonesty, insider trading, conflicts of interest, and the rest, triggering the collapse of leading banks and reputed financial houses, which resulted in unprecedented economic crises and taxpayer bailout of captains of business and industry. China's economic success, on the other hand, exposed the capitalist myth that controls are bad for the conomy, and in the end free and unregulated markets of America had to borrow heavily from the controlled socialist-capitalist economy.

Direct foreign investment has become the buzzword in all emerging economies. It is a fact that most developing economies do not have the accumulated savings and capital necessary for starting export-oriented industries. If the advantage of cheap labour is lost and the multinationals leave, what alternatives do the poor nations have to provide employment for their vast population? Global capitalism is driven by profit, even greed. What other motivation is there for the giant corporations to invest billions of dollars in another country? One must also keep in mind that Western countries do not have the monopoly of TNCs; many developing countries, including India, Nigeria, and Brazil, have several MNCs. For example, Asian Paints, an Indian company, has manufacturing plants in twenty-two countries across five continents and is the market leader in eleven countries. Hindustan Inks is the world's largest with manufacturing branches in Europe and America. India's Hero Honda is the world's largest motorcycle manufacturing company. The world's five largest car companies are procuring their spare parts from India. Multinational business is no longer a one-way traffic. Global capitalism has become a global reality today, and globalization is, in many ways, now an inevitable process. The question is whether developing nations can afford to institute a core standard of relatively high wages and enforce stringent environmental regulations and still do business with multinational corporations. There are lessons from several erstwhile socialist countries. Some of them maintain a state monopoly of all defence-related industries and allow minority participation in other strategic industries. But multinationals are allowed major equity holdings in other areas of the economy. They can also be regulated by national laws designed for the protection of labour and environment. Therefore, the question is not whether global capitalism is good or bad but rather what type of corporations are allowed to operate in what fields and under what conditions.

Study Questions

- Distinguish between the concepts of state and government.
- Discuss the functions of the state.
- Critically examine the nature and role of different types of economy.
- Distinguish between power and authority.
- Define the three types of authority identified by Max Weber.
- Critically examine the power elite and pluralist models.
- Write an essay on the Indian political scene with special reference to the role of caste, corruption, status of women, and coalition politics.
- Critically review the collusion between globalism and corporate capitalism.
- Examine the causes, consequences, and prevention of corruption in India.

References

Bierstedt, Robert, *The Social Order,* New York: McGraw-Hill, 1974.

Dahl, Robert, *Dilemmas of Pluralist Democracy,* New Haven: Yale University Press, 1982.

Dahrendorf, Ralf, *Class and Class Conflict in Industrial Society,* Stanford: Stanford University Press, 1959.

McMichael, Philip, *Development and Social Change,* Thousand Oaks: Pine Forge Press, 2000.

Mills, C. Wright, *The Power Elite,* New York: Oxford University Press, 1956.

Mishra, Lakshmidhar, *Human Bondage: Tracing its Roots in India,* New Delhi: Sage, 2011.

Presthus, Robert V., *Men at the Top: A Study in Community Power,* New York: Oxford University Press, 1964.

Smith, David A. and Jozsef Borocz (eds), *A New World Order,* Westport: Praeger, 1995.

Tischler, Henry L., *Introduction to Sociology*, New York: The Harcourt Press, 2002.

13

Educational System

Sociology of education is a very important field within the discipline of sociology. Sociological perspectives on education have brought about significant changes in the philosophy and structure of education. Lester Frank Ward, the first president of the American Sociological Society, thought of education as a great equalizer. He believed that the unequal distribution of knowledge was the primary source of inequality in society. More and better education would equalize society by diffusing knowledge to all. A defender of 'intellectual egalitarianism', Ward argued that the differences between those at the top and at the bottom of the social ladder were not because of any difference in intellect but because of differences in the opportunity for education and knowledge. A society that provides the greatest opportunity for education for all will also produce the greatest number of individuals with exceptional usefulness.

In earlier societies like hunting and gathering and horticultural societies, there was no social institution called education, and there were no formal facilities called schools. Socialization at home taught the children what they needed to know from their parents; children simply learnt the trade of their parents. In the ancient civilizations of China and Greece learned men taught young boys from upper class families. In ancient India there was the *gurukula* system; young men, usually from the upper castes, lived with great teachers and learnt from them. In feudal Europe, education was the prerogative of the social elites; young men from the upper classes who had nothing else to do went to school to learn the classics. The concept of universal education is a relatively new idea. It was only in the beginning of the twentieth century that most nation-states began to practise the concept of mass education in earnest. Today, the idea that every child has a right to an education that enables him or her to read and write and make an independent choice is widely accepted.

The school has become the primary socialization agency in which modern states invest heavily. The school is a social system with a definite pattern of role and social relationships and a formal organization. Although the structure and functions vary, schools are principal agencies that transmit knowledge, information, and culture. In India, the organizational form of the school is largely structured by state governments. Qualifications of teachers, syllabi, examination system, and rules and regulations may be patterned by the government or other central agencies. Government schools and private-management schools vary in their relationship to community and parent–teacher associations. Private schools more actively engage the community and parents. The school, the community, and the state are interrelated and inter-dependent. The school must be sensitive to the needs and requirements of the community and build on the cultural heritage of the society. It is important to recognize that educational disadvantages at home based on socio-economic status weaken attachment to school. It is also necessary to keep the pedagogy of classroom learning relevant to the lives of all students so that they do not feel isolated and marginal. Schools are an integral part of society, so the whole social system and not just pieces must be part of the process to improve education and student learning. However, schools in India largely ignore the cultural character of local communities and the personal needs of children. They seldom take into account local conditions such as agricultural seasons, public health issues, and employment situation. School officials tend to define success in terms of numerical attendance records, drop-out rates, and test scores. They completely ignore dimensions of schooling that are difficult to quantify, such as creativity and enthusiasm. Teachers have little latitude in what and how they teach their classes. Therefore, the school as a social system is in disequilibrium.

FUNCTIONS OF EDUCATION

Every society needs skilled professionals as well as an informed citizenry. Individuals have to be trained to create new knowledge and to transmit society's cultural traditions from one generation to the next. Education is the social institution responsible for these functions which may be classified under the following categories.

Socialization

Socialization begins at home but continues at school. There are significant differences. At home children identify the rules with their parents. In school for the first time they are exposed to impersonal rules, those made by teachers, schools, and the larger society. In school they are also in the company of children from diverse backgrounds. As children progress in their education, they spend more and more time with their peers away from home. So they learn a distinct set of values, norms, and attitudes. In the old traditional society the family was the primary agent of socialization; children learnt almost everything from their parents. But as societies become more complex with new roles and technologies, we need formal organizations like schools to prepare children for adult roles. Engineers, doctors, managers, computer scientists, and researchers can only be produced by formal centres of education.

Cultural Transmission

Schools play a major role in transmitting the cultural heritage of society from one generation to the next. First, they teach the core values of one's own culture. Moral education is a very important part of the process. In addition to the traditional ways of thinking and acting, which constitute the core values, schools teach self-respect, competition, hard work, achievement orientation, self-discipline, and individualism. School curriculum is a good indication of what the society expects the students to learn. Schools are designed and equipped to pass on society's accumulated knowledge in the fields of science, technology, philosophy, and the arts to new generations of students.

Social Placement

First of all, when children start school, society recognizes them in the new status as students. Second, the prestige of the schools may also be attached to the new status. For example, students from top-ranking schools are often sought after by private companies. Third, social placement also means career opportunities. Education is the key social institution that prepares students for important roles in society. In a democracy we believe that children's success in life is fundamentally linked to their performance in schools. Therefore, parents are eager to send their children to the best schools possible. And, the best schools nurture the students' talents, develop their academic skills, encourage competition and hard work, and motivate them to achieve. Many higher education institutions also sponsor job fairs and career weeks and encourage corporations to come to the campus for recruitment. In recent years, the social placement of education has also highlighted the importance of *credentialism*, that is, the emphasis on formal training and qualifications. Certain credentials are required for certain jobs. The qualifications specify the degree, grade or rank, and years of experience. Credentials make it easy for the system to filter people and assign them appropriate statuses and roles in private and public sectors.

Innovation

Schools must do more than just transmit cultural heritage, they must create new knowledge and new technology. Research is, therefore, one of the key functions of education. Advances in scientific knowledge are essential for social and economic progress. That is why institutions of higher education are encouraged to engage in research that yields discoveries and innovations. Not only in engineering, medicine, and information technology, but also in the arts and social sciences, there is a constant need for new innovations, ideas, and perspectives. Schools are also required to equip students with the knowledge and skills necessary to adapt to a rapidly changing world. Take the demands of globalization, for example. Most educational institutions now find it necessary to offer courses in the areas of information systems, computer science, and managerial skills that are required to take on the challenges of globalization.

Social Integration

Social integration, or what we in India call national integration, is a key function of education. This function is particularly important in a pluralistic society like India with thousands of castes and many religious and linguistic groups. To begin with, schools offer the unique opportunity for students from diverse backgrounds to come together and learn. As we mentioned before, education at all levels emphasizes the core values of society such as nationalism, patriotism, equality, equal reverence for all religions, and other values embedded in the Indian culture. The concept of national integration in India is based on the philosophy of 'unity in diversity'. Core curriculum, national anthem, and numerous national schemes and cultural programmes are designed to forge a mass of people from diverse social and cultural backgrounds into one unified whole.

Critical Thinking

Of what use is education if it can only transmit the accumulated knowledge of the past to the new generation? What good is it to repeat in a parrot-like fashion the great systems of thought handed down from the past ages? Every thesis has an antithesis which leads to a synthesis which then becomes the new thesis that must be re-examined and so on. Schools should not be expected to teach students to accept everything as it is. While they teach traditional core values such as human dignity, compassion, and social justice, they must also stimulate intellectual inquiry and critical thinking. Teaching students to think independently and creatively is probably the most important function of education. Schools must stimulate intellectual curiosity and the ability to debate and critically evaluate any and all systems of knowledge. Uncritical acceptance of ideas is tantamount to mental slavery.

So far we have concentrated on the manifest functions of education. Now let us briefly turn to some latent functions of education. Child care is one of the latent functions of education. Many parents are happy to see that the children are in school rather than at home. For nuclear families where both parents are working, the child care function of the school is particularly important. A related service performed by schools in India is to provide at least one good meal per day especially for children from low-income families. Schools also keep children off the streets and away from trouble. Schools allow young people with plenty of energy, enthusiasm, and free time to channel their resources into productive enterprises. Matchmaking may be another latent function of education. Many young people find life partners with similar interests, education, and social background. Occasionally, educational institutions also facilitate mixed marriages. A significant latent function of schools is to establish social networks and friendship circles. Some of these relationships last a lifetime and are mutually supportive.

Conflict theorists agree that schools perform most of these functions but they also see a hidden agenda of education in society. They say that schools emphasize unthinking obedience and discourage creativity and independence. They argue that the educational system is a means of maintaining status quo in society by insisting on implicit conformity to rules. According to them, even the values espoused by the educational system are the values of the dominant majority. As Szymanski and Goertzel (quoted by Tischler 2002: 366) put it, the function of the school is 'to produce the kind of people the system needs, to train people for the jobs the corporations require and to instill in them the proper attitudes and values necessary for the fulfillment of one's social role.' Students who tow the official line and opt for unthinking obedience are regarded as best students while those with an open mind and critical attitude are considered troublemakers.

The thrust of the conflict perspective, however, is that the educational system is controlled and manipulated by those in power. The American system of education, for instance, extols the values of capitalism, profit, competition, and democracy. The communist government in the former Soviet Union used schools for total indoctrination of children into socialist ways of thinking. Many governments in the Middle East use education to advance their brand of religion and even to disparage other faiths. In some states in India political rulers have revised the school curriculum to glorify their leaders. The recent controversy over the revision of Indian history under BJP rule and the debate over the 'invasion' or 'migration' of Aryans are also indicative of the way the governments in power set their own agenda for education.

INEQUALITY IN EDUCATION

Inequality in education is one of the most disturbing social problems today. Because of the poor and deteriorating quality of government schools, more and more middle class parents send their children to private schools. These schools generate greater interest in learning because of smaller class size, higher academic standards, more student–teacher contact, and greater discipline. Family income is the most crucial factor affecting access to education. Government schools in remote and many rural areas are almost non-functional, making it impossible for members of Scheduled Castes (SCs), Scheduled Tribes (STs), and poor families to have equal access to quality education. As a result, literacy rates among Scheduled Castes (SCs) and Scheduled Tribes (STs) are far below the national average. For example, the literacy rate of 30 per cent among the tribal populations is less than half of the national average. In spite of several special affirmative action projects, vast majority of Scheduled Castes and Scheduled Tribes have been unable to break out of the clutches of traditional occupation and the cycle of poverty. The socio-economic status of the children not only determines their access to quality schools, but even when they are in equal schools, the cultural resources they bring to these schools heavily influence their performance. Thus, inequality in education perpetuates and even augments prevailing stratification systems.

Such gross inequalities in education are highlighted by Pierre Bourdieu's theory of cultural production. Bourdieu makes effective use of the term 'cultural capital' which refers to forms of knowledge, skills, education, and any advantages a person has which give him a higher status in society. Parents provide children with cultural capital, the attitudes and knowledge that make the educational system a comfortable and familiar place in which they can succeed. Cultural reproduction illustrates how existing disadvantages and inequalities are passed down from one generation to the next. This is especially due to the educational system. Capitalist societies depend on a stratified social system, where the working class has an education suited for manual labour, and levelling out such inequalities would break down the system. Thus, schools in capitalist societies will always be stratified. The inequality of performance at school of children from different social classes yielding 'success at school' is primarily due to the cultural capital they bring to school, not the effect of their natural aptitude. Bourdieu's work emphasized how social classes, especially the ruling and intellectual classes, reproduce themselves even under the pretence that society fosters social mobility, particularly through education. According to Bourdieu, the social and cultural capital accumulated in the ranks of upper classes get multiplied through the education system which, rather than level out the differences, enhances the inequalities of the stratified social system.

In a similar vein, the Brazilian educator, Paulo Freire (1970), talks about the way wealth gap stratifies children by access to quality education and school achievement. He has bluntly stated that schools provide a 'pedagogy of the oppressed'. The oppressed are a social class unspecified by race, gender, ethnicity, language, and culture. His work has stimulated over three decades of international dialogue on educational philosophy. Similarly, Ivan Illich's, *Deschooling Society* (1971: 1–9) argues that students, especially those who are poor, are schooled by the educational system to confuse process and substance. 'The pupil is thereby "schooled" to confuse teaching with learning, grade advancement with education, a diploma with competence, and fluency with the ability to say something new. His imagination is "schooled" to accept service in place of value'. The institutionalized system of education leads to physical pollution, social polarization, and psychological impotence. According to Illich:

It should be obvious that even with schools of equal quality a poor child can seldom catch up with a rich one. Even if they attend equal schools and begin at the same age, poor children lack most of the educational opportunities which are casually available to the middle-class child. These advantages range from conversation and books in the home to vacation travel and a different sense of oneself, and apply, for the child who enjoys them, both in and out of school for advancement or learning. The poor need funds to enable them to learn, not to get certified for the treatment of their alleged disproportionate deficiencies.

EDUCATION AND THE UN MILLENNIUM DEVELOPMENT GOALS

In September 2000, world leaders adopted the United Nations Millennium Development Goals which included the following educational goals:

1. Achieve universal primary education: ensure that by 2015 all boys and girls complete a full course of primary schooling.
2. Promote gender equality and empowerment of women: eliminate gender disparity in primary and secondary education, preferably by 2005, and at all levels by 2015.

This means ensuring access to education for over 115 million children who do not attend school today. There is general consensus that the best way to reduce the gap between rich and poor is by ensuring universal education. Without formal education children are starting a life with a severe handicap that ensures they will remain in abject poverty, and the gap between the rich and the poor will continue to widen. In an increasingly integrated world, such socio-economic disparity is a major source of instability. As Amartya Sen put it, 'Illiteracy and innumeracy are a greater threat to humanity than terrorism' (quoted in Brown 2006).

The World Bank has taken the lead with its Education for All plan which will grant financial support for any country with a well-designed strategy to achieve universal primary education. The scheme calls for three principal requirements: that a country submit a sensible plan to reach universal basic education, commit a meaningful share of its own resources to the plan, and have transparent budgeting and accounting practices. If the plan is fully implemented, all children in poor countries would get primary school education by 2015.

The following passage from Lester Brown's *Plan B 2.0* (2006): The benefits of education are many, particularly for women. The achievement level of children correlates closely with the educational level of their mothers. Children of educated mothers are better nourished not necessarily because the family income is higher but because their mother's better understanding of nutrition leads to better choice of foods and healthier methods of preparation. Educating women is the key to breaking the poverty cycle.

The education of girls leads to smaller families. In every society for which data are available, fertility falls as female educational levels rise. And mothers with at least five years of school lose fewer infants during childbirth or early illnesses that their less educated peers do. Among other things, these women can read the instructions on medications and they have a better understanding of how to take care of themselves during pregnancy. Economist Gene Sperling concluded in a 2001 study of 72 countries that 'the expansion of female secondary education may be the single best lever for achieving substantial reductions in fertility.' The case of Kerala illustrates this point. Compared with the whole country, infant mortality is one quarter the national rate and the fertility rate is two-thirds that of India's. In fact, at 1.96 births per woman, Kerala has a lower fertility rate than the United States. This is attributed primarily to the educational revolution in the state.

Sperling argues that every education plan should provide for getting to the hardest-to-reach segments of society, especially poor girls in rural areas. Providing scholarships for promising students from poor families to attend schools, in exchange for a commitment to work in a development project for a fixed period of time, is a highly profitable investment. In fact, some countries like Brazil and Bangladesh provide small scholarships for girls where needed. The World Bank estimates that external funding of approximately $12 billion a year is needed to achieve universal primary education in the more than 80 countries that are unlikely to reach the millennium goal by 2015. On the one hand, not only books but personal computers and vast information resources of the internet are available to children of the developed world but access to minimum level of basic education is unavailable to the vast majority of world's children. Moreover, there are almost 800 million illiterate adults in the world who are severely handicapped by lack of education. Therefore, any effective education plan should incorporate adult literacy programmes.

The extent of schooling in any country is closely tied to its level of economic development. In hunting and gathering societies, instruction amounted to knowledge and skills parents transmitted directly to their children. In less developed countries boys and girls spend several years in school learning practical knowledge, civic duties, and cultural traditions. Yet only a small proportion of them go on to colleges and universities to study literature, art, history, and science. In many Islamic countries schooling is closely tied to Islam, and madrasas impart mostly Quranic education. In the former Soviet Union, the communist party made certain that socialist values dominated its schools. But now the Russians are re-inventing education and retraining their teachers; for the first time, private, religious, and even foreign-run schools are allowed. More industrialized countries not only endorse universal education but also encourage access to higher education in science, engineering, and the arts. One of the global trends in education today is the internationalization of education. Satellite technology, distance learning, and open universities have changed the nature of higher education. In the West, most universities today offer a number of courses on the internet. In addition, universities around the world are competing for students from overseas. Many universities in the United States, Australia, and the United Kingdom have set up campuses overseas. Medical colleges in China are aggressively recruiting students from around the world. Globalization of education may offer more choices but it is unlikely to reduce inequality in education.

Education in India

The relationship between education and development has been well-documented and is fairly well understood; therefore, there is no need to reproduce any data here. Lee Kuan Yew attributed Singapore's success to education. World Bank considers primary education 'a significant factor in explaining sustained high levels of growth in export-led economies.' Primary education is thought to be responsible for 58 per cent predicted growth in Japan and 87 per cent of growth in Thailand. South Korea and India became republics almost at the same time. While Korea achieved almost 100 per cent literacy and emerged as an economic tiger, India remained far behind many Asian countries with only 65 per cent literacy (Abraham 1998).

India has over 30 per cent of the world's total illiterates and 22 per cent of out-of-school children (Abraham 1998). While our East Asian neighbours have attained almost 98 per cent literacy, between 1981 and 1991 our primary school enrollment grew only around 3 per cent. A comparison of 1991 and 2001 census figures shows that the literacy rates recorded an increase of 13.17 per cent from 52.21 in 1991 to 65.38 in 2001. The female literacy rate increased by 11.72 per cent. During the two decades, 1980–2000, the female literacy rate increased by a measly 25 per cent. The literacy rate among males jumped from 64.1 per cent to 75.8 per cent during the same period. However, the provisional data from 2011 census show that literacy rate improved sharply among females as compared to males. While the effective literacy rate for males rose from 75.26 per cent to 82.14 per cent, an increase of 6.9 per cent, it increased 11.8 per cent for females, from 53.67 per cent to 65.46 per cent. This means that the gap of 21.59 percentage points recorded between male and female literacy rates in 2001 census declined to 16.68 percentage points in 2011. This being the national average, the literacy rate in some areas is still below 45 per cent. For example, literacy rate for Madhya Pradesh's Alirajpur district is 37.22 per cent. Yet, the national expenditure on education as a percentage of GDP is only 3.1 per cent. Singapore spends almost 19 per cent on education and South Korea about 18.5 per cent. India is one of the very few countries with such low priority in education. No wonder, according to some estimates India will soon have more than 50 per cent of the world's illiterates.

Some statistical facts about education in India are:

- 2001 literacy rate (percentage): male, 75.26; female, 53.67; total, 64.83.
- 2011 literacy rate (percentage): male, 82.14; female, 65.46; total, 74.04.
- State with highest literacy: Kerala, 93.91 per cent.
- State with lowest literacy rate: Bihar, 63.82 per cent.
- Increase in effective literacy rate in the latest census: 9.2 per cent.

India has adopted Universalization of Elementary Education as a national goal. The India 2003 Report states that 94 per cent of the country's rural population have primary schools within a 1 kilometre distance, and at the upper primary stage, 84 per cent of the rural population have schools within a distance of 3 kilometres. The government set the following goals to promote universal education.

1. All children of six to fourteen years of age are in school/Education Guarantee Scheme/bridge course by 2003.
2. They complete five years of primary education by 2007.
3. They complete eight years of schooling by 2010.
4. Bridge all gender and social category gaps at the primary stage by 2007 and at elementary education level by 2010.
5. Universal retention by 2010.

Later, the Government of India passed the Right of Children to Free and Compulsory Education Act 2009 which guarantees free and compulsory education to all children. It is too early to assess the impact of the Right to Education Act.

However, one thing is clear. These are ambitious goals. But there are at least two major stumbling blocks. The first pertains to the percentage of national expenditure allocated to education. Almost 48 per cent of the country's primary schools are run in makeshift shelters, seven out of ten schools have only one or two teachers, 55 per cent of the students have no access to drinking water, and almost 80 per cent of the schools have no toilets. A World Bank document estimated that government schools in Uttar Pradesh spend a bare Rs 96 a year educating a child and 96 per cent of the primary education budget goes towards paying salaries. According to a survey conducted by the National Council for Educational Research and Training, in 1990 there were 1,694 primary schools in the country without a single teacher. According to the Fifth All India Educational Survey, 66 per cent of the primary schools in the country have fewer than three teachers and 16 per cent of primary school teachers in rural India have not even matriculated. When 96 per cent of the budget goes to pay teachers' salaries, there can be no playground, and there are no toys, games, or creative arts. We spend so little on primary education that facilities are pathetically inadequate and education so boring that over 60 per cent of the children drop out at the primary level. Indeed, nearly 50 per cent of the children drop out during the first three years because of poor quality of schooling, boring curriculum, and pressures of poverty. Despite the government's claim that 83 per cent of all children attend school, reliable reports indicate that almost half of the children and some one-third of their teachers regularly fail to show up for class.

The second issue pertains to child labour. If our goal of universal elementary education is to become a reality, then we must tackle the issue of child labour first. Child labour must be made illegal not only in hazardous industries, as is the case now, but anywhere and in any form. Every child must have free and easy access to quality primary education. Then, how do we force poor parents to send their children to school when their help is needed at home? This is possible only if we adopt flexible hours and a school calendar that takes into account local climatic and agricultural cycles. For example, instead of the two regular months of summer holidays, the schools may be closed during the busy agricultural season when farmers need the help of their children. Similarly, it is also possible to have two separate morning and afternoon shifts if special circumstances warrant them. In any event, the facts are clear. So long as millions of India's children work full time in lock industry, carpet weaving, match-box making, almond thrushing, diamond polishing, and jewellery making, their right to educaton will only be a dream. The Right to Education Act will be no more effective than the anti-dowry, anti-corruption, and anti-foeticide acts.

We began this chapter with Ward's idea that education is a great equalizer. It is also a status stabilizer and the most important factor in social mobility. Today India boasts of the largest pool of scientists and engineers in the world. Even in the United States, a significant percentage of doctors and engineers are from India. It is the remarkable growth of education that made India the information technology hub of the world, the economic powerhouse, and a major destination for foreign direct investment. Yet, can we say that education in India is the great equalizer? Consider the controversy over Mandal I, 1990, and the issue of reservation for OBCs in 2006, dubbed by some as Mandal II. Students took to the streets to protest 27 per cent reservations in the country's premier educational institutions like the Indian Institutes of Technology (IITs), Indian Institutes of Management (IIMs), and All India Institute of Medical Sciences (AIIMS). The main argument against the reservation was that it would compromise the merit of students and the reputation and standard of these elite institutions. In this highly charged emotional atmosphere, caste became the focus of discussion. However, as N.R. Levin (2009: 107–8) points out:

In all the debates that raged in the media and in popular discussion, it was often not acknowledged that the focus on merit itself made caste merely invisible, though it was very much present. For instance, during these agitations and the debates around it, it was discovered that backward caste members had a marginal presence in the mainstream media (considered a bastion of meritocracy) and that there was an absence of their voices of dissent. Merit is determined objectively through entrance examinations, marks secured, etc. But it was only students who had access to a particular kind of education at elite institutions and had the benefit of coaching classes, who lay the maximum claim to that merit. It is well known among policy makers and educational experts that the majority of these winners are particularly drawn from urban, upper-caste households. What is disturbing is that a vast majority of the rural, backward caste students are not able to acquire the merit, and remain tied up with traditional jobs or end up as informal labourers in urban areas.

It is obvious that education is an equalizer only if everyone has equal opportunity.

Let us consider the reality of equal opportunity. Government-run schools, especially in the rural areas, are notoriously inefficient, understaffed, and poorly equipped. Very little instruction takes place in these schools which are mostly attended by students who cannot afford better equipped private schools. Middle class parents choose top schools for their children, provide private tuition, and use highly-priced guides and sample tests. Private schools now make up at least ten per cent of the total. Poor students who are forced to attend the inferior government schools and have no access to other support facilities are at a serious disadvantage. Even in the state of Kerala which is proud of its high literacy rate, many government schools record a dismal five to ten per cent pass in the Secondary School Leaving Certificate (SSLC) examination. The Janshala programme jointly sponsored by the Government of India and the United Nations supports special efforts aimed at achieving universal elementary education. Janshala is a block-based, community-centred primary education designed to benefit regions with low female literacy, incidence of child labour, and concentration of the ST and SC population. There are also other special national schemes such as reservations, book banks, hostels, and coaching facilities for the weaker sections of the population.

There is an irony in the way we determine our priorities in education. We have a system of education that heavily subsidizes university education for the upper middle class and spends crores of rupees on postgraduate and technical education. The cost of college education per student per year is approximately Rs 35,000 but the fees charged by the universities make up a fraction of the university's total expenditure. There is something wrong with the system when 15 per cent of the population gets almost free higher education whereas 85 per cent receive so little for primary education. To make matters worse, most graduates are unable to find jobs matching their technical skills or professional preparation. Our system of education does not inculcate dignity of labour; on the contrary, it breeds false pride and makes people shun away from jobs that involve physical labour. Nor does our education encourage or prepare graduates to start a business, industry, or projects on their own.

India has a long way to go to establish a uniform standard of education. However, National System of Education envisaged in the National Policy of Education talks about a national curricular framework which contains a common core along with other flexible, region-specific components.

Absence of critical thinking at all levels is another major problem plaguing education in India. In Indian education, conformity is equated with discipline and the two are substituted for creativity and imagination. Knowledge often centres on cramming lessons, and evaluation focuses on testing memory. Imagination and creativity are irrelevant. At the level of higher education sycophancy and political cronyism are widespread. Indeed, this is a very unique and disturbing situation in India. Universities are supposed to be centres of learning where people debate ideas and evaluate them critically. On Indian campuses, students protest if their political bosses are not invited and they protest if the opposition leaders are invited. They clamour for banning books and boycott textbooks which present any ideas contrary to their own. Just consider the recent case of the Academic Council of Delhi University abruptly deleting from the syllabus the celebrated essay on Ramayana by the eminent scholar A.K. Ramanujan because Hindu fundamentalists objected to the essay and a handful of right-wing activists vandalized the university's history department. *The Hindu* (28 October 2011) newspaper ran an interview with the noted historian Romila Thapar under the caption, 'The Richness of the Ramayana, the Poverty of a University'. Imagine ninety out of 100 'free-thinking' scholars at the university succumbed to external pressure and voted against academic freedom. This is a dangerous trend. The citadels of learning must be open to all ideas, beliefs, and philosophical systems. Open debates are the only way to advance intellectual integrity; censorship for whatever reason encourages mental slavery and breeds ignorance. Teenagers and young adults in the West adore celebrities and throng to their concerts to catch a glimpse of them; there is no question of mental slavery here. But the Indian phenomena of sycophancy, uncritical acceptance of ideology, and blind following of political leaders is unique and deplorable. In this context, I would like to narrate a personal experience which occurred while I was a PhD student at Michigan State University. Lyndon B. Johnson, the then president of the United States, was scheduled to visit the campus during the following week for a major policy speech. It so happened that one of my graduate classes met at the same time the president's speech was scheduled. Therefore, the professor announced in the previous class that he would cancel next week's class so that we could attend his lecture. One of the students protested. She said that she had paid a large amount in tuition fee to attend the class and to learn something from it: 'I am not throwing away my money to hear some politicians. I will be here in the next class to learn and you will be here to teach. I can read in the newspapers what the President said.' The professor immediately replied that he would hold the regular classes. Students use politics to make the politicians more accountable and not to curtail academic pursuit; they never become stooges of politicians. Indeed, the students would never fight to curtail academic freedom or vandalize public property in response to calls by political parties or religious fundamentalists.

Recently the literary journal *Little Magazine* (Vol. 6 [1 and 2], 2005) invited a large number of writers, teachers, philosophers, historians, and education experts to discuss the state of education in India. How is it possible, several of them ask, that a country famous for its scholarly traditions has fallen so far behind? Few other countries can boast such rich history of intellectual, cultural, metaphysical, and artistic exploration, but the country's educational system today is in crisis. The main criticism of the educational system is that it is intellectually stultifying. Children are not taught, but tamed. Education isn't geared towards encouraging students to be creative and critical but rather to turn out mechanical drones who cannot think independently. Nor do children learn to see themselves as part of a greater whole. The school system holds them captive in a self-image of belonging to a specific population group in a specific country with a specific culture. What is missing throughout India's educational system is the space for a more experimental form of education, such as boosting the imagination, encouraging the arts, and exploring the capacity for self-reflection. The contributors warn that India can no longer afford to ignore the world around it. This is indeed a wake-up call.

Another frequent criticism of our educational system is that it is highly irrelevant. Education has become merely a passport for jobs. And society itself has become highly credentialized. Credentials have become a rite of passage and a degree or diploma has become necessary to perform a variety of tasks. Of course, qualifications are necessary not only to fill the jobs but also to filter numerous applicants in a fair and just manner. The question is how much of the education is relevant to the needs of society. In response to the challenges of globalization, universities have started numerous programmes in information technology, computer science, and global entrepreneurial management. But there does not seem to be a similar emphasis on programmes and courses directed towards rural and sustainable development. Appropriate and rural technology, environmental science, rural health and sanitation, cooperation and Panchayati Raj, grass roots leadership development, small entrepreneurship, and even agriculture and horticulture do not receive half as much attention from our institutions of higher education. For example, nobody seems to ask why Sri Lanka, Vietnam, and Guatemala are able to produce ten to fifteen times more black pepper per hectare than India. Even when it comes to environmental pollution, microhydel projects, low-income housing, solar power, and many other rural development projects, our institutions of higher education act like ivory towers and are too happy to leave those mundane enterprises to voluntary agencies.

Universities must also initiate closer cooperation between institutions of higher learning and corporations. Local industries and businesses provide excellent resources for students to gain practical experience. Students may work with local handicrafts, rural industries, manufacturing units, fisheries, spices, microelectronics, cooperatives, and local governments and earn credit for practicum. Moreover, every institution of higher learning must have an emphasis on community service. Just like teaching and research, community service is also an important function of the university. In addition to seminars, debates, sports events and cultural programmes, universities must also sponsor regular social service programmes. Many problem-related research projects might evolve from these social service programmes.

Finally, higher education in India is all about specialization. Students who successfully complete the secondary school education go in for professional studies such as medicine, engineering, or business, or a programme of study in science or liberal arts. In other words, right from high school, young students can go directly into professional courses without any background in a broad-based liberal arts education. They will completely miss the rich heritage of humanity's arts and classics. This is simply unthinkable in the United States. After high school every student is required to complete almost two years of general education in the arts and sciences before they move on to a field of specialization. The core curriculum usually includes such courses as introduction to sociology, principles of economics, introduction to logic, American history, history of the state, and a few courses in the classics in addition to core courses in language, mathematics, and science. In other words, you cannot get a degree in medicine, engineering, or business without a number of courses in liberal arts and classics. Such a broad-based liberal arts education is necessary for the development of a well-rounded personality. Every student must be taught to appreciate his rich cultural heritage first, encouraged to think critically, and then prepared to be an effective participant in society before he becomes a doctor, lawyer, or engineer. Liberal education, based on critical thinking, is the only guarantor of economic and political freedom.

Study Questions

- What are the functions of education? Explain in detail.
- How does education relate to UN Millennium Development Goals?
- Write an essay on the status of education in India with special reference to systemic inequality.
- Critically examine the controversy surrounding reservation in education.

References

Abraham, Francis, *The Agony of India,* Madras: East West Books, 1998.

Bourdieu, Pierre, *The Field of Cultural Production,* New York: Columbia University Press, 1993.

Brown, Lester R., *Plan B 2.0,* New York: W.W. Norton & Company, 2006.

Freire, Paulo, *Pedagogy of the Oppressed,* New York: Seabury, 1970.

Government of India, *India 2003*, New Delhi: Publications Division, 2003.

Illich, Ivan, *Deschooling Society*, New York: Harper & Row, 1971.

Levin, N.R., 'The Changing Social Structure in Contemporary India', in Neera Chadhoke and Praveen Priyadarshi (eds), *Contemporary India: Economy, Society, Plitics,* New Delhi: Pearson, 2009.

Sperling, Gene B., 'Towards Universal Education', *Foreign Affairs,* September/October, pp. 7–13, 2001.

Tischler, Henry L., *Introduction to Sociology,* New York: The Harcourt Press, 2002.

United Nations, Millennium Development Goals Indicators Database, August 2005.

14

Religion

There is nothing in the world which has at once been the object of such deep reverence and the centre of such severe criticism as religion; it has been equated with salvation and characterized as the opiate of the people. On the one hand, it is viewed as the 'group-supported road to salvation', the path to eternal bliss, or the light of mankind. On the other hand, it is said to be a survival of the primitive, or simply a vestige of an illusion or collective phantasmagoria. Philosophers and scientists seldom agree on the nature and function of religion. And, what Gibbon (1914: 49) wrote of the religion of the Roman Empire could very well be said about contemporary forms of worship in the twentieth century: 'The various modes of worship, which prevailed in the Roman world, were considered by the people as equally true; by the philosopher, as equally false; and the magistrate, as equally useful.'

The sociologist, of course, is not concerned with the truth or falsity of any given religion; he only takes an objective look at religion—its functions, social foundations, and social consequences. He does not study religion per se, but the effect of religious beliefs and practices on the social and cultural systems, socialization process, and personality development. More specifically, the sociologist is concerned with the myriad ways in which society and religion interact, with profound consequences for the individual.

Although the viewpoints and perspectives on religion vary greatly, there seems to be a universal human impulse towards sacredness which manifests itself in the institution of religion, a codified system of beliefs, symbolic expressions, and rituals. Of all creatures, humans alone recognize their own mortality and ponder over death. This awareness induces in them a sense of awe and reverence for what is construed as the supernatural and gives rise to an elaborate system of rituals and ceremonies intended to propitiate the divine force that presides over human destiny. Thus, according to Freud, religion develops from the need to exorcize the horrors of nature, particularly the cruelty of death and also to compensate for the deprivations which culture imposes on the individual. According to Durkheim, religion begins with the division of the world into two kinds of phenomena: the profane and the sacred. The *profane* is concerned with the ordinary aspects of everyday life; it has nothing to do with religious beliefs. The *sacred* refers to all objects and aspects of life set apart from the ordinary, regarded as holy and related to the supernatural. The latter forms the foundation of every religion. Anything that is sacred is so special to the believers that it cannot be questioned.

According to Durkheim (1926: 47), '*Religion* is a unified system of beliefs and practices relative to sacred things, uniting into a single moral community all those who adhere to those beliefs and practices.' Paul Tillich says that religion is that which concerns man ultimately. In sociological terms, religion is simply a system of beliefs, practices, rituals, and symbols that somehow relate to a community's orientation to the supernatural or the life beyond. Religion entails a form of worship, obedience to divine commandments, and a concern with transcendental realms that are beyond the rational and the empirical.

There are eleven world religions today. Christianity has the largest group of followers with over 2.1 billion believers. Islam is the second largest religion with over 1.5 billion followers, and the Hindus constitute about 900 million worldwide and Buddhists about 376 million. Whereas Christianity is the dominant religion of the West, Hinduism, Sikhism, Jainism, and Zoroastrianism are practised primarily in India. Taoism and Confucianism are traditional Chinese religions, and Shintoism is the ancient Japanese religion. Buddhism is concentrated in East and Southeast Asia and Islam in West Asia but with large followings in Asia and Africa. The followers of Judaism are concentrated in Israel and the United States. The Baha'is make up over 7 million worldwide.

RELIGIONS AMONG THE 'PRIMITIVE' PEOPLE

In the process of evolution, man came to believe that there are some powers outside him that control the forces of nature as well as his own well-being. He believed that these powers can be propitiated with gifts and other actions. Rituals and ceremonies developed to take care of the interests of these supernatural powers. Shamans, medicine men, and priests emerged to mediate between man and those powers he held in awe. Objects that represented or were associated with these powers were treated as sacred. Gradually, these beliefs, practices, and their practitioners tended to become part of the tribal social structure.

Primitive religions have taken at least three major forms: animism, naturism, and totemism. Animism is the belief that all things, animate and inanimate, are endowed with personal indwelling souls or spirits. This involves belief in spiritual beings such as ghosts, spirits, and souls. For example, the Native Americans believed in the Great Spirit that exists in all objects and beings and spoke to them through animals and trees. Naturism is the belief in the personified forces of nature which control human destiny. Throughout history humans believed that gods or other supernatural beings controlled the forces of nature, and once again, they sought to appease them for blessings. Not only thunder and lightning, wind, fire, and mighty ocean but also dreadful diseases such as smallpox were believed to be controlled by certain gods or goddesses. Finally, most tribal societies have a totem, an animal, plant, or natural object, that is set apart as sacred and towards which members of the community feel a special relationship. Totemism is a 'form of social organization and religious practice typically involving an intimate association between sibs and their totems, which are regarded as ancestors or as supernaturally connected with an ancestor, which are tabooed as food, and which give the sibs their names' (Henry Pratt Fairchild 1968: 321). Animism, naturism, and totemism have several elements in common. People believe that they can communicate with these powers or spirits and influence them to enhance the community's well-being. Attitude of the community involves veneration of ghosts, spirits, and other supernatural beings. Rituals and ceremonies often involve magic and scacrifices. There are sacred objects, places, and people that are taboo. Very often celebrations of the spirit involve magic, dance, and ritual sacrifices.

James Frazer, British social anthropologist and classical scholar, analysed primitive religions and a vast range of exotic beliefs and customs in terms of man's search for true knowledge and effective control of his environment and his conditions. He delineated the evolution of human psyche in three phases: magical, religious, and scientific thought. Magical thought assumed that the universe is regulated by impersonal and unchanging laws, and the magician, like the modern day scientist, used his knowledge in a quasi-technical manner to accomplish things. As the failures of magic became apparent, it was gradually discredited, and people turned to religious thought. In this phase, supernatural beings were supposed to control the world, and they began to venerate and propitiate them. Finally, recognizing the limits of his own powers and gradually applying logico-experimental methods, man arrived at the scientific stage.

ELEMENTS OF RELIGION

Members of a religion share a set of beliefs, a system of philosophy, forms of rituals, and some type of organization.

Any proposition about an aspect of the universe that is accepted as true may be called a belief. Religion is founded on many such *beliefs*, although they are not usually universal or easily demonstrable. A systematic belief, doctrine or theology is not necessarily a universal component of religion; not even belief in God—personal or transcendental—is essential to the existence of a religion. As a matter of fact, several major religions of the world like Buddhism, Confucianism, Shintoism, and Taoism do not involve a particular god-figure; they constitute certain ethical and philosophical systems that emphasize correct behaviour and a moral way of life.

Based on beliefs of members, religions are divided into two types, *monotheistic* and *polytheistic*. The former believes in only one god, the omnipresent, omnipotent, supernatural god. Polytheistic religions like the natural religions of the ancient Greeks and Romans and many primitive religions of today worship several gods who preside over numerous forces of nature. Hinduism which believes in one supreme being, the *atman*, sees the manifestation of god in myriad forms. Thus, Hinduism is a loose association of numerous local systems of beliefs and rituals which seek to propitiate different deities that preside over particular villages, castes, or clans. Whether it is the Trimurthys of the Hindus, the concept of 'no god but Allah' of Muslims, the one transcendental god of the Christians, a beautiful female deity of the Eskimos, the whale god of the Cherokee American Indians, the totem of the Australian aboriginals, or the Greek gods of Mount Olympus, religion throughout the centuries was always expressed in terms of a system of beliefs. This is why followers of any religion are called believers or 'the faithful' and non-members are characterized as 'infidels' or those who 'lost' their faith.

The creation of the *sacred* is another important element of religion. Myths, legends, and sacred texts provide a framework of knowledge within which the supernatural and the phenomenon outside the ordinary experience become meaningful to the believers. Similarly, the profuse use of *symbols* by believers is part of an attempt to explain the ultimate and the unknown in terms of the mundane and the ordinary, while transcending the objects to the heights of veneration and sanctity. Thus, knowledge of a superhuman figure and his 'demands' is transformed into a pattern of rituals and ceremonies. With this knowledge, doctrines and beliefs like karma or retributive justice, last judgement, forgiveness, absolution, and salvation become meaningful.

The practice of every religion involves a variety of rituals. In addition to various *rituals* and offerings at the temple, the Hindu must also perform several life cycle ceremonies connected with childbirth, naming, attainment of puberty, marriage, death, and death anniversary, etc. Catholics observe Lent and Muslims have Ramadan. Christians celebrate mass and communion while the Buddhists have their prayer wheels and prayer ships. Other rituals include lighting of candles, lighting of the sacred lamp, burning incense, kneeling and bowing, offerings, scripture readings, religious processions, singing of devotional songs, chanting of mantras, circumambulation, etc. As Malinowski (1936: 34) observes:

To us the most essential point about magic and religious ritual is that it steps in only where knowledge fails. Supernaturally founded ceremonial grows out of life, but it never stultifies the practical efforts of man. In his ritual of magic or religion, man attempts to enact miracles, not because he ignores the limitations of his mental powers, but, on the contrary, because he is fully cognizant of them. To go one step further, the recognition of this seems to me indispensable if we want once and for ever to establish the truth that religion has its own subject-matter, its own legitimate field of development; that this must never encroach on the domain where science, reason and experience ought to remain supreme.

Emotionalism is another important aspect of religion. Religious experience is a profound personal experience. It is hard to find a uniform pattern but the emotional experience depends on the intensity of one's faith, the doctrinaire orthodoxy of a religion, form of rituals, and the formative influence of different sects. Some religious experiences include self-torture, collective hallucination, piercing parts of the body, trance, mass hysteria, magical dances, and a host of other emotionally charged experiences. Festivals, ceremonies, prayers, pilgrimages, and certain annual events are occasions for collective enthusiasm and unique personal experiences among the believers of a particular faith. They are the manifest expressions of solidarity, identity, and feeling of awe among believers of the same faith.

Members of most religions have a sense of *community* in that their beliefs, rituals, and practices unite them into a common fold. Some religious groups such as the Catholic Church have a hierarchical organizational structure but most are loosely formed associations of members. Whether there is a formal organization or not, members of every religion have a sense of mutual identity. The bonds that unite members can be very weak or extremely strong. Most religious groups also have some form of organizational structure to train religious leaders, teachers, monks, or priests. The organization promotes communication among members, fosters a sense of unity and group solidarity. Even among the Hindus who lack a universal formal organizational structure, temples, mutts, and other organizations serve as rallying points for the faithful. Some religions have formal means of enforcing conformity to group norms and punishing members for violation.

In summary, we may enumerate the following elements of religion:

1. An irresistible obsession with the sacred, variously defined as god, totem, supernatural, divine, or the ultimate.
2. Symbols—any sacred objects like *trishul*, a cross, fire, totem, beads, prayer wheels, etc.
3. A social form with networks of institutional arrangements and status-roles (priests, temples, monks, churches, shrines, monasteries).
4. A moral philosophy which unites the mundane and the supernatural in a mystical blend.
5. Holy texts believed to be based on revelation and containing the tenets of faith and rules of conduct.
6. A system of rituals including festivals, ceremonies, prayers, religious services, feasts, sacrifices, fasts, offerings, pilgrimages, etc.
7. An expressive culture—particularly visual and performing arts—including dancing, singing, chanting, processions, possession, mystical ecstasy, trance, alteration of psychological states through drugs and deprivation.
8. Congregation which includes meetings, discourses, and devotional gatherings.

SOME RELATED CONCEPTS

Magic

In pre-literate societies magic served some of the same functions as religion. Magicians and shamans were probably the first practitioners of medicine and religion. *Magic* refers to an active attempt to manipulate spirits or supernatural forces in order to attain desired results. Magic does not necessarily involve the worship of a god or gods. Magic is a set of techniques intended to coerce the spirits to grant certain wishes, and almost always is a means to an end. Whereas religion is a cohesive force that unites all believers into a moral community, magic is performed for the benefit of an individual or a group that uses it. In the Middle Ages most people in Europe believed in sorcery, werewolves, witchcraft, and black magic. Elaborate techniques of magic were practised in Asia and Africa. The importance of magic has declined with the development of science and new perspectives on religion. However, magic is still practised by several tribal communities, and several elements of magic are incorporated into the practices of some religious sects and cults.

Sect

A *sect* is an exclusive, highly cohesive group of believers who strictly adhere to a religious doctrine and reject many beliefs and practices of the general society. Membership into a sect is voluntary, usually by conversion. In other words, members join a sect rather than follow their inherited faith. Sects repudiate the existing order and adopt several unconventional beliefs and forms of worship. Sects usually stress equalitarian ideals among its members as new converts and old members are all treated with equal respect. They also expect active participation, strict conformity, and personal commitment on the part of their members. As small breakaway groups from more established religions, sects are less formal than organized religions and celebrate personal experience. Since sects deviate from established norms and hold rigidly to their own religious convictions, their members sometimes suffer harassment at the hands of the general society. According to Thomas O'Dea (1968: 131),

All sects display a considerable degree of totalism in dominating the lives of their membership. Ideological domination is usually supplemented and supported on the social level by measures which set the group apart, such as endogamy, limitations on the forms of participation with outsiders, refusal to take part in significant common societal activities, peculiar habits of eating and abstinence, and with some groups, even peculiarities of dress. Related to these social forms of segregation is the notion of the sect members as comprising the 'elect', some kind of religious elite.

It must be noted that a sect makes no attempt to influence the religious lives and behaviour of those who are outside its fold. As a voluntary group, membership is in fact restricted to those who are qualified to be members. This often requires some test of religious or ethical eligibility such as proof of religious commitment. Normally members are not born into the sect but admitted into it; therefore, the children of existing members have to make a positive affirmation of faith when they are old enough to do so. The sect is a small grouping which aspires inward perfection and values direct personal fellowship among its members. It is either indifferent or hostile to the state and the larger society and often upholds visions of an alternative society. Sects usually, but not always, spring from the lower classes and those who feel oppressed by the state and by society. In a sect, charisma is attached to the religious leader whereas in the organized church it is attached to an office.

Sects are in many ways religious experiments which offer the sociologist an opportunity to study religiosity in its purest forms uncontaminated by the complexities of motive, organization and doctrine which characterize the long established churches and denominations. Sects also offer the opportunity to study what are often radically new ideas and beliefs, styles of organization and life and the processes through which they emerge. Since a large proportion of their membership may be very recent converts, they offer an opportunity to study the process of conversion to unorthodox and 'deviant' beliefs and practices and how such deviance is maintained against the pressure of the wider society. They offer insights into religious change and the emergence of new religious traditions. They are, in short, something of a laboratory for the sociologist of religion. (Hamilton 2001: 229)

Bryan Wilson (Sills 1968: 133) has shown that it is possible to classify sects in terms of their ideological orientations based on the group's self-definition. He has distinguished four types of sects:

1. *Conversionist sect*—which seeks to convert others and thereby to change the world.
2. *Adventist sect*—which expects drastic divine intervention and awaits a new dispensation.
3. *Introversionist sect*—which is pietistic in its orientation, withdrawing from the world to cultivate its inner spirituality.
4. *Gnostic sect*—which offers some special esoteric religious knowledge.

Some sects take a militant posture towards the world, and actively seek to change it, while other sects seek to withdraw from the world, and seek to remain as removed from society as possible.

Cult

A *cult* is an amorphous type of religious organization which is often inspired by a charismatic leader. People voluntarily follow a leader who preaches new beliefs and practices. Since many cults hold unconventional doctrines and adhere to different lifestyles, they evoke negative sentiments in the popular mind. Cults are often at odds with the larger society but they are not necessarily deviant or evil. In fact several of the organized religions began as cults. Cults often last only as long as their leader. There were several millenarian cults that appeared at the end of the twentieth century. These groups believed that the end of the world was near and prepared themselves to be saved by god as a select group of faithful.

According to Stark and Bainbridge (1979), the process of sect development is one of schism in the face of social division and stratification, but the process of emergence of cults is quite different. They set out three mutually compatible models of the process of cult emergence: the psychopathology, entrepreneur, and subculture-evolution. The first model holds that mentally ill persons invent novel compensators and accept them as rewards. The entrepreneurial model recognizes that cults are in many ways like any business; cults are created by individuals with entrepreneurial flair because such individuals believe that they can profit from them. The third model draws upon sociological work on deviant subcultures including delinquent subcultures. Religious cults often begin as magical cults. A magical cult is one that offers specific compensators but not of a supernatural kind. These models are certainly controversial, especially the mental illness model. The authors seem to have been influenced by their own work on spirit possession and shamanism in which hysterical-like behaviour is attributed in some societies to invasion of the individual by powerful and demanding spirits, cults, and movements. The Moonies, People's Temple, Jesus People, Scientology, Rajneeshis, and Ananda Margis are often thought of as cults.

Cults have often attracted controversy because of their alleged techniques of recruitment, lifestyles, and values which are perceived to run counter to those of the larger society. Many of the cults have been accused of kidnapping, brainwashing, using hypnosis, and other mind-control techniques and drugs. They have also been charged with manipulation of the young, immorality, and exploitation. Sociologists of religion view cult formation as a response to utilitarian individualism and materialism of modern consumer culture which is characterized by impersonality and moral ambiguity. They think of it as 'anthropological protest against modernity', quest for new identity or simply 'conscious reformation'.

In India, terms like sects and cults are used loosely. For example, Shaivites and Vaishnavites are called sects. In fact, they are part of the mainstream religion, and not a small group of believers who reject the essentials of Hinduism.

Contemporary Sociological Perspectives on Religion

There are numerous philosophical, anthropological, and sociological perspectives on religion by Robert Bellah, Clifford Geertz, Peter Berger, S. J. Tambiah, R. Assaad, Peter Gold, Steve Fuller, and others. We will focus primarily on the works of Geertz, Bellah, and Berger.

Geertz felt that religion should be understood to mean any metaphysical system, including magic. He defines religion as a cultural system that helps people maintain faith in the ultimate meaningfulness of life and the world. Religious perspective differs from the commonsensical in that it moves beyond the realities of everyday life to wider ones and acceptance of them. This is the only way one can account for anomalies in human experience that threaten to undermine the general order of existence. Geertz (1973) refers to three points where a tumult of events which lack not only interpretation but even 'interpretability' threaten to enter into the world. They are: at the limit of people's ability to explain, to endure suffering, and to make sound moral judgements. Repeated confrontations with these limits set 'ordinary human experience in a permanent context of metaphysical concern and raises the dim, back-of-the mind suspicion that one may be adrift in an absurd world. It is at such difficult moments that religion intervenes and affirms the ultimate meaningfulness of the world.' The religious perspective rests on faith in the wider realities which are perceived to be 'really real', and that is why any form of consecrated behaviour, be it a simple ritual or an elaborate ceremony, evokes acceptance and commitment.

According to Geertz (1973: 112–25), anthropological study of religion is 'a two-stage operation: first, an analysis of the system of meanings embodied in the symbols which make up religion proper, and, second, the relating of these systems to socio-structural and psychological processes.' He believes that much of contemporary anthropology concerns itself with the second and neglects the first. Geertz continues:

To discuss the role of ancestor worship in regulating political succession, of sacrificial feasts in defining kinship obligations, of spirit worship in scheduling agricultural practices, of divination in reinforcing social control, or of initiation rites in propelling personality maturation, are in no sense unimportant endeavors, and I am not recommending they be abandoned for the kind of jejune cabalism into which symbolic analysis of exotic faiths can so easily fall. But to attempt them with but the most general, common-sense view of what ancestor worship, animal sacrifice, spirit worship, divination, or initiation rites are as religious patterns seems to be not particularly promising.

In other words, the role and importance of any religious practice is to be understood not in terms of its relation to actual social realities but in terms of their symbolic meaning in relation to wider realities.

Robert Bellah developed a systematic theory of religion based on Parsons' structural model. Although this cybernetic model has been largely ignored by sociologists, Bellah has made significant contribution to two aspects of religion: religious evolution and civil religion. Like Geertz, Bellah also begins with the assumption that the central focus of religious evolution is the religious symbol system itself.

Here the main line of development is from compact to differentiated symbolism, that is, from a situation in which world, self, and society are seen to involve the immediate expression of occult powers to one in which the exercise of religious influence is seen to be more indirect and "rational". This is the process of the "disenchantment of the world" that was described by Max Weber (Bellah 1970: 17).

Bellah sees gradual differentiation of art, science, and other cultural systems from religious symbolism, and as symbol systems become more differentiated, they make greater demand on the individual for decision and commitment. To support this growing religious individualism, specifically religious group structures are needed, whereas at earlier stages religion tends to be a dimension of all social groups. Bellah argues that modern religious consciousness is different from that in previous epochs.

For one thing, a great shift in the balance between elite and mass religiosity has taken place. The unexamined magical and religious conceptions of nonliterate or semiliterate strata, what used to make up the bulk of the religious life in any society, has come more and more under conscious inspection and critical evaluation as levels of literacy and education reach unprecedented peaks. This has involved the erosion of numerous beliefs and practices, some formerly considered essential to orthodoxy, but many peripheral or of doubtful orthodoxy. On the other hand the old elite notion that religion involves a personal quest for meaning, that it must express the deepest dimensions of the self and in no way violate individual conscience, has been generalized as the dominant conception in religion in modern society. (Bellah 1970: 227)

Also, with the continuing decline in the involvement in religious organizations, Bellah perceives religion increasingly a matter of private concern and personal idiosyncrasy; yet, he sees no prospect of collapse of organized religion.

Robert Bellah popularized the concept of civil religion and defined it as a 'substratum of common religious understandings that are quite pervasive in society. It is based on the belief of people that the foundation of their society is somehow part of a divine scheme of things' (Coleman 1970: 76). Coleman defines it as 'the set of beliefs, rites and symbols which relates a man's role as citizen and his society's place in space, time, and history to be conditions of ultimate existence and meaning' (ibid.: 76). Civil religion has nothing to do with religion at all but it is a system of values associated with sacred symbols that is integrated into the broader society. In the former Soviet Union, atheism and socialism were almost like state religion and the events and images associated with Lenin and the Revolution were almost sacred. In India, there are images, ideas, ceremonies, places, and events that evoke almost divine-like feelings in the popular mind: They include Salt Satyagraha, national flag, national anthem, the concept of Bharat Mata, Gandhi Samadhi, Republic Day celebration, and all ideas and ideologies which promote patriotism, nationalism, and national integration. In other words, civil religion is not a religion at all, it is a set of beliefs, rituals, symbols, and images that makes sacred certain secular values of society and helps integrate the citizens into a national community. Any perception of external threat will intensify civil religion and make the symbols even more sacred.

In his book, *The Sacred Canopy*, Berger proposed that from a sociological point of view, the purpose of religion is to construct a sacred cosmos which gives meaning to the apparent chaos of life's realities. Religion offers a protective canopy of transcendental legitimacy, meaning, and order to the precarious constructions that society calls 'reality'. Religion is the most effective nomos, a socially constructed ordering of experience. Berger believes that human beings transform truth, establish symbols, and fashion a world by their own activity. According to him this ordering of the world takes place through a continual three-fold cycle between individuals and society: externalization, objectivation, and internalization. The world thus fashioned has an order, based on a set of principles, which is transposed to society by individuals through externalization and objectivation, and also is internalized in each individual. In this scheme, society is created through externalization, it becomes an apprehended reality through objectivation, and the producing human subject becomes a product of society through internalization. Through socialization, individuals are taught the objectivized cultural meanings of a society and brought to identify with these meanings. This ordering of the world and experience which is a social process as well as an individual one is indeed a nomos. This socially established nomos becomes a shield against chaos and terror. Berger goes to the extent of saying that 'the most important function of society is nomization' (1967: 22). We all need that structuring nomos; it provides us with stability, predictability, and a frame of reference in which to live. For example, when illness, death, and natural disasters disrupt the order, nomos steps in to stabilize order. To be effective, nomos must be taken for granted, it must be self-evident. 'Whenever the socially established nomos attains the quality of being taken for granted, there occurs a merging of its meanings with what are considered to be the fundamental meanings inherent in the universe' (1967: 25). Berger sees this happening in all societies. While the nomos is expressed in religious terms in 'archaic societies', 'in contemporary society, this archaic cosmization of the social world is likely to take the form of "scientific" propositions about the nature of men rather than the nature of the universe'. So this process of world-construction is not always or necessarily religious, but its expression has most often been religious.

Berger argued that the fate of any social order is inevitably bound up with the fate of religion. He identified the sociological processes of secularization and pluralization as closely related historical phenomena that undermine the credibility of traditional western religions. Social life abhors vacuum, he reasons. Human beings are not capable of tolerating the continuous uncertainty of existing without institutional supports. Thus homeless minds, deprived of roots, are deinstitutionalized selves with their own 'naked selves' to rely on. They inevitably find life difficult and seek out what Berger and his associates call 'secondary institutions'. These are less strongly institutionalized than the primary institutions which are characterized by iron cage rigidity and meaninglessness. At the same time, they are sufficiently institutionalized to provide some guidance and thus serve as a refuge and support for homeless minds. Occultism, magic, mystical religion, Pentecostalism, and several new religious movements serve as secondary institutions.

Key Sociological Theories on Religion

As we indicated before, sociologists are not interested in the truth and falsity of any religion; they are concerned with the relationship between religion and society. Structural-functionalists view religion as an integrative force in society whereas conflict theorists see religion as a tool of the upper classes to maintain the status quo.

The Functionalist Perspective

Radcliffe-Brown and Malinowski provided the most thorough-going functional interpretation of religion. According to these authors, every society must, in order to survive, meet a number of functional prerequisites, one of the most important being solidarity of its members, or simply social integration. Religion is regarded as the integrative and legitimizing institution which unites people in a cohesive and binding moral order. Émile Durkheim also emphasized the role of religion in promoting social cohesion. He believed that collective concentration on selected sacred ideas and a sense of common purpose and unity that is provided by religion inspired a moral community based on social solidarity.

Social control is another function of religion. By the threat of punishment in this world and beyond it, religion enforces conformity with group norms. The ethical system of all religions established an inevitable link between moral values and spiritual values. 'Right behaviour', ritualistic or moralistic, became an indispensable part of the means of salvation. And religion exercises its moral authority through sanctions in this world as well as beyond it.

Whether it be the fear of hell and brimstone, which persisted for so long in Christianity, or the injunction to do good work, religions can clearly influence the daily behaviour of its believers. The recognized, established religion can thus control human behaviour and keep people 'in line' making it a useful instrument for ruling classes, and throughout history these classes have appreciated religion's utility, its instrumental value, regardless of the evaluation of religion in any other terms. Louis Schneider quotes F.E. Manuel that even skeptics and atheists in the eighteenth century recognized that 'religion was a mechanism which inspired terror, but terror useful for the preservation of society ...' In short, religion was regarded as a useful discipline of the masses and an effective control of the working classes. (McKee 1969: 520)

Religion is probably the most enduring and imaginative tension-management device ever created by man. Man transformed his fears of the forces of nature into a cult of the unknown and invented a system of rituals in order to propitiate the supernatural, or the deity that presided over the overpowering forces of nature. The main undercurrent of all religions, from the primitive to the most modern, is a fusion of reverence and devotion to the ultimate which will enable man to overcome his fears by linking mundane existence with eternal bliss. Even the psychological interpretation of Freud rested on the assumption that man created religions in an attempt to thwart the anxieties he felt in a world that was beyond his control. According to him, the feelings humans developed in their nearly helpless stages of infancy and childhood towards their parents were in adulthood transferred to the supernatural.

Religion makes the world comprehensible by providing 'answers' to many unanswerable questions. Where did we come from? Is there life hereafter? What is the purpose of life? Religion seeks answers to such cosmic questions, and such answers provide a world view for the believers. For example, the Hindu concepts of dharma, karma, and transmigration of souls constitute the fundamental basis for the Hindu outlook on life. The belief in the transmigration of souls which grew directly out of the universally diffused representations of the fate of spirits after death and in the principle of retributive justice by which the sins of a previous life are expiated in the present life is at the centre of the Hindu view of life. As the ends which individuals pursue are many and varied, so are the means which they adopt. For instance, Jewish and Islamic traditions emphasize correct observance of the religious law. Right behaviour is given primary attention in Hinduism and Buddhism. Partaking of sacraments was stressed in early Roman Catholicism, and strict moral conduct was the cornerstone of Puritan ethic. The Brahmin stressed gnosis, contemplation, and asceticism as sacred means.

Weber believed that Protestant asceticism, particularly Calvinism, was influential in the appearance of the capitalist spirit. He was intrigued by the fact that full-fledged capitalism was developed in predominantly Protestant countries of western Europe and North America, whereas many of the Catholic countries like Spain and Portugal in spite of their earlier glory failed to attain the economic arrangement of capitalism based on rational bureaucracy. Weber identified several values that constituted the essence of Protestant ethic that facilitated the emergence of capitalism. The essence of this ethic was: accept a calling, work hard, be successful in business or profession, but abstain from the pleasures of the world. In effect, to accumulate, save, reinvest in productive process, was the essence of the new religious ethic—a condition par excellence for capitalism. Weber has stated that outside Western civilization we cannot find a religious interpretation comparable to the Protestant ethic. In China and India, there were many conditions favourable to the rise of capitalism but their combination in Calvinism is original and unique.

In short, whereas Marx believed that religion always retards social change, Weber thought there could be values embedded in the religious ethical system that could trigger change and development. Although Weber described how the spirit of capitalism grew in the fertile soil of Protestant ethic, in a broader sense he was talking about the way systems of values facilitate or impede change. Randall Collins applied Weber's thesis to Asian development and found that the foundations for capitalism in Asia, particularly Japan, were laid in the Buddhist monastic economy of late medieval Japan. According to Collins (1997: 855) 'The temples were the first entrepreneurial organizations in Japan; the first co combine control of the factors of labour, capital, and land so as to allocate them for enhancing production.' The ethic of self-discipline and restraint on consumption facilitated high levels of accumulation and investment. In India also, early Buddhism established great centres of learning in philosophy, medicine, and science but there was no mobilization of land, labour, and capital. In summary, Weber's thesis on religion called for scientific attention to three forms of relationships which exist between social organization and religious ideas, which he believed warranted further investigation. These ideas were as follows:

First, social groups with particular economic interests often show themselves to be more receptive to some religious ideas than to others. For example, peasants typically incline toward some form of nature worship and aristocrats toward religious ideas compatible with their sense of status and dignity. Second, religious ideas lead to formation of certain groups, such as monastic orders, guilds of magicians, or a clergy, and these groups may develop quite extensive economic activities. Third, the distinction between the elite and the masses is as pertinent to the religious sphere as to others—the gap between the elite and the masses poses a problem with which each of the great world religions has had to cope. (Bendix 1968: 497)

Some charismatic leaders have also used religion to provide a new world view for their followers. Mahatma Gandhi's struggle for India's independence and Martin Luther King's fight for civil rights in the United States involved effective use of religious symbolism.

In short, the key functions of religion may be summarized as follows:

1. It helps individuals reconcile to the hardships and inequities of society by interpreting failure and frustration symbolically and by advising believers not to take vicissitudes of mundane existence seriously.
2. It promises salvation or nirvana to those who have tread the prescribed path.
3. It provides a kind of psychic insurance policy by uniting believers into a fellowship of shared experience.
4. It offers support when other social institutions are rapidly changing, throwing the individual's life out of gear. This is particularly true of periods of crisis such as sickness, death, depression, natural disaster, war, and the like.
5. It gives the individual a sense of personal identity, meaning and inner experience and may bring transcendence of the same.

The Conflict Perspective

The conflict theorists also agree that religion, as an agent of social control, is an integrative force. But they argue that religion was always used by the ruling class to suppress the masses. Karl Marx saw religion as an enemy of a socialist revolutionary state. He declared (1844/1964), 'Religion is the sigh of the oppressed creature, the sentiment of a heartless world... it is the opium of the people.' By this he meant religion is like a drug that lulls people into a false consciousness. As people escape into religion, their senses are dulled and they feel apathy and lethargy. The idea is that the masses get indoctrinated into the religious doctrines which support the status quo. Marx believed that the dominant religion of a society is that of the ruling class which uses the religious ideas to exploit the masses and keep them in servitude. 'Man makes religion, religion does not make man', he declared. Leaders of religion often side with the ruling classes and legitimize the political and economic domination of the lower classes. The poor and the oppressed were often told that they should accept their fate and not rebel against the system because they will be rewarded in the life hereafter.

There are many examples of the way religion maintained the social order. In Imperial Japan, the Emperor was considered God and could not be questioned. In England the Divine Rights of Kings postulated that the kings received their mandate from God and were only answerable to Him. In India, the untouchables were told that it was their religious duty to be docile and serviceable and they would be rewarded in the next birth. But if they challenged their fate and failed to perform their dharma, they would be reborn as lower forms of animals. Thus religion was used by the ruling elites to legitimize their status and exploit the lower castes. Christianity did the same thing in medieval Europe. Poor peasants were told that they should accept their slave status and work for their masters, for life on this earth was only a short sojourn; those who suffered here and now would enjoy eternal bliss in the hereafter. Some scholars point to the treatment of women as second class citizens in several Islamic countries as another example of how religion subjugates people. Whereas purdah and burka may be viewed as sign of piety and obedience to God, several laws which deny women equal rights in civil society are indicative of the power of the ruling elites. Even Confucianism preached loyalty to the rulers as a moral obligation.

Thus by legitimizing authority and status quo, religion made it possible for the ruling classes to continue to exploit the poor. By endorsing the existing system, religion also inhibited social change. The history of many social revolutions indicates that religion and the priestly class were often on the side of the nobility and against change. That is the reason why when the communists came to power in the Soviet Union they closed most churches and converted many of them into museums of atheism. However, recent years have seen a reversal of the phenomenon. The liberation theology and many other religious movements have taken up the cause of the poor in developing countries and launched numerous programmes for social change and development.

DURKHEIM'S THEORY OF RELIGION

Durkheim proposed a general theory of religion based on his study of the simplest and most 'primitive' religious institution, the totemism, found among the Australian aborigines. He began with a refutation of animism and naturism. The former is worship of spirit as the most basic form of religious expression. The latter refers to the worship of nature's forces. Durkheim rejected both concepts because he felt that they failed to explain the universal key distinction between the sacred and the profane, and because they tended to explain religion away by interpreting it as an illusion, that is, the reductionist fallacy. Moreover, to love spirits whose unreality one affirms or to love natural forces transfigured merely by man's fear would make religious experience a kind of collective hallucination. Neither is religion defined by the notion of mystery nor of the supernatural. Nor is the belief in a transcendental god the essence of religion, for there are several religions such as Buddhism and Confucianism without specific god-figures. Moreover, reliance on spirits and supernatural forces will make religion an illusion. To Durkheim, systems of ideas like religion which have had such considerable place in history, to which people have turned in all ages for the energy they need to live, and for which they are willing to sacrifice their lives, cannot be mere tissues of illusion. Rather, they should be viewed as so profound and so permanent as to correspond to a true reality. And this true reality is not a transcendent god but society. Thus, the central thesis of Durkheim's theory of religion is that throughout history men have never worshipped any other reality, whether in the form of totem or god, than the collective social reality transfigured by faith.

There is no doubt that a society has everything needed to arouse in men's minds, simply by the influence it exerts over them, the sensation of the divine, for it is to its members what a god is to his faithful. For a god is first a being whom man imagines in certain respects as superior to himself, and on whom he believes he depends... the believer feels that he is obliged to accept certain forms of behaviour imposed on him by the nature of the sacred principle with which he feels he is in communication. But society also maintains in us the sensation of a perpetual dependence, because it has a nature peculiar to itself, different from our individual nature, and pursues ends which are likewise peculiar to itself; but since it can attain them only through us, it imperiously demands our cooperation. It requires that we forget our personal interests and become its servants; it subjects us to all kinds of inconveniences, hardships, and sacrifices without which social life would be impossible. So it is that at every moment we are obliged to submit to rules of conduct and ideas which we have neither made nor willed and which are sometimes even opposed to our most fundamental inclinations and instincts.

Society awakens in us the feeling of the divine. It is at the same time a commandment which imposes itself and a reality qualitatively superior to individuals which calls forth respect, devotion, adoration' (Durkheim 1965: 252–5).

Moreover, Durkheim claims that just as societies in the past have created gods and religions, societies of the future are inclined to create new gods and new religions when they are in a state of exaltation. When societies are seized by the sacred frenzy, and when men, participating in ritualistic ceremonies, religious services, feasts, and festivals, go into a trance, they are united by dancing and shouting and experience a kind of phantasmagoria. Men are compelled to participate by the force of the group which carries them outside of themselves and gives them a sensation of something that has no relation to everyday experience. During such moments of sacred frenzy and collective trance, new gods and religions will be born.

Durkheim believed that he had solved the religious-moral dilemma of modern society. If religion is nothing but the indirect worship of society, modern people need only express their religious feelings directly towards the sacred symbolization of society. The source and object of religion, Durkheim felt, are the collective life. Therefore, a secular sociological explanation of religion could sound something like this—the individual who feels dependent on some external moral power is not a victim of hallucination but a responsive member of society.

Recent Trends in Religion

The dawn of the nineteenth century witnessed a scathing attack on religion in general and doctrinaire and organized religions in particular. Religion has become increasingly imageless, having lost its moral authority among the working classes in industrial societies and its symbolic value among the intellectuals. The Darwinian theory of evolution, Marxist theory of communism, the purely intellectual interpretations of religion by Fraser, Comte, Nietzsche, and others, and the development of rational science have shaken the foundations of organized religion.

The new attempts at rationalization had two inevitable consequences: 1. the accelerating process of secularization; and, 2. the reverberating process of resacralization as a counter-offensive to secularization.

Secularization

In his book, *The Secular City*, which so effectively captured the theological mood of the 1960s, Harvey Cox (1966) refers to secularization as the process that 'simply bypasses and undercuts religion and goes on to other things.' He adds: 'The gods of traditional religions live on as private fetishes or the patrons of congenial groups, but they play no significant role in the public life of the secular metropolis.' In traditional rural India people believed that certain diseases were caused by evil spirits or the wrath of a village deity; local priests were called to ward off evil spirits or to propitiate the local deity. In many peasant societies, many agricultural operations were interspersed with religious rituals. Today, more and more people turn to modern science to cure illnesses or to produce better crops.

In McKee's words (1969), 'As a cultural process, secularization is a desacralization of the world, in which there is no overarching religious symbolism for the integration of society, and in which man's understanding of himself and of his society are no longer primarily in religious terms.' In other words, secularization points to a declining influence of religion in everyday life. Thus, the world has become more rational and secular; economic, political, and educational institutions have become separated from religious perspectives. Neither the laws of nature nor the laws of man are any longer interpreted in terms of traditional religious beliefs; rather religion itself is being radically transformed to meet the changing conditions of the modern world. As Peter Berger and Robert Bellah suggest, today's religion has moved away from the institutionalized framework of dogma and devotion; it has become more subjective, personal, and a privatized form of inner faith which retains its influence primarily within the family. As religions themselves become more secular, they talk less about other-worldly affairs like hell and heaven and cycle of rebirths but more about secular affairs such as improving the quality of life.

The secularization thesis has both its defenders and critics. Although secularization has been a gradual historical process, it was only in the 1960s that social scientists made serious attempts to develop a systematic and empirically grounded formulation of the theory of secularization. Peter Berger was among the most influential sociologists to develop the secularization thesis. Following his lead, many social scientists argued that modernization inevitably leads to secularization. They argued that technology undermines religion because it gives better solution to specific problems and reduces the need for recourse to religious explanations and offices. Technology also gives us an increased sense of mastery over our own affairs. Some even supposed that the world was becoming increasingly godless. Others contended that in democracies, pluralism requires the state to become increasingly neutral on matters of faith. The defence of secularism was largely based on the dwindling involvement in religious organizations and the dramatic decline in church religiosity in Western Europe.

According to Herveu-Leger (Hamilton 2001: 112), 'Secularization has for long been associated with the idea of the loss of religion in modern societies, a loss which followed directly from the disenchantment of the world brought about by the irresistible rise of scientific and technological rationality.' The secularization thesis seeks to explain the manner in which and the extent to which religious creeds, practices, and institutions are losing their significance. The transition from oral traditions to literary traditions reduces the authority of clerics as the custodians of revealed knowledge and fosters free inquiry.

The secularization thesis involves three propositions:

1. Differentiation of secular spheres from religious institutions and norms. Various secular spheres such as politics, economics, law, science, art, etc., could come fully into their own, become differentiated from each other.
2. General decline of religious beliefs and practices. Evidence from European societies showed that the closer people were involved in industrial production, the less religious they became.
3. Privatization or marginalization of religion to a private sphere. This refers to the process of religious individuation based on the freedom of conscience.

The critics of secularization thesis argue that much of the evidence was based on the experience of western Europe where church religiosity has been on a steady decline. Even Berger offered a number of reasons for doubting his initial confidence that modernity undermined religion. He points to the following:

1. The growth of conservative and evangelical churches in the United States.
2. The decline of liberal churches.
3. The persistence of interest in religion (if not church-going) in other western societies.
4. The vitality of religion in other parts of the world.

Berger (1998: 782) argues that 'Most of the world today is as religious as ever it was, and in many a good locales, more religious than ever.' Similarly, Bellah (1970: 246), while admitting that the dominance of utilitarian individualism and scientific instrumentalism have pushed religion into the private sphere as a matter of personal faith, emphatically puts it,

My conclusion, then, runs about as contrary to so-called secularization theory as is humanly possible. It is my feeling that religion, instead of becoming increasingly peripheral and vestigial, is again moving into the center of our cultural preoccupations. This is happening both for purely intellectual reasons having to do with the emergence of the religious issue in the sciences of man and for practical historical reasons having to do with the increasing disillusionment with a world built on utilitarianism and science alone. Religion was the traditional mode by which men interpreted their world to themselves. Increasingly modern man has turned to social science for this interpretation. As social science has attempted more and more to grasp the totality of man it has recognized many of the preoccupations of traditional religion. As traditional religion has sought to relate to the contemporary world it has learned more social scientific contributions to the understanding of man.

In short, modernization does not mean the death of God or the end of religion but only a certain type of religious outlook. Even the spread of latest technology around the globe does not seem to obliterate faith in religious traditions. Saudi Arabia and the rest of the Middle East have been at the receiving end of high technology in every field, but there is no commensurate decline of religion. In Sri Lanka, Ames (1963: 53) found that for many adherents of Buddhism, religion has ceased to be 'abstract and other-worldly. It has come back into the world and it is becoming intimately concerned with the day-to-day stresses and strains of a worldly life'. Geertz's (1963) findings in Indonesia and Singer's (1972) report on India establish that there is no obvious conflict between traditional religious faith and modern careers. On the other hand, technological revolution in transportation and communication may have actually furthered certain traditional values and institutions such as the spread of the 'great tradition' into the little communities, pilgrimages to distant shrines, and the formation of caste groups and religious organizations on regional and even national lines. To quote Gusfield (1967: 351–62), 'The acceptance of a new product, a new religion, a new mode of decision-making does not necessarily lead to the disappearance of the older form. New forms may only increase the range of alternatives. Both magic and medicine can exist side by side, used alternatively by the same people.' Here Bellah (1970: 222–3) introduces a crucial point. He points out that unlike in Christianity and Islam, in Eastern religions, beliefs do not have central place; the 'faithful' are free to believe or not to believe in doctrines such as the immortality of soul or even the existence of God. Here inner experience and expressive gesture are far more important than creeds and syllogistic arguments. 'Further evidence that oriental religions are not on the whole based on cognitive belief is the almost total failure of the conflict between religion and science to materialize in Eastern milieu, even though in the minds of some western scholars it "ought" to have.'

The Indian case is a typical example. Most Indians do not see any conflict between religion and science. A man with a PhD in astronomy may consult an astrologer in planning a wedding for his daughter. In the launching of a satellite, scientists may mix rocket science and religious ceremony. Every major surgery may be preceded and followed by prayers. In fact, the use of every technological innovation is interspersed with ritual practices. Every vehicle from a three-wheeler to an eighteen-wheeler may be adorned with portraits of favourite deities. Every public function may begin with a common prayer. In fact, even the state-owned radio begins the day with religious incantations. Millions throng to pilgrim centres and invoke their favourite deities but they also seek out the best in science. Medicine, magic, science, and religion all have their unique place in the everyday life of the Indians. It is simply easier and safer to follow the traditional rules; if they are correct, no trouble would follow, and if they are wrong, no harm is done. As M.N. Srinivas (1966) observes, the strength of a belief may no longer lie in its sacerdotal importance but the rituals may be continued anyway, often in conjunction with, modern scientific practices (more on this in the chapter under Social Change).

Finally, as Herveu-Leger (Hamilton 2001: 112–23) contends, 'The growing awareness of self that characterizes modern individual does not relieve him or her of the need to believe. Indeed, there is now a more urgent need to give a meaning to the experiences of life and to the ultimate questions raised by exposure, now endured in a more personal way, to uncertainty and a sense of incompleteness.' Therefore, the modern rationale of the individualization of belief does not imply the end of religion but a vast reconstruction of the institutional systems of believing and of the regimes of authority associated with them. Thus, the waning of the secularization thesis has led sociologists to focus more on un-institutionalized forms of religion or versions of spiritual and mystical experiences. This takes us to the process of *resacralization.*

Resacralization

Many followers of religion believe that secularization has gone too far by obliterating the elements of mystery in religion. They argue that humans still have a thirst for the mysterious as well as the transcendental. This explains the growing momentum of various religious sects—evangelist, fundamentalist, transcendental, mystical, and revivalist. Young people all over the world, especially in industrial societies, are returning to an appreciation of mysticism, particularly of the great Eastern religions. A variety of new religious movements such as the Krishna Consciousness (Hare Krishna), Zen Buddhism, Integral Yoga Retreats, Transcendental Meditation, Pentacostal groups and numerous revival movements attest to a growing undercurrent of disillusionment about man's ability to transform either himself or his world, and the resultant quest for new religious roots. In India, the Ayodhya temple movement and the politicization of the concept of Hindutva have led to a revival of religious traditions in Hinduism. However, scholars do not agree on the meaning of this religious 'revival'. There is no proof of a mass return to supernatural beliefs; nor is our everyday life more spiritualistic than before. Yet, there has been a definite increase in the search for a new meaning or a new spiritual discipline as evidenced in the growth of various fundamentalist as well as radical religious movements. Finally, the emergence of several radical fundamentalist (rather, fanatical) groups in recent years shows that religion can still demand unconditional obedience from the rank and file, build impenetrable fortresses around 'truth', and manipulate the faithful.

The rise of Taliban in Afghanistan, radical Islamic fundamentalism in much of the Middle East, and evangelical Christian conservatism in America illustrate globalization of new religious movements. The Iranian revolution against the Shah began as a fundamentalist opposition to westernization but was led by an urban network of *mullahs* who sought power through a reassertion of Islamic rule. The fundamentalists attacked various secular interests in Iran, including non-traditional women, leftist organizations, and liberal or centrist political groups, and any individuals and associations who espoused democratic-secular rather than Islamic rule. In Algeria, Pakistan, Turkey, and now in Iraq, fundamentalism has been on the rise. In Egypt, fundamentalists have mounted a cultural offensive against secular institutions including education, courts, media, and the arts. In southern Egypt's public schools, fundamentalist teachers have begun to re-impose veil on girls as young as six. They argue that secularization is destroying Egypt's deep Islamic and Arab roots. But religious fundamentalism is not unique to Islam. In the United States, Christian conservatives have become a dominant political force. They not only oppose abortion and gay marriage but also a host of public policy issues such as support for family planning programmes worldwide. In fact, many political analysts believe that the coalition of Christian fundamentalists has energized and directed recent elections in the country. Even in Russia and China, lesser known cults and sects have resurfaced in recent years. In several parts of Africa, Christian evangelicals and Islamic fundamentalists have been on a collision course.

In sum, the fundamentalist movements springing up around the world have two main features. First, they articulate the uncertainties and stress brought about by the social decay that populations experience as a result of the limits of developmentalism and the increasing selectivity of globalization. Second, they often take the form of a nationalist resurgence against perceived threats to their culture. The combination frequently involves contesting the universalist assumptions of global development along with presenting alternative ways of organizing social life on a national or local level. (McMichael 2000: 244)

Fundamentalism

Macionis (1995: 507) defines fundamentalism as 'a conservative religious doctrine that opposes intellectualism and worldly accommodation in favor of restoring traditional, otherworldly spirituality.' In other words, fundamentalism denotes the unconditional acceptance of the literal truth of the faith; there is no room for debate. The term fundamentalism, although now used in a pejorative sense, does not necessarily have a negative connotation. It simply means strict adherence to the fundamental tenets of faith. Fundamentalists rigidly adhere to their doctrine and practice their faith, and leave the rest of us alone, even though they believe in the exclusive validity of their doctrines. They do not sit in judgement over members of other faiths and brand them as non-believers or sinners. In this sense, the Old Order Amish of Pennsylvania who shun electricity, automobiles, and all other comforts of modern civilization, and choose to lead a life of piety and peasant self-reliance, are a fine example of a community which adheres to fundamentalism. They practise what they preach and make no attempt to convert others to their way of thinking and do not judge others by their standards.

However, fundamentalism has undergone some internal changes during the last several decades. Today's fundamentalism varies from ultraconservatism to absolute fanaticism. Many fundamentalists today believe that their faith alone is true and those of others false. In recent years, many have also resorted to political actions in order to push for their cherished goals in society.

Macionis identifies five characteristics of fundamentalism.

1. Fundamentalists interpret the scriptures literally.
2. They do not accept religious pluralism.
3. They pursue the personal experience of god's presence.
4. They oppose 'secular humanism', the tendency to turn to scientific experts rather than god for answers.
5. Many fundamentalists endorse conservative political goals.

Because of the fact that today's fundamentalism has a tendency to degenerate into fanaticism, let us now define the latter in sociological terms. *Fanaticism* is blind faith in, and excessive devotion to, literal interpretation of one's religion often characterized by intolerance and even animosity towards other belief systems. When people speak negatively of the evils of fundamentalism, they are often referring to fanaticism. The new global terrorism is largely the handiwork of fanatical religious groups. The Al Qaeda and its offshoots spreading terrorism around the world are typical examples. Aum Shinrikyo, a fanatical Japanese religious cult which released a deadly nerve gas called sarin on subway trains in Tokyo, and several Christian prophets of biblical world-ending events or Armageddon are also part of loosely connected global subculture of apocalyptic violence. Robert Lifton (2000), an expert on religious cults, says that his exploration of Aum has led him to the apocalyptic inclinations of American groups like the Charles Manson Family, Heaven's Gate, and People's Temple, and several radical right-wing groups such as neo-Nazis.

RELIGION IN INDIA

The sociology of religion is not interested in the teachings and practices of religion per se; it is concerned with the relationship between religion and society. One of the sociological features of religions in India are their separateness from one another. Although various religious communities may live together in the same village, share several cultural bonds, and participate in several festivals, it cannot be denied that each religious group is a separate community with its own customs, food habits, and marital exclusiveness.

Most of the world religions are represented in India. According to the latest census data, India has a population of 1.21 billion people. Hindus make up 80.5 per cent of the population, Muslims 13.4 per cent, Christians 2.3 per cent, Sikhs about 1.9 per cent, and others 1.8 per cent. The growth rate of major religious groups during the decade of 1991–2001 was: Hindus 20 per cent, Muslims 29.3 per cent, Christians 22.1 per cent, Sikhs 16.9 per cent, and Buddhists 23.2 per cent. The growth rate of Jains remains unchanged at 16 per cent. While the literacy rate in India is 64.8 per cent, the rates for Hindus, Muslims, and Christians respectively are: 65.1, 59.1, and 80.3. Jains have the highest rate of literacy at 94.1 per cent.

In India, religious considerations play a major role in politics, social reforms, and attitudes towards socio-economic development. Religion also provides an outlook on the world and fashions a way of life. Although it is impossible to generalize, it seems safe to make some tendency statements with regard to religion-wise variations. In other words, the names of people, dress styles, languages they speak and how they speak them, the occupations people prefer, and the customs they follow are to some extent determined by religion. Where the Hindus are landlords, the Muslims are traders. The Jains and the Parsis entered commerce and the medical, legal, and academic professions early and were the leading traders in western India. Moplah traders were very prominent not only in Kerala but also Mysore and Tamil Nadu. The Syrian Christians of Kerala played a major role in banking and plantation crops of tea, coffee, and rubber.

Religion also plays a role in politics. The BJP which has led the government on at least two occasions- and leads now- is devoted to Hindu nationalism and Hindutva. The party is dominated by several Hindu religious organizations. Muslims have also formed their own parties, and in Kerala, the Muslim League has often been part of the coalition government. Sikh politics has been connected with the control of gurdwaras, and the Akali Dal and other Sikh-dominated parties play a major role in Punjab politics. Although Christians have not formed a separate party, the Syrian Christians dominate factions of the Kerala Congress.

Culture is an organic growth evolved over time, and in a pluralistic society like India, it represents a synthesis of a multiplicity of cultures, religions, languages, arts, and traditions. If Brahmins were supposed to be the custodians of classical learning, some of the greatest custodians of Indian culture are Muslims, be it in classical Indian music, painting, handicrafts, literature, weaving—whether Persian carpet or Banares saree—or other forms of art and architecture. In many areas, their contributions are indispensable for the celebration of Hindu marriages, festivals, and ceremonies. M.N. Srinivas refers to an old custom called *cati* by which itinerant Muslims exchanged their superior animals for the inferior ones of the Hindus. Now the Muslims could kill the weak cattle the Hindus could not. Muslims provide a large number of goods needed for Hindu festivals. Muslims are invited to Hindu weddings, and sheep and goats are slaughtered ritually by a Muslim butcher so that the Muslim guests could enjoy the wedding dinner. In some regions, Hindu parents employed the services of Muslim brokers to find a suitable groom for their daughter. Through several centuries, many of these customs persisted and established a common bond between people of different faiths. Some of these old customs have vanished but many others continue to reinforce mutual dependence. There have been, of course, occasional communal riots in many parts of India. But there have also been many inter-caste conflicts all over India.

Kerala has one of the oldest synagogues built on the land gifted by a Hindu king. Hundreds of thousands of devotees of Lord Ayyappa flock to Sabarimala in Kerala, but en route they are still required to pray at the Mosque of Vavar who was Ayyappa's lieutenant in the fight against armed robbers. In Tamil Nadu, hundreds of thousands of Christians and Hindus make a pilgrimage to Velankanni Shrine of Mary, but on the way back they stop and pray at a famous mosque. There is a growing movement to Indianize Christianity. Priests of several Christian religious orders now dress like Hindu sanyasins and conduct the worship service in Indian style. The Syrian Christians of Kerala have always followed many of the Hindu traditions and customs on occasions such as weddings, blessing of new homes, funerals, etc.

Hinduism which is not a rigid sect or an exclusive ideology is a form of all-embracing faith in universalism and a way of life. Earliest religious texts do not mention or define Hinduism but extol the common blood pool of all living things. Hinduism represents thousands of years of cultural heritage of a people who lived in the Indian subcontinent. Its doctrine of 'manyness in one' allows believers to see god in any form or shape and worship in any manner, for truth is one; sages have called it by different names. Adi Sankara said that just as different rivers flow in different directions but ultimately join the ocean, different individuals reach Paramatma through different paths. This is the essence of the Hindu worldview which through the ages preached tolerance of different faiths. Mahatma Gandhi elaborated the concept and called it 'equal reverence for all religions' and made it part of his social reconstruction programme.

Today, a new form of religious revivalism is taking shape in India. Sociologists see revival as an attempt to return to the roots, to be more god-centred and sect-like communities. The Hindu revival includes *jagrans*, *karseva* and calls for aggressive proselytization and conversion of tribals. Ceremonies such as *Etatmata Yangna*, different types of *homa* and traditional rites are widely practised. Among Christians also there are new evangelicals and revival groups. The followers of sects like Pentacostals and Jehovah's Witness are growing. More and more young Muslim children attend madrasas and receive religious instruction. There is also a raging controversy over conversion. Although many individuals and some sects within Hinduism speak of Ishta Devatha and thus express a willingness to honour Christ as an incarnation of the Divine, they strenuously object to the Christian emphasis on conversion which implies the superiority of the Christian message.

Now a word about secularization in India. The Constitution grants every citizen the fundamental right to profess, practice, and propagate the religion of his or her choice. It also prohibits discrimination on the basis of religion. In the context of enormous cultural and religious diversities, the state remains largely neutral in matters of religion. But there are three issues that are at the root of secularization debate in India. The first is conversion. While choice of religion based on one's conscience is a basic fundamental right, some argue that a lot of conversion in India is based on certain material rewards and other incentives. There are no reliable statistics on the extent of conversion. It is generally believed that majority of the conversions are from lower castes. In any case, whether conversion of lower castes really improves their social status in a caste-oriented society is a debatable issue.

The second issue pertains to the existence of personal law, particularly among the Muslims. Many Indians believe that there should only be one set of laws that are uniformly applicable to all citizens regardless of sex, creed, religion, or caste. When the government initiated the Muslim Women (Protection of Rights of Divorcee) Bill, it gave a strange definition of secularism: 'non-interference in the religious affairs of any community' (Abraham 1998). To many, this sounded hypocritical because the history of the last fifty years of social legislation in India shows that the government has passed numerous laws to regulate customs and practices among the Hindu community (Hindu Marriage Act, 1955; Hindu Succession Act, 1956; Hindu Religious and Charitable Endowment Act, 1959). There is no doubt that the government has a responsibility to protect the rights of minorities but the question is whether it should also enforce the law of the land regardless of religious orientation. The third issue pertains to the concept of Hindutva which equates Indian identity with Hindu identity. The latter is defined in terms of a combination of territorial and cultural criteria and leads to cultural homogenization. Many would argue that Indian culture is not identical with Hindu culture, and even some of the advocates of Hindutva now tends to define the concept in terms of 'Indianness' rather than 'Hinduness'. Once again, Robert Bellah comes up with an interesting caveat. According to him (1976), there is a central belief shared by the oriental religions and diffused widely outside them.

This is the belief in the unity of all being. Our separate selves, according to Buddhism, Hinduism, and their offshoots, are not ultimately real. Philosophical Hinduism and Mahayana Buddhism reject dualism. For them ultimately there is no difference between myself and yourself, and this river and that mountain. We are all one and the conflict between us is therefore illusory.

Finally, recent years have seen many instances of communal violence. The massacre of Sikhs following the assassination of Indira Gandhi and the terrible carnage in Gujarat are only two of the recent communal clashes. There have been several other instances in other cities and villages. The term 'communalism' is an Indian concoction which belies definition. If it means religious chauvinism and stands for animosity and hatred among religious groups, communalism is not the monopoly of any particular caste, religion, or political party; several political parties and religious organizations have played a role in promoting or at the least abetting it. However, it must be clearly understood that communalism is not the same thing as fundamentalism. Fundamentalism simply means strict adherence to one's beliefs both in letter and spirit; it does not bother about other people's beliefs and practices. Communalism, on the other hand, is based on a fanatic ideology. Communalists' attitude to other belief systems varies from intolerance to imposition to annihilation. They do not appreciate, or even tolerate, other people's belief systems; they want to impose their beliefs, practices, and politics on others. They deny others' legitimate right to have their own beliefs and practices and even obliterate them if they can. The Popular Front of India which draws sustenance from Wahabism and the Rashtriya Swayamsevak Sangh (RSS) and other Hindu extremist groups that derive their strength from variants of Hindutva are generally regarded as communal groups. But Indian culture is a multilayered, pluralistic, and secular culture that has evolved through centuries of liberal philosophical and religious movements (such as Bhakti and Sufi). Ours is a syncretic, secular culture which has withstood numerous foreign invasions, cultural, political, and religious. The rich Indian culture has proved its resilience time and again. The pluralistic, many-layered, colourful, and rich secular Indian culture will continue to withstand the onslaught of communalism from within.

STUDY QUESTIONS

- Write a paragraph on the religions of the primitive people.
- What are the elements of religion? Explain.
- Compare and contrast the functional and conflict perspectives on religion.
- Summarize contemporary sociological perspectives on religion.
- Critically examine Durkheim's theory of religion.
- Write an essay on recent trends in religion with special reference to secularization, resacralization, and fundamentalism.
- Examine the status of religion as a social institution in India today.
- Define the following concepts: animism, naturism, and totemism; profane and sacred; monotheism and polytheism; magic; sect and cult; secularization, resacralization, fundamentalism, and communalism.

REFERENCES

Abraham, M. Francis, *The Agony of India*, Madras: East West Books, p. 178, 1998.

Ames, Michael, 'Ideological and Social Change in Ceylon', *Human Organization*, 22: 53, 1963.

Bellah, Robert, 'The New Consciousness and the Crisis in Modernity', in Charles Glock and Robert Bellah (eds), *The New Religious Consciousness*, Berkeley: University of California Press, 1976.

———, *Beyond Belief: Essays on Religion in a Post-Traditional World*, New York: Harper & Row, 1970.

Bendix, Reinhard, 'Max Weber' in *The International Encyclopedia of the Social Sciences*, New York: Collier Macmillan Company, 1968.

Berger, Peter, *The Sacred Canopy: Elements of a Sociological Theory of Religion*, New York: Doubleday, 1967.

———, 'Protestantism and the Quest of Certainty', *The Christian Century*, pp. 782–96, 26 August 1998.

————, *Peter Berger and the Study of Religion,* New York: Routledge, 2002.

Berger, Peter, Brigitte Berger, and Hansfried Kellner, *The Homeless Mind: Modernization and Consciousness,* Harmondsworth: Penguin Books, 1979.

Coleman, John A., 'Civil Religion', in *Sociological Analysis,* 31(2): 76, 1970.

Collins, Randall, 'An Asian Route to Capitalism: Religious Economy and the Origins of Self-transforming Growth in Japan', *American Sociological Review,* 62 (December), pp. 843–65, 1997.

Cox, Harvey, *The Secular City,* New York: Macmillan, 1966.

Dillon, Michele, *Handbook of Sociology of Religion,* Cambridge, U.K.: Cambridge University Press, 2003.

Durkheim, Émile, *The Elementary Forms of Religious Life,* New York: Macmillan, 1926.

————, *The Elementary Forms of Religious Life*, New York: Fress Press, 1965.

Fairchild, Henry Pratt (ed.), *Dictionary of Sociology*, Totowa, New Jersey: Littlefield, Adam and Co., 1968.

Geertz, Clifford, *Peddlers and Princes,* Chicago: University of Chicago Press, 1963.

————, *The Interpretation of Cultures: Selected Essays*, New York: Basic Books, 1973.

Gibbon, Edward, *The Decline and Fall of the Roman Empire,* New York: Peter Fenelon Collier, 1914.

Gusfield, Joseph R., 'Tradition and Modernity: Misplaced Polarities in the Study of Social Change', *American Journal of Sociology,* 72, 4, pp. 351–62, 1967.

Hamilton, Malcolm, *The Sociology of Religion: Theoretical and Comparative Perspectives,* New York: Routledge, 2001.

Hargrove, Barbara W., *Reformation of the Holy,* Philadelphia: F.A. Davis, 1971.

Lifton, Robert Jay, *Destroying the World to Save it,* New York: Henry Holt and Company, 2000.

Macionis, John J., *Sociology,* Englewood Cliffs: Prentice-Hall, 1995.

Malinowski, Bronislaw, *The Foundations of Faith and Morals,* New York: Folcroft, 1936.

Marx, Karl, *Selected Writings in Sociology and Social Philosophy*, London: McGraw-Hill, 1844/1964.

McKee, James B., *Introduction to Sociology,* New York: Holt, 1969.

McMichael, Philip, *Development and Social Change: A Global Perspective*. Thousand Oaks: Pine Forge Press, 2000.

O'Dea, Thomas F., 'Sects and Cults', *International Encyclopedia of the Social Sciences,* Vols 13 & 14, 1968.

Sills, David L.(ed.), *International Encyclopaedia of the Social Sciences*, New York: The Macmillan Company, 13: 133, 1968.

Singer, Milton, *When a Great Tradition Modernizes,* New York: Praeger Publications, 1972.

Srinivas, M.N., *Social Change in Modern India,* Berkeley: University of California Press, 1966.

————, *Social Change in Modern India,* Berkeley: University of California Press, 1969.

————, *India: Social Structure*, New Delhi: Publications Division (GoI), 1969.

Stark, R. and W.S. Bainbridge, 'Of Churches, Sects and Cults: Preliminary Concepts for a Theory of Religious Movements', *Journal of the Scientific Study of Religion,* 18, 2, pp. 117–33, 1979.

Weber, Max, *The Protestant Ethic and the Spirit of Capitalism,* New York: Charles Scribner's Sons, 1930.

————, *The Religion of India,* Glencoe: The Free Press, 1958.

Yinger, J. Milton, *Sociology Looks at Religion,* London: Macmillan, 1961.

PART V

SOCIAL CHANGE

Population and Urbanization

As the world population continues to increase, social scientists and national leaders have begun to debate the causes and consequences of population growth. The world population reached seven billion in October 2011. Another billion people will be added every 11 to 13 years. While western Europe, Japan, and Russia worry about low birth rates and aging population, sub-Saharan Africa staggers under the double burden of the world's highest birth rates and deepest poverty. The regional population of 900 million in this part of Africa could reach 2 billion in forty years. Some of the developing countries will double their population in less than twenty years. Imagine the social and economic cost of such population explosion for a country that can hardly meet the basic needs of the current population. Overcrowding, environmental degradation, growth of slums, food shortages, unemployment, poverty, malnutrition, and diseases are some of the consequences of rapid population growth. Although census-taking is a routine national affair today, scientists only began to understand population dynamics during the past two hundred years.

THE BASIC CONCEPTS

Demography is the study of human population, its size and composition, as well as the causes and consequences of population changes. The growth of population is influenced by three major factors: fertility, mortality, and migration.

Fertility

First, we must make a distinction between fertility and fecundity. *Fecundity* is the number of children women are capable of bearing. Women between the ages of 15 and 45 are capable of giving birth to more than 25 children. The reality is, however, different; the realistic maximum number of children a woman can have is between 12 and 15. Even this number is seldom realized; even in countries with high birth rates an average woman rarely has more than eight children.

Crude birth rate is the number of live births per thousand persons in a society in a given year. This measure is called 'crude' because it does not make allowances for men in the population, as well as those who are too young or too old to have babies. Therefore, a more accurate statistical measure is *fertility rate*, which is the annual number of births per thousand women of child-bearing age, that is, between 15 and 44. Industrialization, urbanization as well as women's education and employment cause a decline in fertility rates throughout the world.

Mortality

Mortality refers to the frequency of deaths in a population. *Crude death rate* is the number of deaths per thousand persons in a society in a given year. Once again, this rate does not give any age-specific information, such as *infant mortality rate*, which measures the number of children who die within the first year of life per thousand live births in a given year. Infant mortality rate is a significant measure of a society's level of social and economic development. For example, in developing countries, the proportion of infant and child deaths is very high. Childhood diseases, lack of vaccination, lack of nutrition, lack of pure drinking water, and unsanitary conditions account for a high infant mortality rate. The lowest infant mortality rate in the world is found in Singapore (2.0) and Iceland (2.2). The rate is 6.1 in the United States and 50 in India. Infant mortality is a major determinant of *life expectancy*, the average number of years a person born in a particular year can expect to live. Zimbabwe with 46 has the shortest life expectancy whereas Japan has the longest life expectancy of 83 years. The life expectancy in India is about 65.77 for men and 67.95 for women.

Migration

Migration is the movement of population from one geographical region to another. Migration takes two forms: immigration and emigration. *Immigration* is in-migration, which means a population enters a region from another area. *Emigration* is out-migration, that is, a population leaves an area. *Net* migration is the difference between immigration and emigration. Since the term immigration is often used to refer to the movement of people from one country to another, sociologists use the term *internal migration* for movement within a nation's boundary. Kerala has been experiencing a huge wave of emigration to countries in the Middle East; there has also been a notable trend in internal migration or in-migration of persons from Tamil Nadu to work on plantation and construction projects in Kerala.

Most countries do not encourage immigration. However, countries like the United States, Canada, and Australia owe much of their population to immigration.

Population growth is a function of birth rates, death rates, and migration, that is, birth rate minus death rate plus net migration. Natural growth represents the births and deaths in a country's population, and does not take into account migration. The overall growth rate takes migration into account.

Doubling time is the time span necessary for a population to double in size. A growth rate of 1 per cent means that the population will double in 70 years, and with a growth rate of 2 per cent the population of a country will double in 35 years. At an yearly percentage of 0.1, more developed countries will take 809 years to double their population but at a 1.7 percentage rate,

Table 15.1: The World's Ten Largest Countries in Population

2010		2050	
Country	*Population (millions)*	*Country*	*Population (millions)*
China	1,338	India	1,748
India	1,189	China	1,437
United States	310	United States	423
Indonesia	235	Pakistan	335
Brazil	193	Nigeria	326
Pakistan	185	Indonesia	309
Bangladesh	164	Bangladesh	222
Nigeria	158	Brazil	215
Russia	142	Ethiopia	174
Japan	127	Congo, Dem. Rep.	166

Source: The 2010 World Population Data Sheet, Population Reference Bureau.

less developed countries will double their population in 41 years. Oman will double its population in just 18 years, Pakistan in 25 years, and India in 41 years. Japan will need 462 years and the United Kingdom 546 years to double their population. Table 15.1 lists the world's largest countries in population.

THEORETICAL PERSPECTIVES

Malthusian Theory of Population

Thomas Robert Malthus, an English clergyman, philosopher, and economist, was the first to write a systematic treatise on population. In 1798, he published *First Essay on Population* in which he argued that the population will always grow faster than available food supply. Malthus believed that food supply would increase in an arithmetic progression (1, 2, 3, 4, 5, and so on) whereas population would grow at a geometric rate (1, 2, 4, 8, 16, and so on). According to this view, when a population increases sixteen times, the food supply would increase only five times. Thus, if left unchecked, human population would keep on multiplying while the scarcity of food would become increasingly alarming, leading to poverty and a never-ending 'struggle for existence'.

Malthus spoke of two types of checks that could limit population growth. The first was identified as *preventive checks* or practices which would deliberately limit population growth. They include delayed marriage, celibacy, and use of contraceptives (but Malthus opposed it). The second category of checks was called *positive checks* which included famines, wars, and epidemics which would cause large-scale destruction of lives.

Matlhus' essay was severely criticized, and five years later he wrote a revision in which he acknowledged that late marriage and fewer children could prevent a population disaster. However, he opposed birth control because of his religious conviction. He advocated financial rewards to encourage people to have fewer children. Malthus could not have anticipated the revolutionary technological developments in the field of agriculture which have brought about dramatic increase in food supply. He also did not anticipate the kind of family planning practices in vogue today. Moreover, most of the world does not share Malthus' distaste for birth control methods.

Demographic Transition Theory

According to demographic transition theory, societies pass through four stages of population change:

Stage 1: High fertility and high mortality. In pre-industrial societies, the birth rate was very high. Epidemics, absence of effective health care, and lack of knowledge about sanitation and nutrition kept the death rate very high. A large number of children died in infancy.

Stage 2: High fertility and low mortality. People continued to have a large number of children. But innovations in health care, better food, and increased awareness of sanitation began to reduce death rates substantially. The result was rapid increase in population. Most developing countries are at this stage.

Stage 3: Birth rates and death rates drop. Industrialization, modernization, economic development, and education influence fertility rates, and couples begin to practise family planning. Birth rates and death rates become more or less balanced.

Stage 4: Low birth rates and high death rates. During this stage deaths outnumber births and the population shrinks. Indeed, in about fifty countries, the average number of children born to each woman has fallen below 2.1, the number required to maintain a stable population. In some European countries, particularly eastern Europe, the average fertility rate has fallen to 1.4 children per woman, a rate of population growth below the replacement level.

As societies become more advanced economically and technologically, people realize that they do not need large families. Late marriages, the phenomenon of childless couples, abortion, and widespread use of contraceptives have led to a dramatic decline in population in most developed countries.

POPULATION EXPLOSION: CAUSES AND CONSEQUENCES

In 10,000 BC there were about 10 million people in the world. By AD 1, the population had grown to 300 million. By 1850 the population had reached 1.1 billion. In other words, it took more than 1,800 years for the world population to triple. But from 1850 to 2000, the population jumped to 6.08 billion, a six-fold increase in less than 150 years. To be more precise, the world population did not reach one billion until 1804, and it took 123 years to hit the two billion mark in 1927. Then the pace accelerated to 3 billion in 1959, 4 billion in 1974, 5 billion in 1987, six billion in 1998, and now 7 billion in 2011. The United Nations projects that the world population will reach 8 billion by 2025 and 10 billion by 2083. According to the latest population data, 266 babies are born every minute, 239 of those in less developed countries, and 382,351 everyday. In other words, there are 139,558,000 births every year in the world. After we subtract the number of deaths every year, there is a natural increase of 81,078,000 people added to the world population every single year. It takes only about twelve years to add a billion to the world population. By the year 2025, the population is expected to be about 8 billion and by 2050 more than 9.3 billion people. Of that total, more than 8 billion will be in the less developed countries of Asia, Africa, and Latin America.

Let us look at the Population Reference Bureau's Population Clock (2014) (Figure 15.1).

At the moment, the world population is doubling in about 54 years. At this rate, the world population will quadruple in 108 years and increase eightfold to an incredible 40 billion within 153 years. When we consider the fact that we share this planet today with only 7 billion people, can you imagine the state of the world in 153 years with 40 billion people. Some neo-Malthusians claim that in 900 years there will be 60 million billion people, and there will only be standing room on this planet!

The new Malthusians also argue that the world population is following an exponential growth curve. Each successive addition of 1 million people to the population requires less time than the previous addition required, even if the birth rate does not increase. Tischler illustrates the effects of exponential growth by way of an example. Let us say you work for 30 days on a job at the rate of Rs 100 a day. At the end of 30 days you will receive Rs 3,000. Suppose you say that you want only 1 paisa the first day and that you want to double your pay every succeeding day. If your employer agrees, you will get 1 paisa on the first day, 2 paise on the second day, 4 paise on the third day, 8 paise on the fourth day, and so on. Each day you will receive double what you received the day before. Through this process of successive doubling, you would be paid Rs 5.12 on the 10th day. Only on the 15th day would you receive more than the flat Rs 100 a day you could have received on the very first day. Even then, the amount on the 15th day would be only Rs 163.84. However, from that day on, the daily pay increase is quite dramatic. On the 20th day you would receive Rs 5,242.88, and on the 25th day your pay would be Rs 167,772.16. Finally on the 30th day, you would be paid Rs 5,368,709.12, bringing your total pay for the month to more than Rs 1 crore. Now, if you receive Rs 100 a day, your total would be only Rs 3,000 but by receiving only one paisa on the first day and then doubling the amount on each successive day, your total is one crore. This is exactly what happens when the population keeps doubling.

The annual growth rate in the world's population has declined from a peak of 2.04 per cent in the late 1960s to 1.2 per cent in 2011. But this is the world average. Several countries

	World	More Developed Countries	Less Developed Countries
Population:	7,238,184,000	1,248,958,000	5,989,225,000
Births per:			
Year	143,341,000	13,794,000	129,547,000
Month	11,945,083	1,149,500	10,795,583
Week	2,756,558	265,269	2,491,288
Day	392,715	37,792	354,923
Hour	16,363	1,575	14,788
Minute	273	26	246
Second	4.5	0.4	4.1
Deaths per:			
Year	56,759,000	12,328,000	44,432,000
Month	4,729,917	1,027,333	3,702,667
Week	1,091,519	237,077	854,462
Day	155,504	33,775	121,732
Hour	6,479	1,407	5,072
Minute	108	23	85
Second	1.8	0.4	1.4
Natural Increase per:			
Year	86,582,000	1,466,000	85,115,000
Month	7,215,167	122,167	7,092,917
Week	1,665,038	28,192	1,636,827
Day	237,211	4,016	233,192
Hour	9,884	167	9,716
Minute	165	3	162
Second	2.7	0.0	2.7
Infant Deaths per:			
Year	5,507,000	72,000	5,435,000
Month	458,917	6,000	452,917
Week	105,904	1,385	104,519
Day	15,088	197	14,890
Hour	629	8	620
Minute	10	0.1	10
Second	0.2	0.002	0.2

Figure 15.1: Population Clock (2014). This population clock reflects data from PRB's 2014 World Population Data Sheet

Source: Population Reference Bureau, World Population Data Sheet (2014)

such as Niger, Uganda, Zambia, Gambia and Burkina Faso have a growth rate of 3 per cent or better. Most countries in Africa and Latin America have more than 2 per cent annual growth rate. Therefore, the population in most developing countries will double in less than 30 years. Thus, most of the population explosion in the next few decades will take place in less developed countries. By the year 2050, the population of richer countries will increase only by 200 million, while the developing world would have added about 6 billion to its population.

Nearly half of the current 7 billion people in the world are poor. There are three kinds of poverty: extreme or absolute poverty, moderate poverty and relative poverty. Extreme poverty, defined by the World Bank, as getting by on an income of less than $1 a day, means that households cannot meet basic needs for survival. They are chronically hungry, unable to get health care, lack safe drinking water and sanitation, cannot afford education for their children and perhaps lack rudimentary shelter and basic articles of clothing. More than 1.1 billion people live in extreme poverty. Currently more than 8 million people around the world die each year from extreme poverty, that is, more than 20,000 every day. Much of the one-sixth of humanity in extreme poverty also suffers the ravages of AIDS, drought, isolation and civil wars, and is thereby trapped in a vicious cycle of deprivation and death. Moreover, while the economic boom in east Asia has helped reduce the proportion of the extreme poor in that region from 58 per cent in 1981 to 15 per cent in 2001, and in South Asia from 52 per cent to 31 per cent, the situation is deeply entrenched in Africa, where almost half of the continent's population lives in extreme poverty—a proportion that has actually grown worse over the past two decades as the rest of the world has grown more prosperous (*Time*, 14 March 2005, p. 47).

Let us turn once again to the second stage of demographic transition theory. During this stage the birth rate continues to be high but the death rate declines dramatically. How? Advances in medical sciences have considerably reduced the death toll from numerous infectious diseases. Malaria, tuberculosis, smallpox, and many childhood diseases used to claim thousands of lives every year. Now immunization is widespread and several of the infectious diseases have been wiped out. People have also become more aware of the importance of sanitation, better food, and good health care practices. These developments have considerably reduced the death rate. But they have very little impact on the birth rate which can only be reduced by deliberate planning. In other words, birth rates can be reduced only if people choose to have fewer children or if they are forced to have fewer children. China has been fairly successful with the one-child policy which is strictly enforced by the national government with significant rewards and punishments. But governments in most developing countries, democratic or otherwise, have not been able to persuade their people to adopt family planning programmes. With the result, populations in less developed countries have been growing at an alarming rate. Table 15.2 shows annual percentage increase for select regions of the world.

Now let us examine some of the cultural factors that account for population growth. Clearly, religion plays a major role. In the Philippines, the Catholic Church has consistently opposed

Table 15.2: Rate of Natural Increase for Select Regions

Region	Rate of Natural Increase
World	1.2
More Developed	0.2
Less Developed	1.4
Least Developed	2.4
Northern Africa	1.8
Western Africa	2.6
Eastern Africa	2.8
Middle Africa	2.7
Southern Africa	0.7
Northern America	0.5
Latin America/Caribbean	1.2
South America	1.1
Asia	1.1
Western Asia	1.9
South Central Asia	1.6
South East Asia	1.3
East Asia	0.5
Europe	0.0
European Union	0.1
Australia	0.7
Oceania	1.2

Source: Population Reference Bureau.

the government's family planning programmes. In many Muslim countries, there is no official policy to limit the population size.

Women's average age at first marriage is a significant determinant of fertility. Early marriages result in high fertility. In south Asia and sub-Saharan Africa, most women get married between the ages of 15 and 19. In China, the average age at marriage is around 25. In Sri Lanka where the average age of marriage is 24.4, the average woman has 2.3 children whereas in Afghanistan where the mean age at marriage is 17.8, the average woman has 6.3 children.

High infant mortality is another factor which promotes high fertility. In societies where a large number of children die in infancy, parents give birth to more babies than they really want. This is the only way to ensure that at least two or three children reach adulthood.

The preference for sons which is prevalent in many societies also promotes high birth rate. In several Asian cultures a son is needed to continue the patriarchal line of descent. In Hindu society, a son is required to perform essential religious rituals for the benefit of the parents and the ancestors. Therefore, some parents continue to reproduce until they have one or two sons.

In other instances, they abort the female foetus or practise female infanticide. Thus, in a number of developing countries, there are fewer women than men.

In the rural areas of agrarian societies, children are still considered to be assets. They work in the fields and perform a number of odd jobs. In the absence of any social safety nets, parents depend on their children for support in their old age. Therefore, parents are inclined to produce several children for their economic value as well as old age support.

Now let us turn to the problems of overpopulation.

Overcrowding is only one of the problems. Although neo-Malthusians' 'standing room only' scenario is too far-stretched, there is no denying the fact that overpopulation exerts tremendous pressure on limited land space. Consider the crowded cities and the sprawling slums. Overcrowding is responsible for unsanitary conditions and the spread of epidemics. Undue pressure on the land also leads to the destruction of forests and wildlife.

Neo-Malthusians argue that in spite of all scientific advances in agriculture, there will be scarcity and problems of distribution. Erosion and overuse will gradually deplete even the most fertile soil. 'Green Revolution' and miracle seeds require too much water and fertilizer. Frequent use of chemical fertilizers and pesticides means that they will seep into the groundwater and also destroy many useful organisms. Water scarcity is already a major problem worldwide and cities in industrialized countries have started to recycle water; in some cases even sewage is treated and converted into potable water.

Overpopulation leads to environmental degradation and pollution. Already, the industrialized societies are finding it hard to dispose of all the waste that their population generates. Overpopulation will also deplete the natural sources of energy such as petroleum and natural gas.

Another consequence of rapid population growth is the large proportion of young people in the population. Countries with a high birth rate also have a relatively young population with almost 40 per cent of the population under fourteen years of age. This means a high dependency ratio, the number of people of non-working age in a society for every 100 people of working age.

So far we have documented the consequences of overpopulation in developing countries. It must, however, be noted here that overpopulation is not the only reason for waste, environmental degradation, and the depletion of natural resources. Consider the following facts:

1. People in industrialized nations, who account for 22 per cent of the world's population, consume 70 per cent of its energy, and 85 per cent of its wood. They produce two-thirds of all greenhouse gases and 90 per cent of all ozone-depleting chloro-fluorocarbons.
2. A child born in the United States will, in his or her lifetime, have 35 times the impact on the earth's environment on an average than a child born in India and more than 250 times the impact of a child born in one of the countries in sub-Saharan Africa.
3. 'The United States, with 5 per cent of the world's population, produces 72 per cent of the hazardous waste' (Tischler 2002: 439–40).

In spite of all the doomsday predictions of neo-Malthusians, there are also some signs of optimism. For example, between 1961 and 1994, the global production of food doubled. In fact, there is now more food for each person in the world than there was in 1950, although world population increased two and a half times since 1950. Prices of food have also fallen continually, although 2011 has recorded an increase. New technology is continually discovering and tapping new resources. Moreover, as nations enter the fourth stage of demographic transition, the population will not only stabilize but also begin to shrink.

Yet, the truth is that many of the developing countries are still stuck on stage two of the demographic transition model. Their population continues to rise. There may be surplus food in the world but starvation and famine are a way of life for millions of people. Technology may discover new resources and process them more cheaply, yet most of the poor in the developing world have no access to them.

A Note on Population in India

The population of India, which was 238.4 million in 1901, grew more than four times in 110 years to reach 1.2 billion in 2011. By 2025 India will surpass China to become the world's most populous nation. India accounts for a meagre 2.4 per cent of the world surface area of 135.79 million square kilometres but it supports a whopping 17.5 per cent of the world population. The population of India is almost equal to the combined population of the United States, Indonesia, Brazil, Pakistan, Bangladesh, and Japan. Indeed, the decadal growth of 181 million is roughly equivalent to the entire population of Brazil. Statistics suggest that India is now made up of two contrasting demographic nations. Andhra Pradesh, Karnataka, Kerala, and Tamil Nadu have already achieved the replacement-level fertility of 2.1 children per woman required to initiate the process of population stabilization, while the four large north Indian states of Bihar, Madhya Pradesh, Rajasthan, and Uttar Pradesh have a long way to go. Fifty-one babies are born in India every minute, and eleven of those are in the states that rank the lowest in HDI. However, the good news is that India's annual population growth which was 2.22 per cent in 1981 slowed down to 1.64 per cent in 2011.

Sex ratio, defined as the number of females per thousand males, is an important social indicator to measure the extent of equality between men and women. The sex ratio in India has consistently remained unfavourable to women. It plummeted from 972 in 1901 to 933 in 2001 and increased slightly to 940.27 in 2011. But there is a steep fall in the ratio for the 0–6 age group which accounts for too many 'missing girls' (discussed in the section on women in Chapter 10). Many researchers believe that female foeticide and infanticide are the primary reasons for the declining sex ratio.

Fifty per cent of India's population is under the age 25. It might appear like good news that we have more working hands in the young age. But according to United Nations Population Fund, this 'opportunity clock is ticking fast'. The youth bulge witnessed a peak in 2000, and its effect will be felt only until 2025 when the number of dependents, aided by decreasing mortality rates, begins to rise. The elderly population will be about 173 million in 2026, posing a double challenge for India: to keep its young population usefully employed, and at the same time build support system for increasing elderly population.

India and China have adopted the most comprehensive policy on population control. In China, the one-child norm is strictly enforced. There are exceptions which must be approved by the government. In rural areas, a couple may have a second child if the first child is a female or if the first child is handicapped. The couples who are themselves the only children of their parents may have a second child. Members of the minority groups are also exempted from the one-child norm. China has reached the replacement level of population which is about twenty-one births per thousand.

India has been committed to controlling the population through birth control and sterilization. India's national goal was to reach a birth rate of 2.1 by the year 2000; now India expects to reach that level by 2016. This means instead of stabilizing the population at about 1.5 billion, the country will go to almost 2 billion by the end of the twenty-first century. Although total fertility, that is, the number of children produced by a woman in her total span of productive years, has declined from 3.7 to 2.62, India may not achieve the fertility rate of 2.1 per annum for another ten years. A baby is born in India every 1.2 seconds and if the current rate of growth is unchecked India will surpass China's population somewhere between 2030 and 2035.

The total fertility rate has come down from 6 in the 1950s to 3.6 in 1992. The level of Couple Protection Rate has increased from 10.4 per cent in 1970 to 43.5 per cent in 1992. At the same time sterilization has become less and less important in India's family planning and is generally confined to women. The contribution of sterilization to the annual family planning acceptors has now come down from 32.9 per cent in 1975–6 to 15.8 per cent in 1991–2 but the proportion of tubectomies to total sterilization has increased from 10.4 per cent in 1967–8 to 95.7 per cent in 1991–2. These trends point to the fact that education and empowerment of women are probably significant factors in limiting population growth. Kerala has shown in no uncertain terms that investment in education and health holds the key to population control in India.

India's National Population Policy (NPP) 2000:

affirms the commitment of government towards voluntary and informed choice and consent of citizens while availing of reproductive health care services, and continuation of the target free approach in administering family planning services. The NPP 2000 provides a policy framework for advancing goals and prioritizing strategies during the next decade, to meet the reproductive and child health needs of the people of India, and to achieve net replacement levels (TFR) by 2010.

As stated, the goal was to bring the total fertility rate to replacement level by 2010 and to achieve a stable population by 2045. However, 2011 census shows that the total fertility rate is 2.62, well above the replacement level of 2.1. Yet the NPP 2000 is significant in that it emphasizes quality of life through better management of public health, education, sanitation, and women's

Table 15.3: World Population Growth

	Yearly Percentage Increase	Years Needed to Double the Population
World	1.4	51
More developed countries	0.1	809
Less developed countries	1.7	41
Country		
Oman	3.9	18
Palestinian territory	3.7	19
Chad	3.3	21
Zaire	3.2	22
Saudi Arabia	3.0	23
Nicaragua	3.0	23
Jordan	2.9	24
Somalia	2.9	24
Yemen	2.8	25
Pakistan	2.8	25
Syria	2.8	25
Cambodia	2.6	27
Libya	2.5	28
Afghanistan	2.5	28
Ethiopia	2.4	29
El Salvador	2.4	29
Philippines	2.3	31
Mozambique	2.2	32
Kenya	2.1	33

Source: The 2000 World Population Data Sheet, Population Reference Bureau.

empowerment, rather than through numerical targets for the use of specific contraceptive methods which plagued previous programmes.

On the positive side the policy aims at meeting the unmet needs for basic productive and child health services, supplies, and infrastructure. Other goals are keeping girls in schools longer, raising the age of marriage, reducing infant and maternal mortality, and achieving universal immunization of children against vaccine-preventable diseases. Another significant aspect of the policy concerns freezing the number of seats in the Indian Parliament. If the seats are to be revised according to increase in population, states like Tamil Nadu and Kerala would lose between five and ten seats, but some northern states that have not complied with population policies would gain as many as thirty seats. This would amount to rewarding states which fail to implement population policy and penalizing states which have vigorously followed the NPP. Critics also point out that some of the provisions may be open to misuse. For example, cash incentives at birth of a girl child or to mothers who have their first child after they turn 19 years may lead to practical problems. Many argue that education and empowerment of women are the best guarantee of a stable population.

URBANIZATION

The city is a relatively new phenomenon in human history, appearing only within the past 8,000 years. The first city developed in the fertile river valleys of Mesopotamia (modern day Iraq) and later in Egypt, India, and China. Their populations ranged between 7,000 and 50,000. The cities of Harappa and Mohenjo-Daro were not only the largest but also the most advanced. They were carefully planned with central grain warehouses, water systems, underground drainage, and multi-storeyed buildings built of fired bricks. However, these cities were small compared to modern standards and surrounded by small villages in an overwhelmingly rural world.

Urbanization, the process by which cities form and develop, is a recent phenomenon. Consider the following facts:

1. In 1800, 97 per cent of the world population lived in rural areas of fewer than 5,000 people. By 1850, 2 per cent of the world population lived in cities of 100,000 people or more. By 1900, 86 per cent of the population still lived in rural areas.

2. In 1950, only two cities in the world had populations that exceeded 8 million: London and New York. In 2000, there were sixteen such cities and almost 300 'million-plus' cities in the less developed countries.

3. In the industrialized world, urban growth has generally slowed, and there is even a retreat from cities. But the less developed world is urbanizing at a fast pace and 90 per cent of population growth will occur in urban areas of less developed countries. By 2020, a majority of the population of developing countries will live in urban areas.

4. By 2015, there will be twenty-seven megacities, or cities with a population of over 10 million, twenty-two of them in the developing world.

5. In most large cities of the developing world, at least one-quarter of the population lives in absolute poverty, and their numbers are growing.

6. Two-thirds of Asia's population are expected to be living in urban areas by 2020. China has the largest urban population in the world, but India continues to have the largest absolute increase in urban population of any country in the world—and India is still 70 per cent rural.

7. By 2015, with a population of over seventeen million people, Mumbai will be the fourteenth largest metro in the world. Except for New York and Tokyo, eight of the top largest cities will be in the developing world.

8. For the first time, the world population is evenly divided between urban and rural areas. By 2050, urban residents are likely to make up 70 per cent of the world's population.

As the population increases, more and more people will live in large cities. Already there are more than 400 cities with over 1 million people, and nineteen megacities with over 10 million inhabitants. In 1975, there were just three megacities, and only one of them in a less developed country. But by 2025, there will be twenty-seven megacities, and twenty-one of them will be in less developed countries (see Table 15.4).

Table 15.4: Top 10 Largest Urban Agglomerations (1975, 2000, and 2025)

1975		2000		2025	
1. Tokyo, Japan	26.6	1. Tokyo, Japan	34.5	1. Tokyo, Japan	36.4
2. New York–Newark, US	15.9	2. Mexico City, Mexico	18	2. Bombay, India	26.4
3. Mexico City, Mexico	10.7	3. New York–Newark, US	17.9	3. Delhi, India	22.5
4. Osaka–Kobe, Japan	9.8	4. São Paulo, Brazil	17.1	4. Dhaka, Bangladesh	22
5. São Paulo, Brazil	9.6	5. Bombay, India	16.1	5. São Paulo, Brazil	21.4
6. Los Angeles–Long Beach–Santa Ana, US	8.9	6. Shanghai, China	13.2	6. Mexico City, Mexico	21
7. Buenos Aires, Argentina	8.8	7. Calcutta, India	13.1	7. New York–Newark, US	20.6
8. Paris, France	8.6	8. Delhi, India	12.4	8. Calcutta, India	20.6
9. Calcutta, India	7.9	9. Buenos Aires, Argentina	11.9	9. Shanghai, China	19.4
10. Moscow, Russian Federation	7.6	10. Los Angeles–Long Beach–Santa Ana, US	11.8	10. Karachi, Pakistan	19.1

Source: United Nations, World Urbanization Prospects: The 2007 Revision.

Between 2007 and 2050, Asia is expected to more than double its urban population with an increase of 1.8 billion people. In 1901, only less than 11 per cent of the population in India lived in urban areas, but in 1991 that percentage had increased to 25.7. According to the 2011 census, the urban population in India is 30 per cent and there are over thirty million-plus cities in India. Urbanization in India is due to both 'urban pull' and 'rural push'. Many are pushed out of the rural areas by poverty, lack of employment, caste discrimination, and the decline of traditional occupations. At the same time, millions are attracted to the city because of what they perceive to be better opportunities and facilities.

The urban explosion is caused by the mass exodus of rural migrants as well as by the natural increase resulting from lower death rates. There are differences of opinion as to whether urban

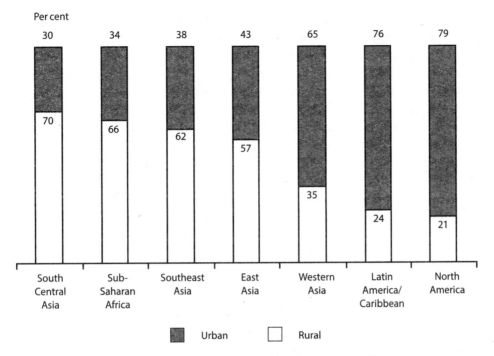

Per cent

Figure 15.2: Much of the World Still Remains Rural

Source: PRB, *2005 World Population Data Sheet.*
Note: Though the world has become increasingly urban, two-thirds of the populations of the world's poorest regions—sub-Saharan Africa and South-Central Asia—still live in rural areas.

concentration in developing countries is a positive or negative factor in national development. Higgins (1967: 117) claims that 'urbanization and economic development have been closely related ever since the industrial revolution of the seventeenth and eighteenth centuries.' According to him no country can be considered advanced with more than one third of its national income produced in the agricultural sector, or more than 40 per cent of its labour force engaged in that sector. The kind of trained, skilled professionals needed to launch and sustain industrialization like to live in urban centres. Even the rural migrants to the city are exposed to mass media, prepared for political participation, and ultimately for national integration. The city provides better health facilities and greater educational opportunities and motivates people to attain higher levels of education necessary to meet the needs of new technology.

Breese (1966) enumerates the following as 'urban roles for emerging nations':

1. *Points of contact with the outside world.* The large city, especially the one that stands at the head of the developing country, serves as a major point of contact with the outside world, facilitating economic and political transactions.

2. *Locus of power.* The city is the centre of political organizations with dominant influence as well as the locus of economic power, with the concentration of industrial, commercial, and other enterprises.

3. *Agency and diffusion point of social change.* In the city evolve new ideas of national policy, patterns of leadership, and new national programmes.

4. *Receptacle of talent and manpower.* The principal city will attract the nation's highest talent, the bulk of its manpower, and major investment funds.

5. *Place of investment.* Large shares of domestic as well as foreign investments will be concentrated in the major cities.

Critics of urbanization argue that the modernizing role of cities is exaggerated. They point to the failure of the metropolitan area to cope with the pressing demands for basic facilities and services. Since in-migrants settle in vastly scattered areas, the complex, high-capital-cost facilities such as potable water supply, sewage disposal, and public transportation cannot be expanded rapidly enough to catch up with the demand. In fact, the 'over-urbanization' perspective is based on the assumption that urban population in developing countries is too large in relation to the extent of their economic development. In other words, countries in the early stages of industrialization suffer an imbalance in both the size and distribution of their urban populations, that is, they have a higher percentage of population living in cities and towns than is 'warranted' at their stage of economic development; they experience excessive migration of unemployable as well as unemployed and underemployed rural folk to the cities in advance of an adequate economic base that can sustain them. For example, the rapid rate of urbanization in Asian countries did not involve a corresponding growth of industry but a shift of people from low productive agricultural employment to yet another type of low productivity employment in handicraft production, retail trading, and domestic services in the urban area. The most visible consequence of rapid urbanization in developing countries is the mushrooming slums or shanty towns which cause the government to allot large proportion of scarce resources to social investment at the risk of reducing productive investments. Moreover, Hauser (1970: 203) contends that the primate cities of Asia are not the result of indigenous economic development, but developed as links between colonies and foreign powers. Hauser also enumerates problems of 'internal disorder, political unrest and governmental instability fed by mass misery and frustrations in the urban setting' and inadequacy and ineffectiveness of infrastructures to plan for and provide health and welfare services, education, culture, and recreational activities. He contends: 'Thus, the underdeveloped areas of the world are "over-urbanized", in that larger proportions of their population live in urban areas than their degree of economic development justifies.'

In an attempt to provide work for unemployed and underemployed immigrants from rural areas, governments usually encourage labour-intensive techniques which, in the long run, tend to discourage labour-saving technological developments, thereby adversely affecting the growth of the nation's net aggregate product. Inadequate urban services, uncontrolled competition for space, overcrowding, ineffective commercial and marketing arrangements, and deteriorating environment characterize the primate cities in many developing countries.

THEORETICAL PERSPECTIVES

How does life in the city affect its residents? This has been the focus of much research in sociology. We will examine two theoretical traditions.

Georg Simmel: Metropolis and Mental Life

Simmel's analysis of the metropolis and mental life provides an accurate insight into his view of modern society. For the sake of self-preservation, modern man tends to develop a defensive reserve around his personality which protects him from the overwhelming social forces that threaten to engulf him. 'The metropolitan type of man—which, of course, exists in a thousand individual variants—develops an organ protecting him against the threatening currents and discrepancies of his external environment which would uproot him. He reacts with his head instead of his heart. In this an increased awareness assumes the psychic prerogative' (Simmel 1969: 48). Individuals living in today's mass society acquire what Simmel calls the 'blasé attitude' which involves antipathy, repulsion, unmerciful matter-of-factness, and utmost particularization. This attitude precludes them from interacting with other men as full, emotional, and concerned human beings. And, precisely because in their everyday life men interact with one another in the most rational, matter-of-fact, and impersonal way, their psychic system is largely unaffected by the destructive consequences of structural disintegration and de-institutionalization.

Louis Wirth: Urbanism as a Way of Life

Louis Wirth's classic essay on urbanism as a way of life, published in 1938, influenced generations of sociologists in their approach to life in the city. He argued that size, density, and heterogeneity of the urban population paved the way for impersonal, transitory, and secondary social relationships based on anonymity, formality, and rational interest. According to Wirth (1969: 153),

increase in numbers limits the possibility of each member of the community knowing all the others personally. Urbanites meet one another in highly segmented roles. The contacts of the city may indeed be face to face, but they are nevertheless impersonal, superficial, transitory, and segmental. The reserve, the indifference, and the blasé outlook which urbanites manifest in their relationships may thus be regarded as devices for immunizing themselves against the personal claims and expectations of others.

Urban life promotes sophistication and rationality, and all social relationships are considered means to other ends. Thus, the urban way of life loses spontaneous self-expression. The segmented character and utilitarian accent of interpersonal relations in the city find their institutional expression in the proliferation of specialized tasks. The city also accentuates division of labour and specialization of occupations. The urban man tends to acquire and develop a sensitivity to a world of artifacts, and becomes progressively farther removed from the world of nature. Since a transitory habitat does not generate binding traditions, the city-dweller is not a true neighbour. The pecuniary nexus which implies the purchasability of services and things has displaced personal relations as the basis of association. Therefore, personal disorganization, mental breakdown, suicide, delinquency, crime, corruption, and disorder might be more prevalent in the urban than in the rural community.

However, recent scholarship indicates that the view that modern urban societies constitute a mass of uprooted, impersonal individuals, disconnected with one another, unloved and alienated, is an exaggeration. There are hundreds of neighbourhoods and little communities right in the heart of the city where people know and relate to one another. New in-migrants to the city also tend to gravitate to neighbourhoods where people from their villages or regions live. Caste groups, religious communities, and linguistic groups provide effective personal networks and support systems. Members of the same caste, people who speak the same language or hail from the same state or members of extended families and clans continue to maintain close social relationships.

URBANIZATION IN INDIA

For the first time since 1921, India's urban population went up by more than its rural population in 2011 census. Migration, natural increase, and inclusion of new areas as urban accounted for this increase. However, the real reason may be the collapse of millions of lives in agriculture and related occupations and despair-driven exodus to cities. At 833.1 million, India's rural population today is 90.6 million higher than it was in 2001. Urban areas account for 30 per cent of the total population. The most urbanized states in India are Tamil Nadu (43.9 per cent), Maharashtra (42.4 per cent), and Gujarat (37.4 per cent). The rate of urbanization is 2.4 per cent. Although less than a third of India's population lives in cities and towns, these areas generate over two-thirds of the country's GDP and account for almost 90 per cent of government revenue.

Sujata Patel (2009: 21) summarizes the process of urbanization in India as follows:

...contemporary urbanization has been characterized by three phases of growth—First the development of capital intensive industrialization which dates back to the 1940s, with the formation of cities such as Bokaro, Bhilai, Durgapur, Rourkela. The second phase is associated with the development of the small scale labour intensive industrialization, which started in the 1960s with provincial towns such as Surat, Faridabad, Ghaziabad, Ludhiana, Kanpur and Meerut, and lastly the service economy associated with globalization, which started in the late 1980s, with cities such as Bangalore and now Hyderabad and Pune. In some cities these phases coexist while in others they remained distinct. This variation is a function of the way the regional and global economies are linked to the local processes as well as of the nature of the migration process, and the role of the State and its policies together with the nature of agricultural growth.

Table 15.5 shows the ranking of cities in India in two census periods.

Table 15.5: Ranking of Select Indian Cities in Two Census Periods

Rank	City Only (Not Metro Area)	Population (2011 census)	Population (2001 census)	State/UT
1	Mumbai	12,478,447	11,978,450	Maharashtra
2	Delhi	11,007,835	9,879,172	Delhi
3	Bangalore	8,425,970	5,438,065	Karnataka
4	Hyderabad	6,809,970	3,637,483	Andhra Pradesh
5	Ahmedabad	5,570,585	3,520,085	Gujarat
6	Chennai	4,681,087	4,343,645	Tamil Nadu
7	Kolkata	4,486,679	4,572,876	West Bengal
8	Surat	4,462,002	2,433,835	Gujarat
9	Pune	3,115,431	2,538,473	Maharashtra
10	Jaipur	3,073,350	2,322,575	Rajasthan
11	Lucknow	2,815,601	2,185,927	Uttar Pradesh

Source: Data from two census reports (Indian Census 2001 and 2011).
Note: UT = union territory.

It is very difficult to generalize on the Indian urban phenomenon. However, we may note a few points. From 1971 onwards, the urban population grew at a higher rate than the total population, and today a significant percentage of people who lead urban life live in Class I towns, that is, towns with more than one lakh population. There is considerable debate on the rural–urban divide. Some scholars argue that it does not make much sense to talk about urban and metropolitan phenomena in the Indian context because social life in the city looks like almost an extension of life in the country. However, Rao (1974: 2) posited that 'In the traditional urban context, the institutional framework and the constraints in which religion, caste and kinship operated are not the same as those in the villages'. For instance, the jajmani (hereditary service) relations were pronounced in the villages but the mahajan or guild organization prevailed in cities. However, Patel (2009) points out that caste and kin linkages together with community may be a factor influencing people's decision to move to the city. 'Thus urban growth in some cases may be triggered due to the history of caste networks that has propelled migration.' Patel (2009: 22) continues:

This urban population is internally segmented on the basis of caste, language, ethnic and religious identities with gender crisscrossing these. Some of these segmentations are spatially organized in settlements and neighborhoods within towns and cities affirming these identities over that of the working class. These trends have not led primordial identities to decline; rather the economy has become cluttered by the way caste and kinship networks, as well as affiliation to gender, ethnicity and religion has trapped it into its fold not allowing it to grow and be competitive.

Slums now account for one-fourth of all urban housing. In Mumbai more than half of the population lives in slums. A report compiled by the National Buildings Organization (NBO) of the Ministry of Housing and Urban Poverty Alleviation shows about 7.6 million children, in the age group 0–6 years, live in slums, and they constitute 13.1 per cent of the total child population of the urban areas in the country. More than 20 per cent of Chandigarh's children are in slums. Maharashtra has 1.7 million and Uttar Pradesh has 0.97 million children living in urban slums.

Another important aspect of the urban phenomenon is that the number of people living in the core city has declined and the peripheries have expanded with high densities. Because of the exhorbitant land prices in the city core, more and more people are moving out to the suburbs, forcing long commutes. Mumbai city, for instance, had a negative population growth rate of 5.75 per cent in the last decade, but Thane, its suburb, which is about 40 kilometres away, recorded 36 per cent growth. Such a sprawl means huge loss of agricultural land and mounting pressure on infrastructure development such as transportation, water supply, and sanitation.

STUDY QUESTIONS

- What is demography? Define the basic concepts of fertility, mortality, and migration and their relation to population growth.
- Critically examine the Malthusian theory of population.
- Summarize the demographic transition theory.
- Write an essay on population explosion and its causes and consequences with special reference to developing societies.
- Summarize the NPP and the population growth in India.
- Critically examine the process of urbanization and its impact on developing countries.
- Write a paragraph each on the following: Georg Simmel on metropolis and mental life; and Louis Wirth on urbanism as a way of life.
- Review the process of urbanization in India with special reference to its social consequences.

REFERENCES

Breese, Gerald, *Urbanization in Newly Developing Countries*, Englewood Cliffs: Prentice-Hall, 1966.
Hauser, Philip, 'The Social, Economic and Technological Problems of Rapid Urbanization' in Bert Hoselitz and Wilbert Moore (eds), *Industrialization and Society*, Paris: UNESCO-Mouton, 1970.
Hauser, Philip and Leo Schnore (eds), *The Study of Urbanization*, New York: John Wiley and Sons, 1965.

Higgins, Benjamin, 'Urbanization, Industrialization, and Economic Development', in Glenn Beyer (ed.), *The Urban Explosion in Latin America,* Ithaca: Cornell University Press, 1967.

Patel, Sujata and Kushal Deb, *Urban Studies,* New Delhi: Oxford University Press, 2009.

Rao, M.S.A., *Urban Sociology in India: Reader and Source Book,* New Delhi: Orient Blackswan, 1974.

Simmel, Georg, 'The Metropolis and Mental Life', in Richard Sennet (ed.), *Classic Essays on the Culture of Cities,* pp. 47–60, 1969.

Tischler, Henry, *Introduction to Sociology,* Philadelphia: The Harcourt Press, 2002.

Wirth, Lewis, 'Urbanism as a Way of Life' in Richard Sennet (ed.), *Classic Essays on the Culture of Cities,* New York: Appleton-Century-Crofts, pp. 143–60, 1969.

16

Collective Behaviour and Social Movements

During the time of the Kumbh Mela, hundreds of thousands of devotees throng the banks of the Ganga to partake in religious rituals which sometimes work them into a frenzy. There are festivals during which devotees pierce their cheeks, hang hooks on their skin to carry sacred objects and then work themselves into a trance. The recent communal riot in Gujarat illustrated how violent and unpredictable human behaviour can be during moments of collective excitement. When a fire broke out in a theatre in Delhi, panic led to mass hysteria and a stampede that killed several people. During temple festivals in Kerala just the rumour that an elephant in the procession has gone mad is enough to cause panic and a stampede. The annual meeting of the World Trade Organization always attracts hundreds of protesters and occasionally the protest turns violent. Peaceful marches sometimes turn violent and lead to looting and vandalism. Workers go on a rampage and destroy property during strikes. Thousands of young men and women imitate the fashions, fads, punk styles, and dances of their peers around the world. Thousands gather to listen to a pop star or flock to a religious revival.

Some of these actions are predictable, others are not. A crowd attending a music concert may disperse peacefully, or an untoward incident during the event may trigger panic or violent frenzy. It is precisely the character of unpredictability that makes a form of behaviour 'collective behaviour'.

According to *A Modern Dictionary of Sociology, collective behaviour* is

interrelated and similar, but unstructured, reactions and patterns of behavior on the part of a number of persons who are responding to a common influence or stimulus. Collective behavior is nontraditional, in the sense that it is not subject to clearly defined, culturally established norms. Cultural definitions and social norms, of course, to a certain extent determine and limit all social behavior, but in the case of collective behavior the cultural expectations are general and nonspecific and may be contradictory, leaving the situation largely unstructured and undefined. Collective behavior is not group behavior, for there is not sufficient organization and interaction for the persons involved to be considered a social group.

Collective actions can cause unpredictable behaviour, unleash powerful social forces, and lead to major social disruptions.

THEORIES OF COLLECTIVE BEHAVIOUR

The first thing we know about collective behaviour is that it is unstructured and unpredictable. We know about the destruction caused by the tsunami but we could never have predicted exactly how people would respond to this terrible crisis. We do not know exactly when a crowd turns into a mob and goes on a rampage. We do know that such behaviours do not follow any established norms. Some types of collective behaviour such as bandhs, strikes, hartals, religious revivals, and even riots are used as means to certain ends, often to achieve political goals. But sometimes crowds are worked into a frenzy and they resort to antisocial behaviour. How do we explain such types of behaviour? Let us look at some general theories of collective behaviour.

Contagion Theory

One of the oldest theories was proposed by a French sociologist, Gustave Le Bon. The essence of his theory is that the condition of anonymity can turn individuals in a crowd into beasts. In a crowd people lose sense of their values, their place in society, and are then swept off their feet. In other words, in a crowd, individuals become less civil: 'Isolated, he may be a cultivated individual; in a crowd, he is a barbarian—that is, a creature acting by instinct. He possesses the spontaneity, the violence, the ferocity, and also the enthusiasm and heroism of primitive beings' (Le Bon 1952: 32). In other words, individuals in a crowd lose their individuality and acquire a collective mentality which transforms them from cultured human beings into destructive anti-social elements. Robert Park and Ernest Burgess (1921), American sociologists, were influenced by Le Bon and added the concepts of social unrest and circular reaction. According to them, 'Social unrest ... is transmitted from one individual to another ... so that the manifestations of discontent in A (are) communicated to B, and from B reflected back to A.'

Herbert Blumer (1939) synthesized the ideas of Le Bon and identified five stages that precede what he called an *acting crowd*:

1. *Tension or unrest*. When people become disturbed about some condition in society, they become apprehensive and vulnerable to rumours.
2. *Exciting event*. A startling event occurs and people become preoccupied with it.
3. *Milling*. A circular reaction sets in as people start talking about the event.
4. *A common object of attention*. As people's attention becomes riveted on some aspect of the event, they get caught up in the collective excitement.
5. *Common impulses*. People give in to the 'engulfing mood, impulse or form of conduct' and the crowd begins to spiral out of control.

Acting crowds are not always or necessarily destructive.

Emergent Norm Theory

Ralph Turner and Lewis Killian (1972) argue that even when crowd behaviour seems to be out of control, it is not entirely normless behaviour. When established norms do not cover unexpected and unpredictable types of behaviour, new norms emerge which may even justify new forms of collective actions. Thus, emergent-norm theory analyses the process by which a new social standard develops and pushes a crowd in one direction or another. In the absence of prior established standards, some active members in the crowd are likely to take the initiative and suggest a new standard, and even a new course of action. Someone starts throwing stones and bottles and urges others to do the same. As more and more people follow, the emergent norm seems to support the unruly behaviour.

Convergence Theory

The contagion theory cannot explain why a crowd turns into a mob. Why is it that only some people are 'engulfed' and swept off their feet and transformed while others just walk away from the unruly situation? The convergence theory argues that collective behaviour is the outcome of situations which draw together people with similar characteristics, attitudes, and needs. In other words, certain kinds of situations bring together certain kinds of people. Communal riots are an example. Once an incident triggers communal feelings, people with strong emotions are drawn from opposing groups into a communal frenzy. Thus, convergence theory stresses the role of the individual rather than collective excitement and argues that some people are predisposed to certain types of collective actions.

Value-added Theory

In 1962, Neil Smelser proposed the most comprehensive theory of collective behaviour called value-added theory. Smelser (1963) identified six conditions that must be met for collective behaviour to occur:

1. *Structural conduciveness.* The existing social order must be somehow conducive to the emergence of collective behaviour. Physical proximity and the ability to communicate with one another are examples.
2. *Structural strain.* There is the perception of an unjust social situation and the discontent causes disruption of the social system.
3. *Growth and spread of a generalized belief.* People not only perceive that a problem exists but they also develop explanations about it. Soon more people believe something must be done.
4. *Precipitating factors.* There is always a triggering event, an incident or event which suddenly grips the consciousness of the people.
5. *Mobilization for action.* This refers to the actual onset of collective action. In the absence of previously recognized leaders, a group is easily swayed by more boisterous and active members.

6. *Mechanism of social control.* Agents of social control such as law enforcement officials move in to restore order.

According to Smelser, each condition must be met before the next can become relevant.

FORMS OF COLLECTIVE BEHAVIOUR

Crowds

A crowd is a temporary aggregate of individuals with a common focus or interest, in physical proximity, and without a history of previous interaction. When the common activity or interest ends, the crowd usually disperses. Individuals in a crowd are relatively anonymous; they do not interact with one another in any structured manner. The presence of a large number of people in an unstructured social situation has important implications. The first is suggestibility, or the tendency of individuals to go along with the crowd. The conditions of anonymity and impersonality mean that people are less constrained by normal rules of behaviour.

Elias Canetti (1978) enumerates the following characteristics of crowds:

1. *Crowds are self-generating.* Since they have no natural boundaries, crowds may swell and spill over any artificial boundaries, such as barricades set up by law enforcement officials.
2. *Crowds are characterized by equality.* Social positions and distinctions lose their importance in crowds.
3. *Crowds love density.* People in a crowd pack together with no regard for personal space.
4. *Crowds need direction.* Many crowds are in motion and their direction is set by the goals of the crowd which vary with the type of crowd.

Turner and Killian (1972) identify five kinds of participants:

1. The *ego-involved* feel a personal stake in the unusual event.
2. The *concerned* also have a personal interest in the event, but less so than the ego-involved.
3. The *insecure* care little about the matter, but they join the crowd because it gives them a sense of power, security, or feeling of belonging.
4. The *curious spectators* also care little about the issue, but they are inquisitive about what is going on.
5. The *exploiters* do not care about the event, but they use it for their own purpose such as looting.

There are several different types of crowd.

An *acting crowd* is a group of people whose passions and tempers have been aroused by some focal event and who are bent upon action to achieve some limited but seemingly important purpose. Members of an acting crowd come to feed on the emotions of one another, lose sight of the normal social controls of society, and often turn violent.

A *threatened crowd* is an acting crowd in a state of alarm because of the perception of some imminent danger. Crowds panic if a packed theatre catches fire or if an elephant runs amuck during a temple festival. *Panic* is a type of localized collective behaviour in which a large number of people react to a real or imaginary threat. A panic situation occurs only when people feel that they are exposed to a life-threatening situation and that the escape routes are limited or uncertain. The terms *mob* and riot also refer to acting crowds. A mob is a highly charged and emotionally aroused crowd that turns violent, pursues a specific target, and fades away. A *riot* is a violent crowd that directs its hostility towards a wide and shifting range of targets, keeps moving, and attacks different targets. Whereas a mob has a specific target, riots lead to mindless destruction of lives and property and may last for several days.

An *expressive crowd* is a gathering of people who display unrestrained collective excitement and participate in emotionally gratifying events. An expressive crowd has no clearly defined goal or external purpose. The activity, a free expression of emotional feelings, is an end in itself. Dancing crowds, New Year's eve gatherings, revivals, and other religious festivals are examples.

A *conventional crowd* is a gathering of people with a specific purpose and in accordance with institutionalized norms. Such crowds include audiences at lectures and theatres as well as participants in sports events and parades.

A *casual crowd* is a group of people who happen to be at the same place at the same time. Crowds gather to watch an accident or a street performer. These are ad hoc gatherings with no prior information.

It is important to remember that any crowd can shift from one type to another. Rock concerts and football matches have turned violent. Even crowds watching accidents have become agitated leading to altercations and fist fights.

Dispersed Collective Behaviour

Certain types of collective behaviour occur even when people are not in close physical proximity. Some of them are discussed ahead.

Rumour

A rumour is unverified information that is informally communicated from person to person. Rumours are frequently, but not always, false. They arise in ambiguous situations when people want information but cannot find verifiable information. According to Rosnow, rumours are likely to develop and spread under the following conditions when:

1. The rumour provides information that is important to people.
2. There is some general uncertainty suggested by rumour.

3. The rumour produces high level of personal anxiety
4. One's belief in the rumour is strong.

To these we may also add that people are likely to believe a rumour if the bearer is generally credible.

The content of rumour changes over time. As the transmission of the rumour proceeds, the content may get distorted. Rumour may also lead to individual definition of social situations or collective action. Recently in north India many refused vaccination because of a rumour that the vaccine was mixed with drugs that will make people impotent. Someone had spread the rumour that the vaccination was a backdoor attempt to sterilize people.

Gossip is a form of rumour but the focus of the former is other people's private affairs; it is almost always some juicy tale about someone you know.

Mass hysteria 'occurs when large numbers of people are overwhelmed with emotion and frenzied activity or become convinced that they have experienced something for which investigators can find no discernible evidence' (Tischler 2002: 519). It is an intense, frightened, and seemingly irrational reaction to some imaginary threat that cannot be rationally explained. In 2001, there were several reports from New Delhi that a 'monkey man' was stalking and biting people who were sleeping on rooftops during the blistering summer heat. The hysteria spread and many people would wake up at night screaming. Some even jumped off the roof. Then again last year mass hysteria struck the campus of the Indian Statistical Institute in New Delhi when many students claimed to have seen the ghost of a student who had committed suicide. Students were so fear-struck that the institute had to close down for days.

Fads and Fashions

Fads and fashions refer to periodic changes in styles and patterns of behaviour. They are dispersed among a mass, are transitory, and seldom institutionalized. A fad is a new form of behaviour that briefly catches people's attention and fades away. A craze is similar to a fad but has an even shorter life. Fads and crazes appear suddenly, spread by imitation, and vanish fairly quickly. They may be related to clothes, hair styles, jewellery, and types of behaviour. Fashions are relatively institutionalized forms of collective behaviour pertaining to standards of dress and manners. Unlike fads and crazes, fashions change relatively gradually. Some are even durable.

Sociologists are interested in fads and fashions because they are indicators of trends of change in society. The role of social classes in the origin of fashions, the process of transmission and economic implications of consumer behaviour are also of interest to sociologists.

Some scholars argue that collective behaviour approaches are rather outmoded and social movement theories are more appropriate today. But there are several collective phenomena which have no relation to social movements, especially in the Indian context. Consider the case of a traffic accident. In the West someone calls the police who arrive on the scene and handle the situation. There is no crowd formation. In India a large crowd gathers, people pass judgement, and even turn violent. A rumour that a patient has died in a hospital because of doctors' negligence causes a mob to attack the hospital and assault the staff. When a student leader is suspended from a college or when some students do not like a particular speaker invited to the college, a mob gathers and vandalizes the property. These types of collective behaviour have nothing to do with social movements. They are centred on local issues, triggered by particular events, and are short-lived.

Social Movements

A *social movement* is a form of collective behaviour in which a large number of people are united in an attempt to promote or resist social change. Having reviewed several definitions of social movements, Ghanshyam Shah (2004: 18) settled on the idea of 'non-institutionalized collective political action striving for social and political change'. For most people, participation in a social movement is only informal and indirect. Usually, a shared sense of dissatisfaction brings people together. They feel concerted action is necessary to change the situation perceived to be undesirable. But many of them who participate in various activities of the movement may not necessarily join the organization which sponsors it.

There are different types of social movements. *Alterative social movements* seek to alter some specific behaviour. The prohibition movement in India was designed to get people to stop drinking and to force governments to enforce the dry law. *Reformative social movements* advocate fundamental social reforms. Movements against untouchability, sati, child marriage, and dowry are examples. *Transformative social movements* are revolutionary movements that aim at total transformation of society. French, Russian, and Chinese revolutions brought about transformations of the social order. Then there are the nationalist movements, farmers' movements, and labour movements which attempt to bring about systemic changes. *Reactionary social movements* embrace the values of the past or some fundamental tenets of faith and want to return general society to yesterday's values. Fundamentalist religious movements may be classified under this category. *Expressive social movements* simply express personal feelings of satisfaction and general well-being and people join them for mutual support and togetherness. They choose an alternative lifestyle and subscribe to a different set of values. The Hippie movement of the 1960s, Hare Krishna, and various 'communitarian' groups fall into this category. Finally, some are obviously *transnational social movements* in the sense that they are global in their orientation. Many of the ideologically based social movements transcend national boundaries.

Theories of Social Movements

Relative Deprivation Theory

The term relative deprivation refers to deprivation or disadvantage which a group experiences, not in absolute objective terms, but in comparison with a reference group. Relative deprivation is not measured by objective standards but always in reference to another group. For example, the economic situation of school teachers may be improving. However, regardless of how much they are paid and how big a pay raise they get, they might still feel deprived if they perceive other non-gazetted government officials to be doing better. Therefore, relative deprivation is not to be understood in terms of the actual situation of a group of people but in terms of how they judge their situation relative to another group.

There is also a gap between people's aspirations and their achievement. For example, in many agrarian societies which won freedom from colonial rule, people's expectations shot up. In fact, exposure to mass media, political participation, and the spirit of nationalism led to a revolution of rising expectations. But there was no corresponding improvement in their standard of living. This leads to frustration and call for concerted action.

James Davies (1992) proposed a strain theory which is based on the gap between expectations and the capacity to achieve those expectations. If people's expectations continue to rise and their levels of satisfaction decline, or if they perceive that the opportunities to achieve them are somehow blocked, there will be considerable social strain leading to collective action. Anti-untouchability movements and women's movements are explained in part by variants of strain theory or relative deprivation theory.

Resource Mobilization Theory

Structural strain and relative deprivation may spread discontent in society. But widespread discontent is not enough to launch a movement. There must be a leader or leaders who can mobilize the resources—people, money, channels of communication, and commitment of time. Leaders formulate specific goals, provide the ideology, and deliver their messages in such an effective manner that they resonate with the right people. Sometimes an organizational format also becomes necessary to recruit large numbers of people, to assign duties and responsibilities, and to allocate resources.

Resource mobilization theory is helpful in explaining several contemporary social movements. The women's movement, student movements in Assam, the Narmada Andolan, and various religious revivalist movements demonstrate the importance of resource mobilization.

Political Opportunity/Political Process Theory

This theory argues that social movements arise when certain political opportunities offer favourable climate for people to engage in contentious politics. People may have grievances and there may be enough resources to be mobilized but these two factors may not be sufficient conditions for the emergence of social movements. However, if there are appropriate political opportunities, social movements are likely to emerge. Some of the political opportunities that favour the rise of social movements are:

1. Political pluralism, that is, the presence of multiple power centres.
2. Defection within elites; some members of the ruling elites defect and support the movement.
3. Declining capacity and propensity of the state to repress the dissent.
4. Instability in the alignment of ruling elites.

The conditions just mentioned are conducive to potential social movement activity. Thus the success or failure of particular social movements depends on certain political opportunities and processes. However, it must be stressed that most political opportunities are situational, not structural, and they are prone to change. Moreover, these opportunities must be perceived and realized by potential participants in the movement.

New Social Movements

This is a group of theories influenced by European thought. Proponents of this perspective argue that most of the earlier theories focused more on structures than cultures. They see the motivation for movement participation as a form of post-material politics and newly created identities. Environmentalists and social reformers, anti-nuclear and anti-war movements, gay rights and civil rights activists, and feminists and adivasis, all involve new identities. Most of the post-Marxist movements are often termed 'the new democratic struggles' (Mouffe 1984). Boggs (1986), drawing together studies from Europe and the United States, argued that new social movements (NSMs) are linked to four potential issues of conflict: economic stagnation; ecological disequilibria; militarism and nuclear politics; and bureaucracy. In a similar vein, Falk (1987) attributed five basic aims to NSMs: denuclearization, demilitarization, dealignment, development, and democratization. The NSMs do not see their actions and objectives in terms of a necessary historical mission such as a revolution leading to a total transformation of the political structure. For many participants, the experience of collective action is an end in itself. Also for many NSMs, there is a convergence of the global with the local. While the NSM may have a global agenda, it may also involve concern for immediate locality. Environmental movement is a case in point.

David Slater (1991) addresses the construction of new identities and values as a feature of the novelty of NSMs.

For Laclau (1985), the radically democratic potential of the NSMs lies in their implicit demand for a critically open and indeterminate view of society; for Evers (1984), it is the continuous effort at democratization that matters, including the importance of cultural and sociopsychic transformations. Other writers have stressed the fact that NSMs have tended to be oriented toward the control of a field of autonomy rather than to be focused on the conquest of political power (Falk 1987). Together with notions of autonomy, the defense and affirmation of solidarity, and the struggle against hierarchy and alienation (Foss and Larkin 1986) have also become symptomatic elements of the NSMs. Further, one ought not to forget the validation of direct participation and in some cases direct spontaneous action (Offe 1985).

Further, Slater posits that autonomy, solidarity, direct participation, and democracy can all be related to the construction within the NSMs of new political values and practices (Slater 1991: 39–40). Most old movements were centred on poverty–wealth divide. But modern social movements may focus on a single issue such as dowry, construction of a dam, a nuclear power plant, or female infanticide. New social movements also make effective use of new technology such as internet and mass media. For example, much of the success of Arab Spring depended on widespread use of Twitter, YouTube and Facebook.

Rajendra Singh (2001) has offered a postmodernist critique of studies of social movements in India. He claims society and movement are two sides of the same coin—social. Each of them has to be conceptualized as the expressive continuation and extension of the other. According to Singh, classical conceptions of society and social order have overlooked freedom and autonomy of individuals, groups, and communities. The postmodern phase abandons the idea of society as a totality and views society, instead, as a pluralist social entity. Singh relates the development of NSMs to the birth of postmodernist societies. To him, NSMs mirror the image of new society in the making. The NSMs project the need for a new paradigm of collective action, an alternative model of culture and society, and a new self-consciousness of the communities about their future. In his view, the new representation of societies defines itself by 'new' types of movements and collective social action (paraphrased from Nag and Srikant, *Economic and Political Weekly*, 2002).

Social movements usually flourish in democratic political systems. Occasionally, events have triggered social movements against entrenched political elites and for democratic governments. The so-called Arab Spring, or pro-democracy movements in the Middle East, is a case in point. Revolutionary social movements such as Marxist socialist movements have sometimes transformed the whole political, economic, and social systems. Mexico, Russia, China, and Cuba are well-known examples of system substitution. In Iran and Afghanistan, religious movements led to the creation of governments based on fundamentalist ideology. In some cases social movements have led to the creation of new political parties. Solidarity in Poland and several regional political parties in India owe their origin to certain social movements. In some cases the state actively supports issues-oriented social movements such as those against sati, untouchability, female foeticide, and dowry, and for environment and civil rights. Thus in some cases, the state may be a catalyst and encourage social movements, and in other cases seek to suppress them with all its might.

THE LIFE CYCLE OF SOCIAL MOVEMENTS

A number of social scientists have studied the process of a social movement in terms of various stages and models. Armand Mauss identifies five stages through which a typical social movement passes. They are as follows:

1. *Incipience.* The first condition of a social movement is the prevalence of some discontent or frustration among a large number of people. Relative deprivation and discontent usually occur during times of economic crisis, war, and major technological changes. Then there emerge leaders who can channel the frustration of affected people, give a voice to their frustration, define the messages, and tell people that change is possible. But many social movements fail at this stage because leaders are unable to mobilize enough support or resources or effectively convince the people that change is indeed possible.

2. *Coalescence.* During this stage interest groups form around leaders and formulate programmes. They network with other groups and like-minded individuals. They seek the support of well-connected and well-known personalities. They also mobilize other resources such as money, goods, people's skills and time, as well as the attention of mass media.

3. *Institutionalization.* If the movement attracts large numbers of people, it can no longer depend on the charismatic qualities of the leader. The movement needs a formal organization with full-time staff, functional division of labour, a budget, and its own publications. When the movement becomes institutionalized, there is always the danger that it will become 'just another organization'.

4. *Fragmentation.* During this stage conflicts arise over a number of issues—leadership style, doctrine, bureaucratization, and even the message. Rebel groups emerge and claim that the organization no longer represents the original goal or mission of the movement.

5. *Demise.* This is the end of the social movement. The organizations created by the movement may survive but many of the goals of the original movement may have been accomplished.

As a collective activity, social movements have a number of characteristics. In the first place, members of the movement share a sense of unity and subscribe to a common goal. They are inspired by an ideology that justifies their actions. Members of the movement follow certain codes of conduct and patterns of behaviour. They may have their own insignia, badges, colours, slogans, and even dress codes. Movements use a variety of approaches to recruit people. Enlisting the support of influential people, getting the attention of the mass media and mobilizing political support are three key processes involved in the development of social movements. Women's movements, labour unions, and farmers' organizations such as Infarm (Indian Farmers' Movement) seek to win political support through grass roots movements. Many student movements may be actually initiated by political organizations.

Another important strategy of modern social movements is to network with existing agencies and organizations. For instance, much of the movement against globalization is articulated through a number of long established formal organizations. Similarly, the environmental movement is not one specific collective action but a series of collective actions sponsored by numerous national and international organizations.

Yet another characteristic of contemporary social movements is that the bureaucratic form of the institutionalized movement survives as a formal organization. Many caste-based social movements which began to bring about changes within the social system continue to function as formal organizations with only occasional issue-based collective action. In short, most social movements have a definite life cycle pattern: there is an injustice component, that is, people feel that some kind of undesirable situation exists. There is a sense of frustration about it. Leaders emerge and initiate concerted action. An organization is formed to mobilize resources. Very often, the organization survives, even if the original goals have been realized, and continue to sponsor collective actions on a variety of related issues. However, it must be noted that many contemporary social movements in India are small and localized. They are often non-bureaucratic and highly participatory. Student movements, tribal movements, and farmers' movements are examples. At the same time, some of the small localized movements are linked together in global networks. Some of the environmental movements and movements against child labour have global connections. Finally, many of the modern social movements are ideologically inclusive and work in unison. Many global movements for environmental protection, social justice, human rights, peace, nuclear freeze, and elimination of poverty involve a number of global players.

SOCIAL MOVEMENTS IN INDIA

India has experienced many social movements throughout its long history. The Bhakti movement, often compared to Reformation in Europe, effected broad transformation of the social and religious fabric and in the cultural ethos of Indian society. Even before the freedom struggle, there were movements against sati, against untouchability, for protection of the environment, for women's rights, and for other specific social reforms. Today there is a new awakening in India against political corruption. Ghanshyam Shah (2004: 18) made a nine-fold classification of social movements: peasant movements; tribal movements; Dalit movements; backward caste movements; women's movements; working class movements; students' movements; middle class movements; human rights and environmental movements. However, in this section we will focus on three broad categories of social movements: caste-oriented movements; women's movement; and environmental movements.

Environmental Movements

The Chipko Movement

The Chipko movement of early 1970s is actually a collective of several grass roots movements against commercial forestry. It did not begin as a conservation movement but as a spontaneous protest by peasants against the methodical destruction of the region's forest. What followed was devastating floods which washed away bridges, roads, and houses, and inundated farm lands. People could see first hand the relationship between deforestation and landslides and floods.

A local activist named Chandi Prasad Bhatt persuaded villagers to 'hug the trees' to stop the felling of trees, thus forcing the contractors to retreat. Later, in 1974, when the state marked forest trees for felling in Joshimath, hundreds of women turned up to hug the trees and drove out labourers and contractors. The significance of Chipko lay in the fact that it was a spontaneous movement by the poor and deprived villagers who realized how commercial forestry was destroying their means of livelihood. The Chipko grew into major environmental movement and the idea of hugging trees to protect them became a powerful concept that resonated with the global concern for conservation.

The Narmada Bachao Andolan

The Narmada Bachao Andolan (NBA) was another grass roots-level movement against the environmental, social, and cultural damages which would result from Narmada Valley Development Project. The project envisaged the construction of thirty large dams and over 3,000 medium and small dams on the river Narmada. The dams would submerge hundreds of villages and displace over 250,000 people. The NBA argued that the benefits were exaggerated and the damage underestimated. The movement highlighted gross violation of the riparian rights of tribals and peasants, environmental degradation, and the failure of the government to provide for adequate rehabilitation. Like Chipko, this was also a movement of the ordinary people in the rural areas to have the right to control their own forest, land, water, and other natural resources, and to preserve the environment that supported their livelihood.

Women's Movements

Women's movements in the pre-independent India focused largely on issues of justice and equality, particularly women's suffrage. But from mid-1970s, women's groups initiated numerous nationwide campaigns with specific focus on legislation to address many issues of concern to women. Some of the prominent issues were sati, dowry deaths, sex discrimination tests, domestic violence, sexual harassment, and child prostitution. Some of these campaigns led to public awareness first, and later espousal of women's concerns by major political parties.

According to Shah, women's movements in India can be divided into three waves. The first wave comprised social reform movements that began in the nineteenth century and the mass mobilization of women for freedom struggle. The second wave, beginning the late 1960s, involved issue-oriented political movements. Women joined hands with peasants, environmentalists, and industrial workers against price rise, deforestation, and poverty. This period also saw the emergence of women's social organizations such as the Self-Employed Women's Association (SEWA) in Gujarat and Working Women's Forum in Tamil Nadu.

The third wave which began in the mid-1970s had a definite feminist agenda which was inspired by the national report on the status of women which highlighted the deplorable gender inequality in India: adverse sex ratio; gender gap in education; high rates of infant and maternal mortality; and increasing deprivation of women. The third wave, therefore, saw the emergence of numerous autonomous women's groups, goal-oriented, but not necessarily linked to political parties. This period also was marked by the founding of several women's groups such as All India Democractic Women's Association, All India Women's Conference, and National Federation of Indian Women.

In a recent book titled *Indigenous Roots of Feminism*, Jasbir Jain (2011) argues that feminism must be understood in the social and cultural contexts. Throughout Indian history, especially during Bhakti movement, women have asserted themselves and challenged the patriarchy. In stories and legends, women like Shakuntala and Kannagi, though brought up in strict patriarchal exclusion, fought for their moral rights and put the kings to shame. Yet she claims that women have not been visible in our history and their role has been ignored in the Dalit movement aimed at fighting social justice.

Caste-oriented Movements

There are at least three strains of caste-oriented movements: Dalit movement; OBC movement; and Adivasi movement. Unlike the earlier social movements which were propelled by class domination, the NSMs focused on human rights and social justice. The centrality of class domination was replaced by other forms of domination based on caste, ethnicity, gender, and community. However, Shah argues that any conflict with an economic context has a class dimension. But what is more distinctive about the contemporary movements is their 'autonomous' nature and lack of exclusive affiliation with any particular political party.

Although Ambedkar emerged as the chief spokesman of anti-caste movement in the 1930s, the Dalit movement itself started in the mid-nineteenth century inspired by Jyotirao Phule's fight against the evils of caste system. The emergence of Dalit Panthers in 1972 marked the first organized fight against the atrocities of upper castes against the 'ati-shudras'. Although a militant group, it lacked any real political strategy and soon broke up because of internal factionalism. The 1980s saw some sort of alliance between Dalit and OBC groups, especially in the context of the formation of Bahujan Samaj Party. Now the Dalit movement has more or less consolidated itself into organized pressure goups rather than nebulous social movements.

The OBC Movement

To begin with, OBC is not a homogeneous category and there are no universally accepted criteria to classify them. Therefore, a commission was set up to identify OBCs which were eventually included in the Indian Constitution for preferential treatment. M.S.A. Rao classified backward caste movements into four types: the non-Brahmin movements in Maharashtra and Tamil Nadu; movements led by low and intermediate castes in Bihar, Punjab, Gujarat, and Maharashtra; movements by the depressed classes or 'untouchables' against upper and other backward castes (OBCs); and the tribal movements. The Mandal Report and the reservation of 27 per cent seats led to widespread protest as well as politicization of castes in India. However, once again, during the last two decades, OBCs have crystallized themselves as political pressure groups.

The Tribal Movement

The Adivasi movement is not one homogeneous national movement but a series of uprisings by different tribal groups in different parts of the country. The aim of the movement also varied from cessation to integration into mainstream of society, from preservation of tribal culture to improvement of socio-economic conditions. Broadly speaking, we may identify tribal movements in terms of the following: 1. forest-based movements against deforestation and for land rights; 2. movements due to economic deprivation—abject poverty and lack of health services have triggered several uprisings; 3. movement against exploitation by outsiders such as moneylenders, labour contractors, miners, and landlords who have alienated tribal lands; 4. movements by tribes for suitable rehabilitation after they were displaced by huge dams and mining projects; and 5. separatist movements like those of Nagas and Mizos who want their own sovereign states.

STUDY QUESTIONS

- Define collective behaviour.
- Summarize the following theories of collective behaviour: contagion theory; emergent norm theory; convergence theory; and value-added theory.
- Critically examine different forms of collective behaviour.
- Define social movement and explain different types of movements.
- Summarize the following theories of social movements: relative deprivation theory; resource mobilization theory; and political opportunity/process theory.
- Critically examine the perspectives on NSMs with reference to old and new social movements.
- Explain the life cycle of social movements.
- What are some of the major social movements in India? Write an essay on any two contemporary social movements.

REFERENCES

Blumer, Herbert George, 'Collective Behavior', in Robert E. Park (ed.), *Principles of Sociology*, New York: Baraes and Noble, pp. 219–88, 1939.

Boggs, C., *Social Movements and Political Power: Emerging Forms of Radicalism in the West*, Philadelphia: Temple University Press, 1986.

Canetti, Elias, *Crowds and Power*, New York: Seabury Press, 1978.

Davies, James C., 'Toward a Theory of Revolution', *American Sociological Review*, 27 (February), pp. 5–19, 1992.

Evers, T., '"Basisdemokratic" in Search of its Subject: New Social Movements and Political Culture in West Germany', *Praxis International*, 4:2, 1984.

Falk, R., 'The Global Promise of Social Movements: Explorations at the Edge of Time', *Alternatives*, XII, 1987.

Foss, D.A. and R. Larkin, *Beyond Revolution: A New Theory of Social Movements*, Mass.: Bergin and Garvey Publishers, 1986.

Jain, Jasbir, *Indigenous Roots of Feminism*, New Delhi: Sage Publications, 2011.

Le Bon, Gustave, *The Crowd*, London: Ernest Benn, 1952. Originally published 1896.

Meyer, David S., Nancy Whittier, and Belinda Robnett (eds), *Social Movements: Identity, Culture, and the State*, New York: Oxford University Press, 2002.

Mauss, Armand L., *Social Problems of Social Movements*, Philadelphia: Lippincott, 1975.

Mouffe, C., 'Towards a Theoretical Interpretation of "New Social Movements"', in S. Hanninen and L. Paldan (eds), *Rethinking Marx*, Berlin: Argument Sonderband, 1984.

Offe, C., 'New Social Movements: Challenging the Boundaries of Institutional Politics', *Social Research*, 52, 1985.

Park, Robert Ezra and Ernest W. Burgess, *Human Ecology*, Chicago: University of Chicago Press, 1921.

Shah, Ghanshyam, *Social Movements in India: A Review of Literature*, New Delhi: Sage Publications, p. 18, 2004.

Singh, Rajendra, *Social Movements, Old and New*, New Delhi: Sage Publications, 2001.

Slater, David, 'New Social Movements and Old Political Questions', *International Journal of Political Economy*, 1991.

Smelser, Neil, *Theory of Collective Behaviour*, Glencoe, Illinois: Free Press, 1963.

Tischler, Henry L., *Introduction to Sociology*, New York: The Harcourt Press, 2002.

Turner, Ralph H. and Lewis M. Killian, *Collective Behaviour*, Englewood Cliffs: Prentice-Hall, 1972.

17

Social Change, Environment, and Sustainable Development

Social change refers to modifications of social structures and processes over time. In India, the old caste system based on the theory of pollution and purity has undergone a thorough transformation. The rule of law has largely replaced the caste panchayats which enforced caste-based customs and regulations. The traditional joint family system supported by ancestral property has undergone radical changes. The process of democracy has significantly altered the power structures and led to the empowerment of new power elites drawn from the backward classes. The emergence of the 'information society' and globalization has created a vast new middle class with an appetite for latest consumer goods. Demographic transition, urbanization, modernization, Westernization, and numerous technological changes have significantly altered the nature and functions of most Indian social institutions.

According to *Dictionary of Sociology and Related Sciences* (Fairchild 1968: 277), social change refers to 'Variations or modifications in any aspect of social process, pattern or form. ... Social change may be progressive or regressive, permanent or temporary, planned or unplanned, unidirectional or multidirectional, beneficial or harmful.' Social change may be swift and radical as in the case of the French or Russian revolutions, or it may be slow and gradual as in the case of secularization and modernization. All societies evolve over a period of time, and social change is part of the process of growth. As Robert Lauer (1991: 4) points out 'social change is normal and continual. The important questions to ask relate to the direction and rate of change at various levels of social life.' According to him, social change is

an inclusive concept that refers to alterations in social phenomena at various levels of human life from the individual to the global.... Change may be studied at one or more levels, using various units of analysis. Obviously, attitude change in this scheme is as legitimate and important as institutional change. The important point to keep in mind, however, is that changes that are significant at one level are not necessarily significant at other levels. Attitude change may or may not lead to, or reflect, changes in interpersonal relationships, organizations, or institutions. Or there may be a time lag involved, with changes at one level occurring more slowly than changes at another.

Theories of Social Change

Comte conceived sociology in a time of great social upheaval following the French Revolution. Most of the early sociologists, anthropologists, and historians were intrigued by the process of social evolution, and they developed numerous theories to account for the phenomenon of social change. Let us look at some of the main theories.

Evolutionary Theory

Based on the assumption that human culture has undergone progressive and cumulative growth, early anthropologists and sociologists sought to delineate stages such as savagery, barbarism, and civilization, through which all societies passed. Some of them saw evolution as a unilinear process and described almost identical stages through which all human societies progressed. Others simply identified broad types of social organizations which evolved over periods of time. In Chapter 2 we have discussed various types of evolutionary theories. Here we will summarize some major perspectives.

Comte's unilinear evolutionary theory assumed that every society passed through the same fixed stages of development. Spencer believed that all societies followed uniform, natural laws of evolution, passing from simple to various levels of compound societies. Lenski delineated types of societies from hunting and gathering to modern post-industrial society. As early European explorers came into contact with other cultures at various levels of development, they thought of themselves to be superior and civilized and considered the rest of the world to be uncivilized or even barbarian. With the expansion of colonies, many European powers assumed that it was their divine mission to civilize the rest of the world.

In sharp contrast to evolutionary theories, cyclical theories proposed that civilizations rise and fall in an endless series of cycles. Oswald Spengler (1926), for instance, believed that Western civilization would die out just the way other great ancient civilizations such as the Egyptian, Chinese, and Sumerian perished. Like any organism, every culture also passes through a life-cycle of birth, youth, maturity, old age, and death. 'The great cultures accomplish their majestic wave cycles. They appear suddenly, swell in splendid lines, flatten again, and vanish, and the face of the waters is once more a sleeping waste.'

Arnold Toynbee also proposed a cyclical theory of human history. Like Spengler, Toynbee believed that all civilizations rise and fall but that these processes are not necessarily the result of inevitable life cycle changes. Rather, the rise and fall of civilizations depends on the challenges each society faces and the way it responds to those challenges. These challenges may come from the natural environment or human actions. Arid and barren land, extreme climatic conditions, and wars pose serious challenges. Great civilizations rise when societies are able to meet the challenges; they decline and fall when the response is weak or inadequate. Some challenges inspire collective responses and stimulate growth.

Having rejected the unilinear view of socio-cultural phenomena which claims that history never repeats itself and that no two cultural objects are ever the same, Sorokin argued that the socio-cultural phenomena are always recurrent and that the process of social change is essentially cyclical. He believed that every socio-cultural complex was characterized by a central mood or idea which is the predominant view of truth in any specific culture. The three major 'cultural mentalities' which Sorokin identified were sensate, ideational, and idealistic. According to Sorokin, history suggests that the pattern or cycle of rise and fall of each is in this specific order—the sensate followed by the counterpoising ideational, followed by the synthesis of the idealistic. And these categories form the foundation for his theory of social change. Sorokin also proposed the principle of immanent change which postulates that the cause of a change of any socio-cultural system is in the system itself. Sorokin (1937: 645) writes:

Bearing the seeds of its change in itself, any socio-cultural system bears also in itself the power moulding its own destiny or life career. Beginning with the moment of emergence, each socio-cultural system is the main factor of its own destiny. This destiny, or the system's subsequent life career, represents mainly an unfolding of the immanent potentialities of the system in the course of its existence.

Functional Theory

Functionalists see society as a system in equilibrium. Since all parts of society are interrelated and interdependent, a change in any part of society produces compensatory changes in the other parts of society. Similarly, if some forces disrupt the equilibrium of society, there will be counter forces which seek to restore equilibrium. For example, as both parents start to work and nuclear families are unable to care for little children, day-care centres and kindergarten schools have sprung up all over the place. When terrorism and other forms of violence began to disrupt normal life, governments have responded with numerous, sometimes draconian, measures such as MISA (Maintenance of Internal Security Act), POTA (Prevention of Terrorism Act), TADA [Terrorist and Disruptive Activities (Prevention) Act], and similar legislative acts.

Like evolutionary theorists, Talcott Parsons believed that societies evolve from simple to various levels of compound societies. He emphasized three key concepts in the process of evolutionary changes: structural differentiation, functional specialization, and social integration. As communities grow larger and larger, societal units get divided and subdivided. Ancestral families were both units of production and consumption as members of extended families lived and worked together. Now there are several agencies which perform the functions of the old extended family. With the emergence of bureaucracy, organizations have developed numerous agencies and units to deal with various functions. Structural differentiation has also led to the specialization of functions. Just as different departments and agencies specialize in different functions, individuals also tend to specialize in specific occupations. Whereas in the traditional little communities, farmers, traders, artisans, and medicine men served almost all functions, in today's complex societies individuals perform literally millions of specialized roles. Now, differentiation and specialization pose problems of integration. As societal units multiply and specialized occupations tend to grow, it becomes necessary to coordinate all aspects of society. Social integration requires effective coordination of domestic, educational, economic, and political institutions in society.

Conflict Theory

Marx is undoubtedly the master theoretician of social conflict and change. He believed that every social system contained the seeds of its own destruction, that is, until the establishment of the utopian society based on socialism. As long as there were classes based on the economic system of production and distribution, conflicts were inevitable. Conflicts are usually violent and result in the overthrow of the existing system. Although many of his predictions did not come true, he was right on target about conflicts between the rich and the poor, forms of exploitation, corporate greed, and the squeeze of technology on the workers. In Chapter 2, we have discussed the conflict theory in detail. Suffice here to say that Marx's theory of class struggle was the most influential conflict perspective in the twentieth century. Marxist ideology inspired revolutionary social movements around the world. Revolutions in Russia and China resulted in total transformation of political, economic, and social systems. It was not simply a matter of social change but one of total system substitution. After World War II, the entire eastern Europe came under Soviet-dominated communist system. For a while the revolutionary ideology of communism swept across much of Asia, Africa, and Latin America. Cuba, Nicaragua, Vietnam, Ethiopia, and North Korea became showcases of communism. Gradually though, hardcore Marxism gave way to socialism. China and Vietnam embraced capitalism within the framework of totalitarian socialism. Yet the ideology of communism with its emphasis on class conflict and elimination of exploitation has considerable appeal in the Third World as is evident from the experience of several countries in South America, especially Venezuela and Bolivia. Neo-Marxists argue that where there is a rich–poor divide and exploitation of the working class, Marxism is relevant. Dahrendorf, in a similar vein, attributed conflict to differential distribution of power. According to him, social change and conflict are ubiquitous but they need not necessarily be manifest or violent.

SOURCES OF SOCIAL CHANGE

There are internal and external sources of social change. The internal sources refer to factors which originate within a specific society and are responsible for significant changes within that society. External sources of change are the result of contacts with other cultures, diffusion of innovations, or spread of ideologies from other societies. The distinction is, of course, artificial since most changes are brought about by a combination of factors. Even the steam engine, automobile, electricity, transistor radio, socialism, and the concepts of liberty, fraternity, and equality originated somewhere but influenced the course of history everywhere. We may identify the sources of change under four main headings: physical environment, technology, cultural contacts and diffusion, and values and ideology.

Physical Environment

Over the millennia, changes in the natural environment have impacted on the social life of human beings. Loss of forests, desertification, soil erosion, environmental degradation, and climatic changes have significantly influenced the way human beings live in groups. Many of these changes have been gradual and slow. But natural disasters such as floods, tsunamis, earthquakes, and volcanic eruptions have had disastrous consequences. Many of the ancient civilizations may have been wiped out or forced to relocate because of dramatic changes in the environment. Today, air and water pollution, acid rain, the greenhouse effect, and dumping of chemical wastes have led to a worldwide environmental movement. Public awareness has forced national governments and international organizations to act in defence of our planet. In many ways it has changed both the individual and social way of life.

Technology

Rapid changes in technology during the past four or five decades have altered not only social life but also the face of the planet. The planet has been shrunken by the technology of instant communication. In 1947 a trip across the Atlantic took seventeen and a half hours; today it takes only three and a half. And, a message may be sent across that distance in an instant. Revolution in computer science and information technology has transformed social systems and human life in them far beyond what one could have imagined just two decades ago. Internet technology, especially YouTube, Twitter, and Facebook, has triggered as well as sustained political campaigns and social movements. As noted elsewhere, the pro-democratic movements in the Middle East and several environmental protests would not have thrived without the extensive use of internet. Mass media also play a significant role as an agent of social change. They spread ideas and innovations as well as publicize, and even popularize, public campaigns and social movements. The presence of several independent television channels means that millions of people can be informed, inspired, and mobilized almost instantaneously. For example, when Anna Hazarre started his fast against corruption, hundreds of thousands of people took to the streets in major cities across the country in support of his crusade. But developments in technology have introduced not only cellular phones, satellites, and electronic communication but also weapons of mass destruction and deadly pollutants. As Alvin Toffler (1980) said: 'Never before did any civilization create the means for literally destroying not a city but a planet. Never did whole oceans face toxification, whole species vanish overnight from the earth as a result of human greed or inadvertence.' But precisely because of such environmental problems, individuals, corporations and nations have brought about significant changes in the way they do business.

Cultural Contacts and Diffusion

Anthropologist Ralph Linton observed years ago that in any particular society only about 10 per cent of the innovations originate internally and the rest are transmitted through contacts with other cultures. The oldest communication model of social change known as the diffusion model explains that most of the innovations are transmitted through various stages of diffusion and adoption. With the miraculous achievements in transport and communication, and rocketry and satellite technology, the planet we share with over seven billion people has become a global village. In general, the more contacts a society has with other cultures, the greater the opportunity for cultural change. Young people learn types of music, dance, and fashions just as soon as they become popular. People adopt new innovations in technology, medicine, and agriculture which are proven to be useful. They resist innovations which are inconsistent with traditional beliefs and values. Sometimes it takes years for new ideas and techniques to be adopted.

Values and Ideology

As Ogburn pointed out, changes in technology are faster than changes in ideas and values. People are quick to adopt technologies which make life easier or more comfortable. However, values, beliefs, and ideas are steeped in traditions. Yet, the twentieth century has witnessed dramatic changes brought about by the most powerful ideas of three great intellectuals: Marx, Freud, and Darwin. The ideas of these three men have caused reverberations not only in education but also religion, politics, economy, literature, and art. The ideology of racism inspired the rise of Nazism. The Marxist ideology of communism led to revolutionary movements and peasant uprisings in many parts of the world. Darwinism triggered the conservative ideology of the survival of the fittest. Freud's psychoanalysis revolutionized the way people look at themselves and others. The concepts of social justice, human rights, and equality have brought about many legal reforms and social changes. They have also inspired many movements for social and economic reforms, environmental protection, and changes in lifestyle.

THE PROCESS OF SOCIAL CHANGE

Industrialization, urbanization, modernization, and Westernization are considered to be the master processes of social change.

Many social scientists have used industrialization as the prime mover of social change. Wilbert Moore (1965) even equates the logic of industrialism with the ethic of modernity. According to him, not only does industrialization appear to be 'a major and essential ingredient for substantial economic growth' but it also leads to the creation of 'a common culture'. Although the idea of a common culture has hence been given up, Moore identifies a number of minimum essential organizational conditions required by the commercial–industrial system. These conditions include resource utilization, commercial and financial organization, a network of transportation and communication, internal diversification, rational secular orientation, and impersonal markets. Since an industrial population requires agricultural surplus, continued industrialization will lead to further technificaion and rational organization of agriculture. Industrialization involves the gradual shift from subsistence production to commercialized production, establishment of monetary exchange, and the transfer of many workers away from food production into manufacturing and services. Industrialization causes extensive migration which disrupts the large kinship organization and leads to more nuclear family units. Industrialization also fosters education and science, bureaucratization of labour force and gross changes in the occupational structure.

Urbanization is another process that significantly alters traditional social systems. Eisenstadt (1973: 24) observed: 'In the sphere of social organization the most important single "external" manifestation of these changes has been the process of urbanization, the growing conglomeration of continuously growing parts of the population in urban centers in which the more specialized types of economic, professional, and civic activities and enterprises became concentrated and expanded continuously.' The city serves as a window on the world facilitating a cultural mix and the diffusion of innovations—technological, organizational, and ideological—in the social system. The city has greater potential and greater variety for modernization. As cities attract large numbers of rural migrants, they expose them to mass media, organize them for political action, motivate them to attain higher levels of education, and provide for better health and educational facilities. Greater occupational differentiation modifies the traditional stratification system and encourages social mobility. According to Miner (Gugler and Flanagan 1978: 110),

The city provides a social milieu in which economic success may be achieved with less regard for activities which are not primarily economic in nature. In the folk community, because of the close-knit functional organization of its culture, religious and family behaviour have definite economic implications. In fact, it is exceedingly difficult, if not impossible, to say what is economic behaviour and what is familial.

But the market economy of the city requires specialized and individualized activity, rewards secular and impersonal behaviour, and transforms many traditional roles. Although there is no general agreement on the modernizing role of the city, there is no denying the fact that cities with their organizational innovations and institutional infrastructures stimulate and sustain industrialization and represent potentially the most favourable conditions for social mobilization. Moreover, most measures of economic growth are positively correlated with urbanization. Urban explosion, however, is not a sufficient condition for development; the modernizing role of cities without a sound economic base is limited. Often industrialization is the forerunner of urbanization; the former affects the rate of urban expansion, the nature of emerging cities, and the level of economic growth involved in urbanization. Industrialization involves a generous use of material energy, a change from labour-intensive to capital-intensive methods of production, a shift in the labour force out of primary and subsistence production into secondary and commercial enterprises, a series of organizational innovations such as retailing, independent advertising agencies, sales finance corporations, labour unions and professional agencies, expanding role of government, increasing leisure and more social services, welfare, and entertainment.

Although recent scholarship on modernization has produced an abundant crop of literature, scholars are not unanimous on their approach to, or definition of, the concept of modernization. Economists interpret modernization in terms of growth models comprising indices such as economic indicators, standard of living, per capita income, and the like. Political scientists analyse modernization in terms of political participation, social upheavals, and institutional alterations. Sociologists have defined modernization variously but within the framework of an evolutionary perspective which involves a multilinear transition of developing societies from tradition to modernity. According to Rogers (1969: 14), 'modernization is the process by which individuals change from a traditional way of life to a more complex, technologically advanced, and rapidly changing style of life.' Many social scientists use advanced, industrialized societies of the West as a standard of reference to which developing societies are compared in an attempt to delineate the processes of change that tend to transform traditional institutions and values in a way that they approximate the model of modernity. For instance, according to Eisenstadt (1966: 1),

Historically, modernization is the process of change towards those types of social, economic, and political systems that have developed in Western Europe and North America from the seventeenth century to the nineteenth and have then spread to other European countries and in the nineteenth and twentieth centuries to the South American, Asian and African continents. It is essentially an evolutionary perspective which explains stages in transition through which societies pass, although all societies do not necessarily go through the same stages or in a given sequence.

Modernization is a many-layered developmental process which involves economic, social, and psychological dimensions. Economic development is evidenced by higher levels of consumption and standard of living, greater capital intensity, monetary system of exchange, rational bureaucratic organization, upgrading of required skill levels through technocracy and rational cost accounting. It also involves mechanization and automation resulting in labour displacement, greater occupational specialization, means of rapid transportation and communication facilitating market participation and labour mobility. Economic modernization also means a large proportional shift into secondary production and corresponding increases in tertiary production. Such a shift is made possible by movement from traditional and subsistence farming towards mechanization and commercialization of various segments of the economy and effective role in a rational world market. It must, however, be remembered that economic growth is not necessarily synonymous with social development or modernization. The state of Kerala has achieved high levels of social development without significant economic development. The reverse is the case of Punjab which has achieved economic growth without corresponding changes in the social sphere.

The principal elements of social modernization include planned social change, secularism, heavy public expenditure on education, knowledge revolution through expanding means of communication, and shift towards instrumental social relationships and contractual obligations. As people move away from well-knit rural communities to urban centres, traditional obligations give way to formal contractual relationships. Families tend to become smaller, nuclear, and egalitarian. Greater social and political participation leads to empowerment. Political modernization consists in the development of bureaucratic infrastructure, greater political participation by the masses, greater mass media exposure, revolution of rising expectations, relative demographic stability, and greater awareness of the concepts of social justice and human rights.

Psychological approaches to modernization emphasize attitudinal and behavioural changes that initiate as well as sustain socio-economic development. The attitudinal facet implies transformation of traditional attitudes based on customs and religious belief systems into some form of secular rationality based on science and organized scepticism. Other elements include greater achievement motivation, entrepreneurial spirit, higher educational aspirations, emergence of equalitarian attitudes, openness to new experiences, revolt against paternalism and authoritarianism, positive attitude towards life and nature, and above all, a rational world view.

With the dawn of information technology, industrial societies have entered a new phase, the post-industrial society based on services rather than manufacturing. According to Daniel Bell (1976), industrial societies 'are goods-producing societies. Life is game against fabricated nature.... A post-industrial society is based on services. Life becomes a game between persons. What counts is not raw muscle power, or energy; what counts is information.' It is estimated that in another two decades the majority of the world labour force will be working in jobs related to information: management, design, computer, mass media, and high technology. In a similar vein, Alvin Toffler identifies three waves or eras. The First Wave was launched by the agricultural revolution around 8000 BC and ended around 1750. The Second Wave, set off by the Industrial Revolution, shaped the world until about 1955. Then the electronic revolution or miraculous achievements in technology ushered in a new civilization based on jets, computers, space exploration, electronic mass media, genetic engineering, and other advances in high technology. While the industrial era centred around the machine and the manufacturing of goods, the Third Wave revolves around production of information and services. Advances in high technology will continue to generate information and services in education, health, mass media, finances, management, and even social movements.

In summary, we may say that modern societies are more industrialized and urbanized, more literate and open, more secular and rational, and more cosmopolitan than local. However, it must be pointed out that the distinction between traditional and modern societies is for analytical purposes only and that the difference between the two types of systems is one of degree and that many elements of tradition and modernity are to be found in all societies.

Finally, there is the question of convergence. Do the processes of modernization and globalization lead to the establishment of a new world order, a common culture? The convergence theorists believed that modernization will break down cultural barriers and that most of the Third World will acquire the social and cultural characteristics of the West. The reality is, however, different. In the first place, people in the Third World refuse to equate modernization with Westernization. Second, countries in the developing world have chosen different paths to modernization. India, China, Iran, Brazil, Thailand, Saudi Arabia, and Malaysia are all for modernization, but they all tend to follow different political ideologies, economic systems, and cultural ethos. Third, nationalism has become the new 'secular religion' of emerging nations in search of a cultural identity. It fosters a new cultural identity based on traditional culture and local values. Indeed, in many developing countries, there is a widespread movement to reassert traditional values, to reinforce old cultural patterns, and to strengthen ethnic traditions.

Social Change in India

M.N. Srinivas has identified Sanskritization, Westernization, and secularization as the three major comprehensive processes that alter and articulate the social and cultural patterns in Indian society. Sanskritization refers to the process by which the low castes are able to rise to a higher position in the social hierarchy by adopting the symbols of higher status, thus taking over, as far as possible, the customs, rites, beliefs, and ways of life of the higher castes. However, 'mobility associated with Sanskritization results only in positional changes in the system and does not lead to any structural change' (1966: 167). Sanskritization may be a historical process of cultural change but its relevance to contemporary society is limited. In the age of mass political participation and caste-based power politics, numerical superiority is far more important than ritual superiority.

Westernization refers to the complex, many-layered process of diffusion of Western ideas, legal and philosophical systems, Western ways of life and culture in Indian society. The twice-born castes were the first to sense the trend of change and take advantage of the new opportunities. Western education and the development of modern transport and communication accelerated the process. One only needs to look at cable television channels to have a sense of the impact of Westernization on music, fashion, dance, art, and even attitudes. Eating is no longer a ritual act, vegetarianism is not necessarily a virtue, the tuft gave way to cropped hair, traditional dress is being replaced by Western fashions, and the electronic media and cell phones have even changed the way people greet one another. Western ideas have eroded the concept of pollution and purity and lifted the ritual ban on many vocations. The rule of law has replaced caste-based rules in traditional society. Modern education fosters the concepts of equality, social justice, and human dignity. Although caste, ethnicity, and class distinctions survive, there is a greater awareness of the worth and dignity of the individual.

Secularization is another concept which is useful in the analysis of social change in India. In the past, Srinivas indicates, the strength of a belief lay in its sacerdotal importance displayed by ritualistic ceremonies. The only standard of reference was tradition and the only authority was the Sanskritic literature in terms of which a belief or practice would be evaluated and validated. But the introduction of Western education, the British legal system, and various ideological movements either changed or abolished many customs once thought to be part of religion. Traditional ideals of ritual cleanliness and pollution and purity are giving way to the rules of reasoned or rational hygiene. Rituals are not only omitted or abolished but are also telescoped with others. All this 'meant that religious customs had to satisfy the test of reason and humanity if they were to be allowed to survive. As British rule progressed, rationality and humanitarianism became broader, deeper, and more powerful, and the years since the achievement of independence have seen a remarkable increase—a genuine leap forward—in the extension of both' (Srinivas 1966). The growth of towns and cities, increased spatial mobility, the struggle for political freedom, declaration of India as a secular state, constitutional recognition of the equality of all citizens before law, and the introduction of universal adult suffrage gave added impetus to the process of secularization. Above all, secularization is a process of rationalization based on science which provides the only validation for most human actions in modern society.

Yogendra Singh (2002: 19–20) sought to examine whether or not cultural globalization posed a threat to cultural identity at the local, regional, and national levels and has come to the conclusion that Indian culture is resilient and capable of adapting to a wide variety of changes. 'The overarching premise in our analysis of culture change is that despite manifestations of many new dimensions of culture change witnessed in the process of globalization, the response to change, ushered in by globalization remains within the discourse of modernity.' According to Singh, electronic mass media have revolutionized economic growth, trade and banking practices, and exchange of information in health, management and the professions. As growth-oriented businesses continue to establish global linkages, they also empower local communities. In the words of Singh:

A significant consequence of politicization in India is the acute self-consciousness and celebration of identity by castes, ethnic groups and minorities, etc. This change has broken down the traditional bonds of reciprocity and linkages of culture and economy among different castes and ethnic groups…. The breakdown in the traditional pattern of the inter-caste and inter-ethnic economic and cultural reciprocities has also been engendered by industrialization, expansion of education, the policy of positive discrimination in education, job opportunities and political offices, etc., in favor of the weaker sections based on caste and ethnicity. Consequently, a rapid change has taken place in the traditional occupational structure of castes and tribes … and brought about new problems of social and cultural alienation of communities both in the rural and urban society.

With progressive liberalization, the services sector and the information technology industry became the drivers of the economy. India now accounts for 65 per cent of the global business in offshore information technology and 46 per cent of the global business process outsourcing (BPO) industry. Today, these two industries employ about 700,000 people and provide indirect employment to about 2.5 million workers. The services sector dominates the Indian economy today, contributing more than half of our national income. Mahapatra (Chandhoke and Priyadarshi 2009: 134–5) continues:

The software industry has produced a new transnational capitalist class. With increasing mobility, Indian information technology companies service global MNCs based all across the globe, 100,000 Indian professionals leave India every year to take jobs in the USA and 25 percent of Silicon Valley companies are founded or managed by Indians. The new middle class is constructed as a potential promise of the benefits of globalization and the benefits are associated with the particular practices of commodity consumption. Liberalization has created a sharp divide within the middle class, as segments of this group constitute the new rich in Metropolitan India. The prosperous, urban, middle-class consumer is basically the young, urban professional working in MNCs and drawing handsome salaries. This new middle class working in MNCs is also a globalized middle class with consumption patterns typical of their counterparts and colleagues in the developed countries. Consumption so defines us that our transnational identity as a consumer often takes precedence over our identity as a citizen, which is territorially defined. We are as much consumers of coke and cricket as we are Indians.

In recent years, several sociologists have studied the impact of liberalization and globalization on local communities in India. There is hardly any consensus on the consequences of privatization and globalization. On the one hand, the demand for skilled labour force by multinational corporations has led to an explosion in education and new career opportunities as well as an expansion of middle class and consumer choices. According to some sociologists (Lal and Ahmad 2001: 11),

New industries that emerge around the 'global centers of growth' tend to be unfair to the work forces who are low paid, unorganized and lack proper awareness to assert themselves for their due. Such people find accommodation in the degenerated periphery. Such places are unable to find requisite funds to meet the essential primary needs of the workers. State indifference in this regard is likely to slow down the immigration of the poor and is also likely to usher physical fragmentation of urban growth.

ENVIRONMENT

The interaction between environment and society is an area of major concern to modern sociology. The quality of our social life depends on the quality of the natural environment, and human actions have a direct impact on the ecosystem. According to Milbrath (1989: 607), human actions have brought about more changes to the planet during the last two centuries than changes to our planet from all causes over the course of the last billion years. It is estimated that the global economy has expanded more in the last seven years than in the 10,000 years since agriculture began.

The technology that enabled the unprecedented economic growth of the 20th century has had a dramatic effect on our natural resources. Global consumption of wood has doubled, paper use has increased six times, and the use of fossil fuels is up nearly five-fold. Grain consumption has tripled, and fish consumption has increased five-fold. The resulting environmental stress includes shrinking forests and wetlands, eroding soil and coral reefs, pollution of international waters, collapsing fisheries, vanishing plant and animal species, and rising temperatures. Half the world's population lives on coastlines, rivers and estuaries, including rural people who rely on waterways for their livelihoods—fishing, transportation, communication, and irrigation for farmlands. Based on U.N. population predictions, by 2050 one in five people is likely to live in a country with severe shortages of fresh water serious enough to threaten health and economic well-being.

Unlike other creatures, humans make deliberate choices that alter the face of the planet; therefore, they have the primary responsibility for maintaining a healthy and diverse ecosystem. More than at any other time in history, people now realize that the civilization they have built may not survive. The Limits to Growth perspective which emerged in the 1970s points out that unlimited growth is neither desirable nor sustainable. Petroleum, natural gas, clean air, fresh water, and the earth's top soil are all finite resources that will exhaust if we continue to pursue growth at any cost. The Limits to Growth perspective argues that humanity must implement effective policies to control the growth of population, material production, and the use of resources in order to avoid environmental degradation.

Today there is a general consensus that the world cannot be at peace unless all living things truly experience the ecosystem in equilibrium. As crucial relationships between world's species and their environment are altered and even destroyed, the integrity of the planet's life-support system is threatened. An area nearly the size of western Europe has lost most of its productivity from man's abusive use. Another 2.25 billion acres, an area larger than Australia, has degraded, requiring care and restoration. Worldwatch Institute calculates that top soil loss means an annual decrease in grain production of 9 million tonnes. As we deplete precious natural resources and degrade the environment we also destroy its ability to rejuvenate itself. For example, scientists predict that the North Sea will be dead within the next few years. For thousands of years, it was able to absorb the filth of Europe's cities, but it also had the capacity to cleanse itself. Now the assault has become overpowering as European nations dump around 700,000 tonnes of mercury, nitrogen, phosphorus, cadmium, lead, and zinc into this sea every year. Today we share this planet with numerous instruments of total destruction: over 30,000 nuclear weapons and untold quantities of deadly biological and chemical materials. Heavy use of fertilizers, pesticides, and herbicides contaminates rivers and ground water. Ozone depletion, destruction of rainforests, and pollution of waterways have disastrous transnational consequences.

There is also injustice in the way the industrialized world's progress has been paid by developing countries. Every year the industrialized West produces millions of tonnes of industrial and toxic waste and often uses the Third World as a convenient dumping ground. The United States alone produces about 160 million tonnes of solid waste per year. Poor countries such as Haiti, Cameroon, and many others have been 'persuaded' to accept, for a fee, toxic garbage from rich industrialized countries. As much as 70 per cent carbon dioxide emissions, which cause global warming, is from Europe and America. The sea level rise due to global warming could destroy countries like Bangladesh, Thailand, and even Egypt. Abdul Gayoom of the Maldives said in the United Nations: 'Global warming means the death of our country of 1,190 small islands. We did not contribute to this impending catastrophe to our nation and alone we cannot save ourselves.' Japan is the largest importer of timber in the world primarily for paper production and disposable chopsticks. The forests of the Philippines, Thailand, Canada, and Malaysia are being destroyed to fulfill Japan's needs. Almost one billion trees are cut down every year to provide disposable diapers for babies. Although they cover only about 7 per cent of the earth's surface, tropical rain forests are home to almost 70 per cent of all plant and animal species most of which have not yet been identified. The global ecological crisis is leading scientists to a new understanding of the relationship of man with nature, and the need to take a holistic approach to problems.

There is also a development dilemma. The countries that have reduced birth rates have become richer and so more consumptive. Take the case of China. With the one-child policy in place, China has become the world's second largest economy and incidentally the biggest emitter of greenhouse gas pollution. But developing countries argue that their emission is the essential by-product of development, whereas in the industrialized countries, pollution is largely the result of limitless growth, over-consumption, greed, needless accumulation, and waste. As Amartya Sen points out, one additional American typically has a larger negative impact on ozone layer, global warmth, and other elements of the earth's environment than dozens of Indians and Zimbabweans put together. The argument goes that the industrialized nations reached their current level of development through uncontrolled growth, unrestrained environmental degradation, and massive pollution. The developing countries claim that they are trying to reach comparable level of development but undue restrictions hold them back. But there is no room for oscillation or argument. The International Energy Agency (IEA) predicts irreversible climate change in five years. Anything built from now on that produces carbon will continue to do so for decades to come, and this 'lock-in' effect will be the single factor most likely to produce irreversible climate change. If the current trends continue, and we go on building high-carbon energy generation, then by 2015 at least 90 per cent of the available 'carbon budget' will be swallowed up by our energy and industrial infrastructure. By 2017, there will be no room for manoeuvre at all (*The Hindu*, 11 November 2011).

It is heartening to note that at the United Nations-sponsored world summit on climate change held in Durban in December 2011, a deal was finally struck with an agreement by more than 190 nations to work towards a future treaty that would require all countries to reduce emissions that contribute to global warming. The agreement marked a tentative but important step towards the dismantling of a twenty year old system that requires advanced industrialized nations to cut emissions while allowing developing countries, including the economic powerhouses like India, China, and Brazil, to escape binding commitments. The delegates also agreed on the creation of a fund to help poor countries adapt to climate change, and to measures involving the preservation of tropical forests and the development of clean energy technology.

Let us now look at some of the major environmental issues.

Global warming or the greenhouse effect is one of the major concerns of the world today. It has been well documented that chlorofluorocarbons or CFCs which are found in so many household products, when released into the air, accumulate in the upper atmosphere, and reacting with sunlight they form chlorine atoms. These atoms destroy the ozone layer which serves to limit the amount of harmful ultraviolet radiation from the sun reaching the earth. The depletion of the ozone layer is linked to global warming, increase in human skin cancers, disastrous effects on plants and animals, and the re-emergence of diseases such as cholera and viral fevers. Although there is some scepticism about the impact of global warming, there is mounting evidence that it is the planet's biggest environmental problem. There is also no doubt that the advanced industrialized nations are the biggest consumers of energy. Industrialized countries represent roughly 20 per cent of the humanity but utilize over 80 per cent of the world's energy. The poorest 20 per cent in the world consume 1.3 per cent of the world's goods and services and account for about 3 per cent of carbon dioxide emissions. A typical American adult consumes one hundred times more energy every year than the average member of the world's poorest societies. Yet, the United States has failed to ratify the 1997 Kyoto Protocol signed by 160 nations which identified ways industrialized and developing countries can reduce emission of gases responsible for the greenhouse effect. And the latest reports by experts warn that by 2010 aviation emissions alone will wipe out any progress made on emission-reduction through the Kyoto Protocol.

Water conservation is another major environmental issue. The simple truth is that without water life and growth cease. It is estimated that 1,000 tonnes of water are needed to produce a single tonne of harvested grain. Worldwide, agriculture uses about 65 per cent of all water removed from rivers, lakes, and aquifers for human activities, compared with 25 per cent for industries and 10 per cent for households and municipalities. According to current predictions, within the next thirty years, more than a billion people in north Africa and the Middle East will lack necessary water. The global consumption of water, estimated at about 5 billion cubic feet per year, has tripled since 1950 and is expanding faster than the world's population. Given the population growth, nearly three billion people or 40 per cent of the projected world population will live in water-stressed countries by 2015. Ground water mining can lead to a variety of irreversible effects. In coastal areas, overpumping can cause saltwater to invade freshwater aquifers, contaminating supplies. This has occurred in Gujarat where irrigators have heavily overpumped local aquifers. Groundwater depletion can also reduce the earth's natural capacity to store water. Another problem is that many of the major rivers of the world are completely tapped out during the drier part of the year that very little water is lost to the sea during the dry season. This is true of most rivers in India including the Ganga. Some cities dump untreated sewage and partially cremated bodies in the Ganga. Industrial waste, pesticides, and herbicides enter the waterways through dumping as well as run off from farms and homes. Such pollution sometimes causes massive fish kills, and many chemicals become more concentrated as they pass up through the food chain, with the humans receiving the highest doses. In short, there are two issues relative to water. The first is, of course, conservation. Rain water harvests and small check dams are significant measures to conserve water. The second issue relates to cleaning up of the waterways and measures needed to prevent further pollution of the sources of water. Water pollution results not only from intentional dumping but also from the run off of agricultural fertilizers, chemicals, and wastes. Ganga Action Plan, launched in 1985, to clean up the river and restore water quality is an example of a belated initiative on the part of the government.

Asia has less than one-tenth of the waters of South America, Australia, and New Zealand, and not even one-fourth of North America's. Yet the world's fastest growing demand for water for food and industrial production and for municipal supply is in Asia, which now serves as the locomotive of the world economy. Today the fastest growing Asian economies are all at or near water-stressed conditions. Asia is not only the global irrigation hub but also the most dam-dotted continent. China alone has almost half of the world's estimated 50,000 largest dams. About 70 per cent of the world's 301 million hectares of land equipped for irrigation is in Asia alone. Once a continent of serious food shortages and recurrent famines, Asia emerged as a net food exporter riding on the back of unparalleled irrigation expansion. Now according to a five-year study by Chinese researchers, glaciers in the Qinghai-Tibet Plateau, the source of many rivers that sustain China and the Indian subcontinent, are melting faster than ever. Data from three meterological stations over the past fifty years showed a continued rise in the average temperature in the region, with the last year touching a five-decade high. Consequently, 70 per cent of the glaciers in the headwaters of the Lancang River had disappeared, while another group of eighty glaciers near the source of the Yellow River was shrinking.

Deterioration of air quality is another environmental problem. The thick, black smoke belched from factory smokestacks and emissions from motor vehicles constitute the major source of air pollution. The rich countries have taken a number of steps to reduce air pollution. Scientists have devised new technologies to reduce noxious exhaust from factories and automobiles. The coal fires that choked London a half-century ago are now forbidden. However, in many less developed countries people still rely on wood, coal, peat, and other fuels for cooking and heating. In India it took a ruling from the apex court to force automobiles to reduce emissions in the wake of continuous deterioration of air quality in the nation's capital.

Preserving the rain forests is yet another environmental issue. South America, especially Brazil, west-central Africa and South-east Asia are home to regions of dense forestation. The world's rain forests cover an area of some 2 billion acres, roughly 7 per cent of the earth's total land surface. The demand for grazing land, hardwood, and crop land, as well as the construction of huge reservoirs has led to large-scale deforestation. Indeed, the world's rain forests are now just half their original size and continue to shrink by 65,000 square miles every year. At the current rate of destruction, the rain forests will disappear by the end of the next century. India has only 2 per cent of the forest and the continuous loss of tree cover and top soil has led to droughts and floods. Deforestation also impacts on biological diversity because of the shrinking habitat available to faunal and floral species. Logging, mining, grazing, agriculture, industrialization, and urbanization alter terrestrial and aquatic habitats in ways that make them less able to support life or valuable ecosystem services. Consider the case of large dams. There are nearly 40,000 large dams and countless smaller dams around the world. Needless to say, dams and reservoirs are not an unmitigated evil. They increase crop production by providing additional irrigation, check floods, and create opportunities for developing inland pisciculture. But they also mean huge displacement and submergence of vast tracts of land, often precious forest land. There has been no public debate in Laos of the government's decision to feed Thailand's energy appetite by building more than twenty-three dams by the year 2010. In India the Chipko movement raised the level of public consciousness about the dangers to which all forms of wildlife are exposed. And the demands made by the Narmada Bachao Andolan spotlight the development vs. environment debate.

Finally, the *loss of biodiversity* is a significant environmental problem which requires immediate attention. In his hunt for new articles of fancy, man began to kill bird and beast, not to improve the living standards but to satisfy his ego and fancy. Some bird species became almost extinct because they had beautiful plumages with which wealthy women wanted to adorn their hats. The rhino and tiger population suffered because some people believed that their bones and some body parts had aphrodisiac properties. Rain forests are home to almost half of this planet's living species. The disappearance of the rain forests would mean the extinction of thousands of species of plants and animals. Also, thousands of species of plants and animals are being lost each year to wars, pests, diseases, climate change, urbanization, the global marketing of exotic breeding material, and large-scale industrial-agriculture. Our planet's biodiversity provides vast and varied sources of food. Scientists are testing tens of thousands of plants for their medical properties, and many medical and pharmaceutical industries depend on animal and plant diversity in their search for new drugs. Just think of the world without the Bengal tiger, Chinese panda, Australian kangaroo, the African giraffe, or the magnificent elephants. About 12 per cent of animal species, including 41 per cent of all recognized fish species, live in the 1 per cent of the earth's surface that is fresh water. According to experts, at least one-fifth of all freshwater fish species have become extinct, threatened, or endangered in recent years, and entire freshwater faunas have disappeared. Among the major food security threats on the horizon are the loss of diversity of plant and animal species, the emergence of new diseases and food-borne illnesses. The experience of Asian chicken farmers who were forced to bury or incinerate millions of chickens because of the avian flu may foreshadow a larger epidemic on the horizon. Indeed Food and Agriculture Organization (FAO) issued a release at the end of 2011 warning of a 'mutant strain' of the virus that was spreading in Asia and beyond 'with unpredictable risks to human health'. Over ten thousand varieties of wheat used to be cultivated in China, and the Philippines had thousands of varieties of rice. Now there are only a few varieties left. In many countries, the increasing demand for meat, eggs, and milk has forced producers to abandon many local breeds in favour of an increasingly limited number of high-producing livestock. In India, the Navdanya movement is responding to the loss of biodiversity by protecting local varieties of wheat, rice, and other crops by cataloguing them and declaring them common property. Navdanya has also set up locally owned seed banks, farm supply stores and storage facilities, and has helped establish 'Zones of Freedom'—villages that pledge to reject chemical fertilizers and pesticides, genetically engineered seeds and patents on life. In this context it is worth referring to the Global Citizens' Report on GM, 2011, which claims that genetic engineering has failed to increase the yield of any food crop. Although companies promised salt tolerance, drought resistance, and minimum pesticide use, none of it has materialized. On the contrary, in Brazil and Argentina, pesticide use on soya increased two-fold and it increased thirteen-fold on Bt cotton in India.

In the words of Abramovitz (Brown 1996: 77):

We need to see the ecosystems in their entirety; rivers and lakes, along with their entire watersheds and all the physical, chemical, and biological elements, are all part of complex, integrated systems. Human inhabitants are also part of those systems. And we need to learn to manage such systems in ways that maintain their integrity. In such a flexible ecosystem-based approach, resources would be managed over large enough areas to allow their species and ecological processes to remain intact while allowing human activity. On a social level, all stakeholders would be involved in defining issues, setting priorities, and implementing solutions.

SUSTAINABLE DEVELOPMENT

Sustainable development (SD) is the process which effectively balances the needs of development with concerns for the health of the environment. It is characterized by economic and social growth that does not exhaust the resources of a host country; that respects and safeguards the economic, cultural, and natural environment; that involves grass roots participation and builds indigenous institutions; and that is nurtured by eco-friendly policies and programmes. Development is sustainable only when it permanently enhances the capacity of a society to improve its quality of life. Sustainable development requires investment in human capital—in education, health, food security, and the total well-being of the population. The United Nations sponsored two worldwide summits—the Rio Conference on Environment and Development in 1992 and the Johannesburg World Summit on Sustainable Development in 2002—which encouraged governments to partner with NGOs and private industry to make a bold commitment to applying SD principles in every area where humans impact on the environment.

As the *Time* (August 2002: A8) special on Green Century put it:

With 6.1 billion people relying on the resources of the same small planet, we are coming to realize that we are drawing from a finite account. The amount of crops, animals and other biomatter we extract from the earth each year exceeds what the planet can replace by an estimated 20 per cent, meaning it takes 14.4 months to replenish what we use in 12—deficit spending of the worst kind. Sustainable development works to reverse that, to expand the resource base and adjust how we use it so we are living off biological interest without ever touching principal.

Two billion people lack reliable access to safe, nutritious food, and 800 million of them, including 300 million children, are chronically malnourished. Yet, most of the agricultural practices are based on unsustainable development. Just fifteen cash crops such as corn, wheat, and rice provide 90 per cent of the world's food, but planting and replanting the same crops strips fields of nutrients and makes them more vulnerable. We resort to improved varieties which require enormous amounts of water and chemical fertilizers. There is considerable apprehension about genetically modified crops. Better crop rotation and irrigation can help but what is even more important is development of indigenous crops and the use of organic natural nourishment. One case in point is the probiotic fertilizers made of composts of agricultural wastes and animal manure developed by the Ahmedabad-based Institute for Studies and Transformations. Studies have shown that probiotic fertilizers make soils and plants healthier, capable of withstanding pests and droughts.

Although the world is 70 per cent water, only 2.5 per cent of it is fresh and only a fraction of that is accessible. With increasing population growth and urbanization, by 2025 nearly two-thirds of the world population will be facing serious water shortages. Since agriculture accounts for almost two-thirds of the fresh water consumed, the United Nations calls for a 'more crop per drop' approach based on efficient irrigation techniques. Rain water conservation and watershed management and more prudent use of water are important SD principles.

The world's appetite for energy is growing and the demands are met by burning fossil fuels such as oil, coal, and gas which release more carbon dioxide and other greenhouse gases. SD principles require the development and use of cheaper, cleaner, and renewable sources. Wind and solar power can be harnessed very efficiently. Small communities may be encouraged to set up micro-hydroelectric plants from streams and rivers.

It is estimated that 36 million acres of forest are razed annually and more than 11,000 species of plants and animals are threatened with extinction. It is not only that vanishing species provide humans with food and medicine but also that the destruction of their ecosystems may disrupt the balance and lead to disastrous consequences. Only now we have come to realize the perils inherent in the prevailing models of development: the atmosphere filled with toxins, oceans polluted and fished to exhaustion, rain forests chopped down, water contaminated and wasted, soil eroded and turned barren, and essential flora and fauna lost forever. So there is a new urgency to follow the fundamental principle of sustainable development: balancing economic growth with environmental protection. The programme of sustainable development includes the following: use of indigenous technology, grass roots participation in development, eco-friendly agriculture with organic manure and crop diversity, rain water conservation, recycling waste materials, use of renewable source of energy such as solar and wind power, saving rain forests, minimizing all types of pollution, and preservation of biodiversity. *Time* (August 2002: 19) observes:

Those who profess to care about the environment and yet scorn the goal of development only undermine both causes. For the poorest members of the human family in particular, development means the chance to feed, school and care for themselves and their children. But development that takes little account of sustainability is ultimately self-defeating. Prosperity built on the despoliation of the natural environment is no prosperity at all, only a temporary reprieve from future disaster. The issue is not environment vs. development or ecology vs. economy; the two can be integrated. Nor is this a question of rich vs. poor; both have an interest in sustainable development.

Today a new consensus is emerging among all nations of the world on the principle of sustainability: meeting the needs of the present without compromising the ability of future generations to meet their own needs. Earth Policy Institute has proposed a Plan B for the planet in peril. New technologies that make up Plan B are already in the market and many governments have made a policy decision to develop and encourage their use. Denmark, for example, today gets 20 per cent of its electricity from wind and has plans to push this to 50 per cent by 2030. Brazil already uses sugarcane-based ethanol for over 40 per cent of its automotive fuel and will become fully self-sufficient in a matter of years. The new wind turbine can produce as much energy as an oil well. Japanese engineers have designed a vacuum-sealed refrigerator that uses only a fraction of the electricty used by older models. Using an ecologically sophisticated carp polyculture, China has become the first country where fish farm output exceeds oceanic catch. Once a barren and almost treeless country, 65 per cent of South Korea is now covered by forests. Amsterdam has developed a diverse urban transport system, and today 35 per cent of all trips within the city are taken by bicycle. These are just a few examples. The fact is that national governments have generally accepted the principle of sustainability and have formulated policies encouraging sustainable development.

STUDY QUESTIONS

- Critically examine the different theories of social change.
- What are some of the sources of change? Explain.
- Write an essay on the process of social change with special reference to industrialization, urbanization, modernization, and westernization.
- What are the main trends of social change in India?
- Critically examine the intricate relationship between environmental wholeness and the quality of life.
- What is sustainable development? How do we achieve it and why?

REFERENCES

Abraham, Francis M., *Perspectives on Modernization: Toward a General Theory of Third World Development,* Washington DC: University Press of America, 1980.

Bell, Daniel, *The Coming of Post-Industrial Society,* New York: Cillier, 1976.

Brown, Lester R., *State of the World: A Worldwatch Institute Report,* New York: W.W. Norton, 1996, 2005.

Chandhoke, Neera and Praveen Priyadarshi, *Contemporary India: Economy, Society, Politics,* New Delhi: Dorling Kindersley, 2009.

Desai, A.R. (ed.), *Essays on Modernization of Underdeveloped Societies,* Atlantic Highlands: Humanities Press, 1976.

Eisenstadt, S.N., *Modernization: Protest and Change,* Englewood Cliff: Prentice-Hall, 1966.

———, *Tradition, Change, and Modernity,* New York: John Wiley, 1973.

Fairchild, Henry Pratt (ed.), *Dictionary of Sociology,* New Jersey: Littlefield, Adams and Co., 1968.

Gugler, Joseph and William Flanagan, *Urbanization and Social Change in West Africa,* New York: Cambridge University Press, 1978.

Lal, A.K. and Sami S. Ahmad, *Social Change in Post-Independence India,* New Delhi: Rawat Publications, 2001.

Lauer, Robert H., *Perspectives on Social Change,* Boston: Allyn and Bacon, 1991.

Milbrath, Lester W., *Envisioning a Sustainable Society: Learning our Way Out,* Albany: State University of New York Press, 1989.

Moore, Wilbert, *The Impact of Industry,* Englewood Cliffs: Prentice-Hall, 1965.

Rogers, Everett, *Modernization among Peasants,* New York: Holt, Rinehart and Winston, 1969.

Singh, Yogendra, *Culture Change in India: Identity and Globalization,* New Delhi: Rawat Publications, 2002.

Sorokin, Pitirim, *Social and Cultural Dynamics,* Boston: Porter Sargent Publisher, 1937.

Spengler, Oswald, *The Decline of the West,* New York: Alfred A. Knopf, 1926.

Srinivas, M.N., *Social Change in Modern India,* Berkeley: University of California Press, 1966.

Thio, Alex, *Sociology: An Introduction,* New York: Harper & Row, 1986.

Toffler, Alvin, *The Third Wave,* New York: Bantam Books, 1980.

Further Readings

Chapter 1

Beattie, J., *Other Cultures*, 'Introduction', sections on social anthropology, London: Cohen & West, 1964.

Béteille, André, *Sociology: Approach and Method*, chapters 1–3, 9, New Delhi: Oxford University Press, 2002.

Bottomore, T.B., *Sociology: A Guide to Problems and Literature*, Part 1, Boston: Allen and Unwin, 1986.

Carr, E.H., *What is History?*, chapters 1–2, Harmondsworth: Penguin, 1961.

Deshpande, Satish, *Contemporary India: A Sociological View*, New Delhi: Viking, 2002.

Giddens, A., *Sociology*, chapter 1, London: Polity Press, 1997.

Inkeles, A., *What is Sociology? An Introduction to the Discipline and Profession*, chapters 1–2, Englewood Cliffs, NJ: Prentice-Hall, 1964.

Pocock, D.F., *Understanding Social Anthropology*, chapter 1, London: Athlone Press, 1998.

Chapter 2

Bottomore, T.B., *Dictionary of Marxist Thought*, Oxford: Blackwell, 1983.

————, *Sociology: A Guide to Problems and Literature*, Part 1, Boston: Allen and Unwin, 1986.

Inkeles, A., *What is Sociology? An Introduction to the Discipline and Profession*, chapter 3, Englewood Cliffs, NJ: Prentice-Hall, 1964.

Ritzer, George, *Sociological Theory*, various sections, New York: McGraw-Hill Company, 1996.

Chapter 3

Béteille, André and T.N. Madan, *Encounter and Experience: Personal Accounts of Fieldwork*, New Delhi: Vikas, 1975.

Durkheim, Émile, *Rules of Sociological Method*, chapters 8–10, New York: Free Press, 1958.

Hatt, P.K. and William J. Goode, *Methods in Social Research*, New York: McGraw-Hill Book Co., Inc., 1952.

Madge, J., *Tools of Social Science*, chapters 2–3, Garden City, NY: Anchor Books, 1965.

Malinowski, Bronislaw, *Argonauts of the Western Pacific*, London: Routledge & Kegan Paul, 1922.

Radcliff-Brown, *Methods in Social Anthropology*, Delhi: Asia Publishing, 1958.

Srinivas, M., A.M. Shah, and E.A. Ramaswamy, *Fieldworker and the Field*, New Delhi: Oxford University Press, 1996.

Srivastava, Vinay Kumar (ed.), *Methodology and Fieldwork*, New Delhi: Oxford University Press, 2004.

Chapter 4

Bierstedt, Robert, *The Social Order*, chapters 5–7, New York: Basic Books, 1957.
Giddens, Anthony, *Sociology*, chapter 2, London: Polity Press, 1997.

Chapter 5

Bierstedt, Robert, *The Social Order*, selected portions, New York: Basic Books, 1957.

Chapter 6

Goffman, E., *Presentation of Self in Everyday Life*, 'Introduction', chapters 6–7, New York: Doubleday Anchor, 1959.
Ritzer, George, *Sociological Theory*, New York: McGraw-Hill Company, 1996.

Chapter 7

Bottomore, T.B., *Sociology: A Guide to Problems of Literature*, Part 2, chapter 6, Boston: Allen and Unwin, 1986.

Chapter 8

Bottomore, T.B., *Sociology: A Guide to Problems of Literature*, Part 4, chapters 12–15, Boston: Allen and Unwin, 1986.
Radcliffe-Brown, A.R., *Structure and Function in Primitive Society*, chapter 11, New York: Free Press, 1952.

Chapter 9

Bendix, Richard and Seymour Martin Lipset, *Class Status, and Power: Social Stratification in Comparative Perspective*, New York: Free Press, 1966.
Bottomore, T.B., *Sociology: A Guide to Problems of Literature*, Part 3, chapter 11, Boston: Allen and Unwin, 1986.
Giddens, A., *Sociology*, chapter 10, London: Polity Press, 1997.
Grusky, D.V., *Social Stratification, Class Race and Gender*, Parts 1, 3–5, Boulder, Colorado: Westview Press, 1994.
Gupta, Dipankar, *Social Stratification*, New Delhi: Oxford University Press, 1993.
Tumin, M., 'Some Principles of Stratification: A Critical Analysis', *American Sociological Review*, 18, pp. 387–94, 1953.
Turner, J., *Societal Stratification: A Theoretical Analysis*, 'Introduction', New York: Columbia University Press, 1984.

CHAPTER 10

Haimendorf, Christoph Von Furer, *Tribes of India: The Struggle for Survival*, chapters 1 and 8, Berkeley, CA: University of California Press, 1982.

Omvedt, G., *Dalit Visions: The Anti-caste Movement and the Construction of the Indian Identity*, Hyderabad: Orient Longman, 1995.

Shah, Ghanshyam Shah, *Dalit Identity and Politics*, New Delhi: Sage Publications, 2001.

Xaxa, V., 'Transformation of Tribes in India', *Economic and Political Weekly*, pp. 1519–24, 1999.

CHAPTER 11

Fox, R., *Kinship and Marriage*, Cambridge: Cambridge University Press, 1996.

Shah, A.M., 'Basic Terms and Concepts in the Study of Family in India', *Family in India: Critical Essays*, New Delhi: Orient Longman, 1998.

Uberoi, Patricia, *Family, Kinship & Marriage in India*, New Delhi: Oxford University Press, 1997.

CHAPTER 12

Bottomore, T.B., *Elites and Society*. Ringwood: Penguin, 1966.

Lukes, S., *Power: A Radical View* (second edition), Basingstoke: Palgrave Macmillan, 2005.

CHAPTER 13

Bourdieu, Pierre, *Homo Academicus* by Peter Collier (trans.), Stanford: Stanford University Press, 1988.

Bourdieu, Pierre and Jean-Claude Passeron, *Reproduction in Education, Society and Culture* by Richard Nice (trans.), London: Sage Publications, 1990.

Dewey, John, *Democracy and Education*, New York: Macmillan, 1916.

Halsey, A.H., J.E. Floud, and C.A. Anderson (eds), *Education, Economy and Society: A Reader in the Sociology of Education*, New York: Free Press, 1961.

CHAPTER 14

Madan, T.N. (ed.), *Religion in India*, New Delhi: Oxford University Press, 1991.

———, *India's Religions: Perspectives from Sociology and History*, New Delhi: Oxford University Press, 2004.

Madan, T.N., *Modern Myths, Locked Minds: Secularism and Fundamentalism in India*, New Delhi: Oxford University Press, 1997.

CHAPTER 15

Davis, K., 'The Theory of Change and Response in Modern Demographic History'. *Population Index* 29, 1963.

Meadows, P. and E. Mizruchi (eds), *Urbanism, Urbanization and Change, Comparative Perspectives*, chapter 2, Reading, MA: Addison-Wesley, 1969.

Rao, M.S.A., *Urban Sociology*, chapters 1, 9–10, and 15, New Delhi: Orient Longman, 1991.

Rao, M.S.A., Chandrashekar Bhat, and Laxmi Narayan Kadekar (eds), *Urban Sociology,* pp. 305–64, New Delhi: Orient Longman, 1991.

Chapter 16

Shah, G., *Social Movements in India: A Review of Literature*, New Delhi: Sage Publications, 1990.

Chapter 17

Bierstedt, Robert, *The Social Order*, chapter 20, New York: Basic Books, 1957.

Bottomore, T.B., *Sociology: A Guide to Problems in Literature*, chapters 17–18, Boston: Allen and Unwin, 1986.

Guha, Ramachandra, *Environmentalism: A Global History*, Delhi: Oxford University Press, 2000.

Milton, Kay, *Environmentalism and Cultural Theory: Exploring the Role of Anthropology in Environmental Discourse*, New York: Routledge, 1996.

Index

aboriginals: discrimination against 160; marriages among 39

activity theory 165–6

Adorno, Theodore 33

adult socialization 89–90

affirmative action 150, 155, 161

aged population 163–6; social isolation of 166

aggression 80, 123, 127, 161–2

agrarian societies 107–8, 110, 142, 165, 181, 262, 282

agricultural practices 72, 107, 234, 308

alcoholism 49–50, 154, 193

Ambedkar, B.R. 161, 288

anthropology 5–6

anticipatory socialization 114

anti-corruption movement 44

Appadurai 75

Assaad, R. 234

assimilation 160–1

Aung San Suu Kyi 120

authority, types of 205–6, *see also* power, and authority

Bainbridge, W.S. 233

Bales, Kevin 148–9

Bandura, A. 87

Bang, Rani 175

Baudrillard, Jean 42

Bauman, Zygmunt 42

Beck, Ulrich 43–4

behavioural psychology 30, 37–9, 78

beliefs 66

Bell, Daniel 299

Bellah, Robert 27, 234–5, 243–4, 250

Berger, Peter 234, 236–7, 243–4

Bhatt, Chandi Prasad 287

Bierstedt, Robert 117, 205

Blau, Peter, Structural Perspective 40–1

Blumer, Herbert 38, 276

Blunt, E.A.H. 136

Bourdieu, Pierre 34, 217–18; theory of cultural production 217–18

bourgeoisie 32, 145, 200

Breese, Gerald 269

Brown, Lester 219

Buddhists 158, 162, 228, 230, 248

bureaucracy 114–16

business process outsourcing (BPO) 301

Canetti, Elias 278

capitalism 8, 12, 18–19, 33–4, 57, 67, 168, 199–200, 209–11, 217, 238–9, 294; consequences of global 210; as economic system 199; and free trade 210; social movements against transnational 210

capitalist societies 32–4, 168, 217–18

caste system (*see also* stratification) 20, 24, 30, 63, 91, 135–40, 149–53, 158–61, 173, 175, 288, 291, *see also* upper caste

Castells, Manuel 43, 147

castes; backward 140, 150, 173, 288; groups based on 113, 140, 152, 158, 175, 205, 207, 244, 271; high 152, 186, 188–9; lower 30, 135, 139, 145, 152, 155, 159–61, 186–8, 240, 250; lowest 152; movements based on 286, 288–9; subcastes 9, 24, 72, 91, 138–9, 188; superiority 7–8; upper 152

causation 48–9, 54

ceremonies 7, 39, 55, 63, 69, 73, 91, 175,
    189–90, 227, 229–30, 234, 236, 242, 248–9,
    300; life cycle 73, 91, 230
charismatic leaders 206, 233, 239
Christians 7, 65, 111, 140, 158, 162, 186–8,
    229, 248–9, see also Christianity under
    religion
civil religion 235–6
Civil Rights Movement in America 119–20
class conflict 33, 143, 145, 294; Marx's theory of
    13, 145; theory of 32–3
classes 149–53: backward 151, 159, 291; lower
    8, 140–1, 152–5, 232, 240; middle 64, 113,
    141, 153–4, 202, 291, 301–2; and subclasses
    3; system of 3, 34, 53, 108, 135, 140–1,
    152–4, 218, 280; upper 140–1, 153–4, 213,
    218, 237
classless society 12, 32, See also Marx, on stages
    of human history
Cognitive Development Theory 86
cohabitation 191, see also marriage
collective behaviour 275–8, 280–1; contagion
    theory 276; convergence theory 277; of
    crowds 278–9; dispersed 279–81; emergent
    norm theory 276–7; forms of 278–9;
    meaning of 275; theories of 275–8; value
    added theory 277–8
collective: actions 38, 275, 277, 280, 282–6, (see
    also collective behavior); conscience 14, 109
Collins, Randall 239
communal violence/riot 49, 129, 162, 249–50,
    275, 277
communalism 66, 250–1
communication 93–5; mass media and
    communication 20, 42–4, 68, 74, 87, 89,
    109, 185, 269, 282, 284–5, 295, 297, 299;
    non-verbal communication 93–4
Comte, Auguste 3–4, 9–11, 13–14, 19, 22–3,
    26, 29, 41, 44, 57, 97, 242, 291; on human
    evolution 12
conditioned behaviour, Ivan Pavlov study of
    79–80

conflicts 9, 32–3, 35–6, 43, 59, 85, 101, 103,
    113, 145, 168, 207, 210–11, 244–5, 250,
    294; perspectives on 13, 126–7, 168, 206,
    217, 240, 294; theory 23, 26, 31–2, 35,
    40–1, 143, 145, 294
Confucianism 228–9, 241
Connell, R.W. 142
convergence theory 200, 277
conversion 161, 232, 249–50, see also under
    tribals
Cooley, C.H. 36, 82, 86, 112–13, 116; on
    complex relationship 82
corporate capitalism 209–11
corruption/bribery 44, 66, 70, 121–2, 126, 128,
    154, 203, 209, 222, 271, 286, 295
Coser, Lewis, Conflict Functionalism of 20,
    35–6
Cox, Harvey 242
crimes 119–21, 125–30, 171–2, 271; and
    criminals 128–9; Durkheim definition of
    121; of, organic inferiority 122. See also
    deviance
Critical Theory, Frankfurt School and 33–5
crowds, meaning of 278
cultural: capital 34, 217–18; change 73–4;
    contacts and diffusion 295–6; diversity
    72–3; heredity and environment 79–81;
    heritage 7, 67, 72–4, 88, 170, 214–15, 226,
    249; identity 73, 299, 301; imperialism 75,
    (see also globalization); orientation 70–2;
    pluralism 161; production 217; relativism
    71–2; systems 20, 30, 227, 234–5; universals
    73; values 29, 38, 40
culture 63–4, 248; Boas on 64; components of
    66–70; definition of 64–5; elements of 73–4;
    language and 67–8; meaning of 63–6; as
    symbolic 65
customs 4, 7, 15, 30–1, 39, 64, 69, 72–3,
    91, 110, 114, 138, 149, 186–7, 248–50,
    299–300
cyberspace 95, 102, 104
Cyclical Evolutionary Theory 27, 292

Dahrendorf, Ralf 32, 35, 145; on social change and conflict 294

Dalits 59, 71–2, 100–1, 111, 138, 140, 149–50, 159–61, 164, 173–4, *see also* castes

Darwin, Charles 79

Darwinism 296

Davies, James 282

Davis, Kingsley 81, 143–4

de Saint-Simon, Comte Henri 9

democracy 66–7, 74–6, 143, 198–9, 205–6, 208–9, 215, 217, 243, 284, 291

democratic socialism 200–4

Deng Xiaoping 202

Desai, A.R. 20

Deshpande, Satish 173–4

developing countries, mixed economy in 200

developing societies 20, 196, 298

deviance 119–28, 130, 232–3, (*see also* crime); Anomie theory 123–5; biological theories 122; conflict theory 126–7; consequences of 121–2; differential association theory 125; gender and 127; labelling theory 125–6; link between progress and 121; psychological theories 122–3; sociological theories 123–7; theories on behaviour of 122–7; type of 119–20, 122–6

Dialectical idealism of Hegel 12

diffusion 74

disabled persons 162–4

discipline 3, 5, 10, 23, 58, 113, 217, 224, 238

discrimination 48, 69, 72, 80, 119–20, 139, 149, 158–62, 166, 168, 170–1, 173, 250; against aboriginals 160; against Africans 159

diseases 47, 101, 147, 154, 228, 242, 255–6, 261, 266, 304, 307

division of labour 106, 109–10, 115, 137, 145, 168, 271, 285; gender roles in 168

domestic violence 56, 127, 142, 171, 191–3, 287, *see also* spousal abuse

dowry system 48–9, 52, 126, 169, 171, 188–9, 193, 281, 284, *see also* marriage

Durkheim, Émile 3, 14–17, 19, 22, 29, 44, 109, 121, 227, 237, 241–2

economy 4–5, 17, 48, 199–200, 226, 243

education 8, 213, 214–18, 220–6, 269, 296; critical thinking 216–17; cultural transmission 214–15; and development 220; female literacy rates 220–1; female secondary education 219; functions of 214–17; higher 31, 142, 150, 191, 215, 220, 225–6; in madrasas 220; inequality in 217–18; innovation in 215; institutions of higher 150, 215, 225; primary 220–3; private schools in 153, 213, 217, 223; research 215; Russia re-inventing 220; and social integration 215–16; and social placement 215; UN Millennium Development Goals 218–20; universal 213, 219–21; universal elementary 222–3; universal primary 218–19; universities in 115, 117, 140, 201, 220, 223–5

Education for All and World Bank 213, 219

ego 84–5, 123, 307

Eisenstadt, S.N. 27, 297–8

Ekeh, Peter 40

elderly 69, 158, 162–6, 264, *see also* aged population

Engels, Friedrich 13, 168

environment 302–8; climate change 43, 304, 307; Chipko movement 286–7; movements of 286–7; Narmada Bachao Andolan (NBA) 287, 306; problems 295, 304, 306

environment sociology 6, 20

equality 19, 44, 67, 74, 176, 216, 264, 278, 287, 294, 296, 300–1

equilibrium 19, 29, 31, 45, 74, 293, 303

Erikson, Erik 85

ethnic group 158

ethnocentrism 71, 159, 210. *See also* Xenophobia

ethnomethodology 99–100

Evers, T. 283

evolutionary: process 26, 79–80, 228; theory 14, 23, 26–8, 41, 44, 292–3; of Spencer 14

exchange theory 23, 26, 38–41; of Homans 40
exploitation 135, 143, 145, 168, 175, 199, 234, 289, 294

family 87–8, 181–3; children in 190; extended 181–2, 186, 189, 193, 271, 293; functions of 184–5; institution of 181; joint 20, 30, 48, 74, 164, 186, 189–90, 291; and marriage 185–91; nuclear 181–2, 185–6, 190, 216, 293; one-parent 191; as social group 181; teenagers 191; types of 181–2
fanaticism 247
fashion 65, 74, 88–9, 248, 275, 280, 296, 300, *see also* lifestyle
female infanticide 49, 72, 128, 169, 187–8, 262, 284, *see also* sex selective abortions
fertility 107, 219, 255, 262, 264
Festinger's theory, of cognitive dissonance 24
festivals 7, 63, 68, 72–3, 230, 242, 248, 275, 279, *see also* ceremonies
feudalism 12, 18
Finch, H.A. 18
folk-urban continuum, of Redfield 110
folkways 69
food habits 72–4, 78, 91, 153, 161, 248
Frazer, James 39, 229
free trade 199, 201, 210
freedom struggle 286–7, *see also* social movements
Freire, Paulo 218
Freud, Sigmund 84, 227, 238, 296
Fromm, Eric 33
Fuller, Steve 234
Functionalism (*see also* stratification, functional theory of) 8, 14, 16, 19, 23, 26, 28, 29–30, 31, 40–1, 44, 83, 143, 165, 293
fundamentalism, religious 246–7, 251; Macionis' definition of 246

Gandhi, Indira 129, 250
Gandhi, Mahatma 119–20, 206, 239, 249
gay 142, 176, 192, 246, 283

Geertz, Clifford 234–5, 244
Gemeinschaft 19, 110
gerontology 164–5
gestures 65, 81, 83, 93–4, 96, 98
Ghurye, G.S. 20, 139
Giddens, Anthony 43
girls 7, 37, 69, 81, 94, 96, 100, 127, 143–4, 149, 167, 169–72, 175, 187–90, 218–20, 246; education of 219, *see also* education
global warming 43, 303–4
global: capitalism 210–11; culture 20, 74–7; marketing systems 43, (*see also* free trade); society 43–4; stratification 145, 147–8
globalization 20, 34, 42–5, 56, 59, 74–7, 95, 207, 209–11, 215, 225, 246, 272, 285, 291, 301–2; Appadurai on culture of 75; Direct foreign investment 211; process of 75–6, 301
Gold, Peter 234
gossip 130, 280. *See also* rumour
Gouldner, Alvin 20
grand theories 24–5, 27; vs. miniature theories 24

Habermas, Jürgen 33–4
Hauser, Philip 270
Hazarre, Anna 44, 209, 295, *see also* corruption
Hegelian idealism. *See* dialectical idealism
Heidensohn, Frances 127
Henry, William 165
Henslin, James 67
Herveu-Leger 245
heterosexuality 192, *see also* gay; homosexuality; sexuality
Hindu Marriages Act of 1955 187
Hindu Succession Act, 1956 250
Hindu upper castes (HUCs) 174
Hinduism 186, 228–9, 234, 238, 249–50; as faith of universalism 249; Hindutva and 246, *see also* Rashtriya Swayamsevak Sangh (RSS)
Homans, George 20, 39–40; theory of elementary social behaviour 24; exchange

theory 40; on principles of psychology 39; and behavioural perspective 39–40
homosexuality 94, 126, 128, 176, 192; and marriages 192
Hooten, E.A. 122
Horkheimer, Max 33
human behaviour (*see also* psychology) 3–4, 6, 9, 22, 34, 57–8, 79–80, 87, 98, 237
human societies 9, 11, 27, 32, 38, 292
hunting and gathering societies 106–7, 220

ideal culture 65–6, 89
Illich, Ivan 218
impulses 84–5, 123, 276
Indian culture 20, 64–5, 69, 73, 161, 216, 248, 250–1, 301
Indian economy 202; Mahapatra on 301
Industrial Revolution 108, 114, 209, 268, 299
industrial societies 14, 33, 145, 192, 242, 245, 299
industrialism 15, 296
industrialization 56, 108, 164, 256, 258, 269, 296–7, 301, 306; countries of 191–2, 220, 262, 303–4
inequality 141, 143, 147–8, 174, 203, 213, 217–18, 220; structured 135, 143
infant mortality rate (IMR) 170, 256. *See also* fertility
Inkeles, Alex 20
institutionalization 83, 142, 270, 285
institutions 3–7, 13, 15, 20, 24, 29–31, 36, 90, 116–17, 139–40, 185, 188–9, 213–15, 225, 243–4, 291; premier educational 222
intellectual disciplines 3, 10–11
interaction 3, 17, 19, 24, 35–8, 40, 48, 82–4, 93–100, 102–4, 106, 110–13, 116, 125, 139, 160; Goffman and 98; status in 100–1; as symbolic 96
international monetary systems 44–5
intimate partner violence (IPV) 193

Jain, Jasbir 288
Jainism 228

Jains 158, 187–8, 248
jajmani system 138, 140, 273
Johnson, Lyndon B. 224

Kaplan, Abraham 22, 26, 41
Karve, Irawati 139
Killian, Lewis M. 278
King, Martin Luther 119–20, 206, 239
Kluckhohn 64
knowledge 41, 213; acquisition of 4
Koenig, M.A. 193
Kroeber, A.L. 64
Kumar, S. 193

labelling theory of Lemert Edwin 125
labour: bonded 128, 148–9, 172, 203; child 128, 149, 172, 203, 222–3, 286, *see also* division of labour
language 67–8, 94; functions of 67–8
Lappe, Frances Moore 148
Le Bon, Gustave 276
Learning theories 87; of Bandura A. 86
lesbian 142, 176, 192
Lesbian, gay, bisexual, and transgender (LGBT) 176
Levin, N.R. 223
Levi-Strauss, Claude 28, 39
liberalization 210, 301–2, *see also* globalization
life expectancy 147, 153, 163–4, 170, 256
lifestyles 24, 33, 52, 55, 64, 72, 74, 91, 102, 114, 141, 146, 153, 161, 176, 233–4; in advanced industrial societies 191; and life-chances 153–4
Lifton, Robert 247
linguistic groups 113, 158, 183, 187, 208, 215, 271
Linton, Ralph 295
Lofland, Lyn H. 50
Loomis, Charles 110
Lowenthal, Leo 33

macro theories vs. Micro Theories 24–5
Malinowski, Bronislaw 29, 39, 64, 230, 237; functionalism of 29

Mandela, Nelson 120
Mannheim, Karl 33
Marcuse, Herbert 33
marriage: age at 190, 262; child 128, 169–70,
    186, 190, 281; definition of 183; divorce in
    72, 88, 90, 142, 175, 186, 191–2; endogamy
    139, 183, 188, 232; exogamy 183, 188; and
    family 186–92; future of 185–6; *Gandharva*
    186; global trends in 191–2; hypergamy 188;
    inter-caste 139, 151, 183; inter-religious 190;
    minors in 172; patterns of 183–4; polygamy
    64, 120, 138, 175, 183–4, 187; and religious
    rituals in 186; *swayamvara* in 186; types of
    183–4
Marx, Karl 7, 11–13, 19, 23, 31–4, 44, 143,
    145, 206, 239–40, 294, 296; on stages of
    human history 12; theory of social conflict
    32; on utopian society 19
mass hysteria 230, 275, 280
mass society 110, 270
matrilineal system 181–2
McKee, James B. 242
McMichael, Philip 210
Mead, George Herbert 36–8, 83, 86
Mead, Margaret 80, 82, 167
Merton, Robert: defining anomie 124; theory of
    125
micro theories 24–5
migration 156, 217, 255–6, 271, 296; as
    movement of population 256
Milbrath, Lester W. 302
mind 36, 83, *see also* self
miniature theories 24–5
minorities 148, 151, 158–62, 164, 166, 173,
    176, 192, 250, 301; classification of 162; and
    Constitution of India 162; groups of 158–9,
    160–2, 264; and minority relations 160–1;
    National Commission for 162; by sexual
    orientation 176; women as 166–8
mobility 42, 154–6, 166, 211, 218, 222, 297,
    300; types of 154–5
modern: industrial societies 182–3; social
    movements 284–6; sociological theory 29–30

modernity 42–3, 77, 234, 244, 296, 298–9,
    301
modernization 20, 28, 41, 43, 56, 164, 243–4,
    258, 291, 296–9
molecular theories 24–5
Moore, Wilbert 27–8, 143–4, 296
moral education 214
mortality 169, 227, 255–6
movements: Adivasi 288–9; anti-war 283; bhakti
    286, 288; caste-based social 286; Dalit 286,
    288; environmental 283, 285–7; of farmers
    281, 286; global 286; Hippie 281; modern
    social 284; peasant 286; post-Marxist 283;
    pro-democracy 284; revolutionary 281, 296;
    against *sati* 286; social reform 287; students
    282, 285–6; tribal 286, 288–9; against
    untouchability 281; working class 286
Mukherji, Radhakamal 20
Mullins, Nicholas C. 99
multiculturalism 72
Multilinear Evolutionary Theory 27–8
multinational or transnational corporation
    (TNCs) 209, 211
Muslims 7, 30, 72, 111, 140, 158, 161–2, 170,
    174, 186–8, 208, 229–30, 248, 250, *see also*
    Islam *under* religion
Myrdal, Gunnar 148

national integration 73, 215–16, 236, 269
National Policy for Older Persons 166
National System of Education 224
nationalism 20, 42, 72, 161, 210, 216, 236, 282,
    299
natural sciences 3–4, 10, 17, 47, *see also*
    environment
naturism 228, 241
Navdanya movement 307, *see also* Social
    movements
Naxalites 125, 127, 207
new social movements (NSMs) 283–4, 288
nomads 106–7, 174–5, *see also* hunting and
    gathering society
norms 68–70, *see also under* violation

O'Dea, Thomas 232
occupations: among caste groups 152; menial 159; traditional 91, 136, 138, 140, 150–1, 161, 174–5, 217, 268
Occupy Wall Street Movement 210
organization 3, 24, 35, 39, 73, 114–16, 136, 140, 186, 228, 239, 287–8, 292, 297; Self-Employed Women's Association (SEWA) 287; social 116–17
Other Backward Classes (OBCs) 150, 155, 173–4, 222, 288–9; movement of 288–9

Panchayati Raj 151, 225
Pareto, Vilfredo 19
Park, Robert 276
Parsons, Talcott 19, 24, 27, 31, 83, 97, 168, 235, 293
pastoral societies 107, *see also* nomads
Patel, Sujata 272–3
peer groups 37, 70, 78, 87–9, 112, 130
Phule, Jyotirao 288
Piaget, J. 86; principal stages of 86
plastic sexuality 95
pluralism 206–7, 243
political: parties 30, 53, 66, 72, 106, 112–14, 119, 121, 151, 196, 201, 205–8, 224, 250, 284, 287–8; power 33, 143, 155, 206, 208, 283
politics 207–9
pollution 8, 43, 130, 136–7, 139, 159, 262, 291, 300, 302–5, 309
population 263–6; concepts of 255–7; control of 264–5; explosion 258–63; fertility 255–6; growth of 163, 173, 255–8, 262, 266, 303, 305; Malthusian theory of 257–8; migration 256–7; mortality 256; policies on growth of 266; theoretical perspectives 257–8; transition theory 258
positive discrimination 150–1, 301, *see also* affirmative action
postmodernism 42–3, 74–5
poverty 14, 16, 32, 71, 140, 145–8, 154–5, 168, 173, 191, 197, 201–3, 217, 222, 260, 286–7; elimination of 197, 202, 286

power relations 40, 138, 207–8
power: and authority 204–6, (*see also* politics); centres of 206–8; elite model and 206; pluralist model of 206–7; theories of 206–7
prejudice 9, 47, 158–60, 164, 166
pressure groups 151, 208
Presthus, Robert V. 207
primitive: communism 12; instincts of 122; religions 228–9; societies 5, 39, 71, 75, 176, 227–8, 238, 241, *see also* nomads
private property 12, 106–7, 168, 199–200
procreation 182, 184, *see also* fertility
production and distribution 32–3, 40, 108, 145, 199–200, 294
proletariat 12, 32, 145, 190
prostitution 69, 120, 127–8, 149, 172
Protestant ethic 8, 18, 57, 238–9; theory of Weber 19
psychoanalytic theory 84–5
psychology 5–6; Cognitive Development Theory 86; Learning Theory 86–7; theories of 82, 84–7, 122–3

race, stratification based on 142
racial group 158
racism 210, 296
Radcliffe–Brown, A.R. 28–9, 45, 64, 237
Ramanujan, A.K. 224
Rashtriya Swayamsevak Sangh (RSS) 251
rationalization 33, 44, 144, 242, 301
real culture 65–6
rebel groups 208, 285
relationships 3–4, 36, 47–8, 51–2, 93, 95–6, 104, 110, 113, 116, 136, 140–1, 186, 213, 271, 298; social interaction into 96
religion 91, 227, 247–51; animism 228, 241; anthropological study of 234; beliefs in 229; Buddhism 228–9, 238, 241, 244, 250; Calvinism and 238; Christianity 161, 228, 237, 240, 244, 249; community sense in 230; concepts of 231–4; conflict perspective of 240; and cosmic questions 238; Durkheim theory of 227, 241–2; elements of

229–31; emotionalism in 230; functionalist
perspective of 237–9; functions of 239;
gods in 229; Great Spirit 228; Gusfield on
244; Islam 161, 183, 220, 228, 244, 246;
Mahayana Buddhism 250; magic and 66,
229–31, 234, 244–5; Marxist thinking of 8;
of organized 232–3, 235, 242; in politics 248;
priests in 10, 47, 137, 189, 228, 231, 249;
among primitive people 228–9; Protestant
asceticism 238; resacralization 245–6; sect
in 232–3; secularization 242–5; Shintoism
228–9; Sikhism 228; for social control 237,
240; sociological perspectives on 234–7;
sociological theories on 237–40; supernatural
beings 10, 228–9; trends in 242–7
religious: beliefs 72, 78, 227, 243, 299;
communities 55, 121, 158, 186, 191, 248,
271; cults 51, 55, 90, 233–4, 238, 246–7;
evolution 235; fundamentalism Macionis, on
246–7; groups 7, 16, 91, 111, 113, 140, 158,
184, 186, 230–1, 247–8, 250; institutions
90, 241, 243; movements 237, 240, 245–6,
251, 281–2, 284; organizations 90, 108,
185, 233, 235, 243–4, 248, 250; ritualism
65, 186, 230, 242, 249, 262, 275; sects 230,
232–4, 246, 249; symbolism 235, 239, 242
remarriage of widow 90, 169, 175, 186–8
research: methods of 52–7; quantitative
vs. qualitative research 57–9; issues in
sociological 59–60; steps in process 49–52
reservation 140, 150–1, 160–1, 173–4, 207,
222–3, 288; and anti-Mandal position 151
resocialization 90–1
Right of Children to Free and Compulsory
Education Act 2009 221
Riley, John W. 185
Riley, Matilda White 185
risks, definition of 43
rituals 73, 155, 175, 188–9, 227–30, 234, 236,
238, 245, 300
Rogers, Everett 298
Rossi, Alice S. 185
Rossi, Peter H. 185

rumour 275–6, 279–81
rural population 202, 221, 271

Sachs, Wolfgang 76
sanctions 70
Sanskritization 114, 155, 300
Sapir, Edward 68
sati 16, 169, 281, 284, 286–7, see also
movements, against sati
Scheduled Castes (SCs) 150–1, 169–70, 173–4,
217; literacy rates among 217
Scheduled Castes and Scheduled Tribes
(Prevention of Atrocities) Act 173
Scheduled Tribes (STs) 150–1, 169–70, 173–4,
217; literacy rates among 217
Scholte, Jan Aart 20, 42
schooling 170, 214, 220–2, see also education;
learning theories
schools 88–9
Schroyer 34
scientific: approach 47–8; industrial society 10,
26; sociology 58, 97; truth 47
secularization 236, 242–6, 250, 291, 300–1;
Herveu-Leger on 243. See also rationalization
self 36, 83; concept of 37; Herveu-Leger on
awareness of 245; Mead on concept of 37
Sen, Amartya 219, 304
sex ratio 169, 264, 287
sex selective abortions 169, see also female
infanticide
sexism 163, 167; 'santsung' or 'thrice-obeying'
in 167
sexual: regulation 184; relationships 183, (see also
prostitution); violence 193
sexuality 95, 142, 188
Shah, A.M. 190, 246, 287
shared values 31, 41, 111–12
Sharma, Kalpana 169
Sheldon, William 122
Shills, E.A. 18
Shinrikyo, Aum 247
Sikhs 72, 129, 140, 158, 162, 188, 248, 250
Simmel, Georg 19, 22, 35, 97, 116, 270

Singh, Rajendra 284
Singh, Yogendra 301
Skinner, B.F. 80
Slater, David 283
slavery 12, 64, 69, 72, 148–9, 175
slums 255, 273, *see also* urbanization
Smelser, Neil 277
Smith, Adam 199
Smith, Anthony 76
social: behaviour 3–4, 17, 24, 39, 47–8, 68,
    98, 207; control 119, 121, 123, 125, 127,
    129–30, 168, 197, 234, 237, 240, 278;
    Darwinism 14; exchange 38–40, 104; facts
    3, 15; identity 82, 84, 87–8, 90, 100, 165;
    integration 40, 215, 237, 293; justice 173–4,
    197, 202, 210, 216, 286, 288, 296, 298, 300;
    mobility 154–6; psychology 6, 79; reforms 9,
    248, 281, 286
social action 3, 17, 31, 36, 96–8, 129; collective
    284
social change 302–3, process of 296–9; sources
    of 294–6; theories of 291–4
social groups 3, 6–8, 16, 37, 59, 64, 69, 72, 111–
    14, 116, 119, 129, 138, 143, 181, 183–4;
    electronic communities 114; reference groups
    113–14
social interaction 95–9; accommodation
    103–4; competition 103; forms of 102–4;
    structure of 100–2; conflict 103; cooperation
    102–3; dramaturgical approach 98–99;
    ethnomethodology 99; exchange 104; virtual
    networking 104
social movements 33, 43–4, 57, 90, 127,
    162, 211, 279–86, 281, 286–8, 294–5,
    299; Arab Spring 284; life-cycle of 284–6;
    political opportunity/process theory 282–3;
    relative deprivation theory 281–2; resource
    mobilization theory 282; theories of 281–3
social sciences 3–6, 10, 17, 20, 25, 47–8, 215,
    244
social structure 3–4, 6, 11, 13, 16, 24, 28–9, 31,
    33–7, 64, 93, 107–8, 116, 123, 138, 144;

and Anomie of Robert Merton 123; Marxist
    theory of 33; Nadel on 28–9; theory of 28
social systems 3, 5–6, 11, 15, 20, 24–5, 28,
    30–1, 35–6, 40, 44, 52, 74, 97–8, 213–14,
    294; Alter on 98
Socialism 12, 57, 200, 202, 207, 210, 236, 294;
    as economic system 200
socialization 38, 41, 73, 78, 81–7, 89–91, 97,
    129, 181, 184, 213–14, 236; of adult 89–90;
    agents of 87–90, 213; deprived 81–2; Family
    87–8; Peer Groups 88; process of 41, 78,
    81–4, 86, 89, 91, 97, 127, 227; School 88–9;
    mass media 89; theories of 82–7
societies 10, 63, 83; evolution of 106–9; agrarian
    societies 107–8; horticultural 107; hunting
    and gathering 106–7; industrial and post-
    industrial societies 108–9; Lenski and types
    of 292; pastoral 107; Robert Redfield on folk
    and urban 110–111
sociobiology 80
sociological: analysis 17, 23, 29, 31, 57, 97;
    knowledge 4; nominalism 97; perspective
    6–9, 25, 29, 36, 93, 120, 234; theories 22,
    25–5, 42, 82, 123, 237
Sociological theory 22–3, 26, 41–2; 82–4, types
    of 23–5; functions Of 25–6
Sociology 3–4; characteristics of 3–4; Comte's
    definition of 3; Durkheim definition of 3;
    fathers of 9–19, *(see also under separate names)*;
    as general social science 6; of knowledge 13, 17,
    19–20; meaning of 3; Weber's definition of 3
solidarity 15–16, 237; Émile Durkheim on 19,
    109
Sorokin, Pitirim 19, 27, 292–3
Speculative Theories vs. Grounded Theories 23
Spencer, Herbert 13–14, 19, 22–3, 27, 29, 44,
    79, 97, 292
Spengler, Oswald 27, 292
Sperling, Gene B. 219
Spitz, Rene 82
spousal abuse 50, 128, 154, *see also* domestic
    violence; sexual, violence

Srinivas, M.N. 20, 114, 136, 155, 190, 245, 248, 300; and religious rituals 245
Sriram, R. 193
Stark, R. 233
state and government 196–7; autocracy 198; defence 197; democracy 198–9; functions of 197–8; social control 197; totalitarianism 198; types of 198–9; welfare 197–8
stereotypes 89, 159–60, 164
stratification 135–41; caste system 136–40; class system 140–1; dimensions of 143; estate system 135–6; functional theory of 143–4; gender, 141–2; global systems of 145–9; race 141–2; theories of 143–5
structural-functionalism 19, 23, 26, 28–31, 41, 44, 83, 143, 165; Nadel conception of 28–9
subcultures 4, 20, 72, 137, 142, *see also* culture
suicide 14–17, 49, 154, 188, 193, 203–4, 271, 280; Durkheim's study of 23
Sumner, William Graham 19
superego 84–5, 123
Sustainable development (SD) 225, 308–10
Sutherland, Edwin, theory of differential association 125
Symbolic interactionism 23, 26, 36–8, 41, 82, 98, 125
system theory 19, 23–4, 26

Taliban 20, 44, 198, 246
Tambiah, S.J. 234
Taoism 228–9
Taylor, Edward B. 63
technology 70, 295; Ogburn on 57
teenagers 191, 224
Theological-Military society 10
theories 22–3, 41–2; definitions of 22; Merton on 24; value of 41
Tillich, Paul 228
Tonnies, Ferdinand 19, 110
total institutions 90–1
totemism 228, 241
Toynbee, Arnold 27, 292

tribal population 174, 176, 217; land use among 175
tribals 174–6, 196, 228; conversion in 175; of Kotas 187; marriage among 175; into slavery 175; traditions and customs among 175; of Todas 7, 72, 187
trivarnic civilization' 137
Tumin, Melvin 144
Turner, Ralph H. 278
twice-born castes 186–7, 300
Tylor, culture concept of 64

Unilinear Evolutionary Theory 26–7
unity in diversity 73, 161, 216
universal evolutionary theory 27
universal immunization 266
Untouchability (offences) Act, 1955 173
untouchability 7, 50, 56, 59, 64, 69, 91, 120, 139–40, 149, 172–3, 284, 286
upper castes 30, 135, 145, 152, 159, 169, 175, 186, 207, 213, 288; Panini on professions of 152
urban population 267–9, 271–3
urbanization 15, 56, 138, 164, 256, 263, 266–73, 291, 296–7, 306–7, 309; Georg Simmel on 270; Louis Wirth on 270–1; Miner on 297

value-added theory 277
values 31, 33, 37, 39, 67; and Ideology 296; of society 39; study of 19
varna system 137–8, *see also* twice-born castes; castes
violation of norms 69–70, 119–21, 125–6; culture defining 120; punishing for 231
violence 89, 103, 119, 127–8, 151, 167, 170, 193, 276, 293; women as victims of 171
vitro fertilization (test tube babies) 192, *see also* fertility

Wahabism, religion 251
Ward, Lester Frank on education 213, 222

Warner, W. Lloyd 141
water conservation 305
Watson, John 79
wealth 107–8, 126, 135–6, 140, 145–7,
   154, 161, 168–9, 201, 218, 284, 307;
   accumulation of 43, 140, 145; of bourgeoisie
   32; and classification of people 141;
   concentration of 108, 136; as criteria for
   stratification 143; determination of class 140;
   differences in 145; of individuals 145; and
   nomads 106–7; production of 43; unequal
   distribution of 146; of upper class 140–1; of
   Vaishyas 137
Weber, Max 3, 8, 17–19, 22, 33–4, 44, 58, 97,
   115–16, 143, 145, 205–6, 235, 238–9; and
   values 17–19
welfare programmes 202–3
westernization 77, 246, 291, 296, 299–300
Whorf, Benjamin 68

Wilson, Bryan 233
Wilson, Edward, as founder of sociobiology 80
Wirth, Louis 270–1
women: adolescent 192; crimes against 171–2;
   education and 192; in IAS 172; in labour
   force 166; as minority 166–8; movements of
   282, 285–8; population of 169; programmes
   for advancement of 172; subordination 193;
   traffic in 172
world population 145–8, 255, 259–60, 263,
   266–7, 302, 305, 309; Malthusians on 259
Wright Mills, C. 7, 9, 32, 58, 206; on
   Sociological Imagination' 7–8
Wrong, Denis 84

xenophobia 71, 159–60

zamindari system 141
Zoroastrianism 228

About the Author

M. Francis Abraham received his PhD from Michigan State University where he was on a Ford Foundation Fellowship and won the Bobbs-Merrill Award for the most outstanding PhD candidate in sociology in 1969. His areas of specialization include sociology of development and sociological theory. He is the author/editor of thirteen books including *Modern Sociological Theory* (Oxford University Press 1982). He has also co-authored with his mentor, Dr Charles P. Loomis, former President of American Sociological Association and a world-renowned sociologist.

Dr Abraham has teaching experience of almost thirty years at various American universities. He has received numerous Fulbright and other international studies grants from several US Government agencies. He has travelled extensively in 42 countries and conducted Fulbright seminars in 18 of them.

In India, Dr Abraham studied and taught at Gandhigram Rural University for over ten years and has done extensive research in the field of rural social problems. Several of his books are standard texts at major universities and are included in the category of recommended readings for IAS/IPS and other national level competitive examinations.